The Significance of Borders

The Significance of Borders

Why Representative Government and the Rule of Law Require Nation States

By

Thierry Baudet

BRILL

LEIDEN • BOSTON
2012

This paperback is also published in hardback under ISBN 978 90 04 22808 5.

The front cover shows a graphic dramatization of Jan Asselijn's painting *The Threatened Swan* (1652). The Swan represents the Grand Pensionary, one of the most important political officials at the time, fiercely defending the Dutch Republic. A few years before, the Republic had acquired its independence from the Spanish Habsburg Empire.

Photograph back cover: Marie-Jeanne van Hövell tot Westerflier.

ISBN 978 90 04 22813 9

This book is printed on acid-free paper.

Printed by Printforce, the Netherlands

Without a 'we', it won't work.

Paul Scheffer, *The Unsettled Land* (2007)

STRUCTURE

PART I
THE RISE OF BORDERS
National Sovereignty

PART II
THE ASSAULT ON BORDERS
Supranationalism and Multiculturalism

PART III
THE NEED FOR BORDERS
Representative Government and the Rule of Law

CONTENTS

Part III – The Need for Borders

ACKNOWLEDGEMENTS

In writing this book, I have greatly benefited from the personal and intellectual support of friends and colleagues, whose engaged and constructive comments were of inestimable value.

I am most indebted to Paul Cliteur and Roger Scruton for inspiring me to write a book about this theme and for supporting the project throughout its realization. A tremendous stand-by from the very beginning has also been my dear friend Tony Daniels, who has constantly motivated me to improve my work. Paul, Roger and Tony, the three of you formed an incredible team. Thank you so much for your confidence in me, and for all your help in the development of my ideas.

There are also many others who have assisted me with particular aspects of the book: with literature, information and arguments. My gratitude and friendship goes out to Marten Admiraal, Mark Almond, Barbara Becker-Rojzcyk, Hugo Bijleveld, Frits Bolkestein, Bas van Bommel, Diederik Boomsma, Lukas van den Berge, David Chandler, Pascal Bruckner, Chantal Delsol, Afshin Ellian, Alain Finkielkraut, Marc Fumaroli, Frank Furedi, Amos Guiora, Hendrik Kaptein, Roy Kenkel, Andreas Kinneging, Leszek Kolakowski (+), Marijn Kruk, Joes Kuys, Bart Labuschagne, Rick Lawson, John Laughland, Christian Leclercq, Jean-Thomas Lesueur, Noel Malcolm, Pierre Manent, Pablo Mendes de Leon, Gelijn Molier, Douglas Murray, Matthijs Pars, Jeremy Rabkin, Bastiaan Rijpkema, Larry Siedentop, Fred van Staden, Jaffe Vink, Michiel Visser and Geerten Waling.

My greatest gratitude goes to my dear parents, my dear sister, and my darling Esmée. Without their love and support, none of this work would have been possible, and it is a pleasure to dedicate the final result to them.

PREFACE

For almost three-quarters of a century, the countries of Western Europe have abandoned national sovereignty as an ideal. Nation states are being dismantled – by supranationalism from above, by multiculturalism from below. Both supranationalism and multiculturalism undermine the territorial jurisdiction and the shared national culture of the nation state. Moreover, they partake of the same vision of the future. Their vision is one of a world beyond borders and beyond the distinction between 'us' and 'them' that these borders entail. Whether perceived to be causing wars, to be impractical, unnecessary or merely small-sided, borders, demarcating the end of one jurisdiction and the beginning of another, the end of one way of life and the beginning of another, are actively being annulled.

It is the purpose of this book to reconsider the significance of borders. The book argues that representative government and the rule of law can exist only within a nation state. And it suggests that, paradoxically as it may seem, the social and economic advantages that globalization brings about can only be realized through strong, sovereign nation states – however internationally orientated and open to newcomers they may be, and notwithstanding intensive cooperation with one another.

The dominant view in much of modern political and legal theory is that free trade, cooperation between states and internationalism require supranationalism, and that being open to newcomers should entail multiculturalism. This, I contend, is an inversion of reality. For supranationalism thwarts a state's options for free cooperation and internationalism, and takes away the very foundations of classical international law, whilst multiculturalism encourages the Balkanization of sensibilities and the narrowing – rather than the widening – of minds and sympathies, eclipsing the perspective on the national whole.

From the facts of globalization, including mass-migration, multinational corporations, electronic communication and world spanning means of transportation, the conclusion has been drawn that 'the idea of national culture makes little sense, and the project of cultural unification on which many past societies and all modern states have relied for their stability and cohesion is no longer viable today'.[1] Because we can easily *cross* borders, or because there are problems that *transcend* borders, we needn't have them at all.

---

[1] Bikhu Parekh, *Rethinking Multiculturalism. Cultural Diversity and Political theory.* Second edition (London: Palgrave, Macmillan, 2006) 8.

But I argue precisely the opposite: because of these phenomena that transcend borders, there is in fact a need for strong nation states. Only in nation states can newcomers be welcomed and made part of the collective 'we' that is necessary for political representation and a shared rule of law. And it is only through nation states that international cooperation can effectively be brought about. For only when decisions are made by national representatives – who can also be held accountable for these decisions –, such international cooperation can be experienced as legitimate.

I call the open nationalism that I defend *multicultural nationalism* – as opposed to multiculturalism on the one hand, and an intolerant, closed nationalism on the other. The international cooperation on the basis of accountable nation states that I propose, I call *sovereign cosmopolitanism* – as opposed to supranationalism on the one hand, and again a closed, isolated nationalism on the other. Both *multicultural nationalism* and *sovereign cosmopolitanism* place the nation state at the heart of political order, while recognizing the demands of the modern, internationalized world.

Historically, the nation state arose out of the conflict between worldly and spiritual leadership – a conflict which, although present already in the early Middle Ages, became untenable in the time of the Reformation. As a result of the religious civil wars that followed in the 16th and 17th century, it became generally acknowledged that states should be sovereign in their internal affairs and that in order to ensure this, the most fundamental obligation of states should be respect for the territorial jurisdiction of other states – in other words: for their borders. The Medieval organization of politics, characterized by overlapping jurisdictions, thus gradually made way for centralized sovereignty.

To legitimize increased political power and overcome religious and ethnic tensions, the idea that those subjected to this developing sovereign should have the same political loyalty, the same allegiance, was self-consciously developed in this era as well. Thus Richelieu, for example, as early as 1617, had already laid down in an instruction to a minister that in matters of state, no French Catholic should prefer a Spaniard to a French Protestant.[2]

But the state under the *ancien régime* was not yet a nation state. Government was not representative of its people in the way that it is taken to be in nation states. And whatever rule of law was in place in the *ancien régime*, it was not a shared law, as groups and regions had their own sets of rights and duties, and different laws applied depending on personal status.

Symbolized by the American and French Revolutions (1776 and 1789 respectively), the idea of representative government and territorial equality before the law had been developed throughout the 18th century and became common in

---

[2] J.C.L. Simonde de Sismondi, *Histoire des Français*. Vol. XXII (Paris: Treuttel et Würtz, 1839) 388.

the 19th. Implied in the notion of representation is the idea that a collective body of people exists that can be represented not just in terms of separate classes or individual interests, but also as a whole. Democracies presuppose the existence of a *demos* in order that parliament be considered the legitimate forum of deliberation and of ultimate decision-making.

But the rule of law equally implies a *demos*. Not only should the judge that administers the law be recognized as an impartial authority by *both* parties to a conflict, and thus draw upon a shared idea of legitimacy. Even more importantly, the content of the law itself is mostly congealed culture. There can be no shared law without a shared sense of morality, without shared customs and shared manners. No matter how much effort the legislative assembly might put in formulating promulgated laws as clear as possible, precisely what should be understood by essential legal concepts such as 'equity', 'good faith', 'grave reasons' and so on, or how the weighing of conflicting constitutional rights should be conducted (e.g. the freedom of religion against the principle of non-discrimination), is always a matter of interpretation. The question of legitimate legal judgments thus becomes ultimately a question of social authority and that is precisely what lacks at the supranational level.

Moreover, as the courtroom is never more than an ultimate remedy, the 'rule of law' really implies that the individuals in a society generally have a shared, internalized idea of what the law is and that they live more or less according to it. Properly understood, the rule of law is only the tip of the iceberg of social cohesion.

The nation-building operations and national unification movements of the 19th century were undertaken with these considerations in view. The course of these events, while not entirely arbitrary, was not inevitable either: there was no historical inevitability that, for example, the Italian unification should have succeeded, or that the German should have failed until as late as 1871. While it is unlikely, for reasons of language and history, that Spain and France should have merged into one nation state, it was not a settled matter that the Basques, the Bretons or the Catalans should have been included in either. Nor should we consider these processes of national unification as forever fixed. Nations are, like every social phenomenon, always in flux, and it is well possible that in the future, different nation states with different borders will develop.

Nor is there any doubt that too strong an affirmation of national identity can have a dark side. The First and Second World Wars provide terrible examples of this. Though the political leaders at the time did not attempt to create nation states but rather multinational empires, nationalism proved an extraordinary way to channel and increase bellicose collective identity.

But we should not judge a virtue by its excesses – as recklessness is not the essence of courage.[3] Moreover, the fading of national identity would not abolish the human need for a collective identity. Nor would it efface mankind's capacity to resort to violence on the basis of antagonisms drawn from such distinctions. Indeed, there is no reason to assume that the particular expression of collective identity through nationality should not have prevented or assuaged more conflicts than it has actually caused, or that other forms of collective identity, i.e. religious, tribal, or racial ones, have a better track record in this field. Moreover, there is no reason to assume that a deficiency of national identity would bring about consequences necessarily less dangerous or destructive than those of an over-affirmed, aggressive nationalism. The lack of internal cohesion may make the formation of government not only utterly difficult, as the case of Belgium illustrates, it may also cause a civil war, as the events in the former Yugoslavia in the 1990s – as well as those in America between 1861 and 1865 – have most bitterly shown.

Nationality, expressed as patriotism in its normal form, can degenerate into aggressive nationalism or imperialism if it is not sufficiently accommodated. German nationalism was born in 1806, the year that the French revolutionary army triumphantly marched underneath the Brandenburg Gate. The French, in turn, were humiliated by the German annexation of Alsace-Lorraine in 1871, and in the years following this defeat, the French third republic saw the rise of a violent and anti-Semitic nationalism that sought to 'purify' the nation and so restore its pride. There can be no doubt either, that the enormous reparations Germany had to pay after the First World War, while having lost a third of an entire generation of young men, contributed to the rise of an aggressive form of nationalism amongst the population in the 1920s and 30s. It is not unlikely that *respect* for national identities rather than the scorn they currently receive, could prevent (rather than, as is feared, incite) the pathological imperialisms that so terribly disfigured the 20th century.

At present, European national governments are still, in the last instance, sovereign in validating the treaties that bind them – and they could still withdraw from those treaties, or demand reforms. Nor has multiculturalism, exceptions aside, replaced formal equality before the law or the authority of national judges to administer national law. Sharia courts are still rare and not broadly desired by immigrant populations. This means that there still is a choice. Even though in past decades, much has been done to eliminate borders, the keys to the gates are still in national hands.

---

[3] Cf. Alasdair MacIntyre, 'Is Patriotism a Virtue?', in: R. Beiner (ed.), *Theorizing Citizenship* (New York: State University of New York Press, 1995) 209-228.

This is not unimportant. Throughout Europe, politicians with a significantly nationalist agenda have had considerable – and increasing – electoral success in recent years. Indeed, the fact that European elites have taken step after step to dismantle the nation state does not mean that the native European populations are enthusiastic about that. 'Populist' politicians such as Berlusconi in Italy, Le Pen in France, Fortuyn and Wilders in the Netherlands, Klaus in the Czech Republic, Haider in Austria, Timo Soini in Finland, and many more, have all made affirmations of the national culture an important part of their political campaigns, and have consciously demonstrated pride in representing their respective nations. In referenda on the Constitutional Treaty of the European Union, large numbers have expressed disapproval of granting supranational institutions powers that were formerly entrusted to national governments. And on November 29th, 2009, the Swiss voted against the right of Muslim immigrants to manifest their religion in an ostentatious way by building minarets. It is not unlikely that holding such referenda in other European countries, would produce similar results.

If large percentages of native European populations do not wish their political sovereignty to be given away, and their national culture to disappear, should this not cause us to doubt the legitimacy and indeed the very rationale of supranationalism and multiculturalism? If the chances of success of a borderless world do not seem very high, would it not be wise to consider alternatives to the currently dominant trend?

This book is, like Gaul, divided into three parts. The first part seeks to analyze the nation state, both historically and analytically, and I will argue that its two primal characteristics are the shared loyalty of its population proceeding from their sense of social cohesion, and the capacity for centralized decision-making. In other words: nationality and sovereignty.

In the second part, I will show the extent to which we have left this reality behind and how, over the past decades, supranationalism and multiculturalism have constituted what could be called an 'assault on borders'. It gives a flavor of the six supranational institutions that have been installed and explains how they infringe their member states' own legal traditions and self-government. A distinction is made between supranational courts – the International Criminal Court, the European Court of Human Rights, and the International Court of Justice – on the one hand, and supranational organizations – the World Trade Organization, the United Nations Security Council, and the European Union – on the other. The second part also takes multiculturalism into consideration. I discuss its two elements separately: the tendency towards legal pluralism on the basis of cultural or religious backgrounds, and the applauding of the different cultures and loyalties within the state, rather than emphasizing the shared national identity.

Why supranationalism and multiculturalism are inimical to representative government and the rule of law forms the argument of part three. I will show that both representative government and the rule of law can exist only within a nation state – i.e. only when they are embedded in a sovereign framework with sufficient social cohesion. As it follows that supranational and multicultural developments are incompatible with two essential institutions of a free society, the final conclusion takes into consideration some practical alternatives to the current situation.

The main thesis of this book is that representative government and the rule of law require nation states. By dismantling national sovereignty, the countries of Western Europe are thus undermining those institutions. Supranationalism and multiculturalism are incompatible with representative government and the rule of law because they efface the sense of overarching loyalty and ultimate centralized sovereignty that are necessary preconditions for them. Without borders, there can be no 'we' – and 'without a "we", it won't work.'[4]

---

[4] Paul Scheffer, *Het land van aankomst* (Amsterdam: De Bezige Bij, 2007) 401.

PART I

THE RISE OF BORDERS

National Sovereignty

What right have you, a foreigner, to come to me and tell me what I must do?

From: Ernest Hemingway, *For Whom the Bell Tolls* (1940)

INTRODUCTION

Borders define jurisdictions. To uphold borders is to claim jurisdiction; to claim the right to decide on the law. The nation state makes such a claim. It seeks jurisdiction over a particular territory. By implication, the nation state also acknowledges that other jurisdictions may apply beyond that territory. Borders work two-ways, and while they grant the nation state exclusive jurisdiction, they also limit the nation state's claims to the designated territory.

Supranationalism and multiculturalism undermine the idea of exclusive territorial jurisdiction. Supranationalism grants institutions the power to break through national borders and to overrule the nation state's territorial arrangements. In this way, borders become increasingly porous. Multiculturalism, meanwhile, not only delegitimizes the nation state's borders by weakening the collective identity of the people living behind them; it also encourages religious sub-groups to invoke rules from beyond the nation state's borders, thereby undermining the very idea of territorial jurisdiction. 'God's heart has no borders', to put it bluntly.[1]

Supranationalism and multiculturalism are thus antithetical to national sovereignty and to the borders therein implied. Supranationalism dilutes sovereignty, and so brings about the gradual dismantling of borders from the outside; multiculturalism weakens nationality, thus delegitimizing their existence altogether from the inside.

The idea of political organization that fundamentally opposes supranationalism and multiculturalism – the idea of the nation state – has been declared 'outdated' and 'irrelevant' by an overwhelming number of commentators. Yet while supranationalism and multiculturalism have dominated politics and academia over the last several decades, their popularity is questionable and debates about national identity divide most European countries at present.

---

[1] Pierrette Hondagneu-Sotelo, *God's heart has no borders. How religious activists are working for immigrant rights* (Berkeley: University of California Press, 2008) 135: 'There is a spirit that transcends the border'.

Politicians playing the nationalist card have had indisputable electoral success: Le Pen and Sarkozy in France,[2] Fortuyn and Wilders in the Netherlands,[3] Filip Dewinter and Bart de Wever in Flanders,[4] Lech Kaczynski and his twin brother Jaroslaw Kaczynski in Poland,[5] Klaus in the Czech Republic,[6] Haider in Austria,[7]

---

[2] Jean-Marie Le Pen (*1928) founded the euro sceptic and patriotic (anti-immigration) *Front National* in 1972. The party increased its vote during every election from 1983 onwards till 2002, when Le Pen opposed Jacques Chirac in the presidential elections. At the elections of 2007, Nicolas Sarkozy (*1955) was able to steal the *Front National's* clothes by taking over much of its patriotic rhetoric, such as declaring that one is to love France or to leave it. In January 2011, Jean-Marie Le Pen's daughter Marine Le Pen took over the leadership of the party, continuing its emphasis on French national identity, while Sarkozy pursued a more pro-European line.

[3] Pim Fortuyn (1948-2002) founded the LPF (List Pim Fortuyn) in 2001 and would have been a candidate in the national elections of May 15th, 2002, but Volkert van der Graaf, an environmental activist who feared that Fortuyn would threaten Dutch society because of his 'stigmatizing political views', murdered him a few days before, on May 6th. Fortuyn's political agenda was one of national patriotism, stressing that the European Union should not take over national sovereignty, and calling for drastic changes in Dutch immigration policies. After his death, much of his agenda was adopted by Geert Wilders (*1963), a former prominent member of the liberal party, who, while posing as an outcast in the media, has scored significant successes in national and municipal elections. At the elections for the European parliament in June 2009, Wilders' party reached the same number of seats (5) as the largest party in the Netherlands, the Christian Democrats. In 2010, Wilders' party increased its influence by giving parliamentary support to a minority coalition of Liberals and Christian Democrats.

[4] Filip Dewinter (*1962) became leader of the Flemish nationalist party *Vlaams Blok* in 1992 (currently renamed as *Vlaams Belang*). Under his leadership, the party grew until it was the biggest party in Flanders for a time. Yet, partly as a result of the *cordon sanitaire* of the other parties, it has not achieved governmental responsibility. The *Vlaams Belang* strongly opposes Muslim immigration to Belgium and to Europe in general, and is highly skeptical of the European Union. Bart de Wever (*1970) founded the *Nieuw-Vlaamse Alliantie* in 2004, and strongly emphasized Flemish identity. In the elections of 2010, the party won over 30% of the votes.

[5] Lech Kascynski (1949-2010) was mayor of Warsaw between 2002 and 2005, and since then President of Poland until his death in a plane crash in April 2010. He was very skeptical of Poland entering into the Euro currency zone, and had vowed to guard 'Polish morals' from Brussels. He also defended Pope Benedict XVI after his Regensburg address, by stating that Muslims 'are a little too easily offended'.

[6] Vaclav Klaus (*1941) was prime minister of the Czech Republic between 1992 and 1997, and has been president of the Czech Republic since 2003, being reelected in 2008. He is a euro sceptic who did not want to sign the European Lisbon Treaty in 2009. He also criticized the 'excessive openness' of the West to immigrants 'from other cultural environments'.

[7] Jörg Haider (1950-2008) became a member of the FPÖ (Austrian Freedom Party) in 1970. He was a member of Parliament from 1979 till 1983, and became president of the party in 1986. From 1989 onwards, he was also elected as governor of Carinthia (which he remained, with an interruption between 1991 till 1995, until his death). Under the leadership of Haider, the FPÖ achieved a high score in the elections of 1994 (22,7 %), and another victory in 1999, leading to a government coalition with the Christian Democrats from 2000 onwards. In 2005, Haider co-founded a new political party, the Bündnis Zukunft Österreich (League for the Future of Austria). Haider was strongly opposed to multiculturalism and to non-Western immigration.

Berlusconi in Italy,[8] Aznar in Spain,[9] and so on. Also, in referenda on the Constitutional Treaty of the European Union, considerable numbers of voters expressed resistance towards granting supranational institutions powers that were formerly entrusted to national governments.[10] The examples are legion. In June 2009, the French government banned the burqa. Later that same year, on November 29th, the Swiss voted against the right of Muslims to erect new minarets. In Sweden, Muslim leaders called the results of the elections of September 2010 a 'catastrophe' because of the gains of the Swedish Democrats, an anti-Islamic party. In April 2011, the nationalist 'True Finns' party won by a landslide success in Finland. And so on.

But what is in fact this 'nation state' that so many popular (or 'populist') politicians now profess to restore? To be sure, in an attempt to provide a sense of home to its inhabitants, whilst at the same time realizing political organization on a scale far exceeding the possible social circle of each individual inhabitant, the nation state consists of two in principle contradictory elements. The need to realize social cohesion on a national scale has brought nation states to defend and indeed actively foster a particular cultural heritage – often at the cost of regional identities – and the application of strict territorial sovereignty has made tremendous injustices possible.

At the same time, however, national sovereignty has also enabled peoples to govern themselves in accordance with their values and preferences. The nation state has made self-government possible. And it differs from supranationalism and multiculturalism on two points: firstly, on the effort to retain ultimate territorial jurisdiction instead of multilevel competencies such as supranational organizations bring to life; and secondly, on the emphasis on the need for a shared nationality within that framework of territorial jurisdiction, as is underminded

---

[8] Silvio Berlusconi (*1936) founded his own political party in 1993, *Forza Italia*. He became prime minister in 1994, forming a coalition with the *Allianza Nazionale (National Alliance)* and the *Lega Nord (Northern League)*, both nationalistic, eurosceptic parties. After losing the elections in 1996 to the pro-European Romano Prodi, Berlusconi won the elections again in 2001. In 2006, Berlusconi lost again to Prodi, but after the rapid fall of Prodi's administration, Berlusconi was restored to power after the elections of May 2008 until his step-back in 2011.

[9] José Maria Aznar (*1953) was Spanish prime minister between 1996 and 2004, leading the *Partido Popular*. He is well known for his anti-multiculturalism and called his left-wing successor's 'Alliance of Civilizations' a stupid initiative, while also being highly skeptical of 'Moors' (i.e. Muslims) in Spain.

[10] The referendum held in France on May 29th, 2005 resulted in a 'no' of 54,87%, while the main political parties and the main newspapers had been in favor. Three days later, 61,6% of the Dutch rejected the constitutional treaty, even though all major newspapers and journals had supported the treaty, and of the Dutch parliament, only 20 of the 150 members had been against it. Following these two referenda, the British decided not to hold the referendum that was scheduled for spring 2006. The Czech government cancelled their planned referendum as well, and the scheduled Danish, Portuguese, and Polish referenda were postponed. Sweden put ratification on hold. The only countries in which a referendum has actually led to a positive result have been Luxembourg, Spain and Ireland.

by multiculturalism. It is the purpose of the first part of this book to examine these points, the core points of the nation state, in more depth.

CHAPTER ONE

THE STATE

1.1. *The Rise of the State*

To understand national sovereignty, it is first necessary to examine the institution that upholds it: the state.

States of the kind we are familiar with today have certainly not always existed. They gradually gained shape over a period of several centuries, leaving behind the multi-layered organization of power that characterized the Middle Ages. It is, however, not easy to draw a sharp line between feudal and modern statehood: rather, the distinction is ideal-typical. The development towards modern statehood consisted in the slow undoing of feudal structures and in the diminution of the power of the church, in favor of the central political force commonly associated with the monarch.[1] As Samuel Finer writes:

> The Middle Ages were regulated, shaped, and permeated by two great institutions: Christianity and Feudalism. (…) If the cathedral is the stone symbol of the Middle Ages, so, equally is the castle. Feudalism and the feudality embraced them both.[2]

The replacement of the power of the 'stones' of the Middle Ages, the cathedral and the castle, by the paperwork of bureaucratic central administrations, marks the coming of the modern state.[3] Ernest Gellner has written about the influence of modernization on 'the replacement of diversified, locality-tied low cultures by standardized, formalized and codified, literacy-carried high cultures'. He noted that 'the Reformation universalized the clerisy and unified the vernacular and the liturgy, and the Enlightenment secularized the now universalized clerisy and the now nation-wide linguistic idiom, no longer bound to doctrine or class'.[4]

---

[1] In republics, this increase in power was naturally not brought about by a monarch, but by another central political figure. In the United Provinces, for instance, political power increasingly concentrated in the person of the Stadtholder.

[2] S.E. Finer, *The History of Government, Volume II. The intermediate ages* (Oxford: Oxford University Press, 1997) 857.

[3] It is against this background that Edmund Burke wrote: 'Nothing is more certain, than that our manners, our civilization, and all the good things which are connected with manners, and with civilization, have, in this European world of ours, depended for ages upon two principles; and were indeed the result of both combined: I mean the spirit of a gentleman, and the spirit of religion. The nobility and the clergy …', in: Edmund Burke, *Reflections on the Revolution in France. A Critical Edition*. Edited by J.C.D. Clark (Stanford: Stanford University Press, 2001) 241.

[4] Ernest Gellner, *Nations and Nationalism* (Oxford: Basil Blackwell, 1983) 76-78.

This, however, was a process that differed significantly from region to region,[5] and a great number of elements of feudalism can still be found in Europe well into the 19th and 20th centuries (for example in the continuation of certain privileges for aristocracy and church, as well as culturally, for instance in the English idea of the 'officer class'[6]).

Moreover, a pivotal institution in the political organization of nation states, parliament, originated in the counsel that vassals rendered to their overlords – and thus has its roots in feudalism.[7] The same goes for the 'estates' idea – as in 'Estates General' – which originally referred to the different feudalities, summoned by the King.

In addition, while the theory of the modern state developed in the 16th and 17th centuries, it was only in the 18th and 19th centuries that states actually acquired the means to administer central political powers even remotely resembling those of today. Powers concerning taxation and legislation remained mostly decentralized until the breakdown of the *ancien régime* in Europe following the French Revolution. An illustration of this fact is that in the years directly preceding the Revolution, Louis XVI tried in vain to increase taxation when government deficits rose to unacceptable levels following the French support for the American War of Independence (1775-1783): the nobility, however, prevented the state from taking such measures.[8] From the modern perspective, all states

---

[5] As did the rise of feudalism, which certainly did not exist all through Europe in the same amount. Finer writes: 'The German Kingdom in the tenth century was not feudal. Feudalism was introduced there in the twelfth century. The kingdom started off with a powerful but primitive personal type of monarchy. By the fourteenth century this kingship was reduced almost to nullity and the kingdom itself was an almost nominal confederacy of independent units. The kingdom of the Franks, on the other hand, was in the tenth century in a similar condition to what Germany would come to be in the fourteenth, a largely nominal confederation of some half-dozen great territorial duchies and counties under a shadowy kingship; whereas by the thirteenth century it had been pulled together as the paradigm feudal kingdom, under a kingship which exploited to the full all the advantages it could extract from feudal law. England in the tenth century was non-feudal, like Germany, and it too possessed a powerful personalized kingship. Reinforced by the effect of the Norman Conquest, this kingship, a blend of Anglo-Saxon and feudal characteristics, ended up as the most effective and wide-reaching central government of the time, but one whose activities were balanced and controlled by the equal and opposite growth of increasingly institutionalized restraints.' Finer (1997) vol. II, 899.

[6] This was expressed, for instance, by the aristocrats who led in war and who were the first to be killed in the First World War. Cf. David Cannadine, *Class in Britain* (New Haven: Yale University Press, 1998), and Martin Gilbert, *The Somme. Heroism and Horror in the First World War* (New York: Henry Holt and company, 2006), or, from the perspective of fiction, R.C. Sherriff, *Journey's End* (New York: Bretano's Publishers, 1929).

[7] J.H.A. Lokin and W.J. Zwalve, *Hoofdstukken uit de Europese Codificatiegeschiedenis*. Derde, geheel herziene druk (Den Haag: Boom Juridische Uitgevers, 2006) 103.

[8] Attempts to increase taxation were for instance undertaken by Turgot, minister of Louis XVI, in 1774. Cf. Joël Felix, 'The financial origins of the French Revolution', in: Peter R. Campbell (ed.), *The Origins of the French Revolution. Problems in Focus* (New York: Palgrave Macmillan, 2006) 35-62.

that may have been in place in Europe before the French Revolution, with the possible exception of Britain since 1688, were at best 'failed states'.[9]

A central characteristic of the Middle Ages was the feudal organization of power. Feudalism had come up when local communities and peasants sought a new bond to provide for their security as the *pax romana* collapsed.[10] During the several centuries usually denoted as 'dark ages', this security was found in different local princes and potentates, who offered protection in exchange of their counsel and military support.[11] They became their *vassals*.[12] Vassals who had pledged allegiance to an overlord, could in turn establish their own fief over parts of their territories. Through this process, a hodgepodge of regional nobles and local lordships arose upon the collapse of the Roman Empire, each with their own means of the enforcement of order.[13]

During the Middle Ages, society thus became structured as a long hierarchical chain of mutual obligations and duties. And whoever stood at the top of this pyramid (a King and, in the German case, an Emperor) had a role much different from that of current heads of state. An old feudal principle was that *vassallus vassalli mei non est meus vassallus* (a vassal of my vassal is not my vassal), severely limiting the power of the king to interfere in matters on the ground.[14]

As a consequence, the relationship of the monarch with his noblemen was one of mutual dependence. This is illustrated by the fact that until the 15th century, there were in principle no standing armies at the disposal of the King.[15] As a result, the monarch, lacking easy means of enforcement, usually had to rule

---

[9] Another exception may be Sweden since Charles XII (1697-1718). Tilly uses a broader definition of the term 'state', however. In contrast, I am specifically referring to the comparison of the modern state with whatever previous types of states may have existed in the past. Cf. Charles Tilly, *Coercion, Capital, and European States, AD 990-1992* (Oxford: Blackwell, 1989) especially 45ff. I also touch upon the notion of the 'failed state' in chapter 2, section 2.2 on 'internal sovereignty'.

[10] Lokin en Zwalve (2006) 103. Finer writes: '"Feudalism" and "feudal system" may be ill-chosen terms – most medievalists agree on that – but they have acquired a connotation which we still have to use because we can avoid it only at the cost of a tedious and, indeed, obfuscating circumlocution. The fact is that in the West and central parts of Europe between the tenth and fourteenth centuries the form of polity was sharply different from any we have met with so far, and "feudal" is the best name we can give it', in: Finer (1997) vol. II, 864.

[11] The *auxilium* and *consilium* of the vassal. Lokin and Zwalve (2006) 103, fn23.

[12] Cf. Stuart Hall, 'The state in question', in: McLennan, Held and Hall (eds.), *The idea of the modern state* (Philadelphia: Open University Press, 1984) 4-7; Hendrik Spruyt, 'The origins, development, and possible decline of the modern state', in: *Annual Review of Political Science*, Volume 5 (2002) 127-49.

[13] Hall (1984) 4-7.

[14] Cf. W.F. Church, *Constitutional thought in sixteenth-century France. A study in the evolution of ideas* (New York: Octagon Books, 1969) 180ff.

[15] Spruyt (2002) 127-49.

with the consent of his noblemen, for instance concerning taxation.[16] He was *primus inter pares*, not supreme executive.[17]

Nor were any powers in place remotely resembling those of a modern legislature. Law in the Middle Ages was primarily customary law, gradually supplemented with more uniformly applied Roman and Canonical law.[18] John Maitland emphasizes that in England, from the time of Henry II (1154-1189), 'a rapid development of law common to the whole land' came into existence, where 'local variations are gradually suppressed'.[19] Finer likewise notes that 'the great leap forward in expanding royal justice at the expense of the feudatories took place under Henry II'. As a result, '[English] kingship, a blend of Anglo-Saxon and feudal characteristics, ended up as the most effective and wide-reaching central government of the time'.[20]

Government in England nevertheless remained 'by any modern standard quite appallingly incoherent, clumsy, crime-ridden, and corrupt (…) violence was endemic: small private wars, the destruction of manor houses, the breaking of enclosures and rustling of livestock, as well as the crop of robberies, murders, burnings and thefts'. Thus, 'even what passed as the best of its kind for that era' had to go far 'to reach even the minimal standards of justice, fairness, and security'.[21]

It was in the 17th and 18th century, that administration became significantly centralized in most other European countries,[22] and only after the French Revolution that national codifications were realized.[23] Although the rediscovery of the 'Digest' – a compendium of writings of important classical jurists, elucidating the tenets of Roman law –, contributed to some increase in legal uniformity from the 13th century onwards; the law remained mostly a matter of customs and privileges.[24] On the European continent, cities were significantly independent

---

[16] Illustrative in this context is the fact that the French Revolution followed on the bankruptcy of the French state, which had come about because of the King's failed attempts to raise taxes from the local potentates in the provinces. (See also above, footnote 8.)

[17] Cf. Hall (1984) 4-7.

[18] Lokin and Zwalve (2006) 122-123.

[19] John Maitland, *The constitutional history of England* (Cambridge: Cambridge University Press, 1961) 13.

[20] Finer (1997) vol. II, 899-902.

[21] Finer (1997) vol. II, 899-919.

[22] Tocqueville writes for instance in *l'Ancien Régime et la Révolution* (1856): 'Je soutiens que [la centralisation] n'est point une conquête de la Révolution. C'est, au contraire, un produit de l'ancien régime, et, j'ajouterai, la seule portion de la constitution politique de l'ancien régime qui ait survécu à la Révolution, parce que c'était la seule qui pût s'accommoder de l'état social nouveau que cette révolution a créé.' Tocqueville, *op. cit.* (Paris: Éditions Gallimard, 1953) 107: book 2, chapter II. Cf. Lokin and Zwalve (2006) 180ff.

[23] Lokin and Zwalve (2006) 182ff. Some German states had already commenced with codification projects in the years preceding the Revolution. As a consequence, Prussia for example presented its codification as early as 1792.

[24] The *Corpus Iuris Civilis* was issued by Eastern Roman Emperor Justinianus I between 529 and 534. It consists of three books: the 'Institutions' (a handbook for students), the 'Digest' or 'Pandects',

to pass and uphold their own legislation, and so enjoyed an amount of political independence far beyond the scope of municipalities today. As social and economic life was deeply regional, moreover, no effective standardization of measures and weights existed, which could therefore differ significantly from one region to another.[25]

Different rules applied to noblemen, clergymen, students or farmers, and guilds and other intermediary institutions were to a large extent able to make and act according to their own rules and trading decisions.[26] The predominant jurisdictional principle of modern states is territorial equality before the law; this did not exist in the Medieval system, in which there was no overarching law that applied equally throughout the territory. Instead, the principle of personality applied: rights and obligations followed from personal status, not territorial coordinates.[27]

In addition, the connection of nobles with their territories was loose. Titles were inherited, or passed through marriages from one family to another. As the principle of primogeniture did not always apply, fiefs were sometimes divided among the different sons of monarchs or nobles as well.[28] Borders were thus subject to constant change and the connection between rulers and ruled, while depending almost entirely on the personal entitlements of the lord, was weak.[29]

John Gerard Ruggie approaches the matter from another angle: 'the Medieval ruling class', he writes, 'was mobile in a manner not dreamed of since, able to assume governance from one end of the continent to the other without hesitation

---

and the 'Codex' (a collection of imperial laws). Cf. Paul Koschaker, *Europa en het Romeinse Recht.* Nederlandse editie verzorgd door Theo Veen (Deventer: W.E.J. Tjeenk Willink, 2000) 57ff [55].

[25] Andreas Kinneging, *Aristocracy, Antiquity, and History, Classicism in political thought* (New Brunswick and London: Transaction Publishers, 1997) 9: 'Apart from the purely physical restrictions on royal authority due to the poor network of communications – it took a courier a week to travel from Nice to Paris -, and the traditional dependence of the French kings on the advice of their counselors – Louis XV constantly reiterated Louis XIV's advice to take counsel in all things -, there was a wide range of formidable checks upon the exercise of monarchical power. The many municipalities, law courts, guilds, provincial estates, and other corporate bodies, all with a different historical background, a different culture, and a different legal code, together formed a profound barrier against royal despotism.'

[26] Cf. Robert Nisbet, *The quest for community. A study in the ethics of order and freedom* (Oxford: Oxford University Press, 1953).

[27] The same goes for the Roman Empire until the Constitutio Antoniniani of 212 AD, when all inhabitants of the Empire became Roman citizens, and hence subjected to the same, territorially instead of personally applying law. It is true that most modern states still apply some jurisdiction based on the principle of personality; criminal acts committed by subjects abroad are an example.

[28] This was especially the case in the Holy Roman Empire, as will be discussed more in depth below. Cf. Paula S. Fichtner, *Protestantism and Primogeniture in Early Modern Germany* (New Haven: Yale University Press, 1989) 8ff.

[29] Under feudal law, vassals retained the formal right to *diffidatio* as well: to renounce their allegiance to the king. Robert of Gloucester did this, for instance, in 1138, to King Stephen (1135-1154). 'In France', writes Finer, 'if a vassal "defied" the king and levied war, his vassals had to follow him, even against the king', in: Finer (1997) vol. II, 921. Cf. Spruyt (2002) 127-49.

or difficulty'. He quotes the French historian Georges Duby, who ironically wrote of the already mentioned Henry Plantagenet (i.e. King Henry II, 1133-1189):

> This was Henry, count of Anjou on his father's side, duke of Normandy on his mother's, duke of Aquitaine by marriage, and for good measure – but only for good measure – king of England, although this was of no concern to the country in which he spent the best part of his time.[30]

A final aspect of Medieval political organization that contrasts sharply with modern statehood is the role of the church in society. For besides the fragmentation of political power through the mutually dependent and layered power structures of feudalism and decentralized administration, there was unity in Medieval Europe too – the unity of religion. The 'universal' church[31] provided not only spiritual like-mindedness, but also dealt with a wide range of everyday matters of a legal and practical nature, including civil administration, education, and charity – roles that churches to a high extent, if not entirely, have abandoned in modern states.

This involvement of the church with political matters was certainly not always experienced as harmonious. In fact, the power struggle between lay rule and clerical rule – between worldly and spiritual leadership – was one of the major causes of political (and ultimately, armed) conflict in the Middle Ages. This conflict was already a reality by the time pope Leo III crowned Charlemagne as Emperor in 800, and was given a new impulse when, later in the 9th century, the Vatican declared that *Papa caput totius orbis* (the Pope is the master of the world). The struggle for the highest power never left the scene, sometimes more slumbering and indirect, at other times right on the surface: for example at the end of the 13th century, when Pope Boniface VIII claimed worldly sovereignty and the right to levy taxes. This claim was endorsed in his *Unam Sanctam* bull of 1302, in which he stated that he, the Pope, was superior in power over Kings.[32] The French King Philip IV responded to this bull by assembling the council of

---

[30] John Gerard Ruggie, 'Territoriality and Beyond: Problematizing Modernity in International Relations', in: *International Organization*, Vol. 47, No. 1. (Winter, 1993) 139-174, there 149-150. The quote from Duby is from: George Duby, *The Three Orders: Feudal Society Imagined*, translated by Arthur Goldhammer (Chicago: University of Chicago Press, 1980) 286.

[31] The word Catholic comes from the Greek *Katholikos*, meaning 'throughout the whole', or 'universal'.

[32] The bull is known by its incipit: 'Unam sanctam ecclesiam catholicam et ipsam apostolicam urgente fide credere cogimur et tenere, nosque hanc firmiter credimus et simpliciter confitemur, extra quam nec salus est, nec remissio peccatorum …' (In translation: 'We are compelled to believe that there is one holy Catholic and Apostolic Church, and our faith urges us to hold – and we do firmly believe and simply confess – that outside of this there is neither salvation nor remission of sins …').

Bishops and a council of nobles to reject it, and consecutively sent the knight
Guillaume de Nogaret on an expedition to Italy to imprison Boniface in 1303.[33]
     As mentioned before, the development of more centrally organized polities
went slowly, and differed in each region.[34] However, as Finer writes,

> In all feudal [realms] without exception (…), the political process boils down to a
> struggle between king and feudatories, and is marked by what are tritely referred
> to as periods of royal 'expansion' and feudal 'reaction'.[35]

In England, the year 1215 marked such a feudal 'reaction' against the expansion
of central power. By the end of the tenth century, its ruling aristocrats had
recognized England as one indivisible realm, and William 'the Conqueror' of
Normandy reconfirmed this in 1066.[36] Besides some 6,000 armored knights,[37]
he had brought with him a new bureaucratic language (French),[38] had declared
the entire country to be royal property,[39] and had installed a feudal system
loyal to him.[40] It was in the 11th century as well that primogeniture appeared in
England, facilitating the accumulation of wealth from generation to generation.[41]
Despite his attachment to his French duchies, as we saw above, King Henry II
'Plantagenet' (r. 1154-1189) significantly increased the central imposition of law
through the institution of a royal court.[42]

---

[33] The history of the reign of Philip IV (1268-1314) clearly illustrates how decentralized political
power was in the Middle Ages. His constant efforts to centralize power and attempts to have
his jurists install new ways of central government are an insightful illustration. His biographer,
Joseph R. Strayer, concludes his *The Reign of Philip the Fair* (Princeton: Princeton University
Press, 1980) 423: 'Philip drew heavily on the political capital accumulated by his ancestors, but
he also replenished it. He was king of all France in a way that none of his predecessors had been.
He had forced the most independent lords – the king-duke of Aquitaine, the counts of Flanders
and of Bar, the southern bishops – to recognize his superiority. His courts, and especially the
High Court that was the Parlement, retained their reputation for justice and made that justice
available to more subjects than ever before. Provincial loyalties were still strong, but some men
were beginning to see a vision of a *patria* that was the kingdom of France'.

[34] W.G. Grewe, *Epochen der Völkerrechtsgeschichte* (Baden-Baden: Nomos Verlagsgesellschaft,
1984); J.R. Strayer, *On the medieval origins of the modern state* (Princeton: University Press, 2005);
A. de Jasay, *The State* (Oxford: Basil Blackwell, 1985); McLennan, Held and Hall (eds.), *The idea
of the modern state* (Philadelphia: Open University Press, 1984); Held, *Political theory and the
modern state* (Cambridge: Polity Press 1989).

[35] Finer (1997) vol. II, 904.

[36] Finer (1997) vol. II, 899.

[37] Finer (1997) vol. II, 900.

[38] Cf. Jean-Benoît Nadeau and Julie Barlow, *The Story of the French* (London: Anova Books,
2006) 31ff.

[39] William did not keep all the lands for himself. As Finer writes: '[William declared] about
about one-sixth to himself alone, about two-fifth to his soldiers, and about one-quarter as church
lands; the remaining one-fifth stayed in the hands of the petty freemen'. Finer (1997) vol. II, 900.

[40] John Gillingham and Ralph A. Griffiths, *Medieval Britain. A very short introduction,* (Oxford:
Oxford University Press, 2000) 3.

[41] Fichtner (1989) 8ff.

[42] Finer (1997) vol. II, 902.

But when the opposition of the nobility succeeded in having King John (1199-1216) sign the Great Charter (the *Magna Carta Libertatum*) in 1215, they in fact already accepted considerable powers in the hands of the monarch. For acknowledging the central government's right to punish criminal offenses, which the Magna Carta does, was already a significant dilution of feudalism (and a power that certainly did not exist in France at the time, for instance[43]). The nobles only managed to mitigate this power through provisions concerning fair trial and due process.[44] The Charter further contained several limitations on the King's powers of taxation as well as provisions for the participation of nobles in important decisions, and was reissued several times: in 1216, 1217, 1225, and again in 1297,[45] but bureaucratic organization nevertheless continued to grow over the years. This increasingly demanded the active participation of the King's officials who took seat in a 'great council' – more and more frequently to be called a 'parliament',[46] which could also issue 'statutes': modifications in the 'common' law of the land.[47]

Step by step, then, the level of organization of the royal administration in England increased. When two centuries later, King Henry VII (1485-1509) succeeded in ending the civil wars known as the Wars of the Roses, the crown managed significantly to increase its demesne revenues; to rely on lower (and thus more dependent and loyal) aristocrats for administrative tasks; and to preside over a kingdom with an aristocracy with smaller estates and 'smaller [armies] (...), firmly subordinated to the Council [of the King].'[48] The son of Henry VII, Henry VIII, would even defend the Tudor sovereignty against the religious claims from Rome.

Centralization of governing tasks in England in the 15th century had closely been connected to the fact that the Hundred Years' War (1338-1453) had provided opportunities for both the English and the French king to increase their hold over the realm. This is not surprising, as Finer writes: 'the verdict of history – at least European history – is that war calls out a superabundance of military, administrative, and fiscal overkills which largely remain in place when peace returns.'[49]

---

[43] Cf. Finer (1997) vol. II, 921.
[44] An example is Clause 39, reading that 'No Freeman shall be taken or imprisoned, or be disseised of his Freehold, or Liberties, or free Customs, or be outlawed, or exiled, or any other wise destroyed; nor will We not pass upon him, nor condemn him, but by lawful judgment of his Peers, or by the Law of the Land. We will sell to no man, we will not deny or defer to any man either Justice or Right'. The clause was numbered 29 at the restatement of 1297 and can be found online at http://www.legislation.gov.uk/aep/Edw1cc1929/25/9/contents.
[45] Gillingham and Griffiths (2000) 35.
[46] Finer (1997) vol. II, 910-913.
[47] Finer (1997) vol. II, 910-914.
[48] Finer (1997) vol. III, 1271.
[49] Finer (1997) vol. III, 1277.

Indeed, 'war is revolution, and revolution is war', as Robert Nisbet observed.[50] When Hugh Capet became King of the Franks in 987, he presided over people speaking 'German in the extreme north-east, Celtic in western Brittany, Basque in the south-east, while the two main branches of the *lingua populare* – French and Occitan[51] – were mutually unintelligible', with weak resources and very little administrative power over his realm.[52]

By that time, primogeniture had become common practice in France,[53] ensuring that the estates of the Gallic nobility stayed intact. The position of the French king remained – when compared to the English monarchy – relatively powerless until the late 12th century.[54] Finer writes that 'between 1179 and 1337 the Crown won the centralization race against the principalities. In 1349-51 and intermittently till 1445 the process went into reverse'.[55] Duchhardt, on the other hand, still discerns the following trend:

> Considered within the category of the *longue durée* one might say – very coarsely and roughly – that the period from the thirteenth to the sixteenth century was shaped by the decline and erosion of both of the universal powers, Empire and Papacy, from which national states and churches and new confessions became more and more emancipated.[56]

One way in which the French kings managed to increase their influence was through the establishment of increased tax administration through a system of *prevôts*: 'directly salaried and removable agents, drawn from the lesser nobility, and so dedicated to the royal cause'.[57] The French King found another way to enhance his power in his alliance with the Church, enabling him, through hospitality at abbeys and bishoprics, to travel the country more easily.[58] But the third and most important way of increasing his power, the French king found in the establishment of parallel courts, *parlements*, as well as the establishment of an *appeal to the king* 'if a seigneurial court failed to do justice'[59] (a comparable institution existed in England in the form of the court of Chancery).

---

[50] Robert Nisbet, *Prejudices: A philosophical dictionary* (Cambridge, MA: Harvard University Press) 225.

[51] Hence the region *Pays d'Oc.*

[52] Finer (1997) vol. II, 920.

[53] Fichtner (1989) 8ff. Cf. H. Rowen, *The King's State: Proprietary dynasticism in Early Modern France* (New Brunswick, N.J.: Rutgers University Press, 1980).

[54] Finer (1997) vol. II, 922.

[55] Finer (1997) vol. II, 923.

[56] Heinz Duchhardt, 'Münster/Osnabrück as a short-lived peace system', in: A.P. van Goudoever (ed.), *Great Peace Congresses in History 1648-1990*, Utrechtse Historische Cahiers: issue 2, year 14 (1993) 13.

[57] Finer (1997) vol. II, 924. Cf. A. Luchaire, *Histoire des institutions monarchiques de la France sous les premiers Capétiens (987-1180)* (Paris: Alphonse Picard, 1891) 221ff.

[58] Finer (1997) vol. II, 925-927.

[59] Finer (1997) vol. II, 925.

Subjects who appealed to a king's court were under the king's protection until the matter was settled. 'The royal court now swarmed with lawyers versed in Roman law and these *légistes* were to press the royal prerogative against strict feudality; in particular, they would use (for instance) the notion of *utilitas*, the king's overriding duty and right to take any measures whatsoever in the cause of the "public weal". But (…) the legists were equally skilled in turning feudal law itself against the feudatories'.[60]

It was thus through law that bit by bit, the king succeeded in increasing his central influence[61] (and the comparison with the way the European Court in Luxembourg has increased the powers of Brussels in the 20th century is striking – see part II).

The feudal lords attempted to counter these successful attempts of the French king to increase his power at their cost, and this was the most important cause of the Hundred Years' War – a kind of civil war indeed (if it is not anachronistic in itself to speak of such a thing before the advent of modern statehood in the first place). The great feudatories Aquitaine, Burgundy, Brittany and Flanders, in any case, rebelled, in alliance with England, against the French king.[62] This, however, proved ultimately unsuccessful and at the end of the war, the French king began to manage the upkeep of the first standing army in Western Europe since the fall of Rome.[63]

Louis XI moreover, acceding to the throne in 1461, successfully managed to maintain the increased military, financial and administrative powers that the loyal feudatories had granted him to fight the war. He succeeded in appropriating Burgundy in 1477, and in 1514, future king Francis I (1515-1547) married the Duchess of Brittany, thus acquiring that territory for the French monarchy as well.

In the Spanish peninsula, the marriage between Ferdinand of Aragon and Isabella of Castille, and the completion of the 'reconquista' in 1492, meant that the government of the whole of Spain came in the hands of one crown and this

---

[60] Finer (1997) vol. II, 927.
[61] The example of Aquitaine is telling. It was a fief of the King of France, but the Duke was the King of England. Robin Neillands writes: '… the exact boundaries of the duchy had been neither fairly settled nor mutually agreed, which provided (…) cause for argument.' He goes on to point at the nobility of Aquitaine, 'who were perfectly placed to play one king off against the other, and did so at every opportunity. On the one hand, they much preferred to be ruled loosely, and at one remove, by the King of England, who usually resided in his misty northern island and provided a rich market for wine. On the other hand, if there were disputes with their lord the Duke, it was useful to appeal over his head to his suzerain, the King of France, and to the *parlements* of Paris, and not simply face the Duke again, in a higher court, when wearing his crown of England'. Robin Neillands, *The Hundred Years War, revised edition* (London and New York: Routledge, 1990) 28.
[62] Finer (1997) vol. III, 1277. Jonathan Sumption writes in the preface of his three-volume history of the Hundred Years War: 'I have written about England and France together, almost as if they were a single community engaged in a civil war as, in some respects, they were'. Jonathan Sumption, *The Hundred Years War, Volume I. Trial by Battle* (London and Boston: Faber and Faber, 1990) ix.
[63] Finer (1997) vol. III, 1282.

significantly increased the possibilities for centralized government. Nevertheless, the regions conquered from the Moors, most notably those in Andalusia,
were quickly claimed by the 'conquistadores' as their feudal territories, and it
was difficult for the Spanish throne to keep a hold over them. At the same time,
Catalonia was reluctant to surrender more powers to the central government.
These circumstances made Spain 'a loose confederacy held together purely by
the personal union of the monarchs of its two great constituents'.[64] Nevertheless, Isabella of Castille had great ambitions. She desired 'one king, one faith,
one law'[65] – and set out to centralize political power by increasing taxation, by
placing governors in cities who were involved with the administration of justice,
and by use of the Inquisition, which could try such crimes as blasphemy, and
was employed to destroy political opponents as well as fulfilling its religious
mission.[66] The discovery of the New World meant an enormous boost for the
power of the state as well, as colonial revenues flowed directly into the treasury.[67]

It was also in the 15th century, with the conquest of the North African city
of Ceuta in 1415, that the flourishing of the Portuguese kingdom commenced.
In 1484, Bartolommeo Diaz reached the Cape of Good Hope, opening a sailing
route to the treasures of Asia. The treaty of 1494 with Spain divided the colonial
world into two parts: west of current Brazil for Portugal, east of it, for Spain,[68]
enabling Lisbon to increase its revenues and power, and so develop a stronger
grip over the country as well.

The history of the Holy Roman Empire runs along rather different lines from
the general picture of increased centralization, especially in the 15th century.
For the German attempts at centralization of powers experienced many more
drawbacks than in the other parts of Europe, creating a sharp contrast with
France and Britain. In the 11th century, when the German emperor Henry IV
dismissed the claims to political power of Pope Gregory VII, but had to make
his infamous walk to Canossa to beg for mercy, the problematic conflict between
pope and emperor over ultimate sovereignty had left deep traces in the political
awareness of the empire. The relationship between the emperor and his vassals,
the princes of the different *Länder*, moreover, remained rather unsettled until
the beginning of the 15th century. That is to say, the relationship was constantly
redefined, depending on the personality of the emperor and the vassals. When
in 1486, emperor Frederick III asked the nobles for additional taxes to pay for

---

[64]   Finer (1997) vol. III, 1291.
[65]   W.H. Atkinson, *A History of Spain and Portugal* (Harmondsworth: Penguin, 1960) 110.
[66]   Finer (1997) vol. III, 1296.
[67]   Finer (1997) vol. III, 1297.
[68]   In 1580, Portugal entered into a personal union with Castile, but it broke away again in 1640.

his military conflict with Hungary,[69] they united to demand more formal rights of participation, especially in the form of an Imperial Court. The assembly of the electors and other dukes was called *Reichstag*, and it was first assembled by Maximilian (1493-1519) in 1495. At this gathering, a series of bills was passed, denoted together as the *Reichsreform*. In this same year, the Empire also received its new title, the *Heiliges Römisches Reich Deutscher Nation*.[70] From then on the beginnings of more formalized administrative institutions started to take shape. Nevertheless, the Empire remained the least centrally administered political entity in early modern Western Europe.[71] While the 'golden bull' of 1356, issued by Emperor Charles IV, had reinforced the principle of primogeniture that had been introduced in the 12th century concerning the titles of those princes who held a fief directly from the king (the Golden Bull fixed these fiefs to a total of seven),[72] partible inheritance remained common practice amongst lower aristocrats until as late as the eighteenth century, and Paula S. Fichtner observes that 'few aspects of political life in Germany before the eighteenth century seem as remote from current views of the state as partible inheritance'. She continues:

> With this willful redistribution of lands, both private and public, and often the dignities associated with them (...), the German princes of the sixteenth and seventeenth centuries confound our views of rational administrative behavior.[73]

Moreover, under the Emperor Maximilian, who had attempted to increase centralized rule, the Swiss Confederacy saw its *de facto* independence recognized in the treaty of 1499. The Low Countries had been brought under more centralized administrative control by Charles the Bold of Burgundy in the fifteenth century and it was determined at the 'pragmatic sanction' of Charles V that they would stay together and not be divided again. From 1568 onwards, the Dutch successfully fought Habsburg rule and gained *de facto* independence in 1609, and *de jure* in 1648, establishing a confederate commonwealth of 'Seven United Provinces'.[74]

---

[69] The King of Hungary at the time was Matthias Corvinus (1458-1490). He declared war on the Emperor in 1481, and conquered Vienna in 1485.

[70] The empire was called Holy Roman from the 13th century onwards, and the addition 'of the German nation' (Deutscher Nation) was made in the 15th century, in part to emphasize its separateness from the French.

[71] Finer (1997) vol. II, 935-936.

[72] This was introduced by Frederick Barbarossa in 1158. Cf. Fichtner (1989) 8ff.

[73] Fichtner (1989) 4. See also: H. Schulze, *Das Recht der Erstgeburt in den deutschen Fürstenhäusern und seine Bedeutung für die deutsche Staatsentwicklung* (Leipzig: Avenarius und Mendelsohn, 1851).

[74] The Italian peninsula saw a fading of its city-state decentralization and the necessity to organize itself along larger political lines after its defeat at the battle of Marignano in 1515 by Francis I of France, who was able to afford much heavier artillery because of his centralized military apparatus. With the peace of Cateau-Cambresis in 1559, though formally still consisting of different states, most of Italy fell under Habsburg rule or its sphere of influence. East of Venice lay the countries that were heavily affected by the fall of the Eastern Roman Empire in 1453 and the subsequent raids of the Ottomans. The kingdoms of Austria, Hungary, and Serbia struggled with rather fluid borders, but the continuing battles necessitated more centralized political organization as well.

The German empire thus presents the least clear picture of increasing centralization. Indeed, the conflict between worldly and religious authority – and thus of ultimate jurisdiction – brought about an opposite development resulting in the birth of the theory of the modern state exactly *at the cost* of German imperial ambitions. The exploitation of their conflict took place in the reformation, which began when a German monk nailed, as was common practice at the time, the announcement of a debate on the door of the *Schlosskirche* of Wittenberg. The announcement read:

> Out of love for the truth and with the object of eliciting it, a discussion will be held in Wittenberg under the presidency of the reverend father Martin Luther, master of the liberal arts and of the sacred theology as well as professor in the same matter, about the following theses:[75]

The theses that would be debated, 95 in total, contained fundamental criticism of the practices and teachings of the Catholic Church, most notably concerning indulgence.[76] From this followed an internal struggle within the Catholic Church, creating occasions for Luther to express further criticism – for instance concerning the alleged infallibility of the pope, celibacy, and the hierarchy of the church. The papal bull *Exsurge Domine*, in which Luther was summoned to recall his views, was burnt by him in public.[77] The conflict was picked up by some ambitious feudal leaders to play out their own power struggles: with the pope but likewise with the emperor. This certainly contributed to the escalation. What ultimately followed was a bitter war in which the German Lutheran princes, united in the Schmalkaldic League, eventually managed to establish in 1555 the

---

[75] The German text reads: 'Aus Liebe zur Wahrheit und in dem Bestreben, diese zu ergründen, soll in Wittenberg unter dem Vorsitz des ehrwürdigen Vaters Martin Luther, Magisters der freien Künste und der heiligen Theologie sowie deren ordentlicher Professor daselbst, über die folgenden Sätze disputiert werden.' Available online at http://www.effekt-erfolgsplanung.de/ron/freenet/site/de/normal/gothik/bibel/95/95.html.

[76] This also illustrates the remarkable freedoms that could exist in the feudal system. As Tocqueville writes: 'Si Luther avait vécu dans un siècle d'égalité, et qu'il n'eût point eu pour auditeurs des seigneurs et des princes, il aurait peut-être trouvé plus de difficulté à changer la face de l'Europe', in: Alexis de Tocqueville, *De la démocratie en Amérque*, vol. II, book 3, chapter XXI: 'Pourquoi les grandes revolutions deviendront rares'. He also writes in tome I, deuxieme partie, chapitre VII: 'Du pouvoir qu'exerce la majorité en Amérique sur la penséee', that 'En Amérique, la majorité trace un cercle formidable autour de la pensée. Au dedans de ces limites, l'écrivain est libre; mais Malheur à lui s'il ose en sortir. Ce n'est pas qu'il ait à craindre un autodafé, mais il est en butte à des dégoûts de tous genres et à des persecutions de tous les jours. La carrière politique lui est fermée: il a offensé la seule puissance qui ait la faculté de l'ouvrir. On lui refuse tout, jusqu'à la gloire. Avant de publier ses opinions, il croyait avoir des partisans; il lui semble qu'il n'en a plus, maintenant qu'il s'est découvert à tous; car ceux qui le blâment s'expriment hautement, et ceux qui pensent comme lui, sans avoir son courage, se taisent et s'eloignent. Il cede, il plie enfin sous l'effort de chaque jour, et rentre dans le silence, comme s'il éprouvait des remords d'avoir dit vrai'.

[77] Cf. Paul Cliteur, *Moreel Esperanto. Naar een autonome ethiek* (Amsterdam: De Arbeiderspers, 2007) 148-149.

recognition by the emperor that a 'new religion' – denoted as 'augsburgian' –
existed on German soil in such clauses as, for instance:

> § 15. In order to bring peace to the Holy Roman Empire of the Germanic Nation
> between the Roman Imperial Majesty and the Electors, Princes and Estates, let
> neither his Imperial Majesty nor the Electors, Princes, etc., do any violence or
> harm to any estate of the empire on the account of the Augsburg Confession, but
> let them enjoy their religious belief, liturgy and ceremonies as well as their estates
> and other rights and privileges in peace; and complete religious peace shall be
> obtained only by Christian means of amity, or under threat of punishment of the
> Imperial ban.
>
> § 16. Likewise the Estates espousing the Augsburg Confession shall let all the
> Estates and Princes who cling to the old religion live in absolute peace and in the
> enjoyment of all their estates, rights, and privileges.[78]

In later years, historians have concluded that what in fact this agreement amounted
to, was the principle of *cuius regio, eius religio: whose realm, his religion*. And of

---

[78]   The German text reads: § 15 Und damit solcher Fried auch der spaltigen Religion halben, wie
aus hievor vermelten und angezogenen Ursachen die hohe Nothdurfft des H. Reichs Teutscher
Nation erfordert, desto beständiger zwischen der Röm. Rayserl. Maj., Uns, auch Churfürsten,
Fürsten und Ständen des H. Reichs Teutscher Nation angestellt, aufgericht und erhalten werden
möchte, so sollen die Kayserl. Maj., Wir, auch Churfürsten, Fürsten und Stände des H. Reichs
keinen Stand des Reichs von wegen der Augspurgischen Confession und derselbigen Lehr,
Religion und Glaubens halb mit der That gewaltiger Weiß überziehen, beschädigen, vergewaltigen
oder in andere Wege wider sein Conscientz, Gewissen und Willen von dieser Augspurgischen
Confessions-Religion, Glauben, Kirchengebräuchen, Ordnungen und Ceremonien, so sie aufgericht
oder nochmals aufrichten möchten, in ihren Fürstenthumen, Landen und Herrschafften tringen
oder durch Mandat oder in einiger anderer Gestalt beschweren oder verachten, sondern bey
solcher Religion, Glauben, Kirchengebräuchen, Ordnungen und Ceremonien, auch ihren Haab,
Gütern, liegend und fahrend, Land,. Leuthen, Herrschafften, Obrigkeiten, Herrlichkeiten und
Gerechtigkeiten ruhiglich und friedlich bleiben lassen, und soll die streitige Religion nicht anders
dann durch Christliche, freundliche, friedliche Mittel und Wege zu einhelligem, Christlichem
Verstand und Vergleichung gebracht werden, alles bey Kayserl. und Königl. Würden, Fürstl.
Ehren, wahren Worten und Pön des Land-Friedens. § 16. Dargegen sollen die Stände, so der
Augspurgischen Confession verwandt, die Röm. Kays. Mai., Uns und Churfürsten, Fürsten und
andere des H. Reichs Stände der alten Religion anhängig, geistlich und weltlich, samt und mit
ihren Capituln und andern geistlichs Stands, auch ungeacht, ob und wohin sie ihre Residentzen
verruckt oder gewendet hätten (doch daß es mit Bestellung der Ministerien gehalten werde, wie
hie unten darvon ein sonderlicher Articul gesetzt,) gleicher Gestalt bey ihrer Religion, Glauben,
Kirchengebräuchen, Ordnungen und Ceremonien, auch ihren Haab, Gütern, liegend und fahrend,
Landen, Leuthen, Herrschafften, Obrigkeiten, Herrlichkeiten und Gerechtigkeiten, Renthen,
Zinsen, Zehenden unbeschwert bleiben und sie derselbigen friedlich und ruhiglich gebrauchen,
geniessen, unweigerlich folgen lassen und getreulichen darzu verholffen seyn, auch mit der That
oder sonst in ungutem gegen denselbigen nichts fürnehmen, sondern in alle Wege nach Laut
und Ausweisung des H. Reichs Rechten, Ordnungen, Abschieden und aufgerichten Landfrieden
jeder sich gegen dem andern an gebührenden, ordentlichen Rechten begnügen lassen, alles bey
Fürstl. Ehren, wahren Worten und Vermeidung der Pön, in dem uffgerichten Land-Frieden
begriffen.' 'Augsburger Reichsabschied ('Augsburger Religionsfrieden'), 25 September 1555. The
translation is provided by Emil Reich (ed.), *Selected Documents Illustrating Mediaeval and Modern
History* (London: P.S. King & Son, 1905) 230-232. Available online at http://pages.uoregon.edu/
sshoemak/323/texts/augsburg.htm.

course, deciding in matters of *religion* meant in fact deciding a variety of political and legal questions: it meant, in other words, *whose realm, his law*: a dramatic increase in independent government. This treaty of 1555 thus symbolizes a break with the Medieval conception of rulers as 'local embodiments of a universal authority'[79] (church or emperor), a conception that had been inherent in the very idea of the 'respublica christiana'.

With Christianity ceasing to be a single creed, rulers necessarily became representatives of a particular locality, independent from other localities. The birth of the modern state thus coincided with the abandonment of universal jurisdiction, and comes down to the raising and upholding of borders.

But with the Augsburg agreement, the religious unrest in Europe had by no means been brought to an end. Throughout the second half of the 16th and most of the 17th century, the Holy Roman Empire, but France, the Low Countries, Denmark, Sweden and England as well, continued to struggle for internal unity and for religious and political independence. The Holy Roman Empire for instance descended into the devastating Thirty Years' War in 1618, of which historians estimate the death toll over 20% of the entire population.[80] After the English King Henry VIII broke with the Catholic Church in 1534, England faced more than a century of severe internal conflict culminating in a civil war and the execution of King Charles I in 1649, only to be resolved after the accession to the throne of the Dutch stadtholder William III in 1688.

The Netherlands, in the meantime, had been struggling for eighty years with the Spanish rule, in part over their right to religious freedom. In doing so, they also experienced one of the first successful acts of religious terrorism of modern times, when Balthasar Gérard murdered their prince William of Orange in 1584, claiming to act in the name of the Catholic Church. France faced similar challenges in these years. A high point was reached in 1572, when throughout the kingdom several thousands of French Protestants, including many leading figures, were murdered. The massacre had a deeply divisive effect on the aristocratic class, and the attempts of King Henry IV to bring reconciliation to

---

[79] Jeremy A. Rabkin, *Law without nations? Why constitutional government requires sovereign states* (Princeton: Princeton University Press, 2007) 51.

[80] Geoffrey Parker writes: 'Earlier estimates that the war destroyed half or two-thirds of the German population, are no longer accepted. More recent estimates are much more conservative, suggesting that the population of the Holy Roman Empire may have declined by about 15 to 20 per cent, from some 20 million before the war to about 16 or 17 million after it', in: Geoffrey Parker, *The Thirty Years War* (New York: Routledge, 1997) 188. Other historians have made different estimations. Norman Davies estimates the loss to have been about 8 million, in: Norman Davies, *Europe. A History* (Oxford: University Press, 1996) 568. C.V. Wedgwood confirms this, when she estimates that the German Empire probably numbered about twenty-one million people in 1618, and thirteen and a half million in 1648 (a loss of 35%), in: C.V. Wedgwood, *The Thirty Years War* (New York: The New York Review of Books, 1938). Alan McFarlane confirms these figures in *The Savage Wars of Peace: England, Japan and the Malthusian Trap* (Oxford: Blackwell Publishers, 1997).

this internal strive resulted in his assassination in 1610 by the Catholic fanatic
François Ravaillac (see also chapter 1.2).

The year 1648 marks a crucial moment in all these conflicts. In that year, two
treaties were signed in Münster, one between the Low Countries and the Empire
(and its constituting estates), another between France and the Empire (again
together with its constituting estates). A third treaty was signed in Osnabrück,
between the Empire (and its estates) and Sweden. Altogether, these treaties are
generally referred to as the 'Peace of Westphalia'.[81]

Heinz Duchhardt observes that 'the 1648 order of peace consists of two
components, the one regulating and balancing the circumstances within the
complex organism of the Holy Roman Empire and proving extraordinarily
enduring and stabilizing, the other being a rather vaguely perceivable political
philosophy which was hoped to bring about a long-term European peace'.[82]
This consisted in:

> Particularly Richelieu's conception of a security system of all European states based
> upon the principle of the inviolability of frontiers and thus upon the settlement
> of the territorial status quo.[83]

The agreements concerning the internal sovereignty of the German states,
however, were especially significant. While the Treaty of Osnabrück explicitly
reconfirmed the religious peace that was concluded in 1555,[84] and declared such
things as that adherents to the Augsburgian religion would receive rights and
justice in the same way (…) as Catholics,[85] it also determined that states would
have the right to administer their own schools and churches, and so on.[86] 'Taken
together', Lesaffer writes, 'the constitutional and religious settlement amounted
to the construction of a highly federative Empire based on the principles of
territorial sovereignty and sovereign equality of the *Stände*' (i.e. the estates).[87]
This was applied to the relations between European states more generally in

---

[81]   The significance of 'Westphalia' has been disputed in recent studies: A. Osiander, 'Sovereignty,
International Relations, and the Westphalian Myth', in: *International Organization*, vol. 55, issue 2
(Spring 2001) 251–287; Randall Lesaffer, 'The Westfalian Peace Treaties and the Development of
the Tradition of Great European Peace Settlements prior to 1648', in: *Grotiana* NS 18 (1997) 71-96;
Karl-Heinz Ziegler, 'Der westfälische Frieden von 1648 in der Geschichte des Völkerrechts' in
Meinhard Schröder (ed.), *350 Jahre westfälischer Friede* (Berlin, 1999) 99-117; Karl-Heinz Ziegler,
'Die Bedeutung des westfälischen Friedens von 1648 für das europäisches Völkerreht', *Archiv des
Völkerrechts 37* (1999), 129-51; Benno Teschke, *The Myth of 1648: Class, Geopolitics, and the Making
of Modern International Relations* (London: Verso, 2003).
[82]   Durhhardt (1993) 16.
[83]   Durhhardt (1993) 16.
[84]   'Die im Jahre 1555 geschlossene Religionsfriede'. Osnabrücker Friedensvertrag (Instrumentum
Pacis Osnabrugensis), 24 October 1648, article V, § 1.
[85]   'Recht und Gerechtigkeit in derselben Weise und ohne Unterschied (…) wie den Katholiken.'
Ibidem, article IV, § 56.
[86]   *Ibidem*, article V, § 7.
[87]   Lesaffer (1997) 71-96, there 72.

later years, and accounts for at least one reason that 1648 is so significant in the development of modern sovereigns states. 'Though [it] was not present in the text', Lesaffer continues, 'the treaties introduced the idea of sovereign equality among the states of Europe. This was however a broad extension of the recognition of the equality of the German *Stände* regardless of their religion'.[88]

The Westphalian treaties taken as a whole, moreover, contained agreements among several European powers; while the treaty of Münster was between the Empire and France, and the treaty of Osnabrück between the Empire and Sweden, both contained references to the other treaty, and thus implied a '*société des nations*' between them, as scholars have concluded.[89] Moreover, the presence of third parties implied a guarantee by such a 'society of nations', which became common from then on in the course of the 17th century (and still is regular practice today).

Recent scholarship has argued plausibly that a nuanced understanding of the significance of the treaty of Westphalia is necessary, and that it is only with hindsight that it can be regarded as the 'moment of birth' of the modern state. Osiander even goes so far as to speak of the 'Westphalian myth'.[90] It may nevertheless safely be contended that with the end of the Thirty Years' War and the significant decrease of the idea of an overarching, Christian unity within Europe, the modern state system received an important impulse.[91]

But while the powers of central governments increased, and the power of the pope decreased, Europe in the age of 'absolutism' remained politically decentralized and monarchs did not remotely have the powers to influence the life of their inhabitants in the way governments do today. Nevertheless, as one scholar put it, the monarchy always sought 'a supreme, independent, secular authority'. Rivalry with the Vatican and with the papacy's claim for ultimate jurisdiction 'was the germ of the modern conceptions of sovereignty',[92] and it was the persisting desire of 'nie wieder Krieg' – never again so destructive a civil war – that inspired scholars all through Europe to draw up the contours of the sovereign state and defend the need for a shared allegiance to it.

---

[88] *Ibidem.*
[89] Lesaffer (1997) 71-96, there 73.
[90] Osiander (2001) 251–287.
[91] The term 'Concert of Europe' was introduced at the Vienna peace congress in 1815; before that, the formula 'balance of powers' was used, which had been introduced with the peace of Utrecht of 1713. Durchhardt (1993) 16ff.
[92] Hall (1984) 7.

1.2. *Averting Civil War*

In many respects, these 'modern conceptions of sovereignty' were first voiced by
Niccolò Machiavelli (1469-1527).[93] Although credit should be given to Marsilius
of Padua for having introduced, some two centuries earlier, several key concepts
of modern political thought in his *Defensor Pacis,* Machiavelli applied the idea of
political and legislative power as a corporate body, not as a personal privilege, to
political doctrine.[94] He thus broke with the Medieval tradition of understanding
power in terms of an eternal chain of mutual obligations,[95] dependent upon
reciprocal personal favors instead of institutions, and had defended in *Il Principe*
a political realism, to be conducted by the prince of Florence but generally applicable to all rulers at all times, justifying political means from an autonomous
ragion di Stato (*raison d'état*), namely in terms of their ends.

Yet Machiavelli did not ask the question, as M.J. Tooley puts it, 'what a
state is and how it is constructed.'[96] His main subject was how political power
functions, how it could be used and maximized. Nor was the specter of a civil
war, of the kind that all of Europe went through, as we have seen, by the end
of the Middle Ages, predominant in his mind. A more general and systematic

---

[93] The dominant view is that the rediscovery of Roman law formed a first impulse for this
development. The Roman conception of the state as a corporate body possessing permanent as
well as ultimate authority, independent of its temporary occupants (a notion known as *plenitudo
potestatis*), as well as the monopoly of legislation, however, also formed a major inspiration for
papal ambitions. William D. McCready writes: 'When the term *plenitudo potestatis* (…) came
to be used in connection with the papacy, it did not necessarily imply a claim to complete
temporal sovereignty, but simply spiritual sovereignty with temporal consequences, plus temporal
sovereignty in the Papal States and certain other special areas. But by the late 13th and early 14th
centuries the term had taken on a wider significance, at least for the papal hierocratic theorists.
(…) What was meant was that the pope had a supreme authority in temporal affairs, and that he
had this supremacy, not because of the beneficence of any temporal ruler, but simply because of
the authority inherent in the papal office itself'. W.D. McCready, 'Papal Plenitudo Potestatis and
the Source of Temporal Authority in Late Medieval Papal Hierocratic Theory', in: *Speculum*, Vol.
48, No. 4 (Oct., 1973) 654-674. Cf. Arthur Nussbaum, *A Concise history of the law of nations* (New
York: The Macmillan Company, 1961) 39ff; B. Holland, 'Sovereignty as *Dominium?* Reconstructing
the Constructivist Roman Law Thesis', in: *International Studies Quarterly*, vol. 54, issue 2 (June
2010) 449-480.
[94] Cf. Harvey C. Mansfield jr., 'On the impersonality of the modern state: a comment on
Machiavelli's use of Stato', in: *The American Political Science Review*, Vol. 77, No. 4. (Dec., 1983)
849-857.
[95] Bertrand de Jouvenel speaks of the 'ladder of commands' that was typical for the Medieval
political worldview. In: *Sovereignty. An inquiry into the political good* (Indianapolis: Liberty Fund,
1997) 204. Cf. Arthur O. Lovejoy, *The great chain of being. A study of the history of an Idea* (New
York: Harper & Brothers, 1936).
[96] Jean Bodin, *Six books of the Commonwealth.* Abridged and Translated by M.J. Tooley (Oxford:
Basil Blackwell, 1955) 16. David Held writes: 'Bodin was not the first to make [the case for a central
authority]; for example, Machiavelli (1469-1527), a significant influence on Bodin, had done so
earlier. But unlike Machiavelli, Bodin developed this notion into what is commonly regarded as
the first statement of the modern theory of sovereignty', in: Held, *Political theory and the modern
state. Essays on state, power and democracy* (Cambridge: Polity Press, 1989) 219.

discussion of statehood, as a concept, and of the great danger of civil war that it should prevent, was first taken up by Jean Bodin (1530-1596) in France, and then continued by Johannes Althusius (1577–1638) in the Holy Roman Empire, and Thomas Hobbes (1588-1679) in England. The consequences of the international state system that emerged out of the peace agreements of the seventeenth century were first analyzed by Hugo Grotius (1583-1645) in the Republic, by Samuel Pufendorf in the Holy Roman Empire (1632-1694), and were synthesized in the middle of the 18th century by the Swiss diplomat Emer de Vattel (1714-1767).[97] It would strike later commentators that the leading authors in this field since the 17th century were mostly Protestants.[98] Karl von Kaltenborn-Stachau, the significant 19th century historiographer of international law, even went so far as to denote international law as 'a Protestant science'.[99] It is not hard to see why: as international law implies sovereign states, it inevitably meant a diminution of the power of the Vatican and a diminishing of the unity of Europe (is it surprising, then, that the major Eurofederalists in the 20th century were Catholics?[100]).

Despite persistent rumors at the time that he had become a protestant, as were most other theorists of sovereignty, Jean Bodin always claimed to be an adherent to the Catholic faith.[101] Systematic thinking about modern statehood begins with him.[102] His starting point was the war of all against all that has become commonplace in political theory ever since (and that was no doubt inspired by the religious conflict France went through at the time). Breaking with the Aristotelian notion that because man is a social animal, 'the state exists by nature',[103] Bodin wrote in his main work, *Six livres de la République* (1576), that 'reason and common sense alike point to the conclusion that the origin and foundation of commonwealths was in force and violence'.[104] He continued: 'the first generations of men were unacquainted with the sentiments of honor, and their highest endeavor was to kill, torture, rob, and enslave their fellows (…) Force, violence, ambition, avarice, and the passion for vengeance, armed men

---

[97] Vattel was baptized as 'Emer'. Modern commentators have mistakenly Germanized his name as 'Emerich'.

[98] Nussbaum (1961) 136.

[99] Quoted and discussed in Nussbaum (1961) 136.

[100] For instance Jean Monnet, Alcide de Gasperi, Robert Schuman, Konrad Adenauer, and Jacques Delors. Apart from the different religious traditions, the Northern European states also had another legal inheritance from that of Roman law. Both the anglo-saxon common law and the Germanic tribal law may have rendered the inhabitants of Northern Europe different instincts than the former subjects of the Roman empire.

[101] Cf. S. Baldwin, 'Jean Bodin and the League', in: *The Catholic Historical Review*, Vol. 23, No. 2 (July 1937) 160-184.

[102] J.H. Franklin, 'Introduction, An outline of Bodin's career', in: Bodin, *On Sovereignty. Four chapters from the Six books of the Commonwealth*. Edited and translated by Julian H. Franklin (Cambridge: Cambridge University Press, 1992) ix-xv.

[103] Aristotle, *Politics* (London: Penguin Classics, 1992) book I.

[104] Bodin (1955) 56 (Book I, chapters VI and VII concerning the citizen).

against one another (…) The result of the ensuing conflicts was to give victory to some, and to reduce the rest to slavery'.[105]

This being the origin of man's political existence, 'we can say then that every citizen is a subject since his liberty is limited by the sovereign power to which he owes obedience'.[106] Bodin goes on to, in his own words, 'carefully define' the term 'sovereignty', which, being 'the distinguishing mark of a commonwealth', and while 'an understanding of its nature [is] fundamental to any treatment of politics, no jurist or political philosopher has in fact attempted to define […]'.[107]

Bodin identifies two essential characteristics of sovereignty: the perpetual character of the sovereign power, and its absoluteness. It is 'the distinguishing mark of the sovereign that [it] cannot in any way be subject to the commands of another …'.[108] The prince (or sovereign) can therefore not even be bound by his own rules, and the autonomy of communities existing within the sovereign state should be regarded as fundamentally limited. This included thus the power to legislate at will.[109]

It is this element of Bodin's thought that critics called his 'absolutism', and Bodin inspired the attempts of both Richelieu and Louis XIV to centralize state power.[110] Moreover, Bodin claimed that no 'right to revolution' existed, not even if the monarch usurped his power:

> If the prince is sovereign absolutely, as are the genuine monarchs of France, Spain, England, Scotland, Ethiopia, Turkey, Persia, and Moscovy (…), then it is not the part of any subject individually, or all of them in general, to make an attempt on the honor or the life of the monarch, either by way of force or by way of law, even if he has committed all the misdeeds, impieties, and cruelties that one could mention.[111]

The *Vindiciae contra tyrannos*, published by an anonymous author under the pseudonym Stephen Junius Brutus in 1579, emphasized this point of Bodin's theory in contradicting it, and claimed that the sovereign was only the guardian of rights he could not break or alter himself, and that the ultimate source of authority was not the state, but the people.

Another critic of Bodin, the German scholar and Calvinist Johannes Althusius (1577-1638) argued in the same vein. In the preface to the first edition of his main work, the *Politica methodice digesta*, or *Politics*, he stated that:

---

[105] *Ibidem.*
[106] *Ibidem.*
[107] Bodin (1955) 56 (Book I, chapter VIII concerning sovereignty).
[108] *Ibidem.*
[109] Bodin (1955) 80ff (Book I, chapter X).
[110] Though it seems fair to say that these were the aims of the absolutist regimes, in practice, they stayed far behind on them.
[111] Bodin (1992) 115 (Book II, chapter 5).

I maintain the exact opposite [from Bodin], (…) I concede that the prince or supreme magistrate is the steward, administrator, and overseer of these [sovereign] rights. But I maintain that their ownership and usufruct properly belong to the total realm or people.[112]

Althusius argues, while laying out a systematic bottom-up approach of 'the commonwealth' (i.e. the state), that while society consists of the individual citizen and the state, it also has a wide variety of intermediary bodies, such as guilds, cities, and provinces with their own prerogatives. In this sense, Althusius remains near to the medieval idea of society, and clearly conflicts with Bodin (and later with Hobbes). Nevertheless, Althusius concedes to the Bodinian notion of supreme authority – the notion of sovereignty, separating the medieval idea of politics from modern statehood. Their dispute is not over the question whether sovereignty ought to be centralized, but rather over the question who ultimately possesses it. 'If law and freedom from law by a supreme power, are accepted in this sense, I concede to the judgment of Bodin (…). But by no means can this supreme power be attributed to a king or optimates, as Bodin most ardently endeavors to defend', Althusius repeats. 'Rather it is to be attributed rightfully only to the body of a universal association, namely, to a commonwealth or realm, and as belonging to it. From this body (…) every legitimate power flows to those we call kings or optimates.'[113]

Thus while the Frenchman had emphasized a top-down *étatist* approach to political power, the German Althusius took a bottom-up approach, in which sovereignty derives from the people. A difference that would also divide the French and the Germans in discussions over nationality, about two hundred years later (and two paragraphs further down this book).

For both Bodin and Althusius, however, modern political organization required the precedence of secular law over religious law. As Jean Bodin wrote, it is central to citizenship to submit to the ultimate authority of one sovereign, and as long as this is done, different 'communities' may exist, enjoying a degree of toleration and self-government.[114] It is the plurality of the law, the overlapping of jurisdictions; indeed the prevalence of personal ties over institutional arrangements, and therefore the fluidness of competencies which was characteristic of the feudal order,[115] that had to give way to the more centralized, institutionalized,

---

[112] The first edition of the book appeared in 1603, but a later and revised edition was published in 1614.

[113] Johannes Althusius, 'Politics', in: F.S. Carney, *The politics of Johannes Althusius*. An abridged translation of the Third Edition of Politica Methodice Digesta, atque exemplis sacris et profanes illustrata and including the prefaces to the First and Third editions (London: Eyre & Spottiswoode, 1965) 67.

[114] Bodin (1955) 59ff (Book I, chapter VI).

[115] Robert Cooper, *The breaking of nations. Order and chaos in the twenty-first century* (London: Atlantic Books, 2004) 8: 'In the particular circumstances of medieval Europe, empire had become

and hierarchical legal order of the modern state. Even though it would take until well into the eighteenth and nineteenth centuries for national codifications to emerge: these legal systems themselves were the logical and ultimate expression of ideas born two centuries earlier.

Bodin and Althusius indeed both seem to have been permeated with the insight that Europe, especially on matters of religion, would never regain its unity – indeed, for a Calvinist like Althusius, this was not even an attractive idea. Attempting to prevent political entities from descending into civil wars or breaking up into weak localities, the aim was to conceive of political authority in a way that enabled it to stand above the different factions of society. Political power thus became more abstract, yet also more pervasive.

An example of the conflict France went through around this time is formed by the events following the early morning of August 24th, 1572, when about a hundred Parisian noblemen undertook the royally sanctioned[116] assassination of one hundred protestant noblemen. This marked the beginning of the St. Bartholomew's Day massacres, which were to sweep through the country and take at least several thousands of lives.[117] France was seriously threatened with civil war, and it was prevented certainly in part by the religious and political virtuosity of King Henry IV, who, after converting from Protestantism to Catholicism,[118] issued the edict of Nantes in 1598, granting religious tolerance to Protestants. Jean Bodin, when writing his treatise on sovereignty, was well aware of the conflicts dividing France at the time. Himself having been under suspicion of Calvinist sympathies several times,[119] Bodin also wrote a series of imaginary conversations between adherents of seven different beliefs: a proponent of natural religion, a philosophical skeptic, a Jew, a Muslim, a Catholic, a Lutheran, and a Zwinglian,[120] who in the end agreed to cohabitate peacefully.[121] The morale was that political authority can exist independently of, and indeed stand above all these different faiths and these different people adhering to them.[122] Cardinal Richelieu – as we have seen before – argued in the same vein, when in 1617, he laid down in an instruction to a minister that no Catholic should be

---

loose and fragmented. A tangled mass of jurisdictions competed for control: landowners, free cities, holders of feudal rights, guild of the king. Above all the Church, representing what remained of the Christian empire, still held considerable power and authority, competing with the secular powers.'

[116] That is King Charles IX (1560-1574).

[117] T.F.X. Noble et al., *Western Civilization. The continuing experiment* (Boston: Houghton Mifflin Company 1998) 547ff.

[118] Famously declaring that *"Paris vaut bien une messe"*. Cf. Heinrich Mann, *Die Jugend des Königs Henri Quatre* (Reinbek bei Hamburg: Rowohlt Taschenbuch, 1964).

[119] Franklin (1992) ix-xv.

[120] Ulrich Zwingli (1484-1531) was a priest who was important in the Swiss reformation.

[121] Franklin (1992) ix-xv.

[122] A comparable argument is developed by Cliteur (2007).

so blind 'to prefer, in matters of state, a Spaniard to a French Protestant':[123] on the contrary, the national loyalty of the citizen had to take clear primacy over whatever religious loyalties he might feel.

Johannes Althusius insisted on the distinction, well known from Augustine, and reformulated by Aquinas, between the universality of morals and the particularity of temporal legal arrangements. In the words of Thomas Hueglin: 'Althusius claimed (…) that the distinction of what is general moral law and what is particular temporal provision was a political one and therefore a matter of secular government'. Although Althusius emphasized the importance of religion as a general moral code, the purpose was, 'not to turn back to the medieval duality of church and state (…)'. Hueglin continues:

> On the contrary, it seems to me much more plausible to see in the *Politics* an attempt of excluding the church as an unwanted interloper in secular matters. Even though, or perhaps precisely because the staunch Calvinist and church elder Althusius was convinced that the Christian religion, particularly in its Reformed version, was the only true religion, he might have understood that the place which this religion could occupy in his political theory was that of a civil moral code.[124]

---

[123] J.C.L. Simonde de Sismondi, *Histoire des Français*. Vol. XXII (Paris: Treuttel et Würtz, 1839) 388-389: 'L'instruction contient un résumé rapide de ce qu'avoit fait la reine pour maintenir la paix du royaume, de ce qu'avoit fait le prince pour la troubler; elle rappelle les nombreux marriages qui de siècle en siècle avoient uni les familles royales de France et d'Espagne; elle declare "que nul Catholique n'est si aveugle d'estimer, en matières d'État, un Espagnol meilleur q'un Français Huguenot". Sismondi notes a page before that 'Richelieu, qui avoit dressé lui-même avec beaucoup de soin l'instruction de Schomberg …'. This episode is also discussed in Henry Thomas Buckle, *History of Civilization in England*. 2nd edition, vol. 1 (New York: D. Appleton and co., 1859) 387-388: 'It might have been expected that when Richelieu, a great dignitary of the Romish church, was placed at the head of affairs, he would have re-established a connexion so eagerly desired by the profession to which he belonged. But his conduct was not regulated by such views as these. His object was, not to favour the opinions of a sect, but to promote the interests of a nation. His treaties, his diplomacy, and the schemes of his foreign alliances, were all directed, not against the enemies of the church, but against the enemies of France. By erecting this new standard of action, Richelieu took a great step towards secularizing the whole system of European politics. For, he thus made the theoretical interests of men subordinate to their practical interests. Before his time, the rulers of France, in order to punish their Protestant subjects, had not hesitated to demand the aid of the Catholic troops of Spain; and in so doing, they merely acted upon the old opinion, that it was the chief duty of a government to suppress heresy. This pernicious doctrine was first openly repudiated by Richelieu. As early as 1617, and before he had established his power, he, in an instruction to one of the foreign ministers which is still extant, laid it down as a principle, that, in matters of state, no Catholic ought to prefer a Spaniard to a French Protestant. To us, indeed, in the progress of society, such preference of the claims of our country to those of our creed, has become a matter of course; but in those days it was a startling noverly'. As will be discussed in chapter 6, Richelieu's view nowadays becomes increasingly rare again as a consequence of multiculturalism.

[124] Thomas O. Hueglin, 'State and Church in the Political Thought of Althusius', available online at http://polis.unipmn.it/seminari/calvino2009/files/Hueglin7_05_09.pdf. The quoted chapter from the *Politics* that Hueglin refers to is XXXff.

Thomas Hobbes likewise defended the state's political supremacy over religious claims. When he wrote his main contribution to political theory, *Leviathan* (1651), it was in many respects a logical follow-up of earlier works scrutinizing the relation of man to nature, and man to man,[125] working in the tradition Machiavelli had set out. Hobbes had therefore already built an intellectual structure, rationalizing all phenomena, in the typical Enlightenment manner, *ab initio*. For Hobbes, the most devastating political situation was the anarchy in the state of nature. In the first part of Leviathan, *Of Man*, Hobbes sets out his view of greedy human nature and the state of war of all against all when there is no sufficiently powerful state.[126] In the second part, *Of Common-wealth*, he then proceeds to sketch the outlines of what would have to be required to let man step out of this state of nature and into the civilized condition. Essential in this would be to renounce all claims to natural rights, as none exist in the state of nature anyway. More powerful than any other organization on the state's territory, the *Leviathan* of state power could then truly stand above its subjects and bring order to them through its laws.[127] Concerning the relationship between church and state, Hobbes argued plainly that since revelations can only be convincing to those who have received the revelation themselves, it should be the political power that is allowed to determine what the church should, in the last instance, teach.[128]

---

[125] Most notably his book *The elements Law. Natural and Politic* (1640) Edited with a preface and cirtical notes by Ferdinand Tönnies (London: Frank Cass & Co, 1969).

[126] Thomas Hobbes, *Leviathan* (1651). Edited with an introduction by C.B. Macpherson (London: Penguin Books, 1985) 183ff: Part I, Ch. XIII, 'Of the *Naturall Condition* of Mankind, as concerning their Felicity, and Misery'.

[127] The commonwealth in fact begins already to be formed in Part I, especially Ch. XIV, 'Of the first and second *Naturall Lawes*, and of *Contracts*', but goes on in more depth in Part II.

[128] Hobbes (1985) 409ff: Part III, Ch. XXXII, 'Of the Principles of *Christian Politiques*': 'When God speaketh to man, it must be either immediately; or by mediation of another man, to whom he had formerly spoken by himself immediately. How God speaketh to a man immediately, may be understood by those well enough, to whom he hath spoken; but how the same should be understood by another, is hard, if not impossible to know. For if a man pretend to me, that God hath spoken to him supernaturally, and immediately, and I make doubt of it, I cannot easily perceive what argument he can produce, to oblige me to believe it. (…)'. And 428: Part III, Ch. XXXIX, 'Of the *Signification in Scripture* of the word Church': '… a Church, such a one as is capable to Command, to Judge, Absolve, Condemn, or do any other act, is the same thing with a Civil Common-wealth, consisting of Christian men; and is called a *Civill State*, for that the subjects of it are *Christians. Temporall* and *Spirituall* Government, are but two words brought into the world, to make men see double, and mistake their *Lawfull Soveraign*. It is true, that the bodies of the faithfull, after the Resurrection, shall be not onely Spirituall, but Eternall: but in this life they are grosse, and corruptible. There is therefore no other Government in this life, neither of State, nor Religion, but Temporall; nor teaching of any doctrine, lawfull to any Subject, which the Governour both of the State, and of the Religion, forbiddeth to be taught: And that Governor must be one: or else there must needs follow Faction, and Civil war in the Common-wealth, between the *Church* and *State* (…)'.

The mutation, then, of the medieval to the modern conception of statehood, could be signified as the breaking of the 'great chain of duties'[129] into several smaller yet stronger chains, attached, at least theoretically, to a final zenith point – the sovereign. As Bertrand de Jouvenel summarizes it in his book *On Sovereignty*: 'In the Middle Ages, men had a very strong sense of the concrete thing, hierarchy; they lacked the idea of that abstract thing, sovereignty'.[130] Indeed, the Europe of the Middle Ages had, because of feudal decentralized rule and religious uniformity, been both essentially *regional* and *unified*.[131] Europe was often referred to as the *respublica Christiana*, a religious-political unity, without clear jurisdictional demarcation lines.[132] In the 16th and 17th centuries, Europe lost this religious unity, while the different regions gradually developed into more centralized political entities. And even though these new 'states' have often recognized their shared interests, the idea of forming a single political unity with the pope at its top, was definitely lost. A clear example of how political power took ultimate privilege over religious leadership was the England of Henry VIII. In a dramatic attempt to realize the desired annulment of his marriage, which the Vatican denied him,[133] he declared himself head of the Church of England in 1534. Other states made comparable arrangements. With the claim to *universal rule* abandoned, it was replaced with a claim to a monopoly on *territorial* jurisdiction and ultimate political power in the capital of that territory, and it is this transition that marks the fundamental divide between the feudal order and modern statehood. The British diplomat and former advisor to Javier Solana, Robert Cooper, is right to write in his book on supranationalism: 'Thus Europe changed from a weak system of universal order to a pattern of stronger but geographically limited sovereign authorities without any overall framework of law'.[134] It seems indeed that Tocqueville was right when he said that 'in running over the pages of our history, we shall scarcely find a single great event of the last seven hundred years that has not promoted

---

[129] In the words of Augustin Thierry, as quoted by Jouvenel (1957) 171.

[130] Jouvenel (1957) 171.

[131] Rabkin (2007) 47-48: '… medieval Europe surely could not sustain any notion of sovereign states. (…) Feudal conditions made it impossible to distinguish sovereign powers from other kinds of authority. (…) There were different peoples, speaking different languages, but no distinct nations or territorial states to define their boundaries.'

[132] Randall Lesaffer, 'Peace treaties from Lodi to Westphalia', in: Randall Lesaffer (ed.), *Peace treaties and international law in European History, From the Late Middle ages to World War One* (Cambridge: Cambridge University Press, 2004) 11.

[133] Pope Clement VII (1523-1534) was under control of Charles V, who opposed the annulment as Henry VIII's wife was Charles' sister Catherine.

[134] Cooper (2004) 8. See also: Hall (1984) 4-7; and Spruyt (2002) 127-49.

equality of condition'[135] – and, we may add (entirely in Tocquevillian spirit), the likewise increase in the power of the state.

Essential, however, to the character of the modern state, is its power ultimately to make, administer and execute the law.[136] While in general these powers increased, it is not before the end of the *ancien régime* and the introduction of democratic politics, that states fully assumed these powers.

Voltaire was still able to ridicule the legal diversity that existed up until the 18th century: 'we [in France] have more laws than the whole of Europe taken together; almost every village has its own'.[137] Whomever had to travel from Bretagne to the Languedoc, Voltaire wrote satirically, 'changes laws more often than he changes horses'.[138] And indeed,

> Is it not absurd and dreadful that what is true in one village may be found false in another? By what strange barbarity is it possible that fellow countrymen do not live under the same law?[139]

It was because London had been destroyed and rebuilt after the great fire, Voltaire contended, that it had become 'worthy of being inhabited'. 'Observe in Paris the area of *les Halles*, of *Saint-Pierre-aux-Boeufs* and of the *rue Brise-Miche* or *Pet-au-Diable*, and contrast that with the *Louvre* or the *Tuileries*: then you get an impression of our laws'. Voltaire saw chaos in the old neighborhoods of Paris and admired the newer *quartiers* symbolized by the Louvre. He confronted the French with the following choice: 'If you want good laws; burn the ones you have and make new ones'.[140]

Opposing the Enlightenment vision thus expounded by Voltaire, stands the Medieval view, expressed by Montesquieu when he emphasized in his *De l'esprit des lois* that cultural diversity was such that uniform laws would result

---

[135] Alexis de Tocqueville, *Democracy in America*. The Henry Reeve Text as revised by Francis Bowen, Volume 1 (New York: Vintage Books, 1990) 5.

[136] As will be further discussed in chapter 2.

[137] 'Nous avons plus de lois que toute l'Europe ensemble; presque chaque ville a la sienne'. Voltaire, 'Dialogue entre un plaideur et un avocat' (1751), in: Ibidem, *Oeuvres complètes de Voltaire*, vol. XXIII, 'Mélanges II' (Paris: Garnier Frères, 1879) 493-496.

[138] 'Change de lois plus souvent qu'il ne change de chevaux'. Voltaire (1751) 493-496: '... il en est ainsi de poste en poste dans le royaume: vous changez de jurisprudence en changeant de chevaux'.

[139] 'N'est-ce pas une chose absurde et affreuse que ce qui est vrai dans un village se trouve faux dans un autre? Par quelle étrange barbarie se peut-il que des compatriots ne vivent pas sous la meme loi?' Voltaire (1751) 493-496. The 'avocat' in the fictional dialogue that this quote is from, goes on to explain how the different regions of France belonged to different 'barons', and that it is impossible 'que la loi soit partout la meme, quand la pinte ne l'est pas'.

[140] 'Digne d'être habitée' (…) Voyez à Paris le quartier des Halles, de saint-Pierre-aux-Boeufs, la rue Brise-Miche, celle du Pet-au-Diable, contraster avec le Louvre et les Tuileries: voilà l'image de nos lois'. (…) 'Voulez-vous avoir de bonnes lois; brûlez les vôtres, et faites-en de nouvelles'. Voltaire, 'Dictionnaire Philosophique: Lois' (1765), in: *Oeuvres complètes de Voltaire*, vol. 33. 'Dictionaire Philosophique – Tome I' (Paris: Antoine-Augustin Renouard, 1819) 170.

in despotism.[141] Montesquieu's 'final emphasis was on a pluralist conception of society', Norman Hampson writes in his study of 18th century French political thought,[142] and Montesquieu praised 'the prodigious diversity' of the laws and customs within the French kingdom.[143]

The very idea of the social contract, enabling the members to design *from scratch* the laws they intend to live under, not only contends with the Medieval view as voiced by Montesquieu, but is also uniquely suitable for centralized codifications of the kind propounded by Voltaire. Several interpretations have been given to this idea, of course (as will be discussed further in chapter 8). John Locke emphasized, for instance, the inalienable rights of the individual citizens including their right to be represented. Rousseau, in his 1771 advise to the Polish kingdom, underlined the importance of the duties of citizenship, in order that the defense of particular social or class interests 'does not penetrate society at the cost of its patriotism, and that the Hydra of hair-splitting does not destroy the nation'.[144]

Rousseau further argued that the kingdom of Poland needed three codes of law only, 'l'un politique, l'autre civil, et l'autre criminel' – all three 'as clear, short and precise as possible'.[145] It was essential that these codes should be taught in schools and universities, and that what remained of customary and Roman law would be discarded: 'we have no need of other bodies of law. (…) When it comes to Roman law and its customs, whatever still exists of it must be removed from the schools and the tribunals. People should not recognize any other authority than the laws of the state; these laws ought to be uniform in all provinces'.[146]

Without the French Revolution, these ideas would never have been realized, and Napoleon marked the definitive breakthrough thereof, when he

---

[141] Montesquieu, *De l'esprit des lois* (1748) (Paris: Éditions Garnier Frères, 1961), for instance Vol. II, Book XXIX, chapter 18, *Des idées d'uniformité*: 'les memes mesures dans le commerce, les memes lois dans l'État, la même religion dans toutes ses parties. Mais cela est-il toujours à propos sans exception? Le mal de changer est-il toujours moins grand que le mal de souffrir? Et la grandeur du genie ne consisterait-elle pas mieux à savoir dans quell cas il faut l'uniformité, et dans quell cas il faut des differences? A la Chine, les Chinois sont gouvernés par le ceremonial chinois, et les Tartares par le ceremonial tartare: c'est pourtant le people du monde qui a le plus la tranquillité pour object. Lorsque les citoyens suivent les lois, qu'importe qu'ils suivent la même?'

[142] Norman Hampson, *Will and Circumstance. Montesquieu, Rousseau and the French Revolution* (London: Duckworth, 1983) 23.

[143] 'La prodigieuse diversité'. Lokin and Zwalve (2006) 181.

[144] '(…) ne s'enracine dans les corps aux dépens du patriotisme, et que l'hydre de la chicane ne dévore une nation'. Jean-Jacques Rousseau, 'Considérations sur le gouvernement de Pologne et la réforme projetée en avril 1772' (1772), in: *Oeuvres Choisies de J.J. Rousseau. Contrat Social ou Principes du Droit Politique*. Nouvelle édition (Paris: Garnier Frères, no year of publication mentioned) 386-387: 'Chapitre X – Administration.

[145] 'Tous trois clairs, courts et précis autant qu'il sera possible'. *Ibidem*.

[146] '… on n'a pas besoin d'autres corps de droit. (…) A l'égard du droit romain et des coutumes, tout cela, s'il existe, doit être ôté des écoles et des tribunaux. On n'y doit connaître d'autre autorité que les lois de l'Etat; elles doivent être uniformes dans toutes les provinces'. *Ibidem*.

launched a single, unified, *Code Civil* in 1804. And he was perhaps right, when
he remarked that:

> My glory is not that I have won some forty battles or that I have submitted kings
> to my will (…) Waterloo will efface the memory of all those victories (…) But
> what will never be effaced and will live forever, that's my *Code Civil*.[147]

The example set by Napoleonic France was in any case followed by all Western
European states. In the decades to come, they all developed their own national
legal codes, completing the development of the modern state.

1.3. *International Relations*

It is not surprising that with the gradual appearance of modern states, and with
the development of a philosophical legitimation for them in the form of social
contract theory, some system of 'international law' was called for, too. Parallel
with the gradual emancipation of modern statehood from the medieval 'chain of
duties', an autonomous doctrine of international relations emerged. The Dutch
thinker and jurist Grotius can be counted among the very first to have embarked
on this path. Although still with one foot clearly in the Medieval system, with
his 1625 *De jure belli ac pacis*, Grotius could, in the words of James Madison,
be counted as 'in some respects, the father of the modern code of nations'.[148]
Grotius starts off from the new, sovereign state as it had emerged from the late
Middle Ages in the course of the 16th and 17th centuries. 'That power is called
sovereign', Grotius writes in Book I, 'whose actions are not subject to the control
of any other power, so as to be annulled at the pleasure of any other human will'.[149]

Following Bodin, Grotius affirmed that a sovereign cannot be bound by his
own actions, and that there is no right to revolt. What is more, a whole people
can agree to give up all their rights to an absolute ruler.[150] This said, Grotius
introduces principles of 'natural law', which, he argued, would apply to subjects
as well as states, even if they have not been formulated or could not be enforced.
He goes on to accept a limited number of universal crimes, against which it
is the right of other states to act – even militarily.[151] Among the principles of

---

[147] 'Ma gloire n'est pas avoir gagné quarante batailles et d'avoir fait la loi aux rois (…) Waterloo
effacera le souvenir de tant de victoires (…) Mais ce que rien n'effacera et qui vivra éternellement,
c'est mon Code civil'. Charles-Tristan de Montholon, *Récits de la captivité de l'empereur Napoléon
à Ste Hélène* I (Paris, 1847) 401. Quoted in: Lokin and Zwalve (2006) 210.

[148] James Madison, 'Examination of the British Doctrine which subjects to capture a neutral
trade not open in time of peace', in: Gaillard Hunt (ed.), *The writings of James Madison, vol. 2*
(The Rnickerboch Press, 1901) 234.

[149] Hugo Grotius, *The rights of war and peace, including the law of nature and of nations* (1625)
Translated by David J. Hill (New York: M. Walter Dunne, 1901) 62: Book I, chapter III, par. 7.

[150] Grotius (1901) 63: Book I, chapter III, par. 8.

[151] Grotius (1901) 247: Book II, chapter XX, par. 40ff.

natural law that Grotius deduces from reason are for instance that *pacta sunt servanda*, promises are to be kept, and that no entity could claim sovereignty over territories it could not possibly hope to control – hence the *mare liberum*, the free seas.[152] Grotius' work, in the words of Arthur Nussbaum, 'certainly does not form an integrated whole. The show of erudition is far overdone, and the reasoning is often ponderous and discursive.'[153] There is a conflict in Grotius between universal morals and sovereignty, and he is unwilling or unable to fully resolve it (i.e. the conflict between universal morals and temporary legal arrangements in Augustine and Aquinas, as discussed above). Nevertheless, his analysis that the *jus gentium* of the coming age would have to be on the basis of equality and on secular principles has been of paramount importance and influence. In this context it is worthwhile to note that he argued that treaties with Christian peoples had the same standing as those made with non-Christian peoples, for instance the Saracens.[154]

Samuel Pufendorf (1632-1694), seen at his time, despite significant differences, as 'the son of Grotius',[155] advanced from the Grotian starting point to develop his systematic account of natural and international law. 'Like Grotius and Hobbes', James Tully writes, 'Pufendorf took the religious differences over which the wars had been fought to be irreconcilable. Hence, a new morality able to gain the consent of all Europeans [...] would have to be independent of the confessional differences which divided them [...]'. While the former two had written in the midst of European civil and religious wars, Pufendorf was the first to reflect on the emerging state system in the second half of the 17th century. As Tully writes: 'In the specific sense, therefore, of being the first to present a comprehensive theory of the existing European state system, Pufendorf is the first philosopher of modern politics'.[156]

In Book II, chapter 6, of his *On the Duty of Man and Citizen* (1673), Pufendorf describes 'the internal structure of states'. He analyses this as a series of agreements, between individuals, to form a union and to organize this union in a particular way. Most important for our purposes is the final agreement Pufendorf describes, that which establishes sovereignty and subjection to it. 'By this agreement', Pufendorf writes, 'he or they bind himself or themselves to provide for the common security and safety, and the rest bind themselves to

---

[152] Which was also clearly in the interest of his native country, the Republic, of course, as was his claim that treaties concluded with the Ottoman Empire should be upheld in the same way as treaties with Christian powers. Grotius (1901) 253: Book II, chapter XX, par. 48ff. Cf. Nussbaum (1961) 110.

[153] Nussbaum (1961) 113.

[154] Nussbaum (1961) 110.

[155] Nussbaum (1961) 150.

[156] James Tully, 'Introduction', in: Samuel Pufendorf, *On the Duty of Man and Citizen* (Cambridge: Cambridge University Press, 1991) xx.

obedience to him or them. By this agreement, too, all submit their will to his or their will and at the same time devolve on him or them the use and application of their strength to the common defence.'[157] Pufendorf concludes: 'Only when this agreement is duly put into effect does a complete and regular state come into being'. This state, then, lives in a state of nature with other states, as states always primarily care for their self-interest.[158]

The Swiss diplomat Emer de Vattel (1714-1767), who brought together theoretical reflections as well as his personal experiences, analyzed the new reality in a profoundly encompassing way. In 1757, he published *Le droit des gens, ou principes de la loi naturelle, appliqués à la conduite et aux affaires des nations et des souveraines*: 'The law of nations or the principles of natural law, applied to the conduct and affairs of nations and of sovereigns'. In this work, Vattel criticizes Grotius and Pufendorf for allowing too much leeway for princes to govern the people as they may please, and defends restraints on royal power and the importance of an elected legislature. In Book I, chapter IV, par. 39, for instance, he writes: 'It is evident that men form a political society, and submit to laws, solely for their own advantage and safety. The sovereign authority is then established only for the common good of all the citizens; and it would be absurd to think that it could change its nature on passing into the hands of a senate or a monarch. (…) A good prince, a wise conductor of society, ought to have his mind impressed with this great truth, that the sovereign power is solely intrusted to him for the safety of the state, and the happiness of the people, – that he is not permitted to consider himself as the principal object in the administration of affairs, to seek his own satisfaction, or his private advantage'.[159] In this, he clearly follows the Lockean amendments to the Hobbesian doctrine.[160]

However, Vattel sees no possibilities for arranging supranational powers to ensure the just conduct of the several sovereign entities. 'Nations being free and independent', Vattel writes, 'though the conduct of one of them [may] be illegal and condemnable by the laws of conscience, the others are bound to acquiesce in it, when it does not infringe upon their [own] perfect rights. The liberty of that nation would not remain entire, if the others were to arrogate to themselves the right of inspecting and regulating her actions; – an assumption

---

[157] Pufendorf (1991) book II, chapter 6, par. 9.
[158] Pufendorf (1991) Book II, chapter 1, par. 11.
[159] Emer de Vattel, *The Law of Nations, or principles of the Law of Nature, Applied to the Conduct and Affairs of Nations and Sovereigns, with Three Early Essays on the Origin and Nature of Natural Law and on Luxury*. Edited and with an introduction by Béla Kapossy and Richard Whatmore (Indianapolis: Liberty Fund, 2008) book I, chapter IV, par. 39. Cf. Francis Stephen Ruddy, *International Law in the Enlightenment. The background of Emmerich de Vattel's Le Droit des Gens* (New York: Oceana Publications, 1975).
[160] Cf. Vattel (2008) Book I, chapter IV, par. 51 and 54, and Book I, chapter V, par. 16.

on their part, that would be contrary to the law of nature, which declares every nation free and independent of all the others'.[161]

Vattel acknowledges that every state ought 'to labour for the preservation of others, and for securing them from ruin and destruction',[162] but goes on to explain that no nation can be obliged to fulfill duties towards others.[163] Nor does Vattel support punitive wars in the name of violations of natural law. He writes that 'it is strange to hear the learned and judicious Grotius assert, that a sovereign may justly take up arms to chastise nations which are guilty of enormous transgressions of the law of nature, *which treat their parents with inhumanity like the Sogdians, which eat human flesh as the ancient Gauls, etc.*[164] In opposition to Grotius, Vattel states that 'men derive the right of punishment solely from their right to provide for their own safety; and consequently they cannot claim it except against those by whom they have been injured'.[165] He goes on:

> Could it escape Grotius, that, notwithstanding all the precautions added by him in the following paragraphs, his opinion opens a door to all the ravages of enthusiasm and fanaticism, and furnishes ambition with numberless pretexts? Mahomet and his successors have desolated and subdued Asia, to avenge the indignity done to the unity of the Godhead; all whom they termed associators or idolaters fell victims to their devout fury.[166]

In addition to these observations, Vattel distinguishes between two types of international 'law': a 'necessary' law of nations, and a 'positive' law. Necessary international law amounts to the natural law principles applying between states, and is, since it is 'founded on the nature of things (...) immutable'.[167] Under 'positive' law of nations, nations may draft treaties between them. But those treaties can never override the eternal principles of the 'necessary' (or 'natural'[168]) law – the most fundamental of them being the right to non-intervention. 'Every treaty, every custom, which contravenes the injunctions or prohibitions of the necessary law of nations, is unlawful'.[169]

---

[161] Vattel (2008) preliminaries, par. 9.
[162] Vattel (2008) Book II, chapter I, par. 4.
[163] Vattel (2008) Book II, chapter I, par. 5-14.
[164] Italics by Vattel himself. Here, a footnote is included in the text, where Vattel refers to Grotius' *De Jure Belli et Pacis*, book II, chapter XX, par. II, that I have also discussed above.
[165] Vattel (2008) Book II, chapter I, par. 7.
[166] Vattel (2008) Book II, chapter I, par. 7.
[167] Vattel (2008), preliminaries, par. 7.
[168] As Vattel writes about the necessary law: 'This is the law which Grotius, and those who follow him, call the *internal law of nations*, on account of its being obligatory on nations in point of conscience. Several writers term it the *natural law of nations*', Vattel (2008) preliminaries, par. 7.
[169] Vattel (2008) preliminaries, par. 7.

With Vattel, the sovereign state of the kind we have become familiar with today, has been thought out in its entirety.[170] It became the dominant model of jurisdiction, and was affirmed for instance by Immanuel Kant in his treatise *Zum ewigen Frieden* (1795):

> The idea of the law of nations presupposes the distinction between independent states. Although this is a state of war ... it is still, according to reason, better than the fusion of those states by means of a hierarchy of power culminating in a universal monarchy. Laws which are passed for a large area lose their vigour, and such a soulless despotism, after it has hollowed out the germ of goodness, ultimately collapses into anarchy.[171]

---

[170] The principle of statehood was reconfirmed at the important peace treaties of the seventeenth and eighteenth century. It was also re-emphasized through the ideas concerning legal unification that the French *philosophes* articulated. After the disorder Napoleon had caused, the Vienna Congress restored the European State system and established the Holy Alliance to strengthen it. The Holy Alliance was a coalition set up in 1815 by Tsarist Russia, Austria and Prussia, the three major continental powers after the battle of Waterloo. Later, France and most other European nations joined, the common aim of the organization being to maintain the continental status quo. However cohesive its social results were, the political record of the organization is poor, and the different member States largely continued to set out for themselves their own political agendas, even if that would result in military confrontation (e.g. the Crimean war).

[171] Immanuel Kant, *Zum ewigen Frieden. Ein philosophischer Entwurf* (Stuttgart: Philipp Reclam, 2005) 32: zweiter abschnitt, erster zusatz, par. 2: 'Die Idee des Völkerrechts setzt die Absonderung vieler voneinander unabhängiger benachbarter Staaten voraus; und obgleich ein solcher Zustand an sich schon ein Zustand des Krieges ist (...) so ist doch selbst dieser nach Vernunftidee besser als die Zusammenschmelzung derselben durch eine die andere überwachsende und in eine Universalmonarchie übergehende Macht, weil die Gesetze mit dem vergrösserten Umfange der Regierung immer mehr an ihrem Nachdruck einbüssen, und ein seelenloser Despotism, nachdem er die Keime des Guten ausgerottet hat, zuletzt doch in Anarchie verfällt'.

CHAPTER TWO

SOVEREIGNTY

2.1. *INTRODUCTION*

'There exists perhaps no conception the meaning of which is more controversial than that of sovereignty', wrote the renowned German-British jurist Lassa Oppenheim.[1] Indeed, in discussions on statehood the controversy frequently focuses on that particular word, sovereignty. Much debated and disputed, its usage has often been thought to be 'inherently problematic',[2] and sovereignty has been identified as 'the most glittering and controversial notion in the history, doctrine and practice of public international law'.[3] It is therefore not surprising that every now and then someone proposes to discard the word altogether. Louis Henkin writes, for instance:

> Sovereignty is a bad word (…) it is often a catchword, a substitute for thinking and precision. (…) For legal purposes at least, we might do well to relegate the term sovereignty to the shelf of history as a relic from an earlier era'.[4]

As of today, however, sovereignty remains a key concept in the relations between states, as well as in the understanding of modern statehood. In this chapter, we will have a closer look at it.

The word 'sovereignty' finds its origin in the Middle-Latin *superanus*, which means 'above' or 'elevated above others'.[5] One of the oldest recordings of it is in a French charter, dated around 1000 AD, but the development into Early French, as *souverain*, is found from the twelfth century onwards – denoting geographical qualities of higher and lower,[6] as in: mountain A is *souverain* over mountain B. The first record where the word 'souverain' was used in a political sense, was

---

[1] Lassa Oppenheim, *International law. A treatise.* 4th Edition by A.D. McNair (London: Longmans, 1928) 66.

[2] Roger Scruton, *The Palgrave Macmillan Dictionary of Political thought.* 3rd edition (London: Palgrave Macmillan, 2007).

[3] H. Steinberger, 'Sovereignty', in: R. Bernhardt (ed.), *Encyclopedia of Public International Law. Volume Four* (Amsterdam: Elsevier, 2000) 500.

[4] L. Henkin, *International Law: Politics and values* (Dordrecht: Martinus Nijhoff Publishers, 1995) 9-10.

[5] Gerard Kreijen, *State Failure, Sovereignty, and Effectiveness. Legal Lessons from the Decolonization of Sub-Saharan Africa* (Leiden: Martinus Nijhoff Publishers, 2004) 27.

[6] Kreijen (2004) 27.

allegedly in the principal work of the French jurist Philippe de Beaumanoir,[7] entitled *les Coutumes de Beauvaisis*, in which he wrote that 'chacuns barons est souverains en sa baronie …'[8] – every baron is the highest in his own barony. From then on, 'sovereignty' is more often recorded as meaning 'there is no higher political power' over a political unit.

But it is exactly this principle of 'no higher power' that causes confusion. For it may refer to external relations, establishing a rule of non-intervention; but it also implies that internally, the sovereign has effectively established himself as the highest power. In order to have an effective 'community of sovereign states' – in order for external sovereignty to make sense –, it is self-evidently necessary that those sovereign entities actually exercise effective governmental control over their territory. One cannot do business with sovereigns if they cannot enforce agreements at home.

A discussion of sovereignty therefore inevitably leads to an analysis of the internal qualities of the modern state. Indeed, sovereignty and statehood are inextricably linked, doubling the complexity of the picture. There can be no international system of sovereign entities, without those entities possessing the effective governmental control associated with statehood.

The general consensus is that four criteria determine sovereign statehood. The first and most important criterion was already mentioned, which is the exercise of 'effective and independent governmental control' (1). This implies a 'population' (2), and a 'territory' (3), culminating in what is generally referred to as 'internal sovereignty'.

But then, there is the international component to sovereignty. This is 'the capacity to enter into relations with other states' (4),[9] and is encapsulated in the notion of external sovereignty. External sovereignty leads to questions over recognition and legitimacy that we will have a closer look at further down. But first we will examine the meaning and scope of 'internal sovereignty'.[10]

---

[7] Philippe de Rémi, sire de Beaumanoir lived presumably from 1247 until 1296. He was a French administrative official and nobleman. His main work is *Coutumes de Beauvaisis*, written in 1283, and printed in 1690.

[8] Kreijen (2004) 28.

[9] Pierre-Marie Dupuy, *Droit International Public* (Paris: Editions Dalloz-Sirey, 1992) 23: 'une population (…) que l'état stabilise à l'intérieur de ses limites; c'est ainsi qu'à l'époque contemporaine, l'idée d'un Etat nomade est définitivement abolie'; Joe Verhoeven, *Droit International Public* (Louvain: Larcier 2000) 52ff; Malcolm D. Evans (ed.), *International Law* (Oxford: University Press, 2003) 217ff.

[10] For a classic definition in international legal discourse, see the case of the Permanent Court of International Law, in the Lighthouses on Creta and Samos case, available online at http://www.worldcourts.com/pcij/eng/decisions/1937.10.08_lighthouses.htm; for a discussion of its terms, see Pablo Mendes de Leon, *Cabotage in International Air Transport Regulation* (PhD thesis, Leiden University Press, 1992) 162. See also the 1949 Corfu Channel Case of the ICJ, judgment of April 9th, 1949. Available online at http://www.icj-cij.org/docket/files/1/1645.pdf. Cf. J.W. Rees, *The*

2.2. *Internal Sovereignty*

As said, internal sovereignty consists in the exercise of effective and independent governmental control, over a population, on a generally marked-out territory. The most problematic aspect of this is the first criterion: effective and independent governmental control. Questions related to defining a population and a territory, more importantly, are outside the remit of this chapter and will therefore not be taken into account.

We will thus focus on effective and independent governmental control. The first thing that may come to mind when discussing this is Albert Venn Dicey's famous definition of parliamentary sovereignty. Parliament, as the highest institution of a state, embodies sovereignty when any of its acts, 'or any part of an Act of Parliament, which makes a new law, or repeals or modifies an existing law, will be obeyed by the courts.'[11] Dicey continues:

> The same principle, looked at from its negative side, may be thus stated: there is no person or body of persons who can, under the English constitution, make rules which override or derogate from an Act of Parliament, or which (to express the same thing in other words) will be enforced by the courts in contravention of an Act of Parliament.'[12]

In Dicey's definition, however, there is no mention being made of existing power realities on the ground; his understanding of sovereignty is institutional. What will actually happen with verdicts of the courts – whether their magistrates have any bearing on the population or not – is not part of his concern. This leaves Dicey's definition open to the obvious objection that while parliament and courts may officially be fully sovereign, effective governmental *control* may be entirely lacking.[13]

Now, governments are often incapable of enforcing compliance with all their laws, and sometimes incapable of enforcing most of them. Courts may be unable to make sure that judgments are actually carried out. The most extreme examples of this are formed by a number of mostly post-colonial (predominantly African) states that have not succeeded in enforcing their laws and maintaining order within their territory. These states have, in recent years, come to be called 'failed states', rendering the notion of sovereignty in Dicey's institutional sense a dead letter.[14]

---

theory of sovereignty restated, in: Peter Laslett (ed.), *Philosophy, Politics and Society.* First series (Oxford: Oxford University Press, 1975).

[11] Albert Venn Dicey, *Introduction to the study of the law of the constitution* (London: Macmillan, 1939) 40.

[12] Dicey (1939) 40.

[13] As Dicey himself acknowledges as well. Dicey (1939) 82ff.

[14] Cf. Kreijen (2004).

That is why Dicey's understanding of sovereignty in fact already presupposes effective governmental control. His approach helps to locate, within the governmental structure, the ultimate sovereign point. But he does not define what it is that constitutes effective governmental control itself.

Another definition of sovereignty that may therefore be considered, is the definition provided by Black's famous *Law Dictionary*. According to this work, sovereignty is to be understood as the 'supreme political authority'.[15] For several reasons, however, this definition is also problematic.

For the word 'authority' can mean two things. Authority may refer to the individual or the institution that has the power of decision in a given dispute (call it authority-1). The umpire of a tennis game, for instance, may be identified as the 'authority' in determining whether a ball was in or out. A teacher is the 'authority' in the classroom. One may point at the police as the 'authority' on the streets (the examples are endless). In that sense, authority (as authority-1) is relative to the power to decide or to act.

However, authority also refers to a feeling of respect or esteem that people may feel for others (call it authority-2). In this sense, the Pope may be indentified by Catholics as an 'authority' in religious matters.[16] Or the Dalai Lama may be regarded as an 'authority' in practical ethics. Both could lose their 'authority' – as authority-2 – over their followers if they were seen to make wrong decisions. For instance, the sex abuse scandals of 2009 within the Catholic Church have affected the 'authority' of the Pope. In 2008, the Dalai Lama was criticized in an article in *The Guardian* that posed the question whether 'there [has] ever been a political figure more ridiculous than the Dalai Lama'. In the article, the Buddhist leader was reproached for being 'a product of the crushing feudalism of archaic, pre-modern Tibet, where an elite of Buddhist monks treated the masses as serfs and ruthlessly punished them if they stepped out of line'.[17] This, if true, might cause his 'authority' over his admirers to diminish.

---

[15] Bryan A. Garner (ed.), *Black's Law Dictionary,* 8th edition (Los Angeles: West Group, 2004) 1430, and Scruton, *Dictionary* (2007) 655.

[16] Of course, the Vatican has a long history of claiming political sovereignty as well, apart from moral or religious 'authority'. As indeed happened with the *Regnans in Excelsis* bull of 1570, which 'released' all the subjects of Queen Elizabeth of England from their allegiance to her. As will be argued below, states confronted with such rival claims would not lose their sovereignty, as long as they maintain effective control. It is clear that Richelieu, when declaring that in matters of state, no French catholic should prefer a Spaniard to a Huguenot, took position against the idea of papal sovereignty, too. This contrasts sharply with the lack of such a strong defense of territorial sovereignty amongst present-day political elites, for instance after Khomeini issued a fatwa with universal validity for all Muslims to assassinate Salman Rushdie, in 1989. Cf. Cliteur (2007).

[17] Brendan O'Neill, 'Down with the Dalai Lama. Why do western commentators idolise a celebrity monk who hangs out with Sharon Stone and once guest-edited French Vogue?', in: *The Guardian,* May 29th, 2008.

Now, the complexity commences as such 'authority' in the sense of being respected or held in high esteem (authority-2) may also be vested in the umpire, the teacher and the policeman. If the umpire is suspected of being biased against one of the players; or if the teacher appears not to know the matter he is teaching; or if the policeman beats up or arbitrarily arrests an innocent civilian; in such cases their authority in the sense of being respected or held in high esteem (authority-2) may crumble. Nevertheless, their authority as agents endowed with the power to make decisions or to act (authority-1), is not affected. The authority in the sense of the 'right to decide' (authority-1) of the umpire, the teacher or the policeman is not dependent on the recognition of their authority in the sense of being respected (authority-2) by those subjected to their power. The tennis player who feels wronged may submit a complaint, the students may write to the school board, or the citizen may sue the police officer – but whether their complaints will affect the authority-1 of the umpire, the teacher or the policeman, is not up to them.

This applies to sovereignty generally as well. Naturally, it is very difficult to imagine a state that does not have any authority in the sense of being respected (authority-2) by its population. Effective governmental control is extremely difficult to maintain without the consent of at least part of the population. Even dictatorships have a need for a loyal class of *custodes* to carry out orders and support the regime. Moreover, in rare cases only have governments possessed the ability to directly intervene with all matters happening on their territory, usually rendering them dependent on benevolent cooperation by other institutions and groups.

However, should governments rule unjustly and undermine their 'authority' in the sense of being respected or held in high esteem (authority-2), they would nevertheless retain their 'right to decide' (authority-1) as long as they maintained effective control.

This confusion that Black's definition of sovereignty gives rise to, stemming from the semantic ambiguity of the word 'authority', is perhaps overcome through the claim by the legal positivist John Austin that the sovereign is the one or the institution whose 'commands are habitually obeyed'. Though we could again dispute over the several ways in which 'habitually' could be understood, this definition is less ambiguous. Yet we could also accept Black's definition of sovereignty as the 'ultimate authority' if authority is understood as authority-1: the ultimate power to decide.

To identify the sovereign as such, however, must mean that our understanding of internal sovereignty is not connected to any considerations of natural law. The eternal question whether unjust laws can still be properly called 'laws' – and whether unjust government can still be properly called 'government' – is beside the point when trying to identify effective and independent governmental control.[18] For whichever normative position one chooses to defend in this debate, it is irrelevant if the internal sovereign's commands continue to be habitually obeyed (when it comes to external sovereignty, by contrast, our assessment of the relevance of this debate may turn out differently, as will be discussed in the next paragraph).

In establishing obedience to its commands, then, as Max Weber argued, the sovereign must monopolize the use of force. In *Wirtschaft und Gesellschaft* (1922), he analyzed that

> A compulsory political organization with continuous operations will be called a 'state' insofar as its administrative staff successfully upholds the claim to the *monopoly* of the *legitimate* use of physical force in the enforcement of its order.[19]

The use of the word 'legitimate' again confronts us with the confusing double meaning also encountered in the word 'authority'. Legitimacy may mean 'in accordance with its own rules' (call it legitimacy-1), or it may mean 'being experienced as rightful' (call it legitimacy-2). It is to legitimacy-1 that Weber intended to refer to, when identifying the monopoly to the use of force in this case.[20] This means that it is not relevant for the existence of a state whether the force is experienced as 'rightful', but only whether the rules laid down permit it.

This also means, ultimately, that there is no conceptual difference between a state and a concentration camp. The guards and rulers of the camp form a government, and the prisoners a population. In such a concentration camp case, then, the guards have a monopoly to the use of force *in accordance with the rules laid down by themselves* (but may be bound by certain limitations too, in which case the concentration camp has an element of the rule of law – see chapter 6). When a fight breaks out between two prisoners, for example over

---

[18] Thomas Aquinas was already occupied with this problem in his quaestiones, most notably the quaestiones 90-95 of the *Summa Theologiae* (1265), and it was famously taken up once again by Hart and Dworkin in the 20th century. Indeed, as one scholar describes it: 'For the past four decades, Anglo-American legal philosophy has been preoccupied – some might say obsessed – with something called the "Hart-Dworkin" debate', the core question of which seems to be the relationship between law and morality – and the question of the extent to which unjust laws are still proper 'laws'. Steven J. Shapiro, 'The "Hart-Dworkin" Debate: A Short Guide for the Perplexed', *University of Michigan Public Law Working Paper No. 77* (February 2, 2007). Available online at http://ssrn.com/abstract=968657.

[19] Max Weber, *Economy and Society. An outline of interpretive sociology*. Edited by Guenther Roth and Claus Wittich (Berkeley: University of California Press, 1978) 54 (§ 17). The original German text reads: '*Staat* soll ein politischer *Anstaltsbetrieb* heißen, wenn und insoweit sein Verwaltungsstab erfolgreich das *Monopol legitimen* physischen Zwanges für die Durchführung der Ordnungen in Anspruch nimmt'. Max Weber, *Wirtschaft und Gesellschaft, Grundriss der Verstehenden Soziologie*. Studienausgabe herausgegeben von Johannes Winckelmann. Band I (Köln & Berlin: Kiepenheuer & Witsch, 1964) 36 (§ 17).

[20] Cf. Weber (1978) 56: 'the use of force is regarded as legitimate only so far as it is either permitted by the state or prescribed by it'. Weber's strict empiricism has often been discussed (and criticized), for example by Leo Strauss, *Natural Right and History* (Chicago: University of Chicago Press, 1953).

food, they have no right to use force against one another, unless this is explicitly permitted by the rules of the camp (as modern states for instance usually allow some form of self-defense). If the camp guards fail to suppress the use of force by the prisoners effectively, some prisoners may come to develop a parallel power center, challenging the power of the guards. It may come to be that the one whose orders are habitually obeyed over time becomes the leader of a gang of prisoners, if the guards continue to fail to take effective action. Ultimately, such a situation could result in a revolt, which is the same as a 'civil war'.

At such a moment, the internal sovereign becomes divided. The situation in Libya in 2011 exemplified this. Colonel Khadafi, who had ruled the country for several decades and had maintained a strong autocratic rule, was challenged by rebels from the East of the country. After some Western military support, the rebels managed to establish a power base around Benghazi, effectively upholding a new sovereign power (again, this has consequences for external sovereignty as well, as will be discussed below). By contrast, as long as failure of the guards or the state to monopolize the use of force remain exceptions, and their commands thus continue to be habitually obeyed, the internal sovereignty continues to reside with them.[21]

Black's definition of sovereignty also contained the word 'political', as in: 'supreme political authority'. This refers to the power of the state as the ultimate expression of the government of the polity. But it puts us on track of at least three problems related to internal sovereignty. The first is that most states at present have decentralized many governing and legislative tasks; the second is that they have some separation of powers; and the third is that they have committed themselves to supranational organizations; the word 'political' in our definition of internal sovereignty as 'supreme political authority' therefore leads to new confusions; however, as we shall see, it also provides the umbrella concept that enables us to solve these problems.

Let us first address the decentralization of governing and legislative tasks. Most states have, to some extent, decentralized governing and legislative tasks, and therefore, the central – 'sovereign' – government often does not possess all the means to govern as it may please.

The most striking example of such decentralization is perhaps a federation such as the United States, where powers not delegated to the federal government are 'reserved to the states respectively or to the people' (Amendment 10). Some have argued that the whole concept of sovereignty is for this reason altogether fraudulent. Should this be the case, then indeed, supranationalism would not be at odds with the state at all, but rather present an additional layer of governance,

---

[21] See also: Maurice Joly, *Dialogue aux enfers entre Machiavel et Montesquieu ou la politique de Machiavel au XIXe siècle* (Bruxelles, A. Mertens, 1865).

not fundamentally different from the already existing layers such as county, state, province or municipality.[22]

At first sight, this view may seem attractive. However, whether we deal with a unitary or a federal state, however different these two types of states may be,[23] and regardless of how many governing tasks may reside within the member states of a federal union, a number of fundamental attributes of statehood are always – and necessarily so – centralized. These are the ultimate command over the army, and the common defense of borders. This has consequences for external sovereignty too, as will be discussed below, because common defense of borders implies the common conduct of foreign affairs.

Ultimate command over the army, moreover, requires the capacity to pay for it, and therefore implies the final say of the central government in (some of) the taxes to be paid as well. There exists no state, as logically there *cannot* exist a state, neither unitary nor federal, in which the command over the army is not centralized, and connected with that the conduct of foreign relations and the administration of (some of the) taxes. This is illustrated by confederacies.

A confederacy is nothing more than an organized structure of unenforceable cooperation between sovereign states. Even the United Nations (the Security Council not taken into account) could be denoted as such: a form of cooperation between states, which ultimately cannot enforce anything. A confederacy can never be a state, which is why a 'confederate state' is a contradiction in terms (and why, for instance, the American confederacy was denoted as 'Confederate States' in the plural). Another typical example of a confederacy is the Republic of the Seven United Provinces, which existed between 1581 and 1795. In this political structure, the seven provinces deliberated on matters of common interest, most importantly their common defense, yet all of them retained the right to veto every proposal for collective action, and the central deliberative body, the Estates General, had no direct legislative powers over the citizens of the seven provinces. Moreover, the provinces retained a right to withdraw, and

---

[22] Cf. W.J.M. Mackenzie, and B. Chapman, 'Federalism and Regionalism. A Note on the Italian Constitution of 1948', in: *The Modern Law Review*, Vol. 14, No. 2 (Apr., 1951) 182-194. See also Part II, *Introduction*.

[23] In unitary states all decentralized (local or regional) administrative units derive their powers from the central sovereign authority, which ultimately holds the power to retain them. In these types of states the decentralized competencies are typically enacted in a centralized law which the centralized legislative is capable of broadening or narrowing. In a federal state, on the contrary, the central sovereign power recognizes that the decentralized administrative entities (usually indicated as 'states') have their own fields of competence that the federal government has no right to interfere in. The invention of this type of state is typically associated with the summer of 1787 when the representatives of the thirteen former colonies gathered in Philadelphia to found the United States.

no common direct taxation existed.[24] Thus, the variation of decentralization is not infinite. A state ceases to exist if it decentralizes or devolves the fundamental attributes necessary for ultimate control.[25]

There is also another reason why the argument that supranationalism is just another layer on an already layered structure of the state, is untenable. For the rationales of centralization and decentralization are completely opposed. To devolve governing and legislative tasks to a *lower* level, enabling the different regions within a state to choose different arrangements, is not the same as to transfer those tasks to a *higher* level, effectively compelling the different regions to accept uniform arrangements. Precisely why decentralization exists, namely to distinguish legitimate state rule on fundamental activities, from fields of minor importance, is denied by supranationalism; the logic of decentralization is diversity, while that of centralization is uniformity. The larger the centralizing unit, the more oppressive the uniformity will be.[26]

In addition to the problems posed by decentralization, there is a second problem related to internal sovereignty: the separation of powers. No constitutional democracy at present has a monarch whose powers even remotely resemble those Jean Bodin or Thomas Hobbes envisaged for the head of state. This means that the single sovereign individual or institution, not only symbolizing the whole of the state, but actually acting as its only ultimate agent, may not even exist. As Mackenzie and Chapman write:

> There may be a constitutional division of functions between legislature, executive and judiciary: or between central legislature and local legislatures: or there may (as in the U.S.A.) be both divisions. In such cases one may be puzzled to say where true sovereignty lies: does it lie with 'We, the people of the United States' or with 'we, the nine old men of the Supreme Court'?[27]

If sovercignty in modern states, then, is in practice 'divided' amongst three branches of government, what meaning does it still have? Where is sovereignty ultimately to be found?[28]

In most states, a division of powers indeed exists, and since these powers cannot be reduced to one another, it is sometimes argued that there is no central

---

[24] See for instance M. Huizer, *Hoofd en hoogste overheid. De soevereiniteit in Nederland sinds 1543* (Amsterdam: J.M. Meulenhoff, 1967) and Ernst Kossmann, 'Soevereiniteit in de Zeven Verenigde Provinciën', in: *Theoretische Geschiedenis*, vol. 18, issue 4 (dec. 1991) 413-422. For a comparative perspective: T.F.X. Noble et al. (1998) 558.

[25] This is also why the 'Confoederatio Helvetica' – i.e. Switzerland – is really not a Helvetian confederation but a federation.

[26] As discussed in chapter 1, section 2, this applies to the state itself as well. States are compromises.

[27] Mackenzie and Chapman, 'Federalism and Regionalism. A Note on the Italian Constitution of 1948', in: *The Modern Law Review*, Vol. 14, No. 2 (Apr., 1951) 182-194.

[28] This discussion was also touched upon in the previous paragraph.

sovereignty anyway. This could mean that it does not matter anymore where for instance the judiciary is located (in- or outside the state): separation is separation.

This was the argument that Carl Schmitt disagreed with by stating that sovereignty lies with that person or institution that has the power to bring about the state of exception which even in federations lies with the federal executive.[29] Whichever view one takes on the question of where exactly the essence of statehood (i.e. 'sovereignty') is to be located, separation of powers is always much more a dialectic of powers than truly a separation. While it is true that three separate 'functions' of the state can be discerned, the executive, the legislative and the judiciary are never strictly divided among the different organs of the state. Many legislative tasks reside with the executive (and the immense bureaucratic apparatus presently at its disposal), while modern parliaments primarily form a check on the power of the executive. Parliaments are sometimes burdened with some judicial tasks as well, for example trying members of the executive. Moreover, the members of the judicial branch are usually appointed by the executive or by parliament. They are expected to be nationals of the state, and can be held in check by the national legislator if their interpretation of the law is felt to exceed its intended margins.

Internal sovereignty consists in the exercise of all these functions.[30] To remove one of these functions from the state, as is done for instance through 'human rights courts', is to remove it from the control of the other powers and so to upset the established balance.[31] Moreover, the three powers recognized by Montesquieu cannot decide differently on any single issue. In that sense, they are inextricably linked, and such a linkage can only harmoniously continue where there is a similarity of cultural and historical assumptions.[32] Therefore, those

---

[29] 'Souverän ist, wer über den Ausnahmezustand entscheidet'. Carl Schmitt, *Politische Theologie, Vier Kapitel zur lehre von der Souveränität* (München und Leipzig: Verlag von Duncker & Humboldt, 1934) 1.

[30] As Laughland writes, when discussing H.L.A. Hart's understanding of sovereignty (who in turn drew on John Austin): 'If there were legal limits on a sovereign's power, then he would not be a sovereign. This is not to say, of course, that a government cannot be subject to the law as laid down in the courts. On the contrary, a state may well have such mechanisms as part of its constitution, and no doubt this is a desirable thing. But sovereignty is not an attribute of one body within a state but instead of the state as a whole. The theory of sovereignty does not state at what level – national or international – nor in what form – dictatorial or democratic – it is desirable to embody sovereignty: it simply states that the buck always stops somewhere', in: John Laughland, *A History of political trials. From Charles I to Saddam Hussein* (Oxford: Peter Lang, 2008) 27.

[31] Many commentators have suggested that a fourth branch of government power exists: the power of the public opinion. This will be discussed in Part II and Part III, where it will be argued that on the supranational level, public opinions cannot really exercise this power – at least not to the extent that they can do this at the national level.

[32] A clear example of how the judicidial branch can clash with the other branches of government is the *Dred Scott v. Sandford* case of the United States Supreme Court of 1857. In this case, the Supreme Court, dominated, as Robert Bork notes, 'by Southeners', ruled that the Missouri Compromise of 1820, in which it was determined that new States would not allow slavery, was

who demand that a single sovereign point be indicated before they are prepared to accept that such a thing as sovereign statehood exists, would probably be best contented with Schmitt's definition of it as the one who ultimately decides on the state of exception and thus commands the army (which leads us back to effective governmental control).

But what then of already existing supranational entanglements, one may ask, do they make the states that are part of them, less sovereign? States became members of them out of their free will – and could withdraw from them if they so wished. How could those organizations then be an infringement of their sovereignty? I will try to find my way out of this dilemma by distinguishing two meanings of the word sovereignty: a formal or 'ultimate' meaning, and a material or 'practical' meaning.

The first, the *formal* meaning of sovereignty, denotes the constitutional independence of a state. The power of supranational organizations is ultimately based on their recognition by the national member states, which retain their right to withdraw and thereby retain their ultimate, 'formal' sovereignty. The second, the *material* meaning of sovereignty, denotes the location where political decisions are being taken. Though not sovereign in the ultimate, 'formal' sense, supranational organizations have acquired a significant amount of this second, 'material' sovereignty.

Take as an example of this distinction the articles 93 and 94 of the Dutch constitution, which concern the direct effect of international treaties on Dutch law. Article 93 reads:

> Provisions of treaties and of resolutions by international institutions which may be binding on all persons by virtue of their contents shall become binding after they have been published.

And article 94 reads:

> Statutory regulations in force within the Kingdom shall not be applicable if such application is in conflict with provisions of treaties that are binding on all persons or of resolutions by international institutions.[33]

These articles declare the supranational obligations of the Netherlands superior to the national law, thus limiting the *material* or practical sovereignty of the Dutch parliament. Nevertheless, the Dutch parliament retains the ultimate sovereign right to scrap or amend these articles of the constitution, to cancel treaties, or

---

a violation of the Constitutional right to have property (following from the 5th Amendment). As Bork notes, 'There is something wrong, as somebody has said, with a judicial power that can produce a decision it takes a civil war to overturn'. Robert Bork, *The Tempting of America. The political seduction of the Law* (New York: The Free Press, 1990) 28-34.

[33] Text taken from the official translation of the Dutch constitution, to be found on the website of the Ministry of Foreign Affairs, www.minbzk.nl/contents/pages/6156/grondwet_UK_6-02.pdf.

to withdraw from supranational organizations, and so annul the international obligations of the Netherlands. Hence, the *formal* or ultimate sovereignty continues to repose with parliament. Formally, the Netherlands remain entirely sovereign, and would only cease to be so if the country lost its power to withdraw from the supranational organizations of which it is a member, or, what amounts to the same thing, loses its right to abolish or amend those articles that declare international obligations superior to national considerations.

This formal or ultimate sovereignty is what people refer to when they say that sovereignty is by its nature indivisible. When John Laughland for example writes that 'the theory of sovereignty (…) simply states that the buck always stops somewhere',[34] he means this formal sovereignty. This kind of sovereignty is indeed like being pregnant: there is no intermediate stage possible. Either a state has the right to withdraw from treaties, or it does not have that right. Either parliament may amend the relevant constitutional commitments, or it may not.

As implied, however, in the previous example, to recognize that sovereignty (in the formal or ultimate sense) is by nature indivisible is not to say that states cannot engage in far-reaching teamwork. It should only be noted that a state will not cease to be sovereign until it loses its right to resign from its supranational entanglements. This was ultimately the question that the American civil war (1861-1865) was fought over, when the southern American states attempted to secede from the union.[35] The Southern American states fought for their formal or ultimate sovereignty – their right to withdraw from entanglements –, but did not succeed.

Indeed, if, as a sovereign political unit, a state decides to coordinate parts of its government's policy (for example its trade tariffs) with those of other states, this can result in close cooperation. A state may even become a member of an institution that may, by majority vote, decide upon the policy to be followed by its members (in this case, the permitted trade tariffs), without losing its sovereignty as such, understood in the formal or ultimate sense.[36] There is, however, still a fundamental difference between these two situations; between treaties between states as such, and an international body deciding by majority vote on policy regulations for its members. They are not exactly the same thing. And that brings us to sovereignty in the material or practical sense.

For while formal or ultimate sovereignty is the principal authority from which, in the last resort, all powers derive, and is, indeed by definition, indivisible, material or practical sovereignty is the competency to decide *as long and*

---

[34] Laughland (2008) 27.

[35] The very fact is illustrated by the different names for the war: the south called it the 'war between the states', the north called it the 'civil war'.

[36] 'In the last resort, the US might walk away from the WTO. That is an ultimate safeguard of sovereignty …'. Rabkin (2007) 228.

as far as the ultimate sovereign permits it. Thus material or practical sovereignty is there, where the political process is happening – which can be very much divided between organizations. When a state is a member of a supranational institution, apart from the question of its right to withdraw from it, it is, as long as it is a member of that organization, bound by its decisions, even to those with which it may not agree. Though in the formal or ultimate sense, the member state is sovereign as it may still withdraw, as long as it has not done so it has lost elements of its material or practical sovereignty. This distinction is important for the rest of this book, and it will return later on.

2.3. EXTERNAL SOVEREIGNTY

This chapter opened with the observation that part of the reason why sovereignty is such a controversial concept is the fact that internal and external sovereignty are inextricably linked. External sovereignty – the acceptance of a state by others – is linked with the question whether that state successfully upholds internal sovereignty. Whether or not internal sovereignty is successfully upheld, moreover, may be disputed. States may deny an entity its external sovereignty, as many Arab states do with Israel, for instance; they may also grant external sovereignty to new entities, as happened with Kosovo in 2009.

This brings us to the fourth criterion for statehood, which is 'the capacity to enter into relations with other states'. On this subject, two different approaches exist. The descriptive or declarative or realist, and the normative or constitutive or idealist.

The descriptive (or 'declarative' or 'realist') view starts from the observation that when an organization succeeds in establishing internal sovereignty, it has gained a *de facto* capacity to enter into relations with other states. This *de facto* capacity is then viewed as the only criterion in international law, and so the entity is viewed as a sovereign state. You do business with whomever you can make deals with.

This approach echoes the authority as-the-power-to-make-rules (authority-1) approach that we associated in the previous section with Austin and Weber.[37] No matter how wildly unjust the rule of that organization may be or by what ruthless acts of aggression territorial control has been realized, once this effective control has been established, we can speak of a state, period. The descriptive approach thus focuses on effectiveness.[38]

---

[37] Weber (1964) 36.
[38] Cf. James Crawford, *The Creation of States in International Law.* Second Edition (Clarendon Press, Oxford, 2006).

The normative (or 'constitutive' or 'idealist') view, by contrast, holds that the capacity to enter into relations with other states is dependent on the general recognition by those other states, and that therefore, sovereignty is dependent upon a significant number of other states recognizing one as such. It is typically associated with the Congress of Vienna of 1814-5, where the great powers determined what entities would be granted the status of statehood in post-Napoleonic Europe, despite demands of many more regions and groups to be recognized as such at the time.[39] The normative approach takes the international community's recognition of a political entity as a state as the ultimate test, regardless of existing aspirations or even power realities on the ground. It thus focuses on legitimacy (to be granted or withheld by 'the international community'), not on effectiveness.

Carl Schmitt may be identified as a primary defender of the descriptive approach; Hans Kelsen as a defender of the normative approach.[40] While Schmitt stressed the fact that norms cannot enforce anything by themselves, and that thus, ultimately, power determined the order of things; Kelsen concluded that 'sein' did not say anything about 'sollen': whatever *was* the case, according to Kelsen, could never determine what *ought* to be the case – and law was the realm of *ought*, not of *is*.[41] Kelsen argued that Schmitt's approach was not 'realist' but 'apologist', because it assumed that, in the words of Martti Koskenniemi, 'might makes right'.[42]

In practice, these two views are brought into play in turns, depending at least partly on the political interests that are served by them; when they can, states may prefer to act by the normative approach, but ultimately, legitimacy always follows power and the descriptive approach is indeed the more 'realist', the constitutive the more 'idealist' – a luxury states cannot always afford.[43]

A good example of how ambivalent states have been in their choice for either of these two approaches is the declaration drafted at the International Conference on Rights and Duties of States at Montevideo (Uruguay) in 1933.

---

[39] Cf. Adam Zamoyski, *Rites of Peace. The fall of Napoleon & The Congress of Vienna* (London: Harper Perennial, 2007) xiii: 'The Congress of Vienna (…) determined which nations were to have a political existence over the next hundred years and which were not …'; also: N. Rosenkrantz, *Journal du Congrès de Vienne 1814-1815* (Copenhague: G.E.C. Gad, 1953).

[40] Cf. Martti Koskenniemi, *From Apology to Utopia. The structure of international legal argument* (Cambridge: Cambridge University Press 2005) ch. 1 and 4.

[41] Kelsen defended a strict monism between the national legal order and the international order. In other words: international law formed an integral part of national law, in his view. Cf. Hans Kelsen, 'Sovereignty and International Law', in: *The Georgetown Law Journal*, vol. 48 (1960) 637.

[42] Koskenniemi (2005) 227. An insightful account of the debate between Schmitt and Kelsen can be found in Gelijn Molier, 'De soevereine staat en het international recht', in: Gelijn Molier and Timo Slootweg (eds.), *Soevereiniteit en Recht, rechtsfilosofische beschouwingen* (Den Haag: Boom Juridische Uitgevers, 2009) 140ff.

[43] Cf. Robert Kagan, *Of Paradise and Power. America and Europe in the New World Order* (New York: Alfred A. Knopf, 2003).

After reconfirming the three criteria for internal sovereignty (or statehood) in the first article (effective control, territory, people), article 3 of the declaration reads: 'the political existence of the state is independent of recognition by the other states'.[44] Article 8 seems consistent with this descriptive approach: 'No state has the right to intervene in the internal or external affairs of another.' Yet article 11 then reads:

> The contracting states definitely establish as the rule of their conduct the precise obligation not to recognize territorial acquisitions or special advantages which have been obtained by force whether this consists in the employment of arms, in threatening diplomatic representations, or in any other effective coercive measure. The territory of a state is inviolable and may not be the object of military occupation nor of other measures of force imposed by another state directly or indirectly or for any motive whatever even temporarily.

Thus article 11 establishes the legitimacy of the status quo at that specific moment in time, while, in an apparent contradiction, articles 3 and 8 seem to give both to minorities within states as to states themselves the freedoms respectively to declare their own state or to adjust their borders according to their own assessment of what their 'external affairs' demand from them.

An example of policy based on such normative ideas as expressed by article 11 of the Montevideo declaration, is the memorandum that the American Secretary of State Henry Stimson had written to India and China in 1931 stating that the United States would not recognize international territorial changes that were brought about through force (thereby implying support for India and China against rising Japanese imperial threats).[45] An example of policy based on realist ideas expressed by article 8 is the seizure by the United States of several former Axis territories following the end of the Second World War, such as the Ryukyu Islands off the Japanese coast.

Another example of the normative policy of the kind endorsed by article 11 is the message that the United States, with eighteen other (Latin) American states, sent to the governments of Bolivia and Paraguay in August 1932, when hostilities over their (i.e. the Bolivian and Paraguayan) border dispute concerning the Chaco region were increasing. The message contained the following passage:

> The American nations further declare that they will not recognize any territorial arrangement of this controversy which has not been obtained by peaceful means

---

[44] Rights and duties of Statehood, Montevideo convention 1933. Available online at http://avalon.law.yale.edu/20th_century/intamo3.asp.
[45] This memorandum turned out to be the starting point of what would become the 'Stimson doctrine', see on this: Kisaburo Yokota, 'The Recent Development of the Stimson Doctrine', in: *Pacific Affairs*, Vol. 8, No. 2 (June, 1935) 133-143.

nor the validity of the territorial acquisitions which may be obtained through occupation or conquest by force of arms.[46]

Yet when a cease-fire in 1935 brought an end to the full-blown war into which Bolivia and Paraguay, despite American attempts to downplay the conflict, had entered, and most of the disputed *Chaco boreal* region was awarded to Paraguay, the United States supported the 1938 truce confirming this new division of land.[47] Again political realities rather than high principles determined the choice of either approach. When this truce was finally confirmed in a treaty signed in April 2009, the United States was present as one of the guarantors of the new borders.

Many more examples could be given of how descriptive and normative approaches are brought into play in turns, depending on political opportunity. Northern Cyprus forms a recent case in which the normative approach seems to have prevailed. The region declared its independence from Cyprus proper in 1983 and has since – with the strong support of Turkey – realized effective governmental control. Even though Northern Cyprus has now been a *de facto* state for almost 30 years, the fact that it originated from a violent *coup d'état* (as well as the fact of Greek-Turkish animosity and Greece's power as a member of the EU) still stands in the way of recognition by other states, and Turkey is the only state to have recognized Northern Cyprus to this day. When Kosovo declared itself independent from Serbia in 2008, however, it was instantaneously recognized by most Western states. Yet when later that same year the provinces South Ossetia and Abkhazia declared independence from Georgia, their independence was met with skepticism and recognitions were not forthcoming.[48]

Thus, there is no general rule as to how the fourth criterion for sovereign statehood – the capacity to enter into external relations – is to be interpreted, and as a result, it is interpreted according to political interests. Indeed, the distinction between the descriptive and the normative approach is more of theoretical than of practical relevance. For in practice, international recognition will always follow power. As long as disputes are still not settled, states may uphold principles of legitimacy to press for their desired outcome of the conflict; but when they are settled, and principle becomes a denial of reality, states will, ultimately, always

---

[46]   Yokota (1935) 133-143. Yokota is right to write: 'Like its predecessors, however, the Chaco note, in so far as it does not represent a formal treaty among States, cannot be regarded as possessing the force of international law nor as other than a simple declaration of policy' – it is exactly this which is marks the distinction between the descriptive and the normative approach.

[47]   F.O. Mora and J.W. Cooney, *Paraguay and the United States: Distant Allies. The United States and the Americas* (Athens: University of Georgia Press, 2007).

[48]   Of course, there is the distinction in international law between granted and withheld internal self-government. It has been argued, in this respect, that Kosovo was suffering from such a lack of internal self-government, while this self-government had sufficiently been granted to South-Ossetia and Abkhazia. But the question becomes then: who gets to make these analyses? Such criteria therefore do not solve the problem, but merely transpose it.

adjust to the new status quo and accept that they will have to live with it. We will also see this later on when discussing the dispute over Alsace-Lorraine after the Franco-Prussian war.

The final argument for the view that the difference between the descriptive and the normative approach is not essential is that when invoked by states, the normative approach finds itself in a circular argument: 'We do not recognize this political entity as a state, because it is not being recognized as a state'. The opposite is also true: when the descriptive approach is invoked by states, they already implicitly recognize the existence of a state, and therefore comply with the demands of the normative approach: 'We recognize this state, therefore it has been recognized'. To conclude, recognition by other states is ultimately dependent upon existing power realities. Effectiveness, therefore, always trumps legitimacy (which is also why, in the last instance, classical international law is really a political instrument).

CHAPTER THREE

THE NATION

3.1. *Membership*

It is at this point that the question arises what kind of social bond, what kind of shared values, culture or loyalties, if any, are necessary within a sovereign state, to make the exercise of power democratically legitimate and indeed even possible. This brings us to the concept of the nation.

Self-conscious 'national' thinking did not arise much before the downfall of feudalism. As a result of the Reformation and the increased power of monarchs, as discussed in the previous chapters, the first manifestations of national identity became visible during the *ancien régime*, often in conjunction with attempts by sovereigns to increase such national awareness. A particular example is the English case, where historians have identified the rise of a significant 'national' identity already in the 16th century under the house of Tudor.[1] This is expressed in some of Shakespeare's plays, for instance, where proud reference is made to England and Englishness.[2]

---

[1] Cf. G. R. Elton, *England under the Tudors*. Third Edition (London: Routledge, 1991) 160ff. The same may be true of Sweden since the times of Charles XII (1682-1718).

[2] In Shakespeare's Richard II (1595), for instance, Gaunt says in act II, scene I: 'This royal throne of kings, this sceptred isle, This earth of majesty, this seat of Mars, This other Eden, demi-paradise, This fortress built by Nature for herself, Against infection and the hand of war, This happy breed of men, this little world, This precious stone set in the silver sea, Which serves it in the office of a wall, Or as a moat defensive to a house, Against the envy of less happier lands, – This blessed plot, this earth, this realm, this England'. And in Henry V (1599), act III, scene I, Henry says on the eve of the Battle of Agincourt: 'Once more unto the breach, dear friends, once more, Or close the wall up with our English dead!, In peace there's nothing so becomes a man, As modest stillness and humility:, But when the blast of war blows in our ears, Then imitate the action of the tiger; Stiffen the sinews, conjure up the blood, Disguise fair nature with hard-favoured rage; Then lend the eye a terrible aspect; Let it pry through the portage of the head, Like the brass cannon; let the brow overwhelm it, As fearfully as doth a galled rock, Overhang and jutty his confounded base, Swilled with the wild and wasteful ocean. Now set the teeth, and stretch the nostril wide, Hold hard the breath, and bend up every spirit, To his full height! On, on, you noblest English, Whose blood is fet from fathers of war-proof! Fathers that, like so many Alexanders, Have in these parts from morn till even fought, And sheathed their swords for lack of argument. Dishonour not your mothers; now attest, That those whom you called fathers did beget you! Be copy now to men of grosser blood, And teach them how to war. And you, good yeomen, Whose limbs were made in England, show us here, The mettle of your pasture; let us swear, That you are worth your breeding, which I doubt not; For there is none of you so mean and base, That hath not noble lustre in your eyes. I see you stand like greyhounds in the slips, Straining upon the start. The game's afoot! Follow your spirit, and upon this charge cry, God for Harry, England, and Saint George!'. Stanley Wells and Gary Taylor (eds.), *The Oxford Shakespeare. The Complete Works* (Oxford: Oxford University Press, 1999). Cf. Roger Scruton, *England: an elegy* (London: Chatto & Wandus, 2000).

With the beginning of the age of industrialization and democracy, national awareness significantly increased.[3] But before we continue, a caveat seems appropriate. For to locate the emergence of national awareness from the 17th century onwards is not to say, of course, that the cultural identity of European states came into existence only in that period. Nor does situating the rise of nationalism in these centuries imply that particular cultural regions may not have had a chauvinistic attitude towards what they would regard as *their* traditions; or that rising states, as discussed in chapter 1, may not have attempted to increase social unity.[4] With national thinking in this respect is meant the defense of a shared national identity by all inhabitants of a given territory; and thus, in the last instance, the understanding of the state as an expression of that constituting – pre-political – element.

The reasons for the rise of this idea from roughly the 17th century onwards are not difficult to see, since it was also around this time, that the exercise of political power moved away from the regional on the one hand, and the imperial or papal on the other, to the level of the state. We have already discussed the rise of the modern state and the ongoing centralization of its governing powers. This also meant that closed regions slowly began to open up to larger units. The beginning of industrialization, the growth of cities, dawning secularization, increase in grand oversees projects and trade, were all part of this development. Another development was the use of vernacular as an instrument of literary and official communication. The foundation of the *Académie Française* by Richelieu in 1635 symbolizes the responsibility the state began to take up to unify the 'national' language of communication.

But these developments coincided with an increased participation of the people in their governments. The very idea of 'representative government', as

---

[3] Benedict Anderson, *Imagined Communities. Reflections on the Origin and Spread of Nationalism.* Revised Edition (New York: Verso, 1991) 6-7.

[4] The European idea is, moreover, at least as old as the Early Middle Ages, and it might even be argued that rough cultural distinctions between what we presently regard as French and German cultural spheres, find their origin already in the division of the Empire of Charlemagne in the 9th century. Cf. Reginald Dale, 'Thinking ahead: Old lines appear on Europe's map', in: *International Herald Tribune*, 17 January 1995, who writes: 'It is true that Bonn's 'hard core' – Germany, France and the Benelux countries – bears an uncanny resemblance to Charlemagne's German-based empire. Anyone who thinks that such ancient history is no longer relevant should ponder this. The two countries that most stoutly resisted Charlemagne's attempts to introduce a common European coinage – England and Denmark – are still the toughest holdouts against a single currency nearly 1,200 years later.' Another example is N. Grant, *Oxford Children's History of the World* (Oxford: Oxford University Press, 2000) 56: 'Between the 5th and 10th centuries, European tribes formed Christian kingdoms ruled by warrior kings. The most successful were the Franks. Their king Charlemagne created an empire that was the foundation of some of the nations of Europe today'. See also chapter 4.7.

implied in most if not all forms of democratic theory,[5] presupposes the fiction of a common identity that can be represented as a collective whole. Ever since the American and French Revolutions,[6] the democratic ideal has gained momentum and modern sovereign states, at least in Europe, all profess to adhere to it (even if they may suffer from serious democratic deficits[7]).

The democratic ideal brought about changes in virtually all aspects of life (simultaneously giving rise to an attempt to conserve what was left of pre-industrialized, pre-egalitarian life: romanticism[8]). The growth of cities, the growth of the population, the increased division of labor, and so on, all contributed to this. The first steam engine railway became operational in 1830, dramatically opening up isolated regions to a larger whole. Another radical change occurred in the field of warfare. While armies had mainly consisted of noblemen and mercenaries in the *ancien régime*, universal conscription now arose[9] – resulting in an enormous enlargement of the scale of social awareness. The individual peasant or farmer became aware of himself as part of a state, not just as an inhabitant of a particular region or province.[10] There can be no doubt that this influenced the experience of social membership and the political awareness of the people dramatically, starting with the first mandatory national conscription in world history following the French Revolution.

Indeed, all these elements of the increased influence on our lives of the modern state pose the question of membership. What is it that I share with you, from an entirely different region, with perhaps different beliefs and a different ethnicity, that our votes are brought together in the same parliament? That we have to live under the same law? And that ultimately, we may have to stand side by side in the defense of a perceived 'national' interest concerning again another region that forms a part of our state, but that we may have no particular relationship with?

---

[5] The idea of direct democracy being by definition opposed to the concept of representation, it has proved extremely hard if not impossible to realize it. Cf. Meindert Fennema, *De Moderne Democratie. Geschiedenis van een politieke theorie* (Amsterdam: Het Spinhuis, 2001) 7ff.

[6] The classical accounts on this are of course Tocqueville's *De la Democratie en Amérique* (1835-1840) and *L'ancien régime et la Révolution* (1856).

[7] As, through the undemocratic legislation imposed by the EU, all European states now do. See for instance part II, chapter 5, section 3.

[8] Cf. Maarten Doorman, *De Romantische orde* (Amsterdam: Bert Bakker, 2004); Rüdiger Safranski, *Romantik. Eine deutsche Affäre* (München: Hanser, 2007); H.G. Schenk, *The Mind of the European Romantics: An Essay in Cultural History,* (London: Constable, 1966).

[9] See on this for instance Jeremy Black, *A Military Revolution? Military Change and European Society, 1550–1800* (London: Macmillan education, 1991).

[10] 'Omnis determinatio negatio est'. Every affirmation implies a negation, and this seems to be the same with national identities, which have often gained shape in the face of a 'national' enemy. As Carl Schmitt notices the reflections of the economist and sociologist Emil Lederer: 'Wir können sagen, dass sich am Tage der Mobilisierung die *Gesellschaft*, die bis dahin bestand, in eine *Gemeinschaft* umformte'. 'Der Begriff des Politischen', in: *Frieden oder Pazifismus?* (Ducker & Humblot, Berlin, 2005) 204n7.

It is in the light of this question, the 'what do I share with you'-question, that 'national thought' and the much despised ideal of 'nationalism' ought to be understood.

3.2. *IMAGINED TERRITORIAL COMMUNITIES*

But before we continue our inquiry into national loyalty, however, it is worthwhile to make some preliminary comments about the word 'nation', as it is the cause of wide confusion. This is partly so because it is regularly used as a synonym for 'state'. An example is its usage in *United Nations,* an international organization that deals with *states,* not nations.[11] Another confusing usage is *International Law,* which deals with legal associations between states, not nations. And so on. 'Nation' and 'State' are often muddled up. [12]

Another impure usage of the word 'nation' is to denote an ethnic, a religious, or a lifestyle community. This happens for instance when we speak of the 'nation of Islam', a Chicago-based organization that seeks to unite and foster the interests not of a nation but of an ethno-religious group. 'Nationality' is used as synonymous with 'ethnicity' in much everyday talk. And a third example is the 'universal zulu nation', an organization that brings together people who enjoy and produce hip hop music, world wide.

If the word *nation* has a meaning of its own, not as a synonym for state, religion, ethnicity, or lifestyle, it is to denote a form of political loyalty stemming from an experienced collective identity, and would thus be of a sociological, rather than a legal, credal, or ethnic nature. Although a sense of political loyalty is a given of our – settled, political – existence, the expression of this loyalty in terms of nationality is not. Governments are always in need of the political loyalty of their subjects, but this loyalty is not always *national* in nature. Indeed, national loyalty is in fact a rather recent form of political loyalty, which has not been common throughout most of political history.

Many people have been troubled with nationalism as a historical, political and ideological phenomenon, and have disagreed on its proper definition. Literally thousands of books have been written about the subject.[13] Not discouraged by this, nor by the conclusion of the historian Eric Hobsbawm that 'no

---

[11] It is true that the United Nations also has many 'Non-governmental organizations' (NGO's) participating in its debates, but the core of the organization remains to be formed by states; illustrative for this is that to this date, only states have voting rights within the UN bodies. Moreover, NGO's are not coterminous with nations either.

[12] See also: Paul Belien, 'Why Belgium is an artificial state', in: *The Brussels Journal,* August 27, 2007. Available online at http://www.brusselsjournal.com/node/2369.

[13] For an instructive, general overview, see Kenneth R. Minogue, *Nationalism* (Maryland: Penguin Books, 1968) 19ff.

satisfactory criterion can be discovered for deciding which of the many human collectivities should be labeled as a nation',[14] I will in the following try to further the understanding of nationality not through identifying particular qualities that may define membership – e.g. shared language, history, and so on – but through defining it as a specific *type* of membership. I suggest defining a nation as a community that is both imagined and territorial. As such, I will contrast it with unimagined-territorial or 'tribal' communities on the one hand, and imagined-nonterritorial or 'religious' and 'universal' communities on the other.[15]

Understanding the nation as an 'imagined community' was first done by the political scientist Benedict Anderson (*1936). In his book *Imagined Communities,* Anderson focused on the rise of nationalism in former colonies, and he defined nations as 'imagined communities' because people experience themselves to be part of a community of which they do not know most of the members.[16] It is certain that an element of imagination is necessary for any national experience, because it is impossible to be personally acquainted with every other member of your nation (let alone to feel sympathy for each single one of them). However, not all imagined communities are also national communities. This is because it is also possible to experience oneself as part of an imagined, non-territorial community.

Joseph Stalin, the future Soviet leader, had pointed at the territorial element in his 1913 book entitled *Marxism and the national question.* In the book, he observed that 'a nation is a historically constituted, stable community of people, formed on the basis of common language, territory, economic life, and psychological make up manifested in a common culture'.[17] It is remarkable that Stalin wrote about nationalism,[18] as Marxism, of course, emphasized the horizontal loyalty of class and market position, unbound by borders, as contrasted with the vertical loyalty of upper and lower classes as joined under a common allegiance to the sovereign. 'National one-sidedness and narrow-mindedness become more and more impossible', the Communist Manifesto declares,[19] and it continues:

---

[14] Eric Hobsbawm, *Nations and nationalism since 1780, programme, myth, reality* (Cambridge: Cambridge University Press, 1990) 5, quoted in: Mikulas Teich and Roy Porter (eds.), *The national question in Europe in historical context* (Cambridge: Cambridge University Press, 1993) xvii.

[15] This is not an exhaustive classification, and no doubt other loyalties could be identified: professional loyalty is an example.

[16] Anderson (1991) 2ff.

[17] Joseph V. Stalin, *Works 1907-1913* (Moscow, 1953) vol. II, 307, quoted in: Teich and Porter (eds.), *The national question in Europe in historical context* (Cambridge: Cambridge University Press, 1993) xvii.

[18] And a different interpretation of the national differences was one of the main reasons for his conflict with Trotsky.

[19] Karl Marx and Friedrich Engels, *Manifesto of the Communist Party* (1848). Authorised English translation of 1888, edited and annotated by Frederick Engels (London: Lawrence and Wishart, 1888). Cf. Max Eastman, 'The Manifesto of the Communist Party', in: Max Eastman (ed.), *Capital. The Communist Manifesto and other Writings* (New York: The modern library, 1932) 315ff.

> The proletarian is without property; his relation to his wife and children has no longer anything in common with the bourgeois family relations; modern industry labor, modern subjection to capital, the same in England as in France, in America as in Germany, has stripped him of every trace of national character.

The worker, it is assumed, has no nationality; he 'has no country'.[20]

Despite Marxist resistance to nationality, Stalin's understanding of nationality contains an interesting complement to Anderson. For besides the fact that it implies an *imagined community*, the experience of nationality, I propose, indeed encompasses a notion of *territoriality*. A nation claims a particular piece of land and declares that it belongs to her. As such, it permits a social and political order that is also a relation among strangers who may have different ethnicities and religions – united as they are in their common commitment to their land.

Depending on the many manifestations of nationality, membership of this social order can be more or less open to newcomers, welcoming them or chasing them away. These approaches to the criteria for national membership, which may differ from one nation to another,[21] will be discussed in the next section. For now, we may safely contend that nationality, or the experience of national belonging, consists essentially in a shared political loyalty among a group of people, with two defining characteristics:

1. Its scale is imagined, allowing membership to be extended to a large group far exceeding the size of the family or tribe;
2. Its claim pertains to a particular territory, contrasting with those forms of membership – for example religious ones –, that are essentially universal (instead of territorial).

As mentioned before, national loyalty contrasts with at least two other forms of loyalty: tribal or 'unimagined' loyalty, and religious or 'non territorial' loyalty.

The tribal loyalty I called 'unimagined' to juxtapose it to the national, 'imagined' loyalty of a group larger than one may ever know (attaching to ideas rather than to kinship).[22] Tribal loyalties take shape in groups that are more or less knowable and thus have no need to be 'imagined' like a nation. It might seem tempting to argue that they form the infancy of man's political existence, yet tribal loyalty still seems to be predominant in many parts of the world. Many African people do not primarily experience a national – imagined and territorial – membership, and their loyalties tend to reach more towards their

---

[20] Marx and Engels (1888).
[21] Cf. Hugh Seton-Watson, *Nations and States. An enquiry into the origins of nations and the politics of nationalism* (Colorado: Westview Press 1977) 467-469, Teich and Porter (eds.) (1993), and Margaret Canovan, *Nationhood and political theory* (Massachusetts: Edward Elgar Publishing Limited, 1996).
[22] And indeed modern technology such as TV plays an important role in fostering the national awareness, as national newspapers have done in the nineteenth century.

village, their tribe or family, and political life is often divided along lines set by these sentiments.

Tribal loyalty also seems to be the form of loyalty of nomadic people, like, traditionally, Native Americans and Bedouins. Instead of settling on a specific territory, they wander from place to place, their communities are usually small in size, and they often live with strict rules of cohesion, which are also necessary for them to survive in frequently harsh conditions (typically, punishment is severe, as deviant behavior may threaten the entire tribe's survival).[23] Also, the tribe is almost everywhere found to be ethnically homogeneous.[24]

A religious loyalty, in contrast with tribal loyalty, may be very imagined and may therefore pertain to a large group of people, yet it is different from national loyalty in that it is not bound to a territory, nor even essentially *about* a territory.[25] While the tribe tends to limit itself to a close group, religious membership can be experienced wholly separated from others. What is characteristic for a religious loyalty, moreover, is that while it is imagined, it can easily result in placing religious rules above the rules of the actual political community. Europe at the time of the Reformation, for example, went through a conflict between religious and national loyalty, expressed through the dispute on ultimate legal authority.[26] The papal bull *Regnans in Excelsis* is a good illustration of this conflict. Issued in 1570, this bull declared the Protestant Queen Elizabeth I of England an unlawful ruler and charged 'the nobles, subjects, peoples and others (...) that they do not dare obey her orders, mandates and laws'.[27] Another example is formed by the Catholic Spanish King Philip II, who proclaimed in 1580 that 'everyone is authorized to harm, or kill' the Protestant leader of the Dutch Republic, William of Orange. This order was the leading pretext for the devout Catholic Balthasar Gérard to assassinate the Dutch prince in his house in Delft in 1584.[28]

---

[23] There are of course tribes consisting of so large a population that their identity must to some extend be 'imagined' too. Still, however, the experience of loyalty on the basis of ethnic kin is fundamentally different from the loyalty on the basis of shared nationality.

[24] Cf. M. Banton, *West African City. A Study of Tribal Life in Freetown* (London: Oxford University Press, 1957).

[25] Neither of these ideal-typical distinctions are without exceptions, of course. The Anglican Church, for instance, promotes a religious loyalty, yet connected to the English nation. There would be many more examples of overlapping loyalties. The purpose here is, however, to distinguish ideal-typical types of loyalty.

[26] See on these and other examples Cliteur (2007) and Cliteur, *The Secular Outlook* (London: Wiley Blackwell, 2010).

[27] The entire text of the bull can be found, in translation, on http://www.papalencyclicals.net/Pius05/p5regnans.htm.

[28] See on this, for instance: Cliteur (2007) 164ff, and: Lisa Jardine, *The Awful end of Prince William the Silent. The first Assassination of a head of state with a Handgun* (London: HarperCollins, 2005), who writes on page 51: 'This act of assassination was, it appeared, the deed of a solitary

Arguably, the questions of the allegiance of Catholic citizens to their Protestant rulers in the age of the Reformation are comparable to current questions related to Islamic terrorism. Indeed, to several observers, they can only be explained properly with this problem in mind, which is also known as the problem of the divine command theory.[29]

National loyalty differs from these other forms of loyalty, in that the primary object of its loyalty is not a tribe or a faith, but a territory and its patrimony. A national loyalty enables a dramatic enlargement of the scale of political organization as compared to a tribal loyalty. It also enables people of different religious beliefs – indeed of every possible different background, be it ethnic, racial, cultural, or religious – to overcome their differences and accept the same sovereign state, given that this state succeeds in attaching its authority to the nationality of its population (hence the packing together of 'nation' and 'state' in the normative conception of the nation state).

3.3. WELCOMING NEWCOMERS

In this section I will develop three idealtypical forms of national membership in order to further our understanding of it. The first I would call the *universalist-enlightened* approach, which is that it is not – or hardly – necessary. According to this approach, political organization can entirely be borne by institutions, and the social experience of membership is at best a useful by-product of this, but is certainly not a constituting element.

Then, there is the approach that I would call *particularist-romantic*, reminding us of the great nationalisms in history. According to this view of nationality, it is necessarily a closed condition; it is impossible to switch from one nation to another, and as a result, foreigners, even those who desire to assimilate, could not be accepted.

The third approach, finally, is that national identity is necessary, but that it can be an open condition; that in principle, nations are indeed closed communities, but that those who wish to belong can become part of the nation through their effort: through integration and assimilation.

For analytical purposes, it may be helpful to associate the first approach with the Enlightenment and the universalist ideals typically connected with the French Revolution; the second approach, then, can easily be associated with Romanticism, emphasizing the element of determinism in life. And finally,

---

fanatic, a loner with an intense commitment to the catholic Church and a faithful upholder of the legitimacy of the rule of Philip II in the Netherlands ...'.

[29] See on this: Cliteur (2007), and Roger Scruton, *The West and the Rest. Globalization and the terrorist threat* (Delaware: ISI Books, 2002).

there is the way out of the dilemma between these two extremes, provided by the concept of *patriotism*. As the word nation originally comes from the Latin *nascor*, meaning 'I am born', the word patriotism is derived from the Latin *patria*, meaning 'fatherland'. The Latin root also returns in words like 'patrimony' and 'patrimonium', referring to something that has been inherited from ancestors, but may also be acquired independently from birth.

The universalist-enlightened model of nationality developed in the eighteenth century, and found an obvious expression in the French Revolution. While it was in part the cry for the sovereignty of the 'nation' that fueled the French revolutionaries,[30] they were not occupied with the question of cultural or ethnic components inherent in this collective. On the contrary: in revolutionary writings, for instance the 1789 essay *Qu'est ce que le Tiers-Etat?*, written by the clergyman Emmanuel-Joseph Sieyès, emphasis is placed on liberating people from their social context: their inherited social position, their class and their ancestors, all had to give way to the new ideal of equality.[31] Indeed, Sieyès argued that a nation is nothing but 'a body of associates living under common laws and represented by the same legislative assembly'.[32] Stressing the need for just laws and nothing else, we see that in the thinking of Sieyès, 'state' and 'nation' are used as synonyms.[33]

The political regime that took power after the revolution attempted to govern in accordance with this view. It had the ideal to define individuals 'by their humanity, not by their place of birth': their race or their class.[34] As Finkielkraut notes:

> This revolutionary project had no intention of trying to create a collective identity (…). On the contrary: by setting [the people] free of all definitive ties, it radically affirmed their autonomy.[35]

In his *Préliminaire de la constitution*, written in 1789, Sieyès derives the desired structure of the French constitution entirely from man's universal qualities and

---

[30] Alain Finkielkraut, *The defeat of the mind*. Translated by Judith Friedlander (New York: Columbia University Press, 1995) 18.
[31] On the French Revolution's abolition of privilege, see: W.H. Sewell jr., *Work and revolution in France: the language of labor from the Old Regime to 1848* (Cambridge: Cambridge University Press, 1980) 78-84.
[32] Emmanuel-Joseph Sieyes, *Qu'est-ce le Tiers état?* (Geneve: Libraire Droz, 1970) 126: 'un corps d'associés vivant sous une loi commune et représentés par la même législature …'.
[33] It is true that Sieyès' thinking is much more complex and layered than can be discussed here; his pleas for a national education in order to instill in all citizens a love of France, for instance, is an interesting example of this. Nevertheless, the focus in his work was hardly on the cultural factors that made French subjects into French nationals. See on this: Thomas Hafen, *Staat, Gesellschaft und Bürger im Denken von Emmanuel Joseph Sieyes* (Wien: Haupt, 1994) 71-88.
[34] Finkielkraut (1995) 12.
[35] *Ibidem*.

inalienable rights.[36] The approach to society is straightforwardly universalist – attempting to deal only with *man*, not *men*. This naturally provoked a reaction. The philosopher Joseph de Maistre answered the 'universal declaration of the rights of man' with the observation (in 1796) that no such thing as 'man' exists: 'il n'y a point d'homme dans le monde'. He continued:

> I have seen, in my life, Frenchmen, Italians, Russians, et cetera, and I even know, thanks to Montesquieu, that one can be Persian: but a man, I declare that I have never run into one in my life: if he exists, it is certainly without my knowledge.[37]

Maistre did not stand alone. In response to the universal ideals of the Enlightenment, many different thinkers began to define the *nation* expressly in contrast with the state: as an organic soul, grown through an historical process, entirely disconnected from political organization – of which only those who shared in its blood could be a part. This happened most notably in the German states, which indeed did not even form such a unified political entity at the time.

The publication of Johann Gottfried Herder's *Auch eine Philosophie der Geschichte zur Bildung der Menschheit* (1774)[38] is often marked as the starting point of this particularist-romantic nationalism. In this work, Herder criticizes the all too universal outlook on mankind that the Enlightenment thinkers, for example Voltaire, had chosen. He reproaches 'den Philosophen von Paris' that they want to educate 'toute l'Europe und tout l'Univers',[39] because that must inevitably lead to a grey, meaningless, sterile society. Making his argument mostly by ironical observations, Herder writes:

> With us, God be praised!, all national characters have been extinguished! We love all of us, or rather no one needs to love the other. We socialize with each other; are completely each other's like – ethically proper, polite, blissful!; indeed have no fatherland, no our-people for whom we live, but are friends of humanity and citizens of the world.[40]

---

[36] Emmanuel-Joseph Sieyès, 'Préliminaire de la Constitution. Reconnoissance et exposition raisonnée des droits de l'homme et du citoyen. Lu les 20 et 21 juillet 1789, au comité de constitution', in: Ibidem, *Ecrits Politiques*. Choix et présentation de Roberto Zapperi (Paris: Editions des Archives Contemporaines, 1985) 192ff.

[37] Joseph de Maistre, 'Considérations sur la France', in: *Oeuvres complètes* (Lyon: Vitte, 1884, reprinted: Genève, Slatkine, 1979) tome I, 75: 'J'ai vu, dans ma vie, des Français, des Italiens, des Russes, etc., je sais même, grâce à Montesquieu, qu'on peut être Persan: mais quant à l'homme, je déclare ne l'avoir jamais rencontré de ma vie: s'il existe, c'est bien à mon insu'.

[38] Translated as: 'This too a Philosophy of History for the Formation of Humanity', in: Johann Gottfried von Herder, *Philosophical Writings*. Translated and edited by Michael N. Forster (Cambridge: Cambridge University Press, 2002) 272-360. Ioannis D. Evrigenis and Daniel Pellerin (eds.), *Another Philosophy of History and Selected Political Writings* (Indianapolis: Hackett Publishing, 2004).

[39] Johann Gottfried Herder, *Auch eine Philosophie der Geschichte zur Bildung der Menschheit*. Nachwort von H.G. Gadamer (Frankfurt am Main: Suhrkamp Verlag, 1967) 83.

[40] Herder (2002) 329. In German, the text reads: 'Bei uns sind Gottlob! alle Nationalcharaktere ausgelöscht! wir lieben uns alle, oder vielmehr keiner bedarf's, den andern zu lieben; wir gehen mit

In *Auch eine Philosophie*, Herder argues for the uniqueness of each nation as a cultural entity. 'Each nation', he writes, 'has its center of happiness in itself, like every sphere its center of gravity!'[41] And in later work, as Isaiah Berlin cites, he calls on the Germans:

> Let us follow our own path (…) let men speak well or ill of our nation, our literature, our language: they are ours, they are ourselves, and let that be enough.[42]

For Herder, 'the plurality of collective souls' is formed through the historical reality of 'nationhood'.[43] Although Herder recognized that in God's perspective, all humans are alike, a human perspective on mankind should not pursue such an abstract viewpoint, he believed.[44]

It is important to note that Herder was, when he published his ideas in 1774, a pioneer of romantic nationalism, and one of the first to voice the particularities of the different nations.[45] But after the defeat and humiliation of the German states by Napoleon in 1806, it became a general vogue to search for a 'true' German identity. Take for example the Grimm brothers, who from 1806 onwards roamed the country to collect German folk tales, the first collection of which was published in 1810; or *Des Knaben Wunderhorn*, a similar collection of tales made available by Achim von Arnim and Clemens Brentano in the same period.[46] No doubt partly in order to compensate their military – and indeed political – powerlessness, the Germans 'embraced everything Teutonic with a passion', as Finkielkraut puts it.[47]

It is also with this atmosphere in mind that Johann Gottlieb Fichte's *Reden an die Deutsche Nation* should be read. In the winter of 1807-1808, in French-occupied Berlin, Fichte declared that Germany could only defend itself against foreign powers by uniting politically. In that way, the romantic idea of an organic national identity entirely separate from political organization was reconnected again to a political structure:

> It is solely by means of the common trait of Germanness that we can avert the downfall of our nation threatened by its confluence with foreign peoples and

---

einander um, sind einander völlig gleich – gesittet, höflich, glückselig! haben zwar kein Vaterland, keine Unsern, für die wir leben; aber sind Menschenfreunde und Weltbürger'. Herder (1967) 94.

[41] In German, the text reads: 'Jede Nation hat ihren Mittelpunkt der Glückseligkeit in sich wie jede Kugel ihren Schwerpunkt!' Herder (1967) 45. The phrase is also discussed by Isaiah Berlin, in: *Vico and Herder* (London: The Hogarth Press, 1976) 186.

[42] Isaiah Berlin (1976) 182.

[43] Finkielkraut (1995) 8-9.

[44] Herder (1967) 105.

[45] Cf. R. Safranski, *Romantik. Eine deutsche Affäre* (München: Hanser, 2007), chapter 1.

[46] See on this: M. Tatar, 'Reading the Grimm's *Children's Stories and Household Tales*: Origins and Cultural effects of the Collection', in: *The Annotated Brothers Grimm* (New York: W.W. Norton & Company, 2004) xxvii and further.

[47] Finkielkraut (1995) 9.

once more win back a self that is self-supporting and incapable of any form of dependency.[48]

Thus two positions, the universalist and the particularist, the former typically associated with the French Revolution and the Enlightenment, the latter with the German defeat by Napoleon and Romanticism, stood radically opposed to each other. And it was more than half a century later before the debate on nationality made further progress.

This was triggered by the Franco-Prussian war. Commencing on July 19th, 1870, this war would last a year, and at the final peace treaty, signed on May 10th, 1871, a united Germany emerged, seizing Alsace and the northern part of Lorraine (la Moselle). German political philosophers concluded that the conquest was legitimate, because, inspired by the Herderian approach to the nation, the territories – fondly denoted as 'unsere Rheinlande'[49] – were identifiably of German cultural origin, and the inhabitants spoke mostly German. Two of the most notable participants in defending this seizure were the German philosophers David Friedrich Strauss and Theodor Mommsen.[50] Two Frenchmen, Ernest Renan and Numa Denis Fustel de Coulanges, offered them a reply.[51]

David Friedrich Strauss, in an open letter he wrote to Ernest Renan in the opening months of the war – when France still possessed Alsace-Lorraine –, spoke of the French 'robbery of the fruits of our flesh';[52] the fact that 'a few rooms of our house' had been appropriated 'by the violent neighbor in earlier times' had already been almost forgotten, he claimed[53] – but now, when France had

---

[48] Johann-Gottlob Fichte, *Addresses to the German nation*. Edited with an introduction and notes by Gregory Moore (Cambridge: Cambridge University Press, 2008) 11. The original German reads: 'Es [ist] lediglich der gemeinsame Grundzug der Deutschheit, wodurch wir den Untergang unsre Nation im Zusammenfließen derselben mit dem Auslande, abwehren, und worin wir ein auf ihm selber ruhendes, und aller Abhängigkeit durchaus unfähiges Selbst, wiederum gewinnen können'. Ibidem, *Reden an die Deutsche Nation* (Hamburg: Felix Meiner Verlag, 1978) 13.

[49] David Friedrich Strauss, *Krieg und Friede 1870. Zwei Briefe von David Friedrich Strauss an Ernst Renan und desen Antwort, mit einem Anhang: Carlyle an die Times* (Leipzig: Im Insel Verlag, 1870) 49. The first letter appeared in the *Augsburger Allgemeine Zeitung* on August 18th, 1870, the second on October 2nd.

[50] David Friedrich Straus (1808-1874) is best known for his theological works, especially his 1835 *Das Leben Jesu, kritisch bearbeitet,* in which he is searching for a new (demystifying) approach to the New Testament. Christian Matthias Theodor Mommsen (1817-1903) is best known for his research in classics. He was also awarded the Nobel Prize in Literature, for his 1854-1856 *Römische Geschichte*.

[51] Ernest Renan (1823-1892) was a writer, philosopher, orientalist, theologian and mathematician. Numa Denis Fustel de Coulanges (1830-1889) was an historian.

[52] David Friedrich Strauss, *Krieg und Friede 1870. Zwei Briefe von David Friedrich Strauss an Ernst Renan und desen Antwort, mit einem Anhang: Carlyle an die Times* (Leipzig: Im Insel Verlag, 1870) 49: 'Beraubung der Früchte unseres Fleisches'.

[53] The region had been part of the Holy Roman Empire roughly since 921. France has throughout its history always been envious of it. By conquest upon conquest, it succeeded to gradually take possession of the region from the mid-16th century onwards, completing this effort in 1798, when

again taken up arms against the Germans, 'these old questions wake up once more as well'.[54]

The French, arguing for the illegitimacy of the announced German occupation of Alsace and Lorraine, were drawn to devising another conception of nationality than the previously predominant universalist one (because that would not help them to argue that any region ever belonged to anyone, whilst only recognizing abstract individuals under a neutral state). In doing so, these Frenchmen developed the conception of nationality that I consider the most helpful for us today.

Renan's answer to David Friedrich Strauss appeared shortly after the battle of Sedan, which had in fact practically decided the Franco-Prussian war.[55] Renan acknowledged that Alsace was German in origin, as Strauss had stressed, but noted that 'it is indisputable that, if we would put the question to the people of Alsace, an immense majority would declare itself in favor of staying together with France'.[56]

A day later, Theodor Mommsen published a letter in the Florentine newspaper *Il Diritto*. The letter was addressed to the political director of that newspaper, Clemente Maraini. In this letter, he argued that the only way to solve the centuries-old conflict with the French would be to turn to 'the sacred principle of nationality' and take back the old German provinces, rendering any possible outcome of a referendum irrelevant:

> the only solution is to stand by the sacred principle of nationality, and to rejoin the regions of German nationality to Germany.[57]

Mommsen admitted that 'the majority of the inhabitants would prefer to stay under French government', but held that a part of a nation may not decide all by itself to leave the nation, as Sicily would not be allowed to leave the Italian union.[58] 'We lay claim to the Germans of Alsace and Lorraine because they are Germans,

---

the city-state of Mulhouse in a referendum voted to become part of the French revolutionary republic. Mulhouse was also the place of birth of Alfred Dreyfus (1859-1935).

[54] Strauss (1870) 49: 'Einige Zimmer (…) unseres Hauses' (…) 'der gewalttätige Nachbar in früheren Zeiten' (…) wachen auch diese alten Fragen wieder auf'.

[55] At the battle of Sedan, which took place on September 2nd, 1870, the French emperor Napoleon III was captured by the Prussian and Bavarian armies, which thenceforth marched on to Paris.

[56] Ernste Renan, 'Lettre a M. Strauss', in: *Ibidem, Histoire et parole. Oeuvres diverses* (Paris: Robert Laffont, 1984) 639-649, there 644-645: 'Il est incontestable que, si on soumettait la question au peuple alsacien, une immense majorité se prononcerait pour rester unie à la France'.

[57] Theodor Mommsen, 'Lettere al sig.Clemente Maraini', in: *Il Diritto* (September 17th, 1870). Available online at http://www.mommsenlettere.org/Letter/Details/323: 'l'unico salvamento è attenersi ai santi principi della nazionalità, riunire i distretti di nazionalità tedesca alla Germania'.

[58] The Italian unification had been brought about in 1861, and comparable discussions were held about the Italian national identity at the time. Cf. Adrian Lyttelton, 'The national question in Italy', in: Teich and Porter (eds.), *The national question in Europe in historical context* (Cambridge: Cambridge University Press, 1993) 63-105.

and because today an immense majority of the German nation wants to reunite them with the common fatherland; I think that makes them good democrats'.[59]

Fustel de Coulanges wrote his *réponse à M. Mommsen* in October 1870, entitled *L'Alsace est-elle allemande ou française?*.[60] 'You believe', Fustel de Coulanges recapitulated, 'that Alsace is a German land; and that therefore, it should belong to Germany'. He continued:

> She speaks German, and as a consequence, you believe that Prussia can take possession of her. In virtue of this reasoning you 'revindicate' her; you want that she be 'restored'. She is yours, you say, and you add: 'we want to take all that is ours, nothing more, nothing less'. You call this the principle of nationality'.[61]

But the question was, of course, what it was that constituted that 'principle of nationality'. Why would Alsace and Lorraine be 'German' instead of 'French'? Fustel de Coulanges comes to his conclusions:

> What singles out nations is not race, nor language. People feel in their hearts that they are the same people when they have a community of ideas, interests, affections, memories and hopes. That is what makes a fatherland. (...) One's fatherland is the land one loves.[62]

Renan argued in practically the same manner. In a second letter written to David Friedrich Strauss, a year later, he stated: 'The individuality of every nation is no doubt constituted by race, language, history, and religion, but also by something a lot more tangible, by actual consent, by the will of the several provinces of a state to live together'. He admitted that Alsace was German in language and race, but,

> She does not want to be part of the German state; that settles the matter. We speak of the right of France, and the right of Germany. But these abstractions touch us much less than the right of the Alsatians, living beings of flesh and bone, not to obey to a power not agreed upon by themselves.[63]

---

[59] Mommsen (September 17th, 1870): 'la maggioranza degli abitanti preferirebbe di rimanere sotto il governo francese' (...) Noi rivendichiamo i Tedeschi dell'Alsazia e della Lorena perché sono Tedeschi, e perché ora l'immensa maggioranza della nazione Tedesca vuol riunirgli alla comune patria; e penso che in ciò siano buoni democrati'.

[60] Nouma Denis Fustel de Coulanges, 'L'Alsace, est-elle allemande ou français?', in: *Ibidem, Questions Historiques* (Paris: Libraire Hachette 1893) 505.

[61] Fustel de Coulanges (1893) 505: 'L'Alsace, à vous en croire, est un pays Allemand; donc elle doit appartenir à l'Allemagne. (...) Elle parle allemande, et vous en tirez cette conséquence que la Prusse peut s'emparer d'elle. En vertu de ces raisons vous la 'revendiquez' ; vous voulez qu'elle vous soit 'restituée'. Elle est vôtre, dites-vous, et vous ajoutez: 'nous voulons prendre tout ce qui est nôtre, rien de plus, rien de moins'. Vous appelez cela le principe de nationalité'.

[62] Fustel de Coulanges (1893) 509: 'Ce qui distingue les nations, ce n'est ni la race, ni la langue. Les hommes sentent dans leur cœur qu'ils sont un même peuple lorsqu'ils ont une communauté d'idées, d'intérêts, d'affections, de souvenirs et d'espérances. Voilà ce qui fait la patrie. (...) La patrie, c'est ce qu'on aime'.

[63] Renan, 'Nouvelle lettre à M. Strauss', in: *Ibidem, Histoire et parole. Œuvres diverses* (Paris: Robert Laffont, 1984) 647-655, there 650-651: 'L'individualité de chaque nation est constituée sans doute par la race, la langue, l'histoire, la religion, mais aussi par quelques chose de beaucoup plus

Once more, Renan stated this definition in 1882,[64] in his famous pamphlet *Qu'est-ce qu'une nation?*. He answers the question posed as follows:[65]

> A nation is therefore a large-scale solidarity, constituted by a feeling of sacrifices one has made and of those one is still prepared to make. It presupposes a common past; it presents itself nevertheless in the present by one concrete fact: the consent, the clearly expressed desire to continue the common life. The existence of a nation is (excuse me for the metaphor) a daily plebiscite.[66]

With the French intellectual debate in the direct aftermath of the Franco-Prussian war, counterweight was thus provided to both the romantic view of the nation as a somehow historically determined, ethnic and static union, as well as against the enlightened-universalist concept. This approach finds connection with both the points emphasized by the two extreme positions, yet reduces each of them to proportions where they can be compromised, and so enters a middle ground. Abstract concepts of 'man' and 'humanity' were, in the last instance, too general, while the determinist – ethnic – conception of nationality gave too little room for man's freedom.

This French approach changed, it must be noted, in the course of the 1880s and 1890s.[67] No doubt in part as an expression of the great national trauma of losing the war against Prussia (as German determinist nationalism had risen as a result of the defeat against Napoleon), a new, determinist and bellicose

---

tangible, par la consentement actuel, par la volonté qu'ont les différentes provinces d'un État de vivre ensemble. (…) Elle ne désire pas faire partie de l'État allemande; cela tranche la question. On parle du droit de la France, du droit de l'Allemagne. Ces abstractions nous touchent beaucoup moins que le droit qu'ont les Alsaciens, êtres vivants en chair et en os, de n'obéir qu'à un pouvoir consenti par eux.'

[64] Finkielkraut reminds his readers that Renan has also contributed to the development of racist ideas, together with the former assistant and friend of Alexis de Tocqueville, Arthur de Gobineau. The 'scientific' concepts of race and culture, however, 'lost their use for Renan after the Franco-Prussian war. (…) To the triumphant ideology of Pan-Germanism, Renan responded with another theory of the nation – insisting on the distinction between national culture and human culture'. Finkielkraut, *The defeat of the mind* (1995) 32-33.

[65] A good article on Renan's national thinking is: M. Zenner, 'Die Nation im Denken Ernest Renans', in: K. Kluxen and W.J. Mommsen, *Politische ideologen und Nationalstaatliche Ordnung. Studien zur Geschichte des 19. Und 20. Jahrhunderts* (München: R. Oldenbourg, 1968) 219-238.

[66] Renan, *Qu'est-ce qu'une nation?*, in: Philippe Forest, *Qu'est-ce qu'une Nation?* (Paris: Pierre Bordas et fils 1991) 41: 'Une nation est donc une grande solidarité, constitué par le sentiment des sacrifices qu'on a faits et de ceux qu'on est disposé à faire encore. Elle suppose un passé ; elle se résume pourtant dans le présent par un fait tangible : le consentement, le désir clairement exprimé de continuer la vie commune. L'existence d'une nation est (pardonnez-moi cette métaphore) un plébiscite de tous les jours.'

[67] Cf. R. Tombs (ed.), *Nationhood and Nationalism in France. From Boulangism to the great war 1889-1918* (London: Harper Collins Academic, 1991); Or the wonderful description of the French national identity by Fernand Braudel in: Braudel, *L'identité de la France. Espace et histoire* (Paris: Arthaus-Flammarion, 1986), who starts with: 'Je le dis une fois pour toutes: j'aime la France avec la même passion, exigeante et compliquée, que Jules Michelet …', and further down: 'En outre, toute identité nationale implique, forcément, une certaine unité nationale, elle en est comme le reflet, la transposition, la condition …'. (pages 9 and 17 respectively).

72   CHAPTER THREE

nationalism emerged. French philosophers and historians following Georges Vacher de Lapouge started measuring what was called the 'cephalic index' of skulls, found on the graveyards of the Hérault and other regions of France,[68] to determine the essential racial characteristics of the French nation. Vacher de Lapouge described in his book *l'Aryen : son rôle sociale* (1899) in fact exactly the approach to nationality that the French had rejected a mere twenty years before:

> One neither decides to become a member of a family nor a nation. The blood one carries in his veins when one is born, one keeps that all his life. The individual is dominated by his race, he is nothing. The race, the nation is everything.[69]

Nationality thus became once more a question not of choice or culture, but of nature.[70] Consider the influential Charles Maurras (1868-1952), who wrote in *Mes idées politiques* (1937) that 'it is not our choice which makes us French. (…) We do not choose our fatherland, any more than we choose our father and mother'.[71]

This deterministic way of thinking, the nation as ethnicity, judging the man instead of his culture, his inherited past rather than his chosen future, culminated in the Dreyfus Affair, a conflict that commenced in 1894 and deeply divided French society for more than a decade. The originally German-speaking Alfred Dreyfus (1859-1935), who had moved from the Alsace region (he was born in Mulhouse) into France after it was annexed by Prussia in 1871, had recently become a captain in the French army. Yet in 1894, he was convicted for treason, as he was found guilty of passing French military secrets to Germany. It quickly became clear, however, that it was unlikely for Dreyfus to have committed this crime, and that the reason for him being convicted lay more in anti-Semitism, as Dreyfus had Jewish roots. Moreover, Dreyfus spoke French with a suspicious German accent, having been raised in the Alsace region.

The anti-Dreyfusards wanted to defend the infallibility of the French army, and to clear France of what they regarded as impure influences. Finkielkraut summarizes their standpoint as 'Dreyfus was guilty, as the inhabitants of the provinces of Alsace and Lorraine were German, by virtue of ethnicity'.[72]

---

[68] The Hérault is a region near Bordeaux.
[69] George Vacher de Lapouge, *l'Aryen et son rôle sociale* (Paris: 1899) 511, as quoted in: Zeev Sternhell, *La droite révolutionnaire: les origines françaises du fascisme, 1885-1914* (Paris: Editions du Seuil, 1978) 168: 'On n'entre par décret ni dans une famille ni dans une nation. Le sang qu'on apporte dans ses veines en naissant, on le garde toute sa vie. L'individu est écrasé par sa race, il n'est rien. La race, la nation sont tout'.
[70] Cf. Tzvetan Todorov, *Nous et les autres, la réflexion française sur la diversité humaine* (Editions du Seuil, 1989) 333.
[71] Charles Maurras, *Mes idées politiques* (Paris: Arthème Fayard, 1937) 252: 'Ce n'est pas notre volonté qui nous a faits Français. (…) On ne choisit pas plus sa patrie – *la terre de ses pères* – que l'on ne choisit son père et sa mere'.
[72] Finkielkraut (1995) 46.

Although Dreyfus was eventually rehabilitated in 1906, the affaire had a deeply divisive influence on French society, and the belief in a predetermined *Volksgeist* as well as its racist and determinist companions had conquered a strong position in French life. Informal leader of the anti-Dreyfusards was the influential intellectual, writer and member of parliament Maurice Barrès (1862-1923). His reasoning was:

> If we prove that Dreyfus is guilty, the french army as a whole will be strengthened: that is good for France. If on the contrary it will turn out that he is innocent, that would discredit the army and harm the nation. Conclusion: whatever may be the 'absolute' truth, justice for France demands that Dreyfus be condemned.[73]

Note that the word *absolute* is placed between brackets: as if to symbolize that every form of 'objective truth' is always in the eye of the beholder.[74] According to Barrès, then, even if Dreyfus was found to be 'objectively' innocent (but what is 'objective innocence'?), those who had defended him – the *Dreyfusards* – would be guilty. Because, as Barrès writes in his *Scènes et doctrines du nationalisme*, 'their conspiracy divides and disarms France, and they are rejoiced by that. Even if their client would be innocent, they would remain criminals'.[75] Indeed, the argument of the anti-Dreyfusards seems to be that the French nation could not accept any infringements of its prestige after the defeat of 1871, and that the individual interest in 'justice' was subordinate to that objective of paramount importance.

Anti-Semitism, moreover, was to continue to play a dominant role in French national contemplations. What was the reasoning behind anti-Semitic nationalism? Again Maurice Barrès:

> The jews have no fatherland in the sense that we understand it. For us, our fatherland is the soil and the ancestors, it is the land of our dead. For them, it is the place where they find their greatest interest.[76]

A man who certainly disagreed with him was Theodor Herzl, who wrote in his 1896 pamphlet *Der Judenstaat* that the only thing that determines the Jew is

---

[73] Quoted in: Todorov, *Nous et les autres, la réflexion française sur la diversité humaine* (Paris: Editions du Seuil, 1989) 91: 'Si on prouve que Dreyfus est coupable, l'armée française en sort renforcée: cela est bon pour la France. S'il s'avère au contraire qu'il est innocent, cela discrédite l'armée et nuit à la nation. Conclusion: quelle que soit la vérité « absolue », la justice française exige que Dreyfus soit condamné.'

[74] Cf. Leo Strauss, *Natural right and history* (Chicago: Chicago University Press, 1953) especially chapter 1, and Allan Bloom, *The closing of the American mind. How higher education has failed democracy and impoverished the souls of today's students* (New York: Simon & Schuster, 1987) especially part II.

[75] Maurice Barrès, *Scènes et doctrines du Nationalisme* (Paris: Émile-Paul, 1902) Tome I, 138: 'leur complot divise et désarme la France, et ils s'en réjouissent. Quand bien même leur client serait un innocent, ils demeuraient des criminels'.

[76] Barres (1902) Tome I, 67: 'Les juifs n'ont pas de patrie au sens où nous l'entendons. Pour nous, la patrie, c'est le sol et les ancêtres, c'est la terre de nos morts. Pour eux, c'est l'endroit où ils trouvent leur plus grand intérêt'.

anti-Semitism: 'Only necessity makes us cling to the old tribe, only the hatred of our environment makes us different. (…) We are a people – our enemies have made us one against our will, as it has always been throughout history'.[77]

But whatever may precisely be the case, one thing is certain: the Dreyfus affair contributed greatly to the explosive warlike atmosphere that arose in Europe, especially between Germany and France, that led to the First World War. Herzl drew his conclusions from this situation, and went down in history as the founder of a new sort of Jewish nationalism – which has culminated, of course, in a particularly remarkable nation state today, Israel.[78]

To conclude, we may – as has been outlined above – distinguish three approaches to the 'nation'. The first is the radical Enlightened, affirming people's equality and rights whatever their background and culture. The second is the radical Romantic, putting all emphasis on historical determinism and race. And the third is the open yet conditional conception, trying to find a middle road between radical equality and determinist inequality: membership is in principle open to everyone, but requires an effort. In his history of European nationalism, Tzvetan Todorov distinguishes between on the one hand 'a community of "blood", that is to say a biological entity, over which the individual has no hold at all', and on the other a community based on 'an act of the will, on subscribing to an arrangement to live together by adopting common rules, by envisaging a common future'.[79]

It is indeed a complicated distinction we have to make to understand the debate rightly. Of course, the theorists of the sovereign state, as discussed above, like Bodin and Hobbes, had some concept of national unity in mind. They were not drawing the map for a world-government. But they were preoccupied mainly with the organizational apparatus needed to restore political order in times of great social divergence.

The great Enlightenment project was to map out what was reasonable for *man* in general. It focused on mankind's nature, and not so much on *men* in their cultural variety. In doing so, the Enlightenment had a propensity to overlook people's roots and their inclination towards the 'little platoons' that Burke thought were the foundation of civil society. The French Revolution symbolized these

---

[77] Theodor Herzl, *Der Judenstaat* (Osnabrück: Otto Zeller 1968, neudruck der Erstausgabe 1896) 26: 'Nur der Druck presst uns wieder an den alten Stamm, nur der Hass unserer Umgebung macht uns wieder zu Fremden. (…) Wir sind ein Volk – der Feind macht uns ohne unseren Willen dazu, wie das immer in der Geschichte so war.'

[78] Cf. B. Evron, *Jewish state or Israeli Nation?* (Bloomington and Indianapolis: Indiana University Press, 1995) 41ff.

[79] Todorov (1989) 508: 'une communauté de « sang », c'est-à-dire une entité biologique, sur laquelle l'individu n'a aucune prise', accomplir un acte de la volonté, souscrire à un engagement de vivre ensemble en adoptant des règles communes, en envisageant donc un avenir commun'.

universalist ideals, thereby creating, amongst other things, a 10-day week and a cult of humanity, while expropriating the Catholic Church.[80]

This was not the focus of the theorists of the nation in the romantic age. They argued that the nation consisted of a homogeneous population and that this homogeneous population had to be the basis of the political organization of the state. The debate over Alsace-Lorraine clearly illustrates this.

As has been shown above, in the late 19th century and first half of the 20th century, the Romantic approach to the nation became increasingly important in political discourse. Moreover, the idea that it was the German state that ought to bring the German Nation *Heim ins Reich*, and the need as perceived by the French to 'purify' the nation during the third republic (e.g. the Dreyfus affair), were in fact extreme excrescences of the Romantic conception of nationality.[81]

This is certainly the main reason why 'nationalism' and the word 'nation' grips our conscience and provokes negative associations. The term brings about not only intellectual discussion, but also highly inflamed emotions. Words are not really important, however, and there is no intrinsic reason why we should continue to use that contaminated word for the patriotic kind of political loyalty that we associated with Renan and Fustel the Coulanges in the course of the last section of this chapter.

Some would thus distinguish here between nationalism and patriotism. The Germans are inclined to call the open idea of nationality '*Staatsbürgerschaft*'. Following Ernst Cassirer, Jürgen Habermas has spoken of '*Verfassungspatriotismus*'.[82] John Stuart Mill emphasized the importance of 'the principle of cohesion among members of the same community or state'.[83] Hegel, too, suggested a form of national identity when he wrote about the need of societies for some set of essential values that generate a certain minimal point of reference for all,[84] a '*Selbstgefühl*',[85] without which a civil society cannot interact harmoniously with the state. Tocqueville, finally, wrote not about nationality but about 'a certain uniformity of civilization' that he believed to be 'not less necessary (…) than a

---

[80] Scruton, 'Man's second disobedience: reflections on the French Revolution', in: *The Philosopher on Dover Beach* (Indiana: St. Augustine's Press, 1998) 196.

[81] Naturally, there were other sorts of romantic nationalism too. For example the nationalism of Charles Péguy, which cultivated the memory of Jeanne d'Arc, and was not anti-Semitic.

[82] Cf. Deniz Coskun, 'Constitutioneel patriottisme voor Europa. Wat Ernst Cassirer bepleitte in Weimar', in: Ernst John Kaars Sijpesteijn (ed.), *Het Volk en Europa* (Amsterdam: Vereniging Democratisch Europa, 2004) 83-92.

[83] John Stuart Mill, *Considerations on representative government* (1861) (New York: Prometheus Books, 1991) chapter 4.

[84] Georg Wilhelm Friedrich Hegel, *Grundlinien der Philosophie des Rechts* (1821) (Frankfurt am Main: Suhrkamp Verlag, 1970) § 174.

[85] Hegel (1821) § 322.

uniformity of interests' for political society to endure,[86] 'un certain nombre de conditions d'union'.[87] Without such 'homogénéité dans la civilisation', he thought a political system could not survive long.[88]

All these ways of expression are variations on the theme of the 'nation', nationality, nationhood. An example of a state that seems to have been able to develop and sustain such an 'open' nationality is the United States of America. Its unifying principle is not race, or ethnicity, but the 'civic religion' that is sometimes expressed as the *American Dream*, and which is symbolized by the 'constitution' (which almost bears a 'sacred' status), the flag, the anthem and the 'dollar' (though admittedly, that one may have lost some of its credit, lately). Thus it was possible in January 2009 for a man of a minority race to become the president of this nation – because Barack Obama was before everything else an *American*.

It is important not to lose our way in semantic discussions: what the Germans mean by *Staatsbürgerschaft*, or what some other authors refer to as 'patriotism', is what Renan and Fustel de Coulanges meant by nationality: the middle-road between universal citizenship (radical Enlightened thought) and pre-determined ethnic membership (radical Romanticism). Both inherently local, as well as open to people from all different backgrounds, it forms the synthesis of Enlightened universalism and Romantic determinism, and it is realized in the ideal of the tolerant and open nation states based on what I call a *multicultural nationalism*.

---

[86] Tocqueville, *Democracy in America*, vol. I, chapter VIII, 'why the Federal system is not practicable for all nations, and how the Anglo-Americans were enabled to adopt it' (New York: Vintage Books, 1990) 169.

[87] Tocqueville, *De la démocratie en Amérique*, vol. I, chapter VIII (1835), 'Ce qui fait que le système fédéral n'est pas à la portée de tous les peuples, et ce qui a permis aux Anglo-Américains de l'adopter' (Paris: Éditions Gallimard, 1986) 257.

[88] Tocqueville, *De la démocratie en Amérique*, vol. I, chapter VIII, 'Ce qui fait que le système fédéral n'est pas à la portée de tous les peuples, et ce qui a permis aux Anglo-Américains de l'adopter' (Paris: Éditions Gallimard, 1986) 258.

CONCLUSION

We have now examined the three elements that together make up national sovereignty. We have defined the 'state' as the political apparatus that structures political power and enforces the law. We have seen that sovereignty can be understood in a formal and a material sense: the formal sense denoting the constitutional independence of a state, the material sense denoting the location of the political process: the actual place where decisions are made. Both are implied in every serious understanding of self-government. And we have identified the 'nation' as an imagined and territorial loyalty, providing an experience of membership, a collective 'we'. Nationality contrasts with tribal loyalty on the one hand, and religious loyalty on the other; the former territorial yet unimagined, the latter imagined but non-territorial.

A question that lies before us today may be what kind of effort should be demanded from immigrants, and what kind of cohesion should be striven for. What are the factors that create national loyalty, or national identity, and how wide-ranging may the differences between citizens be, before national loyalty is abandoned and replaced with tribal or religious loyalties? Can Western culture as a whole provide such a loyalty – and is a European nationality therefore feasible?

An argument in favor of this idea is that nation states of today have to a great extent been created and 'socially engineered' as well.[1] One obvious example is Italy (which did not even have a uniform language in the 19th century), another is Belgium (which could be described, in many respects, as a disintegrating nation[2]). Since it can hardly be said that the Europe of today consists of natural, unchanging and unchangeable nation states, why not create a new one for the whole continent?

On the other hand, even though radical secessionist minorities have continued to exist in many European states, the experience of national membership of the general population seems to remain rather unproblematic in most Western-European countries. If the Vienna peace treaty, the Versailles peace treaty, or the formation of Eastern Europe after the Second World War had been different, then no doubt there would have been different nation states from the ones we have

---

[1] An example is James B. Minahan, *One Europe, many nations. A historical dictionary of European national groups* (Greenwood Press, London, 2000), which discerns approximately 2000 different ethnic groups which form the built-up of the original European population.

[2] Others have said that Belgium never even formed a nation at all, for instance Paul Belien, *A throne in Brussels. Britain, the Saxe-Coburgs and the Belgianisation of Europe* (Exeter: Imprint Academic, 2005).

now: with different borders. France would perhaps be smaller, the Netherlands would perhaps still include Flanders, and Germany might have stretched deeper into the east and southeast, perhaps including Alsace-Lorraine as well.

But the fact that nations are historical contingencies does not mean that people also experience their nationality as a mere coincidence, interchangeable with any other. Nor even that such an experience may be interchangeable over a course of several generations. The fact is that our identity – the identity of each one of us – is formed by a series of coincidences, but that this identity nevertheless defines who we are. The nations of today are inherited identities, and most have been formed under centuries of aristocratic rule. Not only may there be a natural boundary to the scale on which the experience of national identity may be extended; nation-building on a European scale may also be a form of social engineering that needs pressures from above that are impossible to sustain under democratic regimes. Nations, then, may be a bit like fossil fuels: formed under centuries of incredible pressures from above, they are with us as relicts of an age past, but necessary nevertheless for the flourishing of modern life.

But we will return to this issue in part III – as it is first necessary to discuss the antitheses to national sovereignty, which have gained shape in the past three quarters of a century: supranationalism and multiculturalism.

PART II

THE ASSAULT ON BORDERS

Supranationalism and Multiculturalism

Imagine there's no countries
It isn't hard to do
Nothing to kill or die for
And no religion too
Imagine all the people
Living life in peace

From: John Lennon, *Imagine* (1971)

INTRODUCTION

Opposed to national sovereignty stand supranationalism and multiculturalism. The borders that have been constructed over a period of hundreds of years, to separate one jurisdiction from another, to settle the problem of political loyalty and avoid further civil wars, have been broken down. The idea of national sovereignty has been considered to belong to the past.

In a concerted assault on borders, Western European states in the second half of the twentieth century have adopted a policy of dilution both of national identities and of sovereignty. The nation state has been seriously undermined, by a policy of multiculturalism from the inside, and by supranationalism from the outside. It is the purpose of this part of the book to outline the extent to which those developments have infringed national sovereignty, by discussing them separately, commencing with supranationalism, followed by an examination of multiculturalism.

Supranationalism is entirely different from internationalism. The two are often muddled up, but while internationalism is an expression of sovereignty – and indeed only became possible, as discussed in chapter 1, with the rise of sovereign states –, supranationalism entails an inversion of classical international law and stands at odds with the very foundation of cooperation between states, which is sovereignty. As a synonym to supranationalism, the terms transnationalism or 'transnational jurisdiction' are sometimes used.[1]

One explanation for the confusion over the meaning of international and supranational resides in the confusing use of the word 'nation' (as has been discussed in chapter 3). For what is meant by *supranationalism*[2] is in fact supra-statism: the setting up of institutions that function *supra* the *state*: higher than the state. Supranational are those developments that create legal structures that stand *above* the state. Precisely because of this characteristic, supranationalism is something quite different from internationalism, which creates, as we will observe in more detail, legal affiliations *among* and *between* states. Internationalism is an expression of sovereignty, supranationalism *undermines* sovereignty, or, as John Laughland puts it:

> One of the greatest intellectual faults is to confuse cooperation between States, with their political integration, and to defend the latter in the name of the former.[3]

---

[1] As it is used, for instance, by Scruton (2002) 144.
[2] Or, of course, by *transnationalism*.
[3] John Laughland, *The Tainted Source. The undemocratic origins of the European Union* (Boston: Little Brown & Company, 1997) 299. The 1998 edition says: 'It is dishonest for European federalists

Political integration occurs when the free choice to cooperate is taken from the member states, and having a choice to cooperate or not thus implies that no political integration has occurred. Cooperation and integration are mutually exclusive.

Nor does a supranational organization relate to the state as the state does to its provinces. Supranationalism is not an attempt at enlarging the scope of the state. It is not merely a continuation of the concept of sovereign statehood on a larger scale, like federalism. On the contrary: supranationalism is *an entirely different* approach. Let us first discuss the differences between supranationalism and internationalism, and then those between supranationalism and federalism.

States have never existed in a vacuum. As discussed in chapters 1 and 2, the autarkic state has never truly existed. States have always made agreements, alliances, have set up trade conferences and drawn up covenants, and will probably always continue to do so. That is 'internationalism' (or 'intergovernmentalism'), and is profoundly distinct from 'supranationalism'. While any interaction or any agreement between states is a form of internationalism, supranationalism is the establishment of an organization that may, by some form of non-consensual voting or internal judicial procedure:

(a)   amend the agreed provisions, or
(b)   execute these provisions, or
(c)   interpret these provisions,
      thereby binding the member states to terms not formally agreed upon by their legislature (which is charged with ratifying treaties).

Perhaps the clearest way to illustrate the distinction between supranationalism and internationalism, is through an example that could easily be confused with supranationalism, but is in fact a model-example of internationalism: NATO. The North Atlantic Treaty Organization (NATO) was founded on April 4th, 1949, with the signing of the North Atlantic Treaty in Washington, DC. The member states agreed to regard an attack on one of them, as an attack on all, as article 5 of the treaty reads:

> The Parties agree that an armed attack against one or more of them in Europe or North America shall be considered an attack against them all and consequently they agree that, if such an armed attack occurs, each of them, in exercise of the right of individual or collective self-defense recognized by Article 51 of the Charter of the United Nations, will assist the Party or Parties so attacked by taking forthwith,

---

to have peddled the idea of a single market – which could have united the peoples of Europe by means of free and spontaneous interaction – when what was in fact being hatched was not a free market at all. On the agenda instead is a self-contained and centrally directed economic space which is intended to serve as the basis for a political union. The one cannot be defended in the name of the other, any more than integration can be defended in the name of cooperation'. In: *Ibidem* (London: Warner Books, 1998) 326.

individually and in concert with the other Parties, such action as it deems necessary, including the use of armed force, to restore and maintain the security of the
North Atlantic area.[4]

This simple clause marks the essence of NATO, which is therefore in fact nothing
more than an ordinary defense alliance, comparable to any other in history, from
the defense alliance Germany had with Austria in the 1910s, to the one France
had with Britain in the Crimean War of 1853-1856, and so on.

NATO does not have the power to amend, execute, or interpret elements of
its charter by some form of majority vote, or by some form of court decision. If
they no longer adhere to its principles, member states can withdraw (as, indeed,
France partially did in 1966). As all its decisions necessarily have to be taken
by consensus, article 10 concerning the extension of NATO membership reads:

> The Parties may, by unanimous agreement, invite any other European State in a
> position to further the principles of this Treaty and to contribute to the security
> of the North Atlantic area to accede to this Treaty.

Therefore, membership of NATO does not affect any of the powers attributed
to statehood of any of its members but, quite the contrary, it is an *expression* of
those powers. The state remains in place and is only bound by duties explicitly
agreed upon. Indeed, the NATO treaty does not even prescribe *the type of*
assistance states are obliged to offer one another in case of armed attack. Once
again article 5:

> The Parties (…) agree that (…) each of them (…) will assist the Party or Parties
> so attacked by taking (…) such action as it deems necessary.

'Such action as it deems necessary': the decision is in the hands of the member
state itself, *not* in the hands of NATO.[5]

For NATO to have supranational powers, a board would be required that, by
majority vote or executive decision, could determine whether or not there has
been an attack on any of its members; as well as what would be the appropriate
assistance demanded from other members. This, in turn, would also imply that
NATO would have instruments to enforce its decisions, for instance imposing
fines or even the possibility of assuming direct control over a reluctant member
state's military forces. It is clear that this requires an amount of trust that NATO's
member states are not prepared to grant each other, and realizing this helps us
anticipate the question of what it is, that makes us comfortable with our own

---

[4] Available online at http://www.nato.int/cps/en/natolive/official_texts_17120.htm.
[5] As was shown in 2003, when Turkey asked for military support from its NATO allies, and
France, Belgium and Germany opposed any such assistance, on the ground that providing it
would seem to endorse an attack on Iraq. See on this Jeremy A. Rabkin, *The case for Sovereignty.
Why the world should welcome American independence* (Washington, DC: AEI Press, 2004) 180ff.

governments exercising these powers, but uneasy about the thought of other governments exercising them over us.

Two other organizations that can be described as *international* (or inter-governmental) instead of *supranational* are the United Nations (the Security Council not taken into account[6]) and the OECD, the Organization for Economic Co-operation and Development. What is typical for them as international and not supranational organizations, is the following.

The United Nations (not taking into account the Security Council), can only pass resolutions that *suggest* things or set up again new organizations or commit-tees that make recommendations or organize conferences to enhance support for a certain cause. Even the payment of a contribution cannot be enforced by the General Assembly, and the only thing it can do when member states fail to pay, is suspend their right to vote. The UN – apart from the Security Council – is an instrument of international lobbying and policy making, of coordinating inter-national development aid, and a facilitating device for diplomacy. Without the endorsement of the Security Council, the UN cannot enforce any of its decisions.

The same goes for the OECD: established in 1961, the Organization for Economic Co-operation and Development[7] functions as an important means to achieve agreement on proposed international trade and entrepreneurial regula-tions: as an organization it cannot force its resolutions on its members should they, after extensive rounds of negotiations, not find their interests satisfactorily recognized by the forthcoming resolutions or recommendations.

So much for the difference between *supranationalism* and *internationalism*. Now let us have a look at the differences between supranationalism and the attempt to enlarge statehood in some federal form. As previously stated, the supranational organization does not relate to its member states as the state relates to its provinces. It is not the aim of any supranational organization to form a new state (neither on a European, nor on a global level). Supranational organizations undertake a replacement *of the entire concept* of statehood by something that in fact resembles more the medieval organization of power.

Whatever the different ways and forms in which states may have centralized or decentralized their government (which range from a centralized unitary state such as France, to a decentralized unitary state such as the Netherlands, to a federal state like the US, to name a few examples), there are always a number of unique attributes of the state that place it above its decentralized elements.

---

[6] While other bodies of the UN can occasionally draft resolutions that demand direct action, these require affirmation by the Security Council to take effect.

[7] The OECD is the successor to the Organization for European Economic Cooperation (OEEC) that was established in 1947 to coordinate the Marshall plan. In 1960, the United States and Canada joined, and the organization attained its new name and adjusted mission in 1961. Presently, the OECD has 34 member states, from all regions of the world.

As discussed in the first part, a state necessarily retains control over the army, the maintenance of foreign relations, and, correspondingly, the power of direct taxation.

Supranational organizations do not desire to take over all these attributes of the sovereignty of their member states: they merely desire to take over a *particular element* of it. 'Multilevel jurisdiction' is the key-word for supranational thinking.[8] Indeed, supranationalism is an attempt to siphon off any claim for centralized decision-making the state could make. Supranationalism entails – as Jean Monnet put it when he spoke of European integration – 'the abnegation of sovereignty on a limited, but decisive field'.[9]

In the course of the past decades, six supranational institutions have been erected, namely, the International Criminal Court (ICC), the European Court of Human Rights (ECHR), the International Court of Justice (ICJ), the World Trade Organization (WTO), the United Nations Security Council (SC) and the European Union (EU). These institutions take over, in their several ways, a limited aspect of the sovereignty of their member states, binding them by rulings, compelling them to follow policies they might not have accepted or pursued had they retained veto power, or by interpreting existing rules through some form of executive or judicial process. We will examine them in turn, and map out how they take over elements of the self-government of states attached to them.

But before we do so, it may be useful to make two general comments on the supranational philosophy. We can discern in principle two arguments for supranationalism.

---

[8] 'Multilevel jurisdiction' is also the well-chosen name of a research department of the faculty of law at Leiden University in the Netherlands, as the literature using this terminology is almost endless. Cf. I. Bache, *Europeanization and multilevel governance. Cohesion policy in the European Union and Britain* (Maryland: Rowman & Littlefield Publishers Inc., 2007); G. Baldacchino and D. Milne (eds.), *The Case for Non-sovereignty: Lessons from Sub-national Island Jurisdictions* (London: Routledge, 2008); A. Benz and C. Zimmer, 'The EU's competences: The "vertical" perspective on the multilevel system', in: *Living Reviews in European Governance*, Vol. 3 (2008) available online at: http://www.livingreviews.org/lreg-2008-3; O. Budzinski, *Mehr-Ebenen-Governance, Leitjurisdiktionskonzepte und globaler Wettbewerb* (April 14, 2009) available online at http://ssrn.com/abstract=1379608; G.B. Doern and R. Johnson (eds), *Rules, Rules, Rules, Rules: Multi-Level Regulatory Governance* (Toronto: University of Toronto Press, 2006); H. Yamamoto, 'Multi-level Governance and Public Private Partnership: Theoretical Basis of Public Management', in: *Interdisciplinary Information Sciences*, Vol. 13, No. 1 (2007) 65-88; A. van Hoek et al. (eds.), *Multilevel governance in enforcement and adjudication* (Antwerpen: Intersentia, 2006.); L. Hooghe and G.Marks, 'Unraveling the central state, but how? Types of Multi-Level Governance', in: *The American Political Science Review*, Vol. 97, No. 2 (May, 2003) 233-243; F.C. Mayer, 'Multilevel Constitutional Jurisdiction', in: A. von Bogdandy and J. Bast (eds.), *Principles of European Constitutional Law* (Oxford and München: Hart Publishing and Verlag C.H. Beck, 2010); R. Münch, *European Governmentality. The Liberal Drift of Multilevel Governance* (London: Routledge, 2010).

[9] Jean Monnet, *Mémoires* (Paris: Fayard, 1976) 316. The quote is discussed by Neill Nugent, *The Government and Politics of the European Community* (London: Macmillan, 1991) 35ff.

The first argument is that the decisions that are made on the supranational level are 'universal' or stem from a strict economic rationale, and that they are, therefore, 'nonpolitical'. Those who argue this often add that issues that require a political choice remain within the competence of the member states. An example of this is the European Court of Human Rights, which claims to administer only universal, nonpolitical standpoints. As clearly many of the Court's rulings and rules (such as the prohibition of the death penalty) go against the views of large minorities and even majorities in many European states, cursory observation already shows the tension this universal appearance brings about. We also see this idea of the supposed 'universality' of decisions in the policies of the EU's Economic and Monetary Union (EMU), establishing a common European currency, in which the interest rate would be set, and the inflation rate would be aimed for along 'nonpolitical' lines. It is thus widely assumed by those defending supranational developments that a large number of decisions that were formerly entrusted to the national political authorities, can now be made by application of universal laws of economics or ethics, and therefore that many economic or ethical questions are somehow non-political. As John Laughland puts it:

> Above all, it is the economist or unpolitical assumptions underlying the European construction which threaten democracy and the rule of law. It is widely assumed in Europe (and not just at a European level) that politics is simply the administration of the economy, and that it is sufficient to do this well, even in the absence of democracy. (…) To holders of such views, statehood and the activity of politics appear messy and illogical. Far better, it seems, to organize the world rationally, to overcome division and squabbling, and to put in place politico-economic systems which encourage harmony rather than conflict.[10]

'The language of economics has displaced the language of politics', Larry Siedentop notes in his book *Democracy in Europe*.[11] This is as clear in the EU as it is in the World Trade Organization, as will be shown in depth below. The question that supranationalists avoid by presenting arrangements in such a 'universal' way is where the political authority for these arrangements comes from, because what is beyond the political obviously doesn't stand in need of political legitimation.

The second argument that is generally advanced to support supranational developments is made by those who, while acknowledging the political implications of these supranational developments, argue that the loss of sovereignty and (thereby of) political independence is somehow compensated by economic growth or other benefits. This is most clearly seen in defenses of the World Trade Organization, which is supposedly in the self-interest of all of its members, even though in individual cases it may nevertheless act against certain members'

---

[10] Laughland (1997) 149.
[11] Larry Siedentop, *Democracy in Europe* (London: Penguin Press 2000) 102.

interests or wishes. The same argument is plain in discussions on the EU, the Euro currency, and the common market, which, as the proponents of the EU's current supranational direction continue to stress, are to the advantage of everyone, no allowance being made for the possibility of this being to the disadvantage of *some* of its member states.

Let us begin our examination of the workings of the six supranational institutions. For the purpose of clarity, I have divided them into two groups: supranational courts on the one hand, and supranational organizations on the other. Under the first fall the International Criminal Court, the International Court of Justice, and the European Court of Human Rights; under the second the WTO, the Security Council, and the European Union.

I will present the institutional structure and some emblematic examples of the workings of each of these institutions, not to provide an exhaustive account, but to give a flavor of their implications. What follows, thus, is a bird-eye's view of them. All these organizations have developed fairly recently and as yet, their powers are relatively limited. But altogether they form a network of decision making institutions, creating multilevel jurisdiction, constituting the first element of the two-pronged assault on borders.

CHAPTER FOUR

SUPRANATIONAL COURTS

4.1. *The International Criminal Court*

The International Criminal Court (ICC) is the first supranational tribunal with a permanent mandate, devoted to trying individuals, not states. As such, it has the power to start, upon state or Security Council request, or upon its own initiative, a procedure for the trial and conviction of individuals who are nationals *of* any of its member states, or that have committed acts *in* any of its member states.

Although the idea of a permanent international court which could try individuals and not states was already proposed in the 1930s,[1] and again in the 1940s and 1950s,[2] still 'in the early 1990s', as Michael Struett notes, 'the possibility of establishing a permanent ICC seemed remote and fanciful'.[3] After a few years of negotiations, however, a conference in Rome led to the Rome Statute on July 17th, 1998, in which it was agreed to establish the ICC as of July 1st, 2002.

It is widely assumed that the International Criminal Court is the natural successor of *ad hoc* war crimes tribunals, 'like that of Nuremberg'.[4] But the ICC, though superficially resembling the Nuremberg tribunal, is in many ways not comparable with it, and differs on crucial issues of sovereignty.[5] Not that even the Nuremberg trials themselves were uncontroversial at the time. Harlan Fiske Stone, the chief justice of the United States Supreme Court, 'who viewed the International Military Tribunal with great suspicion',[6] refused, as Jeremy Rabkin notes, 'to take part in a swearing-in ceremony for the US-appointed judges to the IMT'. He was said to have argued in private that the whole undertaking

---

[1] The Council of the League of Nations approved the Convention for the creation of an International Criminal Court in 1937; see John Laughland, *A History of Political Trials. From Charles I to Saddam Hussein* (Oxford: Peter Lang, 2008) 112.

[2] Cf. M.J. Struett, *The politics of constructing the International Criminal Court. NGOs, discourse, and agency* (New York: Palgrave Macmillan, 2008) 49ff.

[3] Struett (2008) 68.

[4] As has been done by, amongst many others, Costas Douzinas, *The end of Human Rights* (Portland: Hart Publishing, 2000) 121 and further, Antonio Cassese, *International Law* (Oxford: University Press, 2001) 250, and Peter H. Kooijmans, *Internationaal Publiekrecht* (Deventer: Kluwer, 2000) 34.

[5] Comparable considerations apply to the Tokyo tribunals. See on this: Michael P. Scharf, 'The ICC's jurisdiction over the nationals of non-party states: a critique of the U.S. position', in: *Law & Contemporary Problems*, vol. 64, issue 1 (Winter 2001) 67-118, there 106; B.V.A. Röling, *The Tokyo trial and Beyond. Reflections of a peacemonger, edited and with an Introduction by Antonio Cassese* (London: Polity Press, 1993); Laughland (2008) 163ff: 'Politics as conspiracy: the Tokyo trials'.

[6] R.E. Conot, *Justice at Nuremberg* (New York: Harper & Row Publishers, 1983) 63.

was 'a high-grade lynching party'.[7] Winston Churchill was well-known for his opposition to the idea of an allied trial of Axis war criminals as well,[8] as were many others, such as the US Senator Robert Taft and US Supreme Court Justice William O. Douglas.

John F. Kennedy, the future President, noted: 'These conclusions [that the tribunal was based on *ex post facto* law and that its legitimacy was questionable] are shared, I believe, by a substantial number of American citizens today. And they were shared, at least privately, by a goodly number in 1946'.[9]

The main crime for which the Nazi-leaders were tried was not the holocaust nor even 'crimes against humanity'. Indeed, Telford Taylor confesses in his memoir that when he accepted his position as the United States Deputy Chief prosecutor at Nuremberg after the surrender of Germany, 'I remained ignorant of the mass extermination camps in Poland, and the full scope of the Holocaust did not dawn on me until several months later, at Nuremberg'.[10] The main aim of the tribunal was to try 'crimes against peace', and the 'crimes against humanity' were only actionable if understood in the context of waging an 'aggressive war'.[11] As the judges ruled:

> With regard to crimes against humanity, there is no doubt whatever that political opponents were murdered in Germany before the war, and that many of them were kept in concentration camps in circumstances of great horror and cruelty. The policy of terror was certainly carried out on a vast scale, and in many cases was organised and systematic. The policy of persecution, repression and murder of civilians in Germany before the war of 1939, who were likely to be hostile to the Government, was most ruthlessly carried out. The persecution of Jews during the same period is established beyond all doubt.
>
> To constitute crimes against humanity, the acts relied on before the outbreak of war must have been in execution of, or in connection with, any crime within the jurisdiction of the Tribunal. The Tribunal is of the opinion that revolting and horrible as many of these crimes were, it has not been satisfactorily proved that they were done in execution of, or in connection with, any such crime. The Tribunal therefore cannot make a general declaration that the acts before 1939 were crimes against humanity within the meaning of the Charter, but from the beginning of the war in 1939 war crimes were committed on a vast scale, which were also crimes against humanity; and insofar as the inhuman acts charged in the Indictment, and committed after the beginning of the war, did not constitute

---

[7] Jeremy A. Rabkin, 'Nuremberg Misremembered', in: *SAIS Review*, The Johns Hopkins University Press, Vol. 19 no. 2 (1999) 81-96, there 81-82.

[8] Cf. Laughland (2008) 113.

[9] John F. Kennedy, *Profiles in Courage* (New York: Harper & Row, 1963) 184, chapter 9.

[10] Telford Taylor, *The anatomy of the Nuremberg trials. A personal memoir* (New York: Alfred J. Knopf, 1992) xi.

[11] Cf. *Judgment of the International military tribunal for the trial of German major war criminals: The Law Relating to War Crimes and Crimes Against Humanity*. Available online at http://avalon. law.yale.edu/imt/judlawch.asp.

war crimes, they were all committed in execution of, or in connection with, the aggressive war, and therefore constituted crimes against humanity.[12]

In contrast with the great resonance of the term 'crimes against humanity' today, the Nuremberg tribunal thus understood by them solely those crimes which were committed in the context of an aggressive war – and for that reason, the judges refused to assert jurisdiction over crimes committed before the outbreak of the war, September 1st, 1939. It is not surprising then to note, as Rabkin does, that 'not one of the twenty-four defendants was indicted solely for "crimes against humanity"'.[13]

Moreover, the Nuremberg tribunal was set up with explicit reference to the sovereign legislative power of Germany – executed, at the time, by the four major allied powers.[14] The charter of the Nuremberg tribunal – formally called International Military Tribunal (IMT) – explicitly stated that:

> The making of the Charter was the exercise of the sovereign legislative power by the countries to which the German Reich unconditionally surrendered; and the undoubted right of these countries to legislate for the occupied territories has been recognised by the civilised world.[15]

For the same reason – that it was 'the exercise of the sovereign legislative power by the countries to which the German Reich unconditionally surrendered' –, the accusations were not brought forward by an entity denoted as 'humanity' or 'the United Nations' – as was indeed proposed at a certain point[16] – against Nazi-Germany, but as:

> The United States of America, The French Republic, The United Kingdom of Great Britain and Northern Ireland, and The Union of Soviet Socialist Republics – against – Hermann Wilhelm Goering, Rudolf Hess, Joachim von Ribbentrop …(etc).[17]

Nor were any judges appointed from other allied or neutral countries:[18] only the US, France, the UK and the USSR conducted the trial. When in 1947 additional

---

[12] *Judgment of the International military tribunal for the trial of German major war criminals: The Law Relating to War Crimes and Crimes Against Humanity.* Available online at http://avalon. law.yale.edu/imt/judlawch.asp.

[13] Rabkin (1999) 81-96, there 84.

[14] The promulgation of the International Military Tribunal Charter was 'the exercise of the sovereign legislative power by the countries to which the German Reich unconditionally surrendered', Judgment, Official Documents of the Tribunal, Vol. 1, 171.

[15] 'The law of the Charter', in: *Judgment of the International military tribunal for the trial of German major war criminals: The law of the Charter.* Available online at http://avalon.law.yale. edu/imt/judlawch.asp.

[16] John Laughland, *Travesty. The trial of Slobodan Milosevic and the corruption of international justice* (Michigan: Pluto press, 2007) 60; Rabkin (1999) 81-96, there 87.

[17] Available online at http://avalon.law.yale.edu/imt/count.asp.

[18] Laughland (2007) 67.

alleged war criminals were tried in Nuremberg[19] – this time by the United States alone –, the judges, drawing on the Charter of the IMT and the jurisprudence of the original trial, further recalled that:

> On 5 June 1945 the Allied Powers announced that they 'hereby assume supreme authority with respect to Germany, including all the powers possessed by the German Government, the High Command, and any state, municipal or local government or authority'[20] (…)

And that:

> On 2 August 1945 at Berlin, President Truman, Generalissimo Stalin, and Prime Minister Attlee, as heads of the Allied Powers, entered into a written agreement setting forth the principles which were to govern Germany during the initial control period.

Quoting a number of 'modern scholars of high standing in the field of international law', the judges found that these scholars had agreed that

> the situation at the time of the unconditional surrender resulted in the transfer of sovereignty to the Allies.[21]

They furthermore asserted that 'by virtue of the situation at the time of unconditional surrender, the Allied Powers were provisionally in the exercise of supreme authority, valid and effective until such time as, by treaty or otherwise, Germany shall be permitted to exercise the full powers of sovereignty', and that 'We sit as a Tribunal drawing its sole power and jurisdiction from the will and command of the Four occupying Powers'.[22]

The tribunal went on to declare that '[the] universality and superiority of international law does not necessarily imply universality of its enforcement' and that 'within the territorial boundaries of a state (…) a violator of the rules of international law could be punished only by the authority of officials of that state. The law is universal, but such a state reserves unto itself the exclusive power within its boundaries to apply or withhold sanctions'.[23]

---

[19] The defendants were Josef Altstoetter, Wilhelm von Ammon, Paul Barnickel, Hermann Cuhorst, Karl Engert, Guenther Joel, Herbert Klemm, Ernst Lautz, Wolfgang Mettgenberg, Guenther Nebelung, Rudolf Oeschey, Hans Petersen, Oswald Rothaug, Curt Rothenberger, Franz Schlegelberger, and Carl Westphal. The indictment is available online at http://www.mazal.org/archive/nmt/03/NMT03-T0001.htm.
[20] *Trials of war criminals before the Nuremberg Military Tribunal under Control Council Law No. 10*, Volume III, Case no. 3, 'The Justice Case', United States *against* Josef Altstoetter, *et al.* (Washington DC: U.S. Government Printing Office, 1951) 959: 'Under Source of authority of C.C. Law 10'. Available online at http://www.mazal.org/NMT-HOME.htm.
[21] *Trials of war criminals before the Nuremberg Military Tribunal under Control Council Law No. 10*, Volume III, Case no. 3, 'The Justice Case', United States *against* Josef Altstoetter, *et al.* (Washington DC: U.S. Government Printing Office, 1951) 962. Available online at http://www.mazal.org/NMT-HOME.htm.
[22] 'The Justice Case', 963-964.
[23] 'The Justice Case', 963-964.

The point was thus once again made that the power the Allied forces had assumed in Germany upon its unconditional surrender was 'a power which no international authority without consent could assume or exercise (…)'.[24] The contrast could not be greater with the Criminal Tribunal for the former Yugoslavia (ICTY) – which was based on the idea, as the first ruling of the ICTY Trial Chamber asserted, that 'the sovereign rights of States cannot and should not take precedence over the right of the international community to act appropriately as they [i.e., the crimes against humanity] affect the whole of mankind and shock the conscience of all nations of the world'.[25]

It is not surprising, therefore, that former Nuremberg prosecutor, Walter J. Rockler, has pleaded not only against the legality of the war in Kosovo but also against the legality of the Yugoslavia tribunal,[26] and lamented that

> As a primary source of international law, the judgment of the Nuremberg Tribunal in the 1945-1946 case of the major Nazi war criminals is plain and clear. Our leaders often invoke and praise that judgment, but obviously have not read it.[27]

Nor is it surprising that, for the most elementary reasons of self-interest, the Nuremberg tribunal was not set up as a universal court, trying whatever horrific deeds might have been committed in the name of any government or army whatsoever, but only those committed by Nazi-Germany; nor that it explicitly connected the crimes against humanity with crimes against the peace. The London agreement between the Allied forces, which gave birth to the Tribunal, was concluded two days after the 'Little Boy' nuclear bomb had been dropped on Hiroshima and a day before 'Fat Man' was dropped on Nagasaki – instantly killing an estimated 100 thousand civilians. The British and American air raids on German cities, moreover, had been examples of deeply questionable allied actions, and had cost an approximate total of 500 thousand civilian lives – far more than the German bombings of Britain had cost.[28]

Moreover, one of the main allied powers – the Soviet Union – had itself been Nazi-Germany's ally for several years, and had collaborated in waging an aggressive war, helping itself, as John Laughland puts it, 'to chunks of eastern

---

[24] 'The Justice Case', 970-971.
[25] Quoted by Laughland (2007) 63-64. Laughland gives the following reference (footnote 19): 'Prosecutor v. Dusko Tadic, Trial chamber decision on the defence motion on jurisdiction, 10 August 1995, paragraph 42; this passage was quoted and reaffirmed by the Appeals Chamber in its own decision in Tadic on the defence motion for interlocutory appeal on jurisdiction on 2 october 1995, at paragraph 59'.
[26] Laughland (2007) 68.
[27] Walter J. Rockler, 'War crimes applies to U.S. too', in: Chicago Tribune, 23 May 1999.
[28] J. Friedrich, Der Brand. Deutschland im Bombenkrieg 1940-1945 (München: Propyläen Verlag, 2002). Cf. Telford Taylor, The anatomy of the Nuremberg trials. A personal memoir (New York: Alfred J. Knopf, 1992) 326; Laughland, A history of political trials. From Charles I to Saddam Hussein (Oxford: Peter Lang, 2008) 117.

Poland, the Baltic states and Bessarabia under the terms of the secret protocol of the Molotov-Ribbentrop Pact signed on 23 August 1939'.[29] Laughland claims that the Nazis even 'provided their Bolshevik allies with huge quantities of fuel, food and war materiel for the purposes of conquering and occupying eastern Poland'.[30] After the Red Army's advance into Germany, it is certain that the Soviet soldiers looted for days on end and mass-raped the female population – clearly a war crime of tremendous proportions.[31] And so for all these reasons, the charter plainly stated that a tribunal would be set up

> for the Prosecution and Punishment of the major war criminals of the European axis[32]

– and not for any others.

In order, however, to prevent the defense of *tu quoque* (to which Hermann Goering nevertheless resorted), the 'charges against the Germans for having launched air attacks on British cities were removed: Goering, head of the Luftwaffe, was not indicted for this'.[33] As prosecutor Telford Taylor remembers: 'The great city air raids of the war – Hamburg, Berlin, Dresden, Tokyo, Hiroshima, and Nagasaki – had been conducted by Britain and the United States, which made it most unlikely that the prosecution would make a big thing out of the Germans' earlier raids which, destructive as they were, paled by comparison'. Taylor concludes that it is therefore 'not surprising that Goering's responsibility for the German attacks (…) played no part in the Tribunal's judgment'.[34]

The tribunals in the countries occupied by Nazi-Germany, meanwhile, had extraordinary jurisdiction, usually installed under a special post-war law – but in each case by the national government. These tribunals specifically dealt with crimes committed by the national collaborators under the German occupation.[35]

In contrast, the ICC has been set up without a specific war to condemn or a specific regime to judge. This implies great difficulties, and in any case makes the ICC a very different institution from the Nuremberg tribunal.[36] The legitimacy of the ICC should not be judged by the legitimacy of the Nuremberg trials;[37] the ICC is fundamentally different from the Nuremberg tribunal, and

---

[29] Laughland (2007) 60-61.
[30] *Ibidem.*
[31] Cf. Antony Beevor, *Berlin. The Downfall 1945* (London: Viking Penguin, 2002); Antony Beever, 'They raped every German female from eight to 80', in: *The Guardian* (1 May 2002), available online at http://www.guardian.co.uk/books/2002/may/01/news.features11.
[32] Nuremberg Trial Proceedings Vol. 1, London Agreement of August 8th 1945.
[33] Laughland (2007) 61.
[34] Taylor (1992) 326.
[35] Cf. Laughland (2008) 77ff.
[36] Cf. Michael Lief, H. Mitchell Caldwell, and Benjamin Bycel, *Ladies and Gentlemen of the Jury: Greatest arguments in Modern Law* (New York: Simon & Schuster, 1998).
[37] Cf. Chantal Delsol, *Unjust justice, against the tyranny of international law* (Delaware: ISI Books, 2008) 52-53, who voices the same view but from a different perspective: 'Thus, Nuremberg

it should be considered on its own account. What follows is an examination of its supranational capacities.

Currently, the Court has 116 member states;[38] though this may seem a very large number, many of the states that have decided not to ratify the Rome Statute are important ones, for example, the United States, Russia, China, India, Pakistan, Turkey, and Iran. Many other countries that are likely to be involved in serious armed conflicts in the near future have also decided not to join the ICC, such as Iraq, Kazakhstan, Syria, Saudi Arabia, Egypt, Lebanon, Algeria, Israel, Morocco, Zimbabwe, Somalia, Sudan, North Korea and South Korea.[39]

That is not surprising. The ICC's supranational powers are vast, and it is uncertain what direction its rulings will take, even though formally the Court has jurisdiction over 'the severest crimes of international concern' only.[40] As article 5 of the Rome Statute reads:

> 1. The Jurisdiction of the Court shall be limited to the most serious crimes of concern to the international community as a whole.

It continues:

> The court has jurisdiction in accordance with this Statute with respect to the following crimes:
> (a) The crime of genocide;
> (b) Crimes against humanity;
> (c) War crimes;
> (d) The crime of aggression.

Note that 'crimes against humanity' have now become independent of the 'crime of aggression' (while the two had been connected at the Nuremberg tribunal). Moreover, paragraph 2 of article 5 decrees that the Court would not exercise jurisdiction over the 'crime of aggression', until it would have been 'properly defined' at a later stage. An attempt to do so was undertaken at the Review Conference held in Kampala, Uganda, in 2010, but it was also decided there that the jurisdiction of the ICC over the 'crime of aggression' should have to be reviewed once again after 2017.[41] Not that the other three crimes, (a), (b), and

---

represents a unique instance in which all the requisite circumstances for an unprecedented trial came together, including an unwritten law that condemned those who had followed a written law. The trial was made possible only by an act of conscience and by the remorse of an entire culture. (…) It seems to me, then, that if Nuremberg was justified by the remorse that a culture felt when confronted with its own development, the European tribunal that recently judged the massacres of Rwanda cannot claim the same legitimacy. In the absence of its own conscientious remorse, we see here a sanction applied from the outside to a people who do not understand it'.

[38]   That is, as of June, 2011.
[39]   http://www.icc-cpi.int/Menus/ASP/states+parties/.
[40]   Article 5 of the Rome Statute.
[41]   The resolution was adopted on June 11th, 2010. Available online at http://www.icc-cpi.int/iccdocs/asp_docs/Resolutions/RC-Res.6-ENG.pdf.

(c) are that 'properly defined' either. Articles 6, 7, and 8 attempt to provide more precise definitions, but hardly succeed.

When article 7 (defining 'crimes against humanity') for example declares that 'torture' is punishable, it leaves the judges with the task of defining what counts as such. Although it is true that the terms used in these articles were mostly borrowed from treaties already in force (such as the Convention against torture, and the Geneva Conventions), their interpretation remains disputable. Paragraph 2 of article 7 tries to present a guideline for the notions presented in this article (such as 'torture'), but does not make it much clearer:

> (...) (e) 'Torture' means the intentional infliction of severe pain or suffering, whether physical or mental, upon a person in the custody or under the control of the accused [i.e., the accused before the ICC]; except that torture shall not include pain or suffering arising only from, inherent in or incidental to, lawful sanctions;

What exactly is 'severe pain or suffering, whether physical or mental'? What is the reach of the 'lawful sanctions' that can exonerate the accused? Or take article 8 (defining 'war crimes'). It says that

> war crimes means:
> (...)
> (iii) Willfully causing great suffering, or serious injury to body or health;
> (...)
> (iv) Extensive destruction and appropriation of property, not justified by military necessity and carried out unlawfully and wantonly;
> (vii) Unlawful deportation or transfer or unlawful confinement;

Here again, the meaning of terms such as 'willfully causing', 'great suffering', 'serious injury', 'extensive destruction', 'not justified by military necessity', 'unlawful deportation' is certainly not self-evident and needs interpretation. But what is even more worrying is that some – if not most – of these deplorable actions are probably unavoidable by any of the parties involved in an armed conflict (the problem of 'collateral damage'[42]).

---

[42] The prosecutor of the ICC, Luis Moreno-Ocampo, has commented on this problem in statement made on 9 February, 2006. 'Under international humanitarian law and the Rome Statute, the death of civilians during an armed conflict, no matter how grave and regrettable, does not in itself constitute a war crime. International humanitarian law and the Rome Statute permit belligerents to carry out proportionate attacks against military objectives, even when it is known that some civilian deaths or injuries will occur.' Moreno-Ocampo goes on: 'A crime occurs if there is an intentional attack directed against civilians (principle of distinction) (Article 8(2)(b)(i)) or an attack is launched on a military objective in the knowledge that the incidental civilian injuries would be clearly excessive in relation to the anticipated military advantage (principle of proportionality) (Article 8(2)(b)(iv).' Obviously, this only transposes the question to defining 'intentional attack', 'clearly excessive' and 'anticipated military advantage'. Available online at http://www2.icc-cpi.int/NR/rdonlyres/F596D08D-D810-43A2-99BB-B899B9C5BCD2/277422/OTP_letter_to_senders_re_Iraq_9_February_2006.pdf.

Sub (v) of the above mentioned article 8.2, sums up the acts that could lead to prosecution. It includes:

> Attacking or bombarding, by whatever means (…), buildings which are undefended and which are not military objectives;

A plausible reading of this article could suggest that NATO was guilty of 'war crimes' when bombing Serbia's civil infrastructure in the spring of 1999, or that the United States were guilty of 'war crimes' when striking a pharmaceutical factory in Sudan on February 20th, 1998 in retaliation for the bombings of American embassies in Kenya and Tanzania which killed 224 people (of which twelve American nationals) and injured 5,000 others.[43] The factory, Sudan's primary source of pharmaceuticals, covering the majority of the Sudanese market, was claimed to have been instrumental in the production of chemical weapons, but evidence of this has never been made public. The German ambassador to Sudan between 1996 and 2000, Werner Daum, estimated that the attack probably caused tens of thousands of civilian deaths.[44] Yet both the Clinton and the second Bush administrations have refused to offer apologies to the Sudanese government, and it is not unthinkable that the ICC would have been interested in asserting jurisdiction (had the United States, of course, been a member). The President of Sudan even called for 'the international prosecution of the US officials behind the airstrike'.[45]

In such a case, the United States might then be asked to prove that the factory was rightfully thought to be a military objective (the burden of proof lying clearly on the side of the defendant in this case[46]). The Pentagon would have to present its sources, which would be evaluated by the Prosecutor under the superintendence

---

[43] Cf. Michael P. Scharf, 'The ICC's jurisdiction over the nationals of non-party states: a critique of the US position', in: *Law & Contemporary Problems*, vol. 64, issue 1 (Winter 2001) 67-118.

[44] Werner Daum, 'Universalism and the West. An agenda for understanding', in: *Harvard International Review*, vol 23 (2) (Summer 2001) 19-23.

[45] Scharf (Winter 2001) 67-118.

[46] Cf. the 1927 *Lotus Case* of the Permanent Court of International Justice (PCIJ), which is often referred to in international law discourses as having set a 'precedent' (even though the Court at the time was divided by six judges in favor and six against, and the President of the Court had to decide the case, and indeed even though the very concept of 'precedent' itself is questionable in classical international law). In this case, however, it was held that when a state seeks to withhold jurisdiction from another state, the burden of proof is on the state claiming that such jurisdiction is indeed lacking; not on the state asserting jurisdiction. This principle has been used in later years to expand the scope of international law, as jurisdiction was assmed to exist, as Michael Scharf notes, 'unless it can be shown that this violates a prohibitive rule of international law'. He continues: 'So long as states have a legitimate interest in establishing such an arrangement, the question is not whether international law or precedent exists permitting an ICC with this type of jurisdictional reach (…), but rather whether any international legal rule exists that would prohibit it'. Case of S. Lotus (France v. Turkey), 1927 P.C.I.J. (ser. A) No. 10. Cf. Michael P. Scharf, 'The ICC's jurisdiction over the nationals of non-party states: a critique of the U.S. position', in: *Law & Contemporary Problems*, vol. 64, issue 1 (Winter 2001) 67-118, there 72-74.

of the world press and the secret services of other states. Even though the Court may decide that certain evidence be presented or witnesses be heard behind closed doors, this is a situation that no great power would ever accept.

It was also agreed that the ICC will amend (and possibly extend) the list of crimes under its jurisdiction.[47] This happened for instance at the review conference in Uganda in 2010 (as mentioned above). Some states desire to add terrorism and drug trafficking to the list of crimes covered; so far, the member states have been unable to agree on a definition of terrorism and it was decided not to include drug trafficking as this might overwhelm the Court's limited resources. India lobbied to have the use of nuclear weapons and other weapons of mass destruction (WMD's) included as war crimes, but did not succeed in this (and did not join the ICC).[48]

These, then, are the first important observations concerning the ICC that undermine the claims to political impartiality or the non-political nature of the court: the vagueness of the crimes that fall within its jurisdiction, the fact that those crimes are surely next to unavoidable in any military dispute, and the great consequences for national security that producing evidence could entail.

A further question concerning the ICC is not *what* it will prosecute, but *who*. The ICC has discretionary powers in deciding who should be prosecuted, as article 15 denotes:

> 1. The Prosecutor may initiate investigations *proprio motu* [i.e. on its own initiative] on the basis of information on crimes within the jurisdiction of the Court. (...)
> 3. If the Prosecutor concludes that there is a reasonable basis to proceed with an investigation, he or she shall submit to the Pre-Trial Chamber a request for authorization of an investigation (...). Victims may make representations to the Pre-Trial Chamber, in accordance with the Rules of Procedure and Evidence.
> 4. If the Pre-Trial Chamber, upon examination of the request and the supporting material, considers that there is a reasonable basis to proceed with an investigation, and that the case appears to fall within the jurisdiction of the Court, it shall authorize the commencement of the investigation (...).

Article 16, then, enables the Security Council to defer an investigation or prosecution for a period of 12 months with the possibility of renewal. To do so would however require a majority in the Security Council (9 out of 15 votes), and requires that none of the permanent five Security Council members (i.e. the United States, the United Kingdom, France, the Russian Federation, and China) use its veto power.

---

[47] Cf. articles 121 and 123 of the Rome Statute.

[48] Geert-Jan Knoops is one of the many who criticize the fact that 'the use of poisoned arrows' is a war crime under the ICC, but the use of nuclear weapons is not: Geert-Jan Knoops, *Blufpoker. De duistere wereld van het internationaal recht* (Amsterdam: Uitgeverij Balans, 2011) 104.

The prosecutor of the ICC is elected by the Assembly of States for a nine-year term. As is often the case with such international appointments, they serve political interests and are subject to diplomatic rather than professional considerations. The current prosecutor, the Argentine Luis Moreno-Ocampo, was elected, typically unopposed, in 2003. Moreno-Ocampo has a long record of legal experience in trying state officials and in extradition cases. He has also been involved in some alleged scandals, amongst others an alleged rape-case on the afternoon of March 29th, 2005 in Cape Town.[49] The whistleblower, Christian Palme, who submitted the complaint to the President of the ICC, Philippe Kirsch at the time, was fired by Moreno-Ocampo after a panel of three judges dismissed the complaint on the ground of lack of evidence, but on July 9th, 2008, the International Labor Organization (the Administrative Tribunal of which has jurisdiction over labor disputes of several international organizations including the ICC), ruled that Palme had had good reason to bring the case to the attention of the ICC, that Moreno-Ocampo was not justified in discharging him, and Palme was awarded damages.[50]

The way this incident was hushed up, even if the allegations were entirely false, is typical of the problems that a supranational organization finds itself in: its top functionaries not being subject to the kind of power-balancing framework a national state provides for its appointments, elections often being political ones, and a shared international standard of decent behavior not existing. The personal character of top-functionaries that would be relevant in national circumstances is not usually investigated due to political nomination.

The pre-trial chamber, which has to consider if there is a 'reasonable basis' to proceed with an investigation, consists of six judges but is divided into groups of three judges deciding by majority vote. Thus only two judges need vote in favor of an investigation for it to proceed. Currently (as of spring 2011), the judges at the pre-trial chamber are:

Sylvia Steiner (Brazil)
Hans-Peter Kaul (Germany)
Ekaterina Trendafilova (Bulgaria)
Sanji Mmasenono Monageng (Botswana)
Cuno Tarfusser (Italy)
Silvia Fernández de Gurmendi (Argentina)

---

[49] Moreno-Ocampo allegedly took the car keys of a South African journalist who had conducted an interview with him, and did not give them back unless she agreed to come to his room in the Lord Charles Hotel and have sex with him. The scheduled meeting with the journalist was removed from his agenda after the incident, thus suggesting nothing had ever happened.
[50] *Palme v. ICC, International Labor Organization*, Judgment No. 2757, 105th session.

Deciding on whether an investigation will proceed is thus in their hands. In the hands of Sylvia Steiner from Brazil, Hans-Peter Kaul from Germany, Ekaterina Trendafilova from Bulgaria, Sanji Mmasenono Monageng from Botswana, Cuno Tarfusser from Italy, and Silvia Fernández de Gurmendi from Argentina. The supranational structure makes it particularly difficult to know who these people are. It is a question supranationalists evade by focusing on the technical, perceived non-political nature of the procedures and rules.[51]

But the same problems apply with regards to the other judges of the ICC. Currently 18 in total (but the number is not fixed[52]), they are elected for a nine year period by the Assembly of States. They should be nationals of an ICC member state, and no two judges may be nationals of the same state.[53] Further, 'the states parties shall', according to article 36, paragraph 8 (a):

> In the selection of judges, take into account the need, within the membership of the Court, for:
> (i) The representation of the principal legal systems of the world;
> (ii) Equitable geographical representation; and
> (iii) A fair representation of female and male judges.

Now, these principles for selecting judges are certainly based on questionable philosophical principles. For does 'the representation of the principal legal systems in the world' not imply that there should be a number of judges representing countries that accept Sharia law? And does 'equitable geographical representation' and 'fair representation of female and male judges' provide the legal basis for a policy of affirmative action? Those are certainly worrying considerations.

And if we think of the procedures that surround appointments of judges in national situations – at least when it comes to the appointment of senior judges –, such as approval by a representative council (for instance in the United States after profound personal and professional investigations and several hearings and interviews by the Senate[54]), we should not take for granted that these appointed ICC-judges are necessarily competent to be the arbiters of military conflicts all over the world. Nor is it self-evident that these judges, put forward by the member states of the ICC, will fulfill their jobs without personal or political agendas: this is even more so, while many member states of the ICC are not

---

[51] Cf. on the often misty and political selection of international judges: Ruth Mackenzie, Kate Maleson, Penny Martin and Philippe Sands, *Selecting International Judges. Principle, Process and Politics* (Oxford: Oxford University Press, 2010).

[52] Rome Statute, article 36.

[53] Rome Statute, article 36. This contrasts with how judges function in national circumstances, where nominations are usually for life in order to safeguard their independence. Cf. Cliteur, P., 'De onafhankelijkheid van de rechterlijke macht: acht vormen', in: J.P. Loof (ed.), *Onafhankelijkheid en onpartijdigheid. De randvoorwaarden voor het bestuur en beheer van de rechterlijke macht* (Leiden: Stichting NJCM-boekerij 36, 1999) 9-31.

[54] Cf. Bork (1990) 287ff.

only high on corruption lists[55] but have a history of decades of dictatorial or totalitarian administration.

Apart from starting procedures on its own initiative, the ICC can also begin an investigation at the request of a member state.[56] This option follows from articles 13 and 14 of the Rome Statue. Article 12, paragraph 2 (a) adds that 'the jurisdiction of the Court (…) can also be exercised if the state *on the territory of which* the conduct in question occurred (…) is a member of the ICC'.

This means that the court can very well claim jurisdiction over nationals of a non-ICC member state if those nationals (e.g. soldiers) have committed acts that the ICC believes to fall under any of the 'crimes' it has jurisdiction over. Countries that have chosen not to recognize the ICC may in this way be submitted to its jurisdiction anyway. This has motivated the United States to set up bilateral immunity agreements with other countries, and even to pass the *American Service Members Protection Act* as an amendment to the National Defense Authorization Act in August 2002.[57] This document is also known as the 'Hague Invasion Act', because it authorizes the President to use 'all means necessary and appropriate to bring about the release of any US or allied personnel being detained or imprisoned by, on behalf of, or at the request of the International Criminal Court'.[58]

The third and final way for the ICC of asserting jurisdiction is an even more remarkable instance of supranationalism, and follows from article 13 (b) of the Rome Statute, reading:

> The court may exercise its jurisdiction with respect to a crime referred to in article 5 in accordance with the provisions of this Statue if (…) a situation in which one or more of such crimes appears to have been committed is referred to the Prosecutor by the Security Council acting under Chapter VII of the Charter of the United Nations;

The Security Council of the United Nations can thus assign jurisdiction to the ICC if it deems so necessary, even if the alleged 'crimes' have not been perpetrated by an ICC member state nor even have been committed on the territory

---

[55]   See for example the yearly statistics on corruption produced by *nationmaster*, available online at http://www.nationmaster.com/graph/gov_cor-government-corruption.

[56]   One example of this was in 2006, when Uganda requested the ICC to prosecute members of the Lord's Resistance Army, an insurgency that had been active in the northern regions of Uganda for over twenty years.

[57]   Available online at http://www.state.gov/t/pm/rls/othr/misc/23425.htm.

[58]   Cf. John R. Bolton, 'The risks and weaknesses of the International Criminal Court from America's perspective', in: *Law and Contemporary Problems,* vol. 64, no. 1 (Winter 2001) 167-180. Available online at http://www.law.duke.edu/shell/cite.pl?64+Law+&+Contemp.+Probs.+167+(Winter+2001).

of a member state. This happened in 2005, when the Security Council passed resolution 1593,[59] containing, amongst others, the following phrases:

> Acting under Chapter VII of the Charter of the United Nations,
> 1. Decides to refer the situation in Darfur since 1 July 2002 to the Prosecutor of the International Criminal Court;
> 2. Decides that the Government of Sudan and all other parties to the conflict in Darfur, shall cooperate fully with and provide any necessary assistance to the Court and the Prosecutor pursuant to this resolution and, while recognizing that States not party to the Rome Statute have no obligation under the Statute, urges all States and concerned regional and other international organizations to cooperate fully;

Not surprisingly, the President of Sudan, Omar al-Bashir, denied jurisdiction, but an international arrest warrant has in the meantime been issued against him. Before discussing questions related to this international arrest warrant, it is necessary to examine the inevitability of choice in whom to prosecute. There are actions that are obvious atrocities, such as those committed in 2008 in Darfur, but there are also actions that are open to several different interpretations. Justified retaliation or excessive use of force? Pre-emptive defense, or act of aggression?

And the ICC has additional problems. For it is unsure what is 'a reasonable basis to proceed with an investigation', of the kind article 15 sub 1 of the Rome Statute provides as a legitimate ground for trying individuals.[60] The prosecutor and his pre-trial chamber may decide that although no knockdown evidence is ever likely to be produced, an investigation should be commenced anyway. As a result, the accused can be put under all kinds of restraints (including being held in custody in The Hague) and will certainly be brought under a grave public shadow. Indeed, with the ICC, the accused is not innocent until proven guilty,[61] but, in the eyes of the world, guilty even when *not* proven guilty[62]).

There is much to be said for the view that this is an inevitable hazard of any criminal prosecution. But unlike at the national level, there is at the supranational level no counterbalance to the discretionary powers of the prosecutors. States differ greatly in their constitutional structures, but what most modern democracies share is some check – whether ultimately derived from a parliament, a senate, or a senior council of state – on these discretionary powers (the balance or dialectic of power, see chapter 2). In the Netherlands, the executive power – in the person of the minister of justice – is ultimately responsible for the policy of

---

[59] The resolution passed with the vote of 11 in favor and 4 abstentions, amongst which were the United States, and is available online at http://www.un.org/News/Press/docs/2005/sc8351.doc.htm.
[60] Article 15 sub 1 of the Rome Statute.
[61] Which is the official position of the ICC, article 66 of the Rome Statute.
[62] As happened to, for example, Milosevic, who was never convicted after six years of trial. I do not argue that he was innocent, but rather that he *could* have been innocent – as he was never convicted after six (!) years of trial. Cf. John Laughland, *Travesty. The trial of Slobodan Milosevic and the corruption of international justice* (London: Pluto Press, 2007) 2.

the prosecutor, and can be held accountable by parliament. Similarly, the Dutch law provides a procedure following article 12 of the code of criminal procedure, which enables concerned parties to file a complaint against the Prosecutor at the Court of Appeals. These sorts of checks and balances are fundamentally impossible to realize at the supranational level as they presuppose the existence of a full state. As a result, supranational prosecution will necessarily remain arbitrary and the powers of such institutions necessarily unchecked by balancing powers.[63]

Nor is it certain that the Court will accept justice done to 'war criminals' on national levels. For the ICC retains the ultimate authority to decide on whether that function has been adequately exercised,[64] and, if it finds that it has not been, the ICC can reassert jurisdiction.[65] For example Charles Graner and Lynndie England were sentenced to, respectively, ten and three years imprisonment by Court Martial of the US army for crimes committed at the Abu Graib prison in Iraq. The ICC could rule this punishment inadequate, and restart a criminal procedure against them (had the United States been part of the ICC, of course).

And this is a very serious point indeed. By becoming a member of the ICC, states have deputed their power to decide how to react to their own military troops committing mistakes or crimes, to the Prosecutor and his Pre-trial Chamber, to state requests, or to a majority in the Security Council. The ICC may even declare national reconciliation procedures void, thereby taking from the parties involved the decision of what justice requires in the circumstances. After the abolition of the Apartheid regime in South Africa, for example, many former government officials were not punished for crimes committed in the name of the regime if they admitted them before a special tribunal.[66] The ICC might in the future overrule such a reconciliation settlement (as the Prosecutor has for example said in the spring of 2011 that he would not accept immunity for Colonel Khadafi as part of a cease-fire). Even when the ICC has not in advance given notice that it would not accept a particular reconciliation settlement, it may still begin investigations. Whether or not the ICC is going to do so can thus never be guaranteed in advance.[67] This may cause many regimes to refuse

---

[63] As Madison observed: 'The provision for defence must in this, as in all other cases, be made commensurate to the danger of attack. Ambition must be made to counteract ambition. The interest of man must be connected with the constitutional rights of the place. It may be a reflection on human nature, that such devices should be necessary to controul the abuses of government'. Hamilton, Madison and Jay, *The Federalist Papers* (New York: Bantam Dell, 1982) 316, Federalist no. 51 (Madison).

[64] As provided by article 20 of the Rome Statute.

[65] Henry Kissinger, 'The Pitfalls of Universal Jurisdiction', in: *Foreign Affairs*, vol. 80, no. 4 (July/August 2001) 95.

[66] See on this: Afshin Ellian, *Een onderzoek naar de Waarheids- en Verzoeningscommissie van Zuid-Afrika* (Nijmegen: Wolf Legal, 2003).

[67] Here, the example of General Pinochets peaceful resignation is also worth mentioning. The agreement that he would not be tried was violated by the claim to universal jurisdiction,

reconciliation tribunals (and continue fighting), as one cannot be sure that admitted crimes will not be used against one in The Hague. An armed conflict such as the aforementioned operation Desert Storm (1991) might not have been concluded with an armistice if there had been a fair chance that Saddam Hussein would have had to face extradition to The Hague.

Moreover, if the Court wants to be effective in its rulings its members will have to place their armies and police forces at the Court's disposal, because the ICC does not have its own means of enforcing its decisions and warrants. This implies the active participation of the 'international community' in the situations of armed conflict the ICC has chosen to involve itself in.

A glimpse of what this might amount to is found in the aforementioned resolution 1593 on Sudan, when the Security Council urged all states to cooperate with the proposed prosecution of the Sudanese leadership by the ICC. A next step in supranational direction might be that the Security Council (of which we will come to speak in depth in chapter 5 section 2) decides that all states *must* cooperate. While these legal considerations are unlikely to cause much unrest among insurgency and terrorist groups, or among undemocratic regimes, Western states with their rule of law, an obedient police force and respect for international law and diplomacy will always be directly held accountable and easily criticized.

Yet, is it likely that the ICC would ever assert jurisdiction over powerful countries? One critic put it this way:

> Today's international criminal justice only punishes certain criminals, those who can be apprehended because they belong to countries that find themselves in a weak and dependent position. Even if China and Russia were to ratify the treaty establishing the International Criminal Court, would the court be able to judge Chinese authorities for what they have done in Tibet? Or put Putin in the dock for crimes committed in Chechnya? Of course not.[68]

It would, however, be quite likely that regimes may use the ICC to dispose of political enemies. Generals who become a threat to the internal power base of presidents may be handed over to the ICC; some have pointed with suspicion at the fact that Congo's remarkable cooperation with the extradition of opposition leader Jean-Pierre Bemba to the ICC served the political interests of the president, his rival Joseph Kabila.[69]

---

and this may set a precedent that may prevent future dictators from considering resigning from power (think of, for instance, Fidel Castro, who happened to be in Spain when the arrest warrant against Pinochet was issued – not surprisingly, Castro supported the former Chilean dictator in his objections to his prosecution).

[68] Delsol (2008) xvii.

[69] Daniel Howden, 'International justice and Congo "warlord" on trial', in: *the Independent* (23 November 2010): 'Mr. Bemba's supporters in the DRC have accused the ICC of allowing itself to be used to remove the political rivals of the President Joseph Kabila.' Available online at

To entrust all such matters to an international court is to entrust a great moral responsibility to the 'international community'. To do so is not realistic, Saudi Arabia still being a recognized adherent to the Convention to Eliminate All Forms of Discrimination Against Women (CEDAW),[70] as in 2003, the Iraq of Saddam Hussein, then the only regime in place that had ever used weapons of mass destruction on its own population, was chairing the 25th anniversary Disarmament Conference in Geneva, assisted by co-chair Iran.[71] These countries had recently been in a war with each other in which over a million people were killed. China claimed to be in full compliance with the Covenant on Civil and Political Rights, while Amnesty International devoted more pages in its 2006 annual report to Human Rights abuses in Britain and America than to those in Saudi Arabia and Belarus.[72] In addition, the UN Human Rights Commission (now reframed as Council) has not issued a single condemnation of the atrocities committed in Sudan in 2008 while it has repeatedly condemned Israel for its human rights violations, upon neglecting, largely, the abuses of its neighbours,[73] and so on. Is this the 'international community' we are entrusting all these powers to?

Finally, within the ICC, the Prosecutor has discretionary competencies that can have enormous effects. This became clear when in March 2009, Luis Moreno-Ocampo openly requested an arrest warrant against the Sudanese president al-Bashir. But by openly doing so, Antonio Cassese argued,[74] he implicitly warned al-Bashir that attempts at prosecution were at hand, and thereby reduced the ICC's chances of ever trying him. Cassese even suggested that Moreno-Ocampo did in fact not sincerely attempt to further the case against al-Bashir, but might have had other motives.[75] A prosecutor with so much power can only be supported if one accepts the supranational world-view, according to

---

http://www.independent.co.uk/news/world/europe/international-justice-and-congo-warlord-on-trial-2141135.html.

[70]   Rabkin (2004) 107.

[71]   R. Roth, 'Iraq to chair disarmament conference', on: *CNN.com,* 29 January 2003. Available online at http://edition.cnn.com/2003/WORLD/meast/01/28/sprj.irq.disarmament.conference/.

[72]   Amnesty International Report 2006. The report can be found on Amnesty's website, http://www.amnesty.org/en/library/info/POL10/001/2006. See for critical commentary also: 'Many rights, some wrong', in: *The Economist,* March 22nd, 2007.

[73]   26 of its 32 condemnations have been against Israel: R. Farrow, 'Beware of the U.N. Human Rights Council; Obama should be careful about lending legitimacy to bad actors', in: *The Wall Street Journal,* April 5th, 2009.

[74]   Antonio Cassese, 'Flawed International Justice for Sudan', in: *Project Syndicate,* June 15th, 2008, available online at http://www.project-syndicate.org/commentary/cassese4/English.

[75]   As he writes: '(…) if Moreno-Ocampo intended to pursue the goal of having al-Bashir arrested, he might have issued a sealed request and asked the ICC's judges to issue a sealed arrest warrant, to be made public only once al-Bashir traveled abroad.' Antonio Cassese, 'Flawed International Justice for Sudan', in: *Project Syndicate,* June 15th, 2008, available online at http://www.project-syndicate.org/commentary/cassese4/English.

which – and this is the recurring theme of this chapter – *the question for political legitimacy never arises*. It is only in nation states that powerful functionaries can be subjected to checks and balances. It is inherent in the supranational idea that these functionaries are installed *without* those checks, precisely because those checks can only exist within a state and form an integral part of the concept of statehood. For those checks require other elements of sovereignty that a supranational organization can never possess.

Collateral damage is, moreover, an unavoidable consequence of any military involvement in armed conflicts. Though during operation 'Desert Storm' (1991) it was announced that the era of 'clean wars' had commenced, it never, despite impressive technological improvements and conscious efforts, quite arrived. Does this mean that all those who participate in military conflicts will run the risk of being tried by the ICC in the future?

The International Criminal Court is probably not intending to prosecute UN Peacekeeping personnel when they may, as sometimes happens in wars, accidentally have bombed and devastated a village of innocent farmers and craftsmen. A comparable situation occurred for instance when NATO bombed Serbia in 1999. But the ICC *would* want to prosecute the dictator such as Milosevic who has acted similarly. It will prove almost impossible for the ICC to remain 'objective' and 'neutral' while making such choices in military conflicts.

We have arrived at perhaps the most fundamental difficulty for an international court with supranational powers, which is the impossibility of neutrality. It may already be tremendously difficult to decide which is the more legitimate military force in an armed conflict; to decide on whether the amount of force used was 'disproportionate' or imposed too much harm on civilians is clearly a political matter. Why trust an outsider, or the 'international community' to decide such questions?

It was also this dilemma that caused Immanuel Kant to ultimately reject the idea of a supranational court, considering in the *Metaphysik der Sitten* (1797) that

> No war of independent states against each other can be a *punitive war (bellum punitivum)*. The punishment occurs only in the relation of a superior (*imperantis*) to those subject to him (*subditum*), and states do not stand in that relation to each other.[76]
>
> (...)
>
> The right of a state *after a war*, that is, at the time of the peace treaty and with a view to its consequences, consists in this: the victor lays down the conditions on which it will come to an agreement with the vanquished and hold *negotiations* for concluding peace.

---

[76] Immanuel Kant, *The metaphysics of morals*. Translated and edited by Mary Gregor (Cambridge: Cambridge University Press, 1996) 117 (par. 57).

The victor does not do this from any right he pretends to have because of the wrong his opponent is supposed to have done on him; instead, he lets this question drop and relies on his own force. The victor can therefore not propose compensation for the costs of the war since he would then have to admit that his opponent had fought an unjust war. While he may well think of this argument he still cannot use it, since he would then be saying that he had been waging a punitive war and so, for his own part, committing an offense against the vanquished.[77]

Contrary to what is commonly believed, Kant had argued likewise in his well known essay on international relations, *Zum ewigen Frieden* (1795).[78] While stressing that 'war is only a regrettable expedient for asserting one's rights by force within a state of nature, where no court of justice is available to judge with legal authority', Kant found that 'neither party can be declared an unjust enemy, for this would already presuppose a judge's decision', and that it was the outcome of the conflict itself that would determine 'who is in the right', and that for this reason, 'a war of punishment between states is inconceivable, since there can be no relationship of superior to inferior among them'.[79] Acknowledging that 'perpetual peace, the ultimate goal of the whole right of nations, is indeed an unachievable idea',[80] Kant, in his *Metaphysik,* goes on to discuss the possibilities for a congress of states, of the kind that 'took place (...) in the first half of the present century in the assembly of the States General at the Hague'.[81] This, however, would not have supranational powers but would merely be accepted as 'arbiter, so to speak'.[82] Kant finishes with the caveat that 'by a congress is here understood only a voluntary coalition of different states which can be dissolved at any time', and which serves to aid the nations in 'deciding their disputes in a civil way'.[83]

The tradition of organizing such an international conference of 'arbiters' continued until the Hague Peace Conferences of the beginning of the 20th century, and was surely one of the most important reasons why 'the Dutch government, proud of its tradition of offering political asylum and of its respect for international law, resolutely refused to extradite the Kaiser when he sought asylum there' after World War I.[84] The former head of the German state was to be tried by an international tribunal as demanded by the allies under the provisions

---

[77] Kant (1996) 117-118 (par. 58).
[78] Immanuel Kant, *Zum ewigen Frieden. Ein philosophischer Entwurf* (Stuttgart: Philipp Reclam, 2005).
[79] In Kant's vision, the only way in which states could relate to each other in a peaceful manner was by mutual recognition of their sovereign equality. This implied for him the impossibility of judgment of states' behaviors, even in wartime: Immanuel Kant, 'Perpetual Peace', in: *Political Writings.* Edited with an introduction and notes by Hans Reiss. Second, enlarged edition (Cambridge: Cambridge University Press, 1991) 96 (first section, par.6).
[80] Kant (1996) 119 (par. 61).
[81] *Ibidem.*
[82] *Ibidem.*
[83] *Ibidem.*
[84] Laughland (2008) 55-56.

of article 227 of the Versailles treaty,[85] but found refuge in the Netherlands and died in Doorn in 1941.

The aforementioned problems have plagued international tribunals ever since the rise of sovereign statehood (see also chapter 1), and it becomes clear that the two are fundamentally irreconcilable.

4.2. *The European Court of Human Rights*

The same idea as implied in the ICC – that supranational judges and functionaries should uphold abstract rules of 'fundamental value' – underlies human rights discourse. This is evident generally from a great number of UN commissions as well as NGO's labouring for increased 'human rights protection'[86] – and it has become manifest most obviously in the European Court of Human Rights (ECHR). At present, this Court is the only supranational Human Rights-institution that may impose legally binding decisions, and therefore this section is primarily about the Strasbourg bench. However, it is necessary first generally to examine human rights discourse, or, as it has been called, 'rights talk',[87] because deeper and largely neglected questions that should be brought to the fore lie underneath the specific questions related to the Strasbourg court.

Thinking in terms of 'human rights' has gained enormous momentum in the past decades. Rights discourse usually distinguishes between three main categories of 'human rights': classical rights, social rights, and group rights. Rights that fall in the first category concern the negative freedoms of the individual, and include the freedom of speech, a fair trial, *habeas corpus*,[88] freedom of religion, and so on. They require primarily abstention of the state from the arbitrary use of power. The second category encompasses all those rights of which the enforcement requires an active role of the state. They are the rights to education, to an adequate standard of living, adequate food, clothing and housing,[89] and so on. In more recent years, a third category of rights has been developed, the social group rights: people can claim rights because they belong to a certain group, for example an ethnic minority, a sexual minority, or even a generation

---

[85] Available online at http://net.lib.byu.edu/~rdh7/wwi/versa/versa6.html.

[86] Examples are the UN Human Rights Council, the UN High Commissioner on Human Rights, Amnesty International, Human Rights Watch, and so on.

[87] Mary Ann Glendon, *Rights Talk. The impoverishment of political discourse* (New York: The free press, 1991).

[88] The principle of habeas corpus denotes the right not to be held prison without charges being pressed.

[89] International Covenant on Economic, Social, and Cultural Rights (1966), article 11: 'The States Parties to the present covenant recognize the right of everyone to an adequate standard of living for himself and his family, including adequate food, clothing and housing, and to the continuous improvement of living conditions'.

(e.g. 'youth rights'). These rights are what multiculturalism argues for, as will be discussed in chapter 6.

Most advocates of all these universal 'rights', however, speak in metaphors rather than in factual terms. They mistake the wish for the reality. What is often meant – and this applies to all three categories – is not 'rights' in any juridical sense, but 'humanitarian principles', 'Christian values' or 'natural law' that *ought to be installed as rights*. 'Human rights' have become the umbrella concept to denote general principles of justice. It has become a habit to express disapproval of genocide, suppression, severe abuse of power, and so on, as violations of 'human rights' of some sort. We say, for instance, that in a war in Africa 'basic human rights' are infringed, or that the regime in Burma 'gravely violates the human rights' of its citizens. Sometimes it seems that modern man can only conceive of moral ideas when they are expressed as 'rights' of some sort.

Nevertheless, as I said above, all such use of the term 'human rights' is *metaphorical*. Whoever uses the term does not refer to actually existing *rights*: for in order to do that, those 'rights' ought already to have been legislated and to be enforceable by a court. The same goes for the great number of other 'rights' that are currently advocated – for instance 'animal rights' and the 'rights of the environment'.[90] For defenders of the flora and fauna of the world, the word 'rights' has a completely different meaning from that in the positive, *legal* sense. Animals are not legal subjects because they couldn't possibly defend themselves in a court of law. To speak of – or even legislate – animal rights is ultimately about how *we*, as human beings, *ought to treat* animals, and certainly not about what one animal may do to – or invoke against – another animal, for instance.[91] Many national laws forbid certain forms of animal maltreatment, but however important these regulations may be, they amount to something entirely different from considering animals legal subjects and bearers of individual, inalienable 'rights', with an entitlement to enforce them in a court of law against any other mammal or reptile. The same goes, *a fortiori*, for trees and the earth's crust. Those invoking supposedly universal 'human rights', 'animal rights' and the 'rights of the tree' thus do not invoke any actually existing rights, but principles of justice, decent behaviour, responsible stewardship – expressed through the *metaphor* of 'rights'.[92]

---

[90] Cf. the French philosopher Michel Serres who defends the 'rights' of the ocean: Michel Serres, *Le contrat naturel* (Paris: François Boudin, 1990).

[91] The fact that some of such 'animal rights' have now been 'recognized', as has been done for instance in Spain, does not affect this.

[92] To say that it is absurd – in the literal sense – to grant rights to non-rational actors is by no means to say that we are without duties towards them, of course. We are never free from duties towards children, mentally disabled or people suffering from dementia. Nor are we even without duties towards non-living objects, for example a painting of Rembrandt. In fact, there is a good case to be made for the view that rights talk impoverishes moral thinking rather than enriching it.

Though dating back to the second half of the eighteenth century,[93] the several declarations of the universal rights of man have, to this day, never gained legal status either. The United Nations' *Universal Declaration of Human Rights* of 1948 has no legal validity, as it is a *declaration* and not a treaty.[94] The International Covenants on Civil and Political Rights, and on Economic, Social and Cultural Rights (both drawn up in 1966) do not pretend to codify universal 'human rights', but a range of political themes so wide as to annul the very idea of a universal core of natural law. Rather, these treaties sum up the elements a wise government ought to take into account. Even the ominous right of prisoners for their 'reformation' is included, as well as the right of working mothers to 'paid leave or leave with adequate social security benefits', the 'fundamental right of everyone to be free from hunger' and the right to the enjoyment of 'the highest attainable standard of physical and mental health'.[95]

It is clear that these 'rights' do not indicate universal, ultimate boundaries which governments may not cross in any circumstances whatever. They may denote desirable policy proposals (although the 'reformation of prisoners' reminds one of the Gulag archipelago), but they are not universal and inalienable moral imperatives.[96]

Even more importantly, these rights cannot be claimed universally, as there is no world court – let alone a world police force to guarantee the enforcement of the rulings of such a hypothetical court. As a consequence, their interpretation will differ from country to country. Countries like Bolivia or Ghana have different standards of 'highest attainable standards of health' from those of Switzerland or Sweden; China and Saudi-Arabia mean something different by the 'reformation of prisoners' than most Western states. In any event, there is no way of speaking of 'universal' human rights, based on any of the UN's declarations and treaties.

Cf. Roger Scruton, *Animal Rights and Wrongs* (London: Continuum, 2000), Glendon (1991), and the excellent essay by Theodore Dalrymple, 'The demoralization of abortion', in: Claire Fox (ed.), *Abortion: whose right?* (London: Hodder & Stoughton, 2002). On page 38, Dalrymple writes: '(...) I have the right to buy a painting by Rembrandt, if I have enough money. Once such a painting is in my possession I have the legal right to destroy or deface it, if I so desire: but surely no one would argue by way of exculpation or even mitigation, were I to do so, that I had acted within my rights. My rights have nothing to do with the question. A woman who believes that she has a right to an abortion, which should require no further justification than that she wants it, as an instance of her right to self-determination (the 'it's-my-body' argument) overlooks morally important aspects of her own situation.'

[93] A major source of inspiration being, of course, John Locke's *Second Treatise of Government* (1690). John Locke, *The second treatise of Government* (1690) especially chapter XIX: 'Of the dissolution of government'.

[94] J.H. Burgers, 'The Road to San Francisco: the revival of the Human Rights Idea in the Twentieth Century', in: *Human Rights Quarterly*, vol. 14 (1992) 447-477.

[95] UN Covenant on Civil and Political Rights (1966) articles 10, 11 and 12 respectively.

[96] Cf. Cliteur, 'Steeds maar nieuwe rechten. Inflatie als juridisch probleem', in: Cliteur, *Tegen de Decadentie. De democratische rechtstaat in verval* (Amsterdam: De Arbeiderspers, 2004) 161ff.

But not only do universal human rights not exist because they have never been codified and could never be enforced; in the hypothetical situation that we *did* codify and enforce them centrally, their application would hardly be unproblematic.

Suppose we made the 'right to life' a 'universal human right' – applied universally by, in the last instance, a world court. Would that mean a ban on abortion and euthanasia? Many people – including many judges from all over the world – would say yes. Would it mean a ban on the death penalty? Overwhelmingly, European elites think so – while many Americans and Asians do not. Nor is it difficult to reframe the right to life into a positive obligation of the state to provide the basic needs of all.[97] Does standing by without providing a remedy while someone dies violate his right to life or not? Must this not mean that the welfare state follows necessarily from this 'right to life'?

Or take the principle of non-discrimination. Again, this is something that sounds 'fundamental' and important. But consistent application of this principle could justify the prohibition of just about anything from hereditary monarchies to the constitutional rule that in order to become American president, a candidate has to have been born in the US and be at least 35 years of age.[98] Because no two individuals are entirely the same, the principle of non-discrimination is endless in its application – just as consistent application of the principle of 'equal opportunities' would require a ban on private property and the dissolution of families.

Likewise, the prohibition of discrimination inevitably clashes with classic civil liberties such as those of expression, conscience and religion.[99] The privileged positions that many states – for a variety of social, cultural and historical reasons – preserve for a specific religious denomination, for instance the Anglican Church in Britain, or the Lutheran in Denmark, or clubs that discriminate on the basis of sex, are all in violation of this supposedly fundamental principle.[100]

A recent Dutch case against the Christian Orthodox party SGP is an example of how arbitrary the application of the 'fundamental principle of non-discrimination'

---

[97] In the Case of *Osman v. United Kingdom (Application no. 87/1997/871/1083)* Judgment Strasbourg 28 October 1998, the Court for instance ruled that 'Article 2 of the Convention may also imply in certain well-defined circumstances a positive obligation on the authorities to take preventive operational measures to protect an individual whose life is at risk' (B.2, par. 115).

[98] The unavoidability of discrimination will be discussed more extensively in chapter 8 and 9.

[99] A comparable critique of the supposed universal 'right to free speech' has been given by Stanley Fish, *There's No Such Thing As Free Speech. And It's a Good Thing, Too* (Oxford: Oxford University Press, 1994).

[100] An example is the Dutch *Commission for Equal Treatment* ('Commissie Gelijke Behandeling') which found in June 2011 that a café that organized a 'ladies night' was applying intolerable discrimination on the basis of gender, because women received five free consumptions. Cf. 'Café berispt om ladies' night-korting', NOS, June 30th, 2011, http://nos.nl/artikel/252403-cafe-berispt-om-ladies-nightkorting.html.

may in practice turn out to be, when on April 9th, 2010, the Dutch Supreme Court ruled that the Netherlands' oldest political party had violated the 'principle of non-discrimination' by not allowing women to stand for election on behalf of their party. The Dutch court considered, that:

> The prohibition of discrimination outweighs, in so far as it guarantees the franchise of all citizens (…) other constitutional rights involved.[101]

But why did the prohibition of discrimination outweigh other constitutional rights in this case? Well, because the Court thought so.[102] And why was the SGP, which had been denying women the right to stand for election ever since it was founded in 1918, only been prohibited from doing so in 2009? Surely because our views on this subject have proven susceptible to change over time.

The fundamental problem of 'rights talk' is thus that rights (all rights, in all circumstances) are always open to multiple interpretations. Their precise meaning is never obvious. The application of rights, to say the same thing in different words, requires a political choice. This is evident from the situation in the United States too, where judicial appointments to the Supreme Court are in practice political appointments. Through their jurisprudence, these judges may indeed take decisive political decisions in areas such as national security (qualifying practices at Guantanamo Bay as torture), ethics (allowing or prohibiting abortion and euthanasia), criminal justice (capital punishment), immigration (permitting or prohibiting the rejection of asylum seekers), and international law (declaring treaties unconstitutional).[103] American presidents nominate judges with views consistent with their own.[104] The Senate, which must ratify the appointments, can oppose the nomination when the majority has a different political opinion (as happened in 1987 when Ronald Reagan's

---

[101] '[Het] Discriminatieverbod weegt, in zoverre het de kiesrechten van alle burgers waarborgt (…) zwaarder dan de andere grondrechten die in het geding zijn': LJN: BK4547, Hoge Raad, 08/01354, ruling of 9 April 2009.

[102] To arrive at its conclusion, the Court interpreted article 7a of the UN Convention on the Elimination of Discrimination against Women (CEDAW), which had already been entered into force in 1981, in a particular way. Cf. http://www.un.org/womenwatch/daw/cedaw/history.htm.

[103] Another example is the way the American Supreme Court has over time stretched the meaning of the right to free speech, now also encompassing incitement, sedition, and obscenity. Cf. Stanley Fish, *There's No Such Thing As Free Speech. And It's a Good Thing, Too* (Oxford: Oxford University Press, 1994), Ronald Dworkin, 'Why must Speech be free?' and 'Pornography and Hate', in: Ibidem, *Freedom's Law. The moral reading of the American Constitution* (Cambridge, MA: Harvard University Press, 1996) 195-226, as well as Milos Forman's movie *The people vs. Larry Flynt* (1996).

[104] Cf. Bork (1990); Stephen Breyer, *Making our democracy work. A judge's view* (New York: Alfred A. Knopf, 2010); Erwin Chemerinsky, *The conservative assault on the constitution* (New York: Simon & Schuster, 2010); Jeffrey Toobin, *The Nine. Inside the secret world of the supreme court* (New York: Anchor Books, 2007).

candidate Robert Bork was rejected[105]). Americans know where the judges of the Supreme Court stand and weigh their chances to push for certain political changes when a judge is replaced. Democrats are currently hoping that during Barack Obama's term some Republican judges will be replaced by Democrats (and that, for instance, this may lead to the abolition of the death penalty).

There are thus already considerable problems related to 'rights talk' on a national level. But the larger the juridical scope of a court, the greater the difficulties, as different countries arrange their affairs differently. If the writ of the US Supreme Court also ran in Canada, Mexico, Guatemala and Venezuela, the situation would soon get out of hand. Therefore, the application of rights on a supranational level multiplies the problems. What is more, the powers of the US Supreme Court are held in check by the legislature, which may provide countervailing legislation if it does not agree with the court's rulings. That is the idea of constitutional checks and balances: 'ambition must be made to counteract ambition', and different bodies of the state must keep one another in check.[106] This does not – and cannot – exist on the supranational level, as it requires a full state.

It is, however, also an option constitutionally to forbid judges from applying 'fundamental rights' to democratically passed legislation, and so tackle the danger of politicized 'rights talk'. This has traditionally been the Dutch approach.[107] The argument against constitutional review is that reviewing laws on their constitutionality implies interpretation of the constitution, and interpretation of the constitution is inherently political.[108] The more fundamental the rule in question, the vaguer its application by definition becomes. Therefore, critics argue, allowing constitutional review will over time lead to a weakening of the

---

[105] Cf. for a critical account of the events surrounding the nomination, Ronald Dworkin, 'Bork: The Senate's Responsibility', 'What Bork's Defeat Meant', and 'Bork's own Postmortem', in: Ibidem (1996) 261-305.

[106] 'The provision for defense must in this, as in all other cases, be made commensurate to the danger of attack. Ambition must be made to counteract ambition. The interest of man must be connected with the constitutional rights of the place. It may be a reflection on human nature, that such devices should be necessary to controul the abuses of government'. Alexander Hamilton, James Madison and John Jay, *The Federalist Papers* (New York: Bantam Dell, 1982) 316, Federalist no. 51 (Madison).

[107] Cf. on the Dutch view: Paul Cliteur, *Constitutionele toetsing, met commentaren van R.A.V. van Haersolte, J.M. Polak en T. Zwart* ('s Gravenhage: Geschrift 74 van de Prof. mr. B.M. Teldersstichting, 1991) 179ff.

[108] There have been many political thinkers who have opposed constitutional review, ranging from Hegel to Henry Steele Commager, and from James Bryce to Maurice Cranston. For an overview, see Paul Cliteur, *Rechtsfilosofie. Een thematische inleiding* (Amsterdam: Ars aequi libri, 2001) 179ff. For the arguments of John Marshall in the US supreme court case of *Marbury v. Madison* (1803), see Bork (1990) 20ff. Cf. William J. Brennan, jr., 'Why have a Bill of Rights?', in: *Oxford Journal of Legal Studies*, vol. 9, no. 4 (1989) 425-440; and Antonin Scalia, *A matter of interpretation. Federal courts and the law* (Princeton: Princeton University Press, 1997).

primacy of politics in deciding political questions and to a colonization of the
neutral territory of the law by political bias.[109]

It is with this concern in mind that judges in the Netherlands – though allowed
to review the constitutionality of lower (e.g. municipal or provincial) legislation
as well as decisions of the executive ('royal resolutions') –, cannot review laws
passed by the national parliament. Article 120 of the Dutch constitution forbids
a direct appeal to fundamental rights to negate a national legal provision. The
idea is that political primacy should lie with the democratically elected Second
Chamber – held in check through all kinds of constitutional balancing powers
such as the Senate, the Council of State, the Queen, elections, the free press, the
public debate, and so on – and that the Dutch court does not rule on the interpretation of fundamental rights, which is regarded as being inherently political.
The framers of the Dutch constitution thus chose to have the constitutional bill
of rights as a reminder for the legislator to take into account the principles of
justice they point to, and not as 'trumps' in the hands of citizens or judges to
enforce their views through undemocratic means.[110] It is largely for this reason
that the Dutch Supreme Court has, over the years, managed to maintain a fairly
apolitical profile.[111]

But this immediately brings us to the European Court of Human Rights.
Contradictory to the original philosophy of the Dutch constitution, the Council
of Europe, an organization itself installed by the Treaty of London, on May 5th,
1949, drew up the Convention of Human Rights in 1950 including provisions
for the setup of a fundamental rights court.[112] It entered into force in September
1953, counting 14 member states at the time.[113] Today, the Council of Europe
has 47 member states.[114]

---

[109]   As, indeed, the development of the United States Supreme Court seems to show.
[110]   Though J.R. Thorbecke himself was, oddly enough, a defender of Constitutional review;
J.R. Thorbecke, *Bijdrage tot de herziening van de Grondwet* (1848).
[111]   Cf. on the Dutch debate, Joost Sillen, 'Tegen het toetsingsrecht', in: *Nederlands Juristenblad*,
vol. 43 (10 december 2010) 2231-2748.
[112]   Counting 10 formative states, namely, Belgium, Denmark, France, Ireland, Italy, Luxembourg,
the Netherlands, Norway, Sweden, and the United Kingdom. Winston Churchill had (Especially
in his speech of 19 September 1946 in Zurich) promoted the idea of this organization as a means
to bring reconciliation to Europe after the devastation of the World Wars. Article 1(a) of the
Statute explains that 'The aim of the Council of Europe is to achieve a greater unity between its
members for the purpose of safeguarding and realising the ideals and principles which are their
common heritage and facilitating their economic and social progress'.
[113]   New members were: Greece (1949-08-09), Turkey (1949-08-09), Iceland (1950-03-09), and
West-Germany (1950-06-13).
[114]   Austria (1956-04-16), Cyprus (1961-05-24), Switzerland (1963-05-06), Malta (1965-04-29),
Portugal (1976-09-22), Spain (1977-11-24), Liechtenstein (1978-11-23), San Marino (1988-11-16),
Finland (1989-05-05), Hungary (1990-11-06), Poland (1991-11-26), Bulgaria (1992-05-07), Estonia
(1993-05-14), Lithuania (1993-05-14), Slovenia (1993-05-14), Czech Republic (1993-06-30),
Slovakia (1993-06-30), Romania (1993-10-07), Andorra (1994-10-10), Latvia (1994-10-10), Albania
(1995-06-13), Moldova (1995-06-13), FYR Macedonia (1995-11-09), Ukraine (1995-11-09), Russia

The convention recognizes a wide range of rights, complemented by a number of protocols containing additional rights. The rights guaranteed in this code can go pretty far. Take the example of protocols 6 and 13, which establish the prohibition of the death penalty. It is clearly questionable how universal, nonpolitical such a prohibition is. Not only from the standpoint of political theory,[115] but also democratically. A recent poll showed that more than half of the European population is in favor of capital punishment in specific, unusually severe cases.[116] Nevertheless, it has now been declared a violation of 'fundamental human rights' in all circumstances whatever.[117]

The Parliamentary Assembly of the Council of Europe, upon state submission, installs the judges of the Court. Each member state nominates three nationals (who do not need to have worked as judges in their national legal system), and the Assembly then decides who it likes best. With one judge for each member state, Monaco and Azerbaidjan have as much say in the European Court of Human Rights, as do Germany and Britain (although whatever is said during deliberations must obviously be translated, with judges from 47 different countries).

Applicants from all different member states (both citizens and non-citizens) may file a complaint for an alleged violation by any of its member states of the rights recognized in the Convention and protocols. The conditions for admissability of the case are formal: domestic remedies should have been exhausted (art. 35 sub 1 ECHR), no complaint may be anonymously filed, et cetera – but these conditions do not confine the jurisdiction of the Court to for instance 'the severest cases only'. Through its jurisprudence, the Court has in recent years also assumed jurisdiction over behavior of its member states' military forces in occupied territories. Thus the United Kingdom was convicted, for instance, in

---

(1996-02-28), Croatia (1996-11-06), Georgia (1999-04-27), Armenia (2001-01-25), Azerbaijan (2001-01-25), Bosnia and Herzegovina (2002-04-24), Serbia (2003-04-03), Monaco (2004-10-05), and the most recent one, Montenegro (2007-05-11).

[115] Cf. Paul Cliteur, 'Afschaffing van de doodstraf als nationale folklore', in: *Ibidem, Moderne Papoea's. Dilemma's van een multiculturele samenleving* (Amsterdam: De Arbeiderspers, 2002) 106-136. Cliteur discusses the great body of political theory in support of the death penalty, as well as such a case as that of Adolf Eichmann, who was hanged, to the general approval of many, in 1962.

[116] Facts on this are abundant. See for instance Prague Daily Monitor, July 13th, 2009, 'Poll: almost two-thirds of Czechs support capital punishment'; A. Moravchik, 'The new abolitionism: why does the U.S. practice the death penalty while Europe does not?', in: *European Studies* (September 2001), writes: 'European public opinion, and that of other advanced industrial abolitionist nations, views the death penalty positively. In France, for example, President Mitterrand abolished the death penalty in 1982 despite 62% percent of the French being retentionists; only last year did poll support dip for the first time below 50%. Two-thirds of the German population favored the death penalty at the time of its abolition. Today 65-70% of Britons, nearly 70% of Canadians, a majority of Austrians, around 50% of Italians, and 49% of the Swedes favor its reinstatement.'

[117] Cf. J.M. Marshall, 'Death in Venice: Europe's Death-penalty Elitism', in: *The New Republic* (July 31, 2000).

2011, after Iraqi nationals filed a complaint in Strasbourg against the conduct of British soldiers in the Iraqi province of Basrah during a night patrol.[118]

Given the Dutch tradition of withholding from judges the power to interpret constitutional principles, it is not surprising that many government officials in the Netherlands were reluctant to embrace the idea of a Court of Human Rights in the first place. Prime Minister Drees resisted the individual complaints mechanism of the court until the last moment. Amongst his objections was the fear that it would make it impossible for the Dutch state to defend itself against disruptive individuals within its territory (especially, national-socialists and communists),[119] because defence against them would sometimes compel the state to take measures infringing the 'rights' such a Court might want to uphold for them.[120]

In the end, the Dutch government ratified the convention after the advice of several experts in international law who proclaimed that none of the laws of the Netherlands were in contradiction with the Convention.[121] The Council of State, however, was unremitting in its rejection of the Convention. It clearly saw the problems posed by the infringement of the country's sovereignty inherent in the ECHR, and held that should the Netherlands become part of the court, a reservation on the right to individual applications should be made. In any case, accession to the ECHR should, according to the Council of State, be regarded as a constitutional treaty and would thus have required a qualified majority.[122]

But the Council of State and the Prime Minister were overruled by the enthusiasm of the Dutch Parliament for the Convention, and the Netherlands joined the ECHR in 1954 upon unqualified (and uncounted, but generally assumed) majority vote in Parliament.[123]

In the discussion of its legitimacy, the first argument defenders of the ECHR use is that the Court will help emerging democracies such as Bulgaria, Russia and Turkey to function properly. The Court would protect the freedom of expression

---

[118] Grand Chamber judgement in the Case of *Al-Skeini and Others v. the United Kingdom* (application no. 55721/07). For a comparison with previous cases concerning extraterritorial jurisdiction of the ECHR (most notably the case of *Bankovic and others v. Belgium & Others –* 52207/99 [2001] ECHR 890, 12 December 2001), see: Alasdair Henderson, 'Al-Skeini v. United Kingdom (7 july 2011)', in: *Human Rights and Public Law Update* (14 July 2011), available online at http://www.1cor.com/1315/?form_1155.replyids=1402.

[119] The actuality of this argument is illustrated by the way some Islamist radicals use Human Rights to continue their terrorist activities unhindered, as described in: Melanie Phillips, *Londonistan* (London: Gibson Square 2006) 63 and further.

[120] Y.S. Klerk and L. van Poelgeest, 'Ratificatie a contre Coeur: de reserves van de Nederlandse regering jegens het Europees Verdrag voor de Rechten van de Mens en het individueel klachtrecht', in: *RM Themis* 5 (1991) 220-246.

[121] Most notably prof. dr. François and mr. Eijssen, see on this: Klerk and Van Poelgeest (1991) 220-246.

[122] Klerk and Van Poelgeest (1991) 220-246.

[123] *Ibidem.*

and right to a fair trial of journalists and opponents of these governments; it would help to improve living conditions of prisoners, and the position of women.

It is true that the Court frequently slaps those countries on the wrist (though its rulings are often ignored – either because the awarded indemnifications are not paid, or because the demanded amendments to legislation are not made[124]). However, the Court does much more than that. It often focuses on Western Europe and forces mature democracies with a properly functioning rule of law to revise democratically established policies. The ECHR interferes not only with torture and disappearances, with clandestine state practices and incipient ethnic cleansings in Eastern Europe, but also with everyday issues such as the voting rights for prisoners,[125] provisions for public education,[126] policies concerning homebirth,[127] regulations with regards to house searchings,[128] and police interrogations.[129] Moreover, the Court also interferes with important national questions such as political asylum and immigration,[130] national security, and the combating of terrorism.[131]

The question why the judges from Strasbourg should be allowed to impose their views on these issues to the rest of Europe is pressing – even in the view of the ECHR itself. Acknowledging that they are surely an extremely small group that is outside the control of national parliaments, a doctrine of a 'margin of appreciation' has been developed by the Court, that would help it to distinguish between 'fundamental' questions that would fall under its jurisdiction, and less fundamental or everyday ones that should be left at a national level. According to the doctrine of the 'margin of appreciation', the Court should perform a 'marginal' check only and thus function merely as an ultimate 'watchdog' of

---

[124] As of yet, no systematic quantitative research on the compliance with judgments of the ECHR has been undertaken. However, several studies have pointed at the lack of compliance of for instance Russia with the ECHR's rulings. See for instance Julia Lapitskaya, 'ECHR, Russia, and Chechnya: two is not company and three is definitely a crowd', in: *International Law and Politics* (NYU, Vol. 43, 2011) 479-547.

[125] Case of *Hirst v. The United Kingdom* (no. 2) *(Application no. 74025/01),* Judgment Strasbourg 6 October 2005.

[126] Case of *Lautsi v. Italy (Application no. 0814/06)* Judgment Strasbourg 3 November 2009; and Grand Chamber: *(Application no. 30814/06)* Judgment Strasbourg 18 March 2011.

[127] Case of *Ternovszky v. Hungary (Application no. 67545/09)* Judgment Strasbourg 14 December 2010.

[128] Case of *Sanoma Uitgevers B.V. v. The Netherlands (Application no. 38224/03)* Grand Chamber Judgment Strasbourg 14 September 2010.

[129] Case of *Salduz v. Turkey* (Application no. 36391/02) Judgment Strasbourg 27 November 2008.

[130] For instance through interim measures preventing the expulsion of asylum seekers in October 2010. Cf. *MSS v. Belgium & Greece* (application no. 30696/09) Judgment Strasbourg 21 January 2011. Remarkable in this case was the scarcity of evidence the applicant provided for the inhumane situation in Greece he allegedly had been in.

[131] Case of *Kelly and others v. The United Kingdom (Application no. 30054/96)* Judgment Strasbourg 4 May 2001.

the most basic natural law.[132] In the words of the Dutch judge at the ECHR, Egbert Myjer, the Court is the guarantor of 'European minimum standards'.[133]

But the problem with this is that it is the Court itself that decides the width of the margin of appreciation. As a result, we have seen the ECHR appropriate more and more jurisdiction to itself.[134] 'In practice', as the former British high court judge Lord Leonard Hoffmann argued, 'the Court has not taken the doctrine of the margin of appreciation nearly far enough. It has been unable to resist the temptation to aggrandise its jurisdiction and to impose uniform rules on Member States'.[135]

The ECHR has for instance, as mentioned before, ruled against Britain for its refusal to grant the right to vote to convicted criminals while they are in prison. Although the British High Court had considered that:

> if an individual is to be disenfranchised that must be in the pursuit of a legitimate aim. (...) As [the counsel for the Secretary of State] submits, there is a broad spectrum of approaches among democratic societies, and the United Kingdom falls into the middle of the spectrum. In course of time this position may move, (...) but its position in the spectrum is plainly a matter for Parliament not for the courts.[136]

The Strasbourg Court, however, thought differently. 'A general, automatic and indiscriminate restriction on a vitally important Convention right must be seen as falling outside any acceptable margin of appreciation', it held with the vote of twelve in favor to five against.[137] The Court considered, amongst other things, that 'there is no evidence that parliament has ever sought to weigh the competing interests or to assess the proportionality of a blanket ban on the right of a convicted prisoner to vote. (...) It may perhaps be said that, by voting the way they did to exempt unconvicted prisoners from the restriction on voting, parliament implicitly affirmed the need for continued restrictions on the voting rights of convicted prisoners. Nonetheless it cannot be said that there was any substantive debate by members of the legislature on the continued justification in light of modern day penal policy and of current human rights standards for

---

[132] Cf. Jeroen Schokkenbroek, 'The Basis, Nature and Application of the Margin of Appreciation Doctrine in the Case-Law of the European Court of Human Rights', in: *Human Rights Law Journal*, vol. 19, no. 1 (April 1998) 30-36, as well as the other articles in this particular issue of the Journal, which was dedicated entirely to the doctrine of the Margin of Appreciation.

[133] 'Zolang als u maar niet door de Europese minimumnorm zakt', in Buitenhof, 5 December 2010.

[134] In this respect, the Public Choice Theory is interesting, as it provides models for understanding the ever-expanding nature of institutions.

[135] Leonard Hoffmann, *The Universality of Human Rights* (Judicial Studies Board Annual Lecture, 19 March 2009), available online at www.shrlg.org.uk/wp-content/plugins/download.../download.php?id=15.

[136] Case of *Hirst v. The United Kingdom (no. 2) (Application no. 74025/01)* Grand Chamber Judgment Strasbourg 6 October 2005.

[137] *Ibidem*. The Chamber had ruled unanimously against the UK in 2004.

maintaining such a general restriction on the right of prisoners to vote.[138] It is remarkable, to put it no higher, that a supranational court is here not only assessing the legal system of one of its member states, but also goes at some length evaluating the deliberations of its parliament.

In 2010, the ECHR, noticing that the UK had not amended its provisions concerning the prisoners' voting ban, reconfirmed its views on the matter, and concluded that:

> the respondent State must introduce legislative proposals (…) within six months of the date on which the present judgment becomes final.[139]

Days before this ruling, the British Prime Minister David Cameron had declared that the idea of prisoners having the right to vote made him 'physically sick',[140] and he was backed by an overwhelming majority in Parliament resisting to review the provisions in the British criminal code. In February 2011, the British Parliament voted with 234 to 22 votes to continue the ban on prisoners' voting rights. In April 2011, the ECHR rejected (by an anonymous panel of five judges) the British application for appeal to the Grand Chamber, thus making the previous judgment final and so bringing an obligation on the United Kingdom to change its laws before 11 October 2011.[141]

It was not the first time that the Court had had views regarding punishments conflicting with those of the United Kingdom. More than thirty years earlier, in the *Tyrer v. UK* case of 1978, the Court had already interfered with practices on the Isle of Man, which ultimately came down to declaring all forms of corporal punishment to juveniles a form of 'degrading' punishment prohibited in article 3 (although it remains questionable if any child is ever brought up without having received an occasional slap by his parents). In his dissenting opinion, Judge Sir Gerald Fitzmaurice considered:

> I have to admit that my own view may be coloured by the fact that I was brought up and educated under a system according to which the corporal punishment of schoolboys (…) was regarded as the normal sanction for serious misbehaviour, (…). Generally speaking, and subject to circumstances, it was often considered by the boy himself as preferable to probable alternative punishments such as being kept in on a fine summer's evening to copy out 500 lines or learn several pages of

---

[138] *Ibidem.*

[139] Case of *Greens and M.T. v. The United Kingdom (Applications nos. 60041/08 and 60054/08)* Judgment Strasbourg 23 November 2010.

[140] Cameron declared this on November 3rd, 2010, in a debate in Parliament. Cf. B. Quinn, 'Prisoners' voting rights: government loses final appeal in European court. European court of human rights rules UK must draw up proposals to end ban on prisoners voting within six months', in: *The Guardian,* Tuesday 12 April 2011. Available online at http://www.guardian.co.uk/politics/2011/apr/12/prisoners-vote-government-loses-appeal?&.

[141] This information is provided by the British Parliament itself, available online at http://www.parliament.uk/documents/commons/lib/research/briefings/snpc-01764.pdf.

Shakespeare or Virgil by heart, or be denied leave of absence on a holiday occasion. (...) Yet I cannot remember that any boy felt degraded or debased. Such an idea would have been thought rather ridiculous. The system was the same for all until they attained a certain seniority. If a boy minded, and resolved not to repeat the offence that had resulted in a beating, this was simply because it had hurt, not because he felt degraded by it or was so regarded by his fellows: indeed, such is the natural perversity of the young of the human species that these occasions were often seen as matters of pride and congratulation, – not unlike the way in which members of the student corps in the old German universities regarded their duelling scars as honourable – (though of course that was, in other respects, quite a different case).[142]

It was also in this *Tyrer* case, that the Court for the first time declared that 'the Convention is a living instrument which (...) must be interpreted in the light of present-day conditions' – which meant that in theory, the Court was now no longer restrained by a strict, literal interpretation of the text of the Convention.[143]

As a result, ever since this ruling, the Court has given new – and expanding – interpretations to the rights under its jurisdiction. 'The Strasbourg court has taken upon itself an extraordinary power to micromanage the legal systems of the member states of the Council of Europe', Lord Hoffmann observed in 2011.[144]

In 2007, for example, the ECHR ruled that the Somali asylum seeker Salah Sheekh could not be expelled from the Netherlands because expulsion would infringe his right not to be tortured. The Dutch government's agency on immigration had concluded beforehand that Salah Sheekh did not run the risk of torture. Dutch national immigration policy, established after extensive public debate and sanctioned by the democratically elected parliament, has thus been overruled.[145] Following this case, the Chamber of the Court decided in the case of *A. v. the Netherlands* of in July 2010, that a Libyan asylum seeker, who was regarded a threat to national security by the Dutch secret services (AIVD) and

---

[142] Case of *Tyrer v. The United Kingdom (Application no. 5856/72)* Judgment Strasbourg 25 April 1978. The Court has also referred to a 'European consensus', a 'trend', an 'international consensus' (Case of *Christine Goodwin v. The United Kingdom (Application no. 28957/95)* Judgment Strasbourg 11 July 2002), all of which being not even remotely clear in their definition. Should a 'consensus' develop that the Court finds unwelcome – for instance concerning opposition to gay-rights, a viewpoint that a great serious number of member states of the Council of Europe indeed seem to increasingly share – it is unclear what the Court would do. Cf. K. Dzehtsiarou, 'Consensus from within the Palace Walls: UCD Working Papers in Law, Criminology & Socio-Legal Studies Research Paper No. 40/2010' (September 17, 2010) available online at http://papers.ssrn.com/sol3/papers.cfm?abstract_id=1678424.

[143] Case of *Tyrer v. The United Kingdom (Application no. 5856/72)* Judgment Strasbourg 25 April 1978.

[144] Leonard Hoffmann, 'Foreword', in: Michael Pinto-Duschinsky, *Bringing Rights Back Home. Making human rights compatible with parliamentary democracy in the UK* (London: Policy Exchange, 2011) 7.

[145] Case of *Salah Sheekh v. The Netherlands (Application no. 1948/04)* Judgment Strasbourg 11 January 2007.

later by the Dutch government and the courts as well (due to active participation in a jihadist network), could not be expelled because, so the Court believed, he might be tortured in Libya.[146]

It were precisely such cases that were feared by those who objected to granting the Court the right to receive individual complaints – and it was precisely with such cases in view, that guarantees were given to the Netherlands before accession, that its decisions in these matters would not be interfered with.[147]

The examples are abundant, and the potential contradictions between national preferences and the momentary moral whims of a human rights court are endless. In *Lautsi v. Italy*, the ECHR initially ruled that crucifixes in Italian public schools were a violation of the fundamental right to freedom of religion (article 9 of the Convention) taken together with article 2 of the second Protocol, that requires that 'the State shall respect the right of parents to ensure such education and teaching in conformity with their own religions and philosophical convictions', and sentenced Italy to pay 5,000 euros 'non-pecuniary damage'.

The ruling was unanimous, and the wording of the ruling strict and highly critical of Italy:

> The Court considers that the presence of the crucifix in classrooms goes beyond the use of symbols in specific historical contexts.
> (…)
> The Court acknowledges that, as submitted, it is impossible not to notice crucifixes in the classrooms.
> (…)
> The presence of the crucifix may easily be interpreted by pupils of all ages as a religious sign (…). What may be encouraging for some religious pupils may be emotionally disturbing for pupils of other religions or those who profess no religion. That risk is particularly strong among pupils belonging to religious minorities.[148]

But in appeal, the Court reversed its conclusion. With a great majority of fifteen votes to two, the court all of a sudden concluded that, in fact, no violation of the convention had occurred. While 'the decision whether or not to perpetuate a tradition falls in principle within the margin of appreciation of the respondent State', the Court considered that 'a crucifix on a wall is an essentially passive symbol'. In addition, it concluded that:

> There is no evidence before the Court that the display of a religious symbol on classroom walls may have an influence on pupils and so it cannot reasonably be asserted that it does or does not have an effect on young persons whose convictions are still in the process of being formed.

---

[146] Case of *A. v. The Netherlands (Application no. 4900/06)* Judgment Strasbourg 20 July 2010.
[147] Klerk and Van Poelgeest (1991) 220-246.
[148] Case of *Lautsi v. Italy (Application no. 30814/06)* Judgment Strasbourg 3 November 2009.

The Court also reminded the plaintiff that she 'retained in full her right as a parent to enlighten and advise her children, to exercise in their regard her natural functions as educator and to guide them on a path in line with her own philosophical convictions'.[149]

Two other examples of the Court's ambivalence are the case of *Pye v. UK* and that of *Hatton v. UK*. In *Pye v. UK,* the Court considered the extent to which British limitations on land ownership claims were contrary to the 'right to protection of property' (Article 1 of the first Protocol). Initially, the Court ruled that there was indeed a conflict, but the Grand Chamber then considered that England was within its right to decide for itself on these matters.[150] In *Hatton and others v. UK,* the Court ruled with 5 to 2 votes that night flights regulations concerning Heathrow Airport, decided upon by the British Secretary of State upon an assessment of the national economic interest concerned, were a violation of the right to respect for the privacy of those living in the area of the airport. The Grand Chamber overruled this decision again with the vote of 12 to 5.[151]

If the two chambers of the Court could differ so greatly, how 'universal' then could the fundamental principles on which they decided the case have been? Is it not a basic assumption of a supranational Human Rights court – and was it not a basic assumption of the ECHR in Strasbourg – that it would merely deal with principles of basic justice ('self-evident' principles, as it were[152]) that we all agreed with?[153] The whole point of a supranational court of Human Rights is that there are some 'fundamental' values that we all agree upon – and that we have a Court to make sure they are protected – while more ordinary or disputable questions remain within the competence of national politics.

But it is becoming increasingly clear that the European Court of Human Rights does not aim to perform that role. In a significant number of cases, the Court hardly performs 'marginal', 'subsidiary' interpretation of otherwise universal principles, immediately recognized by any civilised nation. While the Court was set up to pass judgment on gross violations of undisputed matters only, it is gradually applying the European Convention of Human Rights as law to the

---

[149] Case of *Lautsi and others v. Italy (Application no. 30814/06)* Grand Chamber Judgment Strasbourg 18 March 2011.

[150] Case of *J.A. Pye (Oxford) Ltd. v. The United Kingdom (Application no. 44302/02)* Judgment Strasbourg 15 November 2005; and Grand Chamber Judgment Strasbourg, 30 August 2007.

[151] Case of *Hatton and others v. The United Kingdom (Application no. 36022/97)* Grand Chamber Judgment Strasbourg, 8 July 2003.

[152] As the American declaration of independence famously denotes such basic principles.

[153] For not only did the Grand Chamber rule completely opposite to the Chamber, the votes of the judges itself show serious discord as well. While the Chamber judgment had *unanimously* held that there had been a violation, the Grand Chamber again overwhelmingly voted (with 15 to 2) that in fact there had *not* been such a violation.

cases brought before it – thus accepting the panel of international judges coming from 47 countries as the ultimate authority in increasingly ordinary disputes.[154]

One of its judges has even considered in a dissenting opinion that speed limits might be a violation of a universal human right, considering that 'it is difficult for me to accept the argument that hundreds of thousands of speeding motorists are wrong and only the government is right'.[155] In other cases, the Court interferes not with its member states' governments, but with its member states' judges. Thus the ECHR overruled the German Supreme Court's decision to allow the publication by the press of pictures of the Princess of Hannover and her children, stating that such publication would violate her right to privacy (Article 8 of the Convention). The Court thought the disputed pictures made no 'contribution (…) to a debate of general interest', while Germany, aware of its particular history of curtailing free expression in public, had thought it best to allow such a publication.[156] The judge from Slovenia in his concurring opinion rose to the occasion to present his own philosophical position on the freedom of speech:

> I believe that the courts have to some extent and under American influence made a fetish of the freedom of the press. (…) It is time that the pendulum swung back to a different kind of balance between what is private and secluded and what is public and unshielded. The question here is how to ascertain and assess this balance …'[157]

Apart from the unusual liberty assumed here by Judge Zupancic to express his views on the alleged American 'fetish' of the freedom of the press and the undoubtedly political viewpoint that 'it is time that the pendulum swung back', it is important to note that he believed it was the task of the ECHR to 'ascertain and assess' this issue.

But not only does Strasbourg – as we have seen in these examples – assume jurisdicton in increasingly far-reaching and political questions, in practice its rulings reach even further, since the rights of the convention and the jurispru-dential course of the Court are also applied by national judges in national courts, as if they were precedents.

---

[154] Sometimes, the European Court also seems to use its Convention as the Constitutional appeal of a supposed 'Federal State of Europe'. As indeed acknowledged by the Court itself in the Loizidou-case (Preliminary objections, March 23, 1995), when the Court described the European Convention on Human Rights as 'a constitutional instrument of European public order'. See R.A. Lawson and H.G. Schermers, *Leading cases of the European Court of Human Rights* (Leiden: Ars Aequi 1995) vii.

[155] Case of *O'Halloran and Francis v. The United Kingdom* (Applications 15809/02 and 25624/02) Judgment Strasbourg 29 June 2007.

[156] Case of *Von Hannover v. Germany (Application no. 59320/00)* Judgment Strasbourg 24 June 2004.

[157] Concurring opinion of Judge Zupancic, Case of *Von Hannover v. Germany (Application no. 59320/00)* Judgment Strasbourg 24 June 2004.

We are already seeing that all kinds of articles of domestic law are being interpreted according to the European Court's jurisprudence. A recent example from the Netherlands was the decision of the Court of Appeal of The Hague, which declared new legislation concerning the eviction of illegal squatters a violation of the European Court's interpretation of the right to family life.[158] On November 8th, 2010, the mayor of Amsterdam, Eberhard van der Laan, was thus prevented from executing democratically passed new legislation on the matter.[159] We have also seen the principal of precedent being applied in the Dutch jurisprudential interpretation of freedom of speech, which was extensively reviewed in the light of Strasbourg jurisprudence during the trial of Geert Wilders, as if it were authoritative law applying directly to the Dutch case.[160]

In *Salduz v. Turkey*, the Court decided that there must be no police interrogation of suspects without the presence of a lawyer. This case created a precedent for the Dutch criminal justice system that has traditionally allowed interrogation of suspects immediately after arrest.[161]

It is possible that there will soon be an Islamic interest group that will challenge the French ban on the burqa in Strasbourg by invoking the right to freedom of religion. Or the Swiss minaret-ban. What will the Court say? Thomas Hammarberg, who works as a 'commissioner for human rights' at the Council of Europe, has already announced on July 20th, 2011, that he saw such a ban as 'a sad capitulation to the prejudices of xenophobes', and Erdogan, the prime minister of Turkey – which is also a member of the Council of Europe – has declared that to his mind, this ban violated the 'freedom of religion'.[162] Perhaps

---

[158] Gerechtshof 's-Gravenhage, November 8th, 2010, published November 11th, 2010; LJN: BO3682, 200.076.673/01. The decision was supported by the Supreme Court on October 28, 2011.

[159] The anti-squatting law had been initiated by five members of Parliament, Ten Hoopen (Christian-Democrats), Slob (Christian party) and Van der Burg (Liberal Party). The Second Chamber passed it in October 2009, and the Senate passed it in June 2010. More information available online at http://www.eerstekamer.nl/wetsvoorstel/31560_initiatiefvoorstel_ten.

[160] Rick Lawson, 'Wild, wilder, wildst. Over de ruimte die het EVRM laat voor de vervolging van kwetsende politici', in: *NJCM-Bulletin*, vol. 33, no. 4 (2008) 481. Cf. Thierry Baudet, 'De vrijspraak van Geert Wilders is uniek in Europa', in: *Trouw*, 25 June 2011. The article has been translated as 'Geert Wilders, a Voltaire for our times?', and is available online at http://www.presseurop.eu/en/content/article/743751-geert-wilders-voltaire-our-times; it was criticized by Rick Lawson, 'Werd Islamcritici de mond gesnoerd? Helemaal niet', in: *Trouw*, 28 June 2011; which was again answered on the weblog *Dagelijkse Standaard*, 'Professor Rick Lawson nu zelf onzorgvuldig', 1 July, 2011, available online at http://www.dagelijksestandaard.nl/2011/07/professor-rick-lawson-nu-zelf-onzorgvuldig.

[161] Cf. Alexander de Swart, 'Toch nog een raadsman bij het politieverhoor? Enkele ontwikkelingen na *Salduz/Panovits*', in: *Nederlands Juristenblad*, no. 4, 29 January 2010, 223-226; Alexander de Swart, 'Update *Salduz*-doctrine. Toch nog een raadsman bij het politieverhoor? Part II', in: *Nederlands Juristenblad*, no. 42, 4 December 2010, 2692-2695.

[162] Quoted in: 'Council of Europe blasts burqa ban', in: *www.euractiv.com* (20 july 2011) available online at: http://www.euractiv.com/en/culture/council-europe-blasts-burqa-ban-news-506689. Cf. 'Penalising women who wear the burqa does not liberate them', in: *The Council of Europe Commissioner's Human Rights Comment*, 20 July 2011. Available online at: http://commissioner.cws.coe.int/tiki-view_blog_post.php?postId=157.

that a ban on the burqa or on new minarets will indeed be found to be in conflict with the 'human rights' of immigrants, nobody can know in advance, but there is now a fair chance in almost any legal dispute that involves moral questions to win your case in Strasbourg. The Court has a waiting list approaching 200.000 cases, growing everyday.

4.3. *The International Court of Justice*

The International Court of Justice has become one of the leading fora for international dispute settlement since its installation simultaneously with the founding of the United Nations.[163] In principle, it is not a supranational court because referral of disputes by states to it is always on a voluntary basis. Article 36 par. 1 reads: 'The jurisdiction of the Court comprises all cases which the parties refer to it'. And it takes two to tango.[164]

Yet, the possibility exists for a state to accept the jurisdiction of the ICJ in any international dispute it may have, and it is then obliged to accept the ruling of the Court. This possibility is given in par. 2 of the same article 36. It reads:

> The states parties to the present Statute may at any time declare that they recognize as compulsory *ipso facto* and without special agreement, in relation to any other state accepting the same obligation, the jurisdiction of the Court in all legal disputes (…).

Making such an article 36 declaration makes the ICJ a supranational institution *for that state* and *for the type of disputes* that have been declared to be falling under the compulsory jurisdiction of the Court. An impressive range of states has accepted this compulsory jurisdiction: 66 in total.[165]

Yet if we look at the provisions in the declarations of these 66 states, we understand that this acceptance of compulsory jurisdiction is often merely *pro forma*: most states have made extensive lists of exceptional circumstances in which they do not recognize the compulsory jurisdiction of the ICJ – circumstances such as border disputes, disputes concerning armed conflicts, disputes where, in

---

[163] The 'introductory note' to the Charter of the United Nations reads: 'The Statute of the International Court of Justice forms an integral part of the Charter of the United Nations.'

[164] Though the ICJ itself goes so far as to denote itself as the 'world court', http://www3.icj-cij.org/jurisdiction/index.php?p1=5. The Permanent Court of International Justice has also been denoted as such, see for instance Michael P. Scharf, 'The ICC's jurisdiction over the nationals of non-party states: a critique of the U.S. position', in: *Law & Contemporary Problems*, vol. 64, issue 1 (Winter 2001) 67-118, there 73.

[165] As of Spring 2011. Information is available online at http://www.icj-cij.org/jurisdiction/index.php?p1=5&p2=1&p3=3.

the case of states such as India, 'other commonwealth or former commonwealth states' are involved, and the like.[166]

Moreover, just as with the ICC, most states that are likely to be involved in serious armed conflicts in the near future have not recognized this compulsory jurisdiction, for example China, Russia, United States, France, Israel, Iran, and others.

What we see in the ICJ is therefore an international organization with embryonic supranational powers. There have been worrying examples of what these capabilities may amount to, however. One is the 1986 case of Nicaragua v. the United States.[167] In this case, the US was condemned to pay indemnification to Nicaragua for its aggression in supporting rebels who opposed the pro-communist Nicaraguan regime at the time. The United States had agreed to accept the compulsory jurisdiction of the ICJ under article 36 (be it with a number of important reservations). The Security Council then proposed a resolution to demand that the United States comply with the rulings of the ICJ. The United States was able to veto this resolution. But if a non-veto power had been in the position of the United States in this case, it might have been obliged to comply with the ruling of an international court that it did not accept (following this affair, the United States withdrew its acceptance of compulsory jurisdiction of the ICJ under article 36 and has never restored it).

---

[166] These and other countries' declarations can be found online at http://www.icj-cij.org/jurisdiction/index.php?p1=5&p2=1&p3=3

[167] Military and paramilitary activities in and against Nicaragua (*Nicaragua v. United States of America*), Merits, Judgment, ICJ Reports 1986.

CHAPTER FIVE

SUPRANATIONAL ORGANIZATIONS

5.1. *The World Trade Organization*

The World Trade Organization (WTO) is a supranational organization that is concerned with the rules of trade between its member states. It is based in Geneva and currently has 153 member states. As the successor of the General Agreement on Tariffs and Trade (GATT), it was founded in 1995 at the end of the so-called 'Uruguay Round Agreements'.

The GATT system, in turn, had been part of a series of developments that followed from the international conference on rebuilding the global economic system after the Second World War, held in the first three weeks of July 1944 at the Mount Washington Hotel in Bretton Woods, a village in New Hampshire.

During this conference, special attention was paid to the prevention of what was considered an important cause of the Second World War: the collapse of the international financial and trade system in the Great Depression (from 1929 onwards). Moreover, one of the driving forces behind the initiatives at this conference was the United States, which had an interest in the dissolution of the European empires that offered favorable trade positions to its colonies and client states and in taking over global economic hegemony through worldwide free trade and the establishment of the dollar as the international reserve currency.

In any case, at this conference in Bretton Woods, initiatives for three new international institutions were launched: the International Monetary Fund (IMF), the International Bank for Reconstruction and Development (IBRD, later becoming part of the 'World Bank Group'), and the International Trade Organization (ITO).

The main functions of the IMF were (and still are) three. The first is the installation of an international system of economic *surveillance*, involving the monitoring of global economic and financial developments, and providing policy advice for states that ask for it, aimed especially at the prevention of financial crises. The second function of the IMF is *lending* to countries with balance of payments difficulties, and advising or imposing economic policies aimed at correcting the underlying problems (the so-called Structural Adjustment Programmes). And the third function of the IMF is to provide countries with technical assistance and training in its areas of expertise, such

as currency devaluations. Thus, however powerful the IMF may be, it possesses
no *supranational* powers.[1]

The IBRD, now part of the World Bank Group, provides loans to developing
countries. It thus differs from the IMF in that it does not lend just to restore the
financial stability of a country, but to help it develop. The IBRD thus functions
as a form of development aid system. (The first country to receive a loan from
the IBRD was France, 250 million US dollars in 1946[2]). Thus, the World Bank
Group does not possess any supranational powers either.[3]

Thirdly, there was the plan to set up an International Trade Organization
(ITO). This plan was not further developed at the Bretton Woods conference,
but, as such an organization was considered a necessary supplement to the
IMF and the IBRD, talks concerning it continued between 1945 and 1949. The
organization was to have been placed under the aegis of the UN, and was to
have a broad regulatory mandate, covering international trade as well as national
employment regulations and business practices.

The United States Congress, however, did not ratify the treaty that was
eventually drafted, and the ITO therefore never came into being (the US of
course being at the time by far the most important economy).[4] At the same time,
however, a number of countries that had been present at the ITO negotiations
(most notably, at the conference in Havana in 1948) had drafted a provisional
program for the regulation of international trade, called the General Agreement
on Tariffs and Trade (GATT).[5] This was not much more than an interim solution,
but it turned out to be long lasting.

After the initial round of negotiations, new rounds followed, encompassing
more tariff reductions on a wider range of products, attracting more and more
states to become a party to GATT. A particularly comprehensive round, that of
Uruguay, lasting from 1986 until 1993, established a permanent international
organization, the World Trade Organization (WTO). This WTO were to cover
a wider range of trade issues and to provide an umbrella institution of which

---

[1] Cf. http://www.imf.org/external/about/whatwedo.htm.
[2] The Marshall Plan was set up alongside the IBRD, as at that time, IBRD revenues were
insufficient to supply all European aid.
[3] See also the website of the Worldbank, available at http://web.worldbank.org/WBSITE/
EXTERNAL/EXTABOUTUS/0,,pagePK:50004410~piPK:36602~theSitePK:29708,00.html.
[4] See on the ITO for instance: Claude E. Barfield, *Free trade, sovereignty, democracy. The future
of the World Trade Organization* (Washington DC: IAE Press, 2001) 20-21.
[5] There was no separate ratification by the US Senate required for the implementation of the
commitments of GATT, because American adherence to it was already authorized under the
Reciprocal Trade Agreements Act (RTAA), a pre-war US statute. There were initially twenty-
three countries party to these agreements, namely: Australia, Belgium, Brazil, Burma, Canada,
Ceylon, Chile, China, Cuba, the Czechoslovak Republic, France, India, Lebanon, Luxembourg,
Netherlands, New Zealand, Norway, Pakistan, Southern Rhodesia, Syria, South Africa, the United
Kingdom, and the United States.

GATT would now become a part,[6] together with the General Agreement on Trade in Services (GATS) and the Agreement on Trade Related Aspects of Intellectual Property (TRIPS).[7]

Any member of the WTO would automatically be part of GATT, GATS, and TRIPS. A new round of negotiations was started at the ministerial conference at Doha in 2001, but this round is still in progress.

In some ways, the establishment of the WTO might be seen as the fulfilment of the promise of GATT (and certainly the WTO can be seen as the answer to the expectations that the failure of the ITO had raised). Yet there are two essential changes in the transformation of GATT to the WTO, which make the WTO not only a permanent forum for negotiating trade agreements, but a supranational organization.

Firstly, GATT had been an agreement with – and between – 'parties'. This meant that every rule that was binding on the parties was necessarily accepted by all of them individually. This had the effect that GATT lacked supranational powers. The WTO, by contrast, is an international organization, with 'members'. While, like GATT, WTO rulings are also to be accepted by unanimity, and article IX under 1 of the WTO treaty determines that the 'WTO shall continue the practice of decision-making by consensus followed under GATT 1947', article IX under 2 reads:

> In the case of an interpretation of a Multilateral Trade Agreement in Annex 1 [i.e. the specific trade rules on goods], they [the ministerial conference] shall exercise their authority on the basis of a recommendation by the Council [i.e. the General Council, a governing body of the WTO] overseeing the functioning of that Agreement. The decision to adopt an interpretation shall be taken by a three-fourths majority of the Members.

A three-fourth majority vote (each country counting for one) is thus sufficient to re-interpret existing agreements and thus possibly to change their scope.

But not only can the WTO interpret previous agreements, it can also amend them. Article X of the WTO treaty provides that 'Any Member of the WTO may initiate a proposal to amend the provisions of this Agreement (...) by submitting such proposal to the Ministerial Conference'. It continues that 'If consensus is not reached at a meeting of the Ministerial Conference within the established period',

---

[6] Until that moment, there had been six rounds, the Annecy Round (1950), the Torquay Round (1951), the Geneva Round (1955-1956), the Dillon Round (1960-1962), the Kennedy Round (1964-1967), the Tokyo Round (1973-1979).

[7] Since that moment, many additional agreements, for instance the Anti-Dumping Agreement (ADA), and the Sanitary and Phytosanitary measures (SPS), have been added to this.

the Ministerial Conference shall decide by a two-thirds majority of the Members whether to submit the proposed amendment to the Members for acceptance.[8]

Following this, again a three-fourths majority is needed to make those amendments binding on all members if they are considered to 'alter the rights and obligations of the members'.[9] States that do not agree with such an amendment, will be offered either the possibility of withdrawing from the WTO, or of accepting it anyway.

In practice, it has so far been impossible to reach this three-fourth majority, and it is unlikely that the WTO, with its 153 members with highly diverging agendas, will do so in the near future. Moreover, as European countries are still among the world's most powerful trading nations, it is unlikely that a three-fourth majority of member states of the WTO will vote against one of the European member states' wishes. Still, it is a fact that the WTO possesses this power, and there can be no doubt it is a supranational power.

The second change in function between GATT and the WTO is in the settlement of disputes between its states. In a situation in which conflict arose over the interpretation of certain trade agreements, GATT rules provided no institution that could pass judgement – and thus did not contain any provisions to place itself above the states that were party to the agreement. GATT functioned as a means to facilitate international trade agreements; it did not have its own mechanism of interpreting provisions and accumulating jurisprudence through precedents.

Article XXIII of GATT stated that 'If any contracting party should consider that any benefit accruing to it directly or indirectly under this Agreement is being nullified or impaired or that the attainment of any objective of the Agreement is being impeded as the result of (…) the failure of another contracting party to carry out its obligations under this Agreement (…)',

> the contracting party may, with a view to the satisfactory adjustment of the matter, make written representations or proposals to the other contracting party or parties which it considers to be concerned. Any contracting party thus approached shall give sympathetic consideration to the representations or proposals made to it.

Paragraph 2 of this article of GATT then continued:

> If no satisfactory adjustment is effected between the contracting parties concerned within a reasonable time, (…) the matter may be referred to the contracting parties.

Under GATT, then, the contracting parties – i.e. all the states that were parties to GATT – would have had unanimously to agree that a state had violated an agreement – which meant that a single state, including the state involved in the dispute in question, could block such a declaration. Furthermore, this declaration

---

[8] WTO agreement, article X under 1.
[9] *Ibidem.*

was all GATT could provide. It did not have any means of its own to enforce its agreements, and the ultimate sanction for non-compliance was retaliation from states that felt injured or wronged. This form of retaliation rested on the decision of the states that wished to employ it. There was no supranational decision-making involved.

The WTO system amended this procedure on two points. Firstly, while under GATT, states could only be judged by consensus, meaning that a single objection could block the conviction; the rulings of the arbitration panel were now, under the WTO, automatically adopted unless there was a consensus to *reject* them.

Secondly, a permanent judicial body was installed under the *understanding on rules and procedures governing the settlement of disputes*, to which states could appeal decisions of the arbitration panel: the *Appellate Body* (AB). This AB would not consist of three ad hoc arbiters, appointed by the disputing states (as was the case under GATT), but of seven 'members', appointed by the assembly of states for a period of four years (with the possibility for one reappointment). Member states have agreed not to retaliate if they do not agree with the decision of the abitration panel (as would have been possible under GATT), but to bring their issues before the AB.

The first important problem this poses, is that it actually places serious restrictions on the exercise of foreign policy, limiting the freedom to install a trade blockade. In history, trade sanctions often played an important role in enforcing foreign policy, coming between mere diplomatic pressure and actual military engagement. As a result of rules governing the WTO, therefore, the possibilities for imposing economic sanctions have been severely limited.[10]

But there is yet more. At its very first ruling,[11] *the United States – Standards for Reformulated and Conventional Gasoline*, the appellate body declared a standard of review for the provision of article 3, paragraph 2 of the Dispute Settlement Understanding (DSU), that reads:

> The dispute settlement system of the WTO is a central element in providing security and predictability to the multilateral trading system. The Members recognize that it serves to preserve the rights and obligations of Members under the covered agreements, and to clarify the existing provisions of those agreements in accordance with customary rules of interpretation of public international law.

---

[10] It is true that under article XXI (b) 'security interests' may allow such a trade blocade, and that article XXI (c) gives members of the WTO the right to comply with UN trade sanctions. But when no UN sanctions have been agreed and no direct 'security interests' are involved, or when member states in their trade sanctions violate the proportionality test that is included in the AB's *standard of review* (as will be discussed further down this section), member states thus violate WTO rules.

[11] The actual first case to be brought under the Appellate Body, *Malaysia – Prohibition of Imports of Polyethylene and Polypropylene*, did not result in a ruling as the complainant, Singapore, withdrew.

According to the AB, these 'customary rules of interpretation of public international law' were also to encompass article 31 of the Vienna Convention on
the Law of Treaties, which states that the interpretation of treaties should be
led by what is called the 'ordinary meaning' of terms. Indeed, this was declared
by the AB to be

> a rule of customary or general international law. As such, it forms part of the
> 'customary rules of interpretation of public international law' which the Appellate
> Body has been directed, by Article 3(2) of the DSU, to apply ...[12]

The curious thing is not that this rule is thought to be itself problematic. Nor
that the application of this article was of decisive impact on the outcome of the
dispute. What is curious, is that the United States – which was the defending
party in this dispute – had never ratified the Vienna Convention on the Law
of Treaties (and still hasn't[13]). In other words, the defendant in this dispute was
not a party to the treaty held by the AB to be 'a rule of customary or general
international law'. A court that is capable of doing such a thing might very well
expand its powers in other cases even more.

An occasion to do so was provided in 1997. India, Malaysia, Pakistan and
Thailand brought a joint complaint before the AB stating that the United States
had violated article XI of GATT, which is concerned with eliminating import
restrictions.

According to the complainants, these restrictions resulted from Section 609
of US Public Law 101–102, enacted in 1989, which obliged shrimp fishers to
use fishing nets equipped with so-called Turtle Excluder Devices (TED's), thus
ensuring that sea turtles would not get caught (and possibly killed) in the process of shrimp fishing. Additionally, this law prohibited the selling on American
markets of shrimp (or of shrimp products) that were caught with nets *not using*
those TED's. In its defence of the prohibition, the United States invoked article
XX, paragraph g of GATT, that reads:

> nothing in this Agreement shall be construed to prevent the adoption or enforce-
> ment by any contracting party of measures (...) relating to the conservation of
> exhaustible natural resources if such measures are made effective in conjunction
> with restrictions on domestic production or consumption;

Both the initial arbitration panel, and the Appellate Body, held that the US
legislation was in violation of free trade provisions of GATT, because of 'its
intended and actual coercive effect'.

---

[12] Available online at http://docsonline.wto.org/GEN_highLightParent.asp?qu=%28%40met
a%5FSymbol+WT%FCDS2%FC%2A%29&doc=D%3A%2FDDFDOCUMENTS%2FT%2FWT%2
FDS%2F2%2D10A7%2EWPF%2EHTM&curdoc=3&popTitle=WT%2FDS2%2F10%2FAdd%2E7.
[13] The fact that US Courts as well as the US Department of State have routinely invoked the
Vienna Convention does not alter the principles at stake here.

The AB went on to say that the American regulation of Section 609 was 'in effect, an economic embargo which requires all other exporting Members, if they wish to exercise their GATT rights, to adopt essentially the same policy …'.[14] This was the case, because, according to the AB:

> the effect of the application of Section 609 is to establish a rigid and unbending standard by which United States officials determine whether or not countries will be certified, thus granting or refusing other countries the right to export shrimp to the United States. Other specific policies and measures that an exporting country may have adopted for the protection and conservation of sea turtles are not taken into account, in practice, by the administrators making the comparability determination.[15]

Ultimately, the AB ruled that the US was allowed to require compliance with certain environmental protection laws of its own, as long as it would not only apply them on a non-discriminatory basis (as is prescribed by the chapeau of article XX), but also as long as the US would perform:

> Ongoing serious good faith efforts to reach a multilateral agreement

on the protection of sea turtles. This meant that there was now a positive obligation on the United States to lobby actively (and continue to do so with 'ongoing serious good faith') for a multilateral agreement to uphold the same environmental standards as it had legislated for itself. Indeed,

> Section 609 of Public Law 101-162 (…) is justified under Article XX of the GATT 1994 as long as the conditions stated in the findings of this Report, in particular the ongoing serious good faith efforts to reach a multilateral agreement, remain satisfied.

It has also become clear that the AB applies the principle of precedent in its rulings,[16] amounting to the accumulation of legislation.[17] The precedent that this ruling concerning shrimp restrictions sets, for instance, is that multilateral agreements set an international standard. This seems to suggest that in fields where such a multilateral agreement *has* been reached, the WTO may actually enforce it – a power of considerable implications, as states might otherwise not have given it a direct effect into their national jurisdiction.

Nor need the WTO hesitate to declare those treaties directly applicable to states that decided *not* to become a party to them (as was the case, for instance, with the US concerning the Vienna Convention on the Law of Treaties). It is

---

[14] WT/DS58/W, consideration 162.
[15] WT/DS58/W, consideration 163.
[16] For example in consideration 150 of the dispute WT/DS58, *United States – Import Prohibition of Certain Shrimp and Shrimp Products*: 'As we stated in United States – Gasoline …'.
[17] The momentous importance of precedent has also been discussed in the previous chapter concerning the ICC, the ECHR and the ICJ.

easy to imagine this principle being applied to Human Rights treaties,[18] such as the International Covenant on Economic, Social, and Cultural Rights, to labor standards following from treaties or conventions of the International Labour Organization, and even to the Kyoto Protocol: indeed, consistent application of this principle may ultimately have such wide-ranging effects, that it would make the WTO, over time, almost preponderant in domestic legislation and litigation.[19]

This point has even become more real, as the AB allowed *amicus curiae briefs* in the already mentioned shrimp case.[20] *Amicus curiae briefs* are requests from third parties, like non-governmental organizations or multinationals, which may contain additional complaints or evidence (or both). By granting locus standi to non-state parties, the WTO opened the door to the more active enforcement of the entire body of international law, and far outgrew its stage of a mere court of arbitration between two states having different interpretations of certain trade agreements.[21]

Several trade disputes have, over the years that followed, caused 'considerable controversy', in the words of expert Peter van den Bossche.[22] They in any case clearly show how the existence of a permanent body dealing with trade issues can have the practical effect of speaking out over an increasing number of political questions.

In September 2007, for instance, the WTO's appellate body ruled that EU rules banning genetically modified organisms (GMOs) from their food-markets needed amending. They ruled that

---

[18] Cf. Elisabeth Burgi, Thomas Cottier and Joost Pauwelyn (eds.), *Human Rights and International Trade* (Oxford: Oxford University Press, 2005).

[19] See on this: Yasmin Moorman, 'Integration of ILO Core Rights Labor Standards into the WTO', in: *Columbia Journal of Transnational Law,* vol. 39 (2001) 555; Robert Howse, 'The WTO and Protection of Workers' Rights', in: *Journal of Small and Emerging Business Law,* vol. 3 (1999) 131; Steve Charnovitz, 'The moral exception in trade policy', in: *Virginia Journal of International Law, vol. 38 (Summer 1989)* 686. A UN advisory body, the International Commission of Jurists, prepared a set of guidelines for implementing the Covenant on Economic and Social Rights in 1997 (the so-called Maastricht Guidelines) which insisted, among other things, that signatory states must 'ensure' that the rights enumerated in the Covenant 'are fully taken into account in the development of policies and programs' of the WTO. The Guidelines were published as 'The Maastricht Guidelines on Violations of Economic, Social and Cultural Rights' in *Human Rights Quarterly,* vol. 20 (Summer 1998) 691-730. Cf. Gary P. Sampson (ed.), *The role of the World Trade Organization in global governance* (New York: United Nations University Press, 2001); Gary P. Sampson (ed.), *The WTO and global governance: future directions* (New York: United Nations University Press, 2008); Lori Wallach and Patrick Woodall, *Whose Trade Organization? Corporate Globalization and the Erosion of Democracy* (New York: Public Citizen, 1999).

[20] Dispute WT/DS58.

[21] Although some have argued that allowing *amicus curiae briefs* would make it easier for non-state actors to influence WTO decision-making, and so bring about more balanced legal developments, the fact remains that the WTO is granting weight to non-state actors and so reduces the relative power the member states.

[22] Peter van den Bossche, *The Law and Policy of the World Trade Organization* (Cambridge: Cambridge University Press, 2008) 169.

None of the safeguard measures at issue were based on a risk assessment.[23]

It is not relevant here to examine whether or not the AB was right in ruling that none of the European safeguards was based on such an assessment; nor is the point that restrictions on genetically modified crops ought or ought not to be reinstalled. The point, firstly, is that it is now up to an international court to decide whether or not evidence is sufficient to suggest the danger of certain products.[24] Whatever 'risk assessment' may have been felt to be sufficient, is thus no longer up to the national parliaments and governments to decide.

Secondly, it also shows that it is up to such an institution to decide *that such evidence is necessary in the first place*. This is to say, that there might be other arguments, i.e. not evidence based ones (but, for instance, arguments of a religious or ethical nature, that are not 'necessary for the protection of public morals',[25] but merely felt to be *preferable* or *desirable*), that might incline a member of the WTO to restrict the entry of certain products into its (food) market. Given the controversy that exists over the use of GMOs, it is not surprising that the question of the legitimacy of the WTO to pronounce on such matters has repeatedly been raised.

Another example of the supranational power of the WTO is the so-called *Gambling case*[26] in which the question was examined whether US legislation against internet gambling was in the legitimate protection of 'public morals'. As former NYU professor and clerk for US Supreme Court Justice Sonia Sotomayer argued:

> Despite the need to constrain the scope of the public morals exception, *Gambling* went too far. The decision, at least implicitly, suggests that States invoking a public morals defense will be expected to present evidence of similar practice by other states. Taken to an extreme, the *Gambling* doctrine might be read as implying that states cannot unilaterally define public morals'.[27]

Comparable questions can be raised with regards to national legislation that limits the admission of foreign workers. The WTO may easily turn out to present legislation contrary to what national preferences might be.

---

[23] Dispute WTO/DS291/R, *European Communities – Measures Affecting the Approval and Marketing of Biotech Products*.

[24] The AB has made it clear that so far, it only marginally tests the undertaken risk assessments. But new jurisprudence may easily increase the criteria of such tests. Cf. Stefan Zleptnig, 'The Standard of Review in WTO Law: An analysis of law, legitimacy and the distribution of legal and political authority', in: *European Integration online Papers (EIoP)*, vol. 6, no. 17 (2002) 24 October 2002. Available online at http://eiop.or.at/eiop/texte/2002-017.htm.

[25] As is the text from article XX, sub (a) GATT.

[26] Dispute WT/DS285/AB/R, *United States – Measures Affecting the Cross-Border Supply of Gambling and Betting Services*.

[27] Jeremy C. Marwell, 'Trade and Morality: the WTO Public Morals Exception after *Gambling*', in: *New York University law review*, vol. 81 (May 2006) 802-842.

During the negotiations of new agreements in 2005, extensive debate was already devoted to the question whether Western countries should provide extended visa provisions to temporary professionals. 'How did immigration wind up on the table at the WTO?', one commentator wondered. He continued:

> Under the global trade body's General Agreement on Trade in Services (GATS), governments can regulate the supply of services performed by foreigners. (...) The wrangling over visas is just one more example of the WTO's mission creep.
>
> Global trade rules are no longer aimed merely at eliminating tariffs on goods that cross borders. (...) And any domestic law, including public interest regulations, can be challenged under WTO rules as 'an unfair barrier to trade'.[28]

Like aiming for a 'level playing field', the bringing about of which has allowed the EU to realize a virtually boundless expansion of its powers, the removal of 'trade barriers' is theoretically endless in its application, and grants the WTO a limitless pretext for overruling whatever national policy it may find in its way.

Take for instance the WTO's rulings on agricultural and technological subsidies. The Appellate Body of the WTO decided on March 3rd, 2005, in the case on US Cotton subsidies,[29] that these Cotton subsidies were in violation of international agreements on agricultural support. Likewise, questions related to European agricultural subsidies may be brought before the WTO some time in the future. With regards to European subsidies for technological industries, this has in fact already happened. On May 18th, 2011, the Appellate Body ruled that some of the European subsidies for Airbus had 'adverse effects to the interests of the United States', and that therefore the European Union ought to 'take appropriate steps to remove the adverse effects or (...) withdraw the subsidy'.[30] But surely the WTO's agreements were not subscribed to with such rulings in mind? Moreover, is it in a world dominated by American giants like Boeing and Lockheed Martin – which received structural state-support in years preceding the WTO's existence – not perfectly reasonable that European states support their own aviation industry?

Since it has been in operation, from January 1st, 1995, the AB has in the past 16 years decided on well over 300 cases.[31] The whole dispute settlement body, including the decisions of the arbitration panels, comprises roughly the same amount. Not all of these cases have stretched the scope of the agreements or

---

[28] Sarah Anderson, 'US immigration policy on the table at the WTO', in: *Global Politician*, 12 March 2005. Available online at http://www.globalpolitician.com/21446-immigration.

[29] Dispute WT/DS267/R, *United States – Subsidies on Upland Cotton*.

[30] WT/DS316/AB/R, *European Communities and Certain Member States – Measures Affecting Trade in Large Civil Aircraft*. Available online at http://docsonline.wto.org/GEN_catalogViewAllBottom.as p?ct=DDFEnglish%2CDDFFrench%2CDDFSpanish&c2=@meta_Serial_Num&q2=11-2462&c3=@ meta_Symbol&q3=%22WT%FCDS316%FCAB%FCR%22&c1=@meta_Language&q1=E.

[31] Information from the website of the WTO, available online at http://www.wto.org/english/ tratop_e/dispu_e/disp_settlement_cbt_e/intro1_e.htm.

increased the power of the WTO. But with each decision or ruling that did, a precedent was created, and the jurisprudence was further tightenened.

It is possible and indeed not unlikely that in the future other cases will be brought before the AB. These case may involve ethical or environmental issues, such as restrictions on bio-industried cattle, meat or crops from radio-active regions (such as Chernobyl), restrictions on ritually slaughtered meat (Halal), and commodities such as textiles produced by child-labour or by de facto (e.g. economic) slavery, as well as trade issues with countries that perform policies inimical to the values of Western countries that they may wish to install trade sanctions against.[32] A policy of cultural protectionism – such as the French law that a certain percentage of songs broadcast on national radio ought to be of French origin – may also easily be found to be in violation of agreements on free trade. Whether or not all these policies are permissible, and whether or not nations have to accept full foreign participation on their national markets and national culture and public sphere is now ultimately in the hands of the WTO.

Now it is not the purpose of this chapter to defend any particular political position. Rather it is to point out that none of the positions claimed by supranational organizations are themselvels universal, i.e. free of political choice. Through the WTO, a neoliberal view has been institutionalized, and this view is certainly not undisputed. Protectionism is not indefensible and indeed not without intellectual support.[33] Since the financial crisis of 2008, this point has even become more serious.

While the hostility of the WTO to protectionism may well be a respectable political position, it certainly is not a universal one. The view that protectionism is no longer of this age is disputable. One can argue for it or against it. If it is the purpose of a national government to act in the interest of its population, it is not self-evident that a supranational organization should be allowed to make the assessment of whether the national market should be opened to foreign products or not.

It is often said, that for international trade to flourish, concessions are required, and that 'we can't have it all our way'. As Jeremy Rabkin puts it, 'the claim that the WTO can impose binding "law" rests on the hope that interests within each country will support the organization and its authority, even if they are disappointed in particular rulings'.[34] But economic 'interests' do not always trump others. There are many things that would, strictly speaking, be in our

---

[32] Cf. Jeremy C. Marwell, (May 2006) 802-842.
[33] Cf. Paul Krugman, *Pop Internationalism* (Cambridge, MA: MIT Press, 1997); Russel Roberts, *The Choice: A fable of free trade and protection*. Third Edition (New Jersey: Prentice Hall, 2006); Tim Lang and Colin Hines, *The New Protectionism: Protecting the Future against Free Trade* (London: Earthscan Publications, 1993), Ralph Nader et al., *The Case against "Free Trade"*: GATT, NAFTA, *and the Globalization of Corporate Power* (Berkeley: North Atlantic Books, 1993).
[34] Rabkin (2007) 229.

economic interests, but that we still do not do. The WTO imposes free trade by unfree choice, irrespective of either national policy or majority opinion, or both.

Whether or not there is a good rationale behind these ethical or cultural modifications of the free-play of merely economic forces is beside the point. The point is that ethical and cultural considerations *can* play a role in the policy of a state, and that it is therefore not always a matter of *evidence* or *efficiency* whether import restrictions should be upheld. Even if a certain measure will make the economy flourish, it can still be against the wish of the population, as could be the case with opening up markets to the products of industrialized farming, or opening borders to the import of cheaper products.

Nor would an alternative to the WTO have to be a return to full protectionism. In 1913, when no supranational organization existed that coordinated national trade barriers, there were proportionally more international investments being made than until well into the 1990s.[35] As this shows, any trade agreement drawn by state parties, any form of international deal, might still be made without a supranational organization seeing to it. And there can surely be many middle ways between the global free-market as propounded by the WTO, and the isolationist extreme of the autarkic state.

5.2. *The Security Council*

In 1816, Lord Byron wrote:

> The Psalmist number'd out the years of man:
> They are enough: and if thy tale be true,
> Thou, who didst grudge him even that fleeting span,
> More than enough, thou fatal Waterloo!
> Millions of tongues record thee, and anew
> Their children's lips shall echo them, and say –
> 'Here, where the sword united nations drew,
> Our countrymen were warring on that day!'
> And this is much, and all which will not pass away.

This poem, part of the *Child Harold's Pilgrimage* ballad, refers to the battle of Waterloo where in 1815 a coalition of mainly British and Prussian armies defeated Napoleon and his dream of a unified Europe. Referring to this poem, Winston Churchill suggested the term *United Nations* to Franklin D. Roosevelt when speaking of the Allied forces that were combating Nazi-Germany's pan-European ambitions. On January 1st, 1942, at an international conference in the United States, the Allied coalition made a *Declaration by United Nations*, expressing

---

[35] Cf. Paul Bairoch, 'European Trade Policy, 1815-1914', in: P. Mathias and S. Pollard (eds.), *Cambridge Economic History of Europe*, vol. 8, 'The industrial economies: the development of social and economic policies' (Cambridge University Press: 1989) 103-126, 'Colonial trade policies'.

their determination to defeat the Axis powers and restore national sovereignty to the states of Europe.

The allies continued to use the term, and after Germany and Japan had been defeated, a permanent international organization, successor to the League of Nations, was established in New York, and called the *United Nations Organization*.

In many respects, the United Nations Organization (which was referred to from the 1950s onwards simply as 'the United Nations', as if it had 'outgrown' being merely an 'organization') was nothing new. Its main deliberative body, the General Assembly, was an extended version of the Assembly of the League of Nations – and the charters of both confirmed the principles of classical international law (see chapters 1 and 2). Most of the work of the United Nations is concerned with streamlining international diplomacy and creating an arena for discussion in which global issues can be addressed.

There was, however, one very new idea involved at the inception of the United Nations, and that was the Security Council. For the first time since the birth of modern states, they have accepted that an international body can approve or disapprove their military interventions and that it can even call for the undertaking of military interventions in its own right. It was largely through the Security Council that the United Nations 'was intended by its founders to be far more than "a method for carrying on relations between states"'.[36] How was this major revolution in international politics possible?

There seem to have been at least two reasons. Firstly, after the devastation of the Second World War, the necessity for international cooperation was felt to exist. In the minds of many, it was at least partly due to the failure of the League of Nations that World War II broke out, and a stronger international governing body would therefore help prevent the occasion of further 'untold sorrow'.[37] Secondly, the Security Council provided a uniquely powerful position in world affairs for the permanent five members. Having won the Second World War, they were able to establish their power on a more permanent basis through the Security Council, taking up the role, in the words of Franklin D. Roosevelt, of 'global policemen'.[38]

If, under chapter VII of the United Nations Charter, the Security Council determines a situation to constitute a

---

[36] Rosemary Righter, *Utopia Lost* (New York: A twentieth century fund press, 1995) 25. The quote is from Alfred Zimmern, *The League of Nations and the Rule of Law, 1918-1935* (London: Macmillan, 1936) 1.

[37] As the preamble of the United Nations Charter starts: 'We the peoples of the united nations determined to save succeeding generations from the scourge of war, which twice in our lifetime has brought untold sorrow to mankind …'.

[38] Quoted in Rosemary Righter, *Utopia Lost* (1995) 25.

threat to the peace, breach of the peace, or act of aggression,[39]

it may, ultimately,

> take such action by air, sea, or land forces as may be necessary to maintain or
> restore international peace and security.[40]

It is important to note that the five permanent members of the Security Council, the United States, the United Kingdom, France, Russia, and China, have a veto power in the Security Council. This means that for those five members, the Security Council does not in fact have supranational powers.

The foundation of the UN's system of international security is the members' abjuration of the right to use force against one another. Article 2, paragraph 4 of the UN Charter states that 'All members shall refrain in their international disputes from the threat or use of force …'. Since in addition to that rule, the charter recognizes only the 'inherent right of individual or collective self-defense' (in article 51), it must follow that article 42 of Chapter VII vests the Security Council with the only other right to the legitimate use of force.

This means that a foreign policy decision by national executives or parliaments to use force – not dictated by strict self-defense – would from now on be dependent on the approval of the Security Council. And this would include the power of the United States, Russia, China, the UK and France to block a resolution to this effect with a veto.

The emergence of the Cold War soon after the end of the Second World War caused the Security Council to be constantly, and deeply, divided. As Rosemary Righter notes, the United Nations was 'ill-constructed for the actual tensions of the post-1945 world'.[41] That is why most Security Council resolutions were ineffective or simply weren't passed in the first forty years of its existence.

Until the fall of the Berlin Wall, use of force was authorized only one single time by the Security Council, and that was when the Soviet delegate was absent: June 25th, 1950 saw not only the invasion by North Korean troops of South Korea, but also an immediate session of the Security Council resulting in an ultimatum to North Korea to withdraw, and ultimately a UN sanctioned military intervention.[42]

But after this event, Russia never missed another session of the Security Council, and until the fall of the Berlin Wall, the Security Council did not issue a single resolution approving the use of force under Chapter VII (while considerable military conflict certainly took place during those years). Indeed, there has

---

[39] UN Charter, article 39.
[40] UN Charter, article 42.
[41] Rosemary Righter (1995) 41.
[42] UN Security Council resolution 82, June 25th, 1950, available online at http://daccess-dds-ny.un.org/doc/RESOLUTION/GEN/NR0/064/95/IMG/NR006495.pdf?OpenElement.

been such a great number of military conflicts that it has been suggested that after so many years of disuse, the UN Charter had lost its legal standing (even if formally, the treaty had not been annulled or altered), on the principle of *non usus*, one of the oldest principles of contract law, formalized by the Romans. When a rule has not been practiced for years on end, it becomes customary law to ignore it.[43]

If we look at the obvious violations of the prohibition to use force that have occurred without the condemnation nor the approval of the Security Council (the Russian interventions in Hungary and Czechoslovakia, the war in Vietnam, the Six Days' War, the Yom Kippur war, the war between Iraq and Iran, the Russian invasion of Afghanistan, the Falkland War, and NATO's intervention in Kosovo, to name but a few), it can hardly be said that throughout the second half of the twentieth century such a thing as 'international law' existed that had anything to do with the Security Council or its Charter.[44]

Nor could it be argued that military interventions since 1945 have always been in direct self-defense. Three clear examples:

First, the invasion of Cambodia by Vietnam in 1978, undertaken while the UN remained incapable of condemning or even of commenting on the mass killings that were being perpetrated from 1975 onwards by the Khmer Rouge in Cambodia (called Kampuchea at the time). The Vietnamese government installed a puppet regime that put a stop to the killings. The only response of the UN was on October 13th, 1980, when the UN General Assembly voted *against* the motion to remove the representative of the Khmer Rouge Regime (which had effectively lost power to the Vietnamese puppet regime) from its seat at the UN.[45]

Second, the pre-emptive strike on Iraqi nuclear plants by Israel in 1981, which were believed by the latter (as well as by many others) to be manufacturing nuclear weapons. Israel was condemned by the Security Council for doing so in its resolution of June 19th, 1981, because Iraq was a signatory to the non-proliferation treaty and the military attack by Israel was 'in clear violation of the Charter of the United Nations and the norms of international conduct.'[46]

---

[43] As the *Encyclopedic Dictionary of Roman Law* defines Desuetudo: 'A long continued non-application of a legal norm. Although *desuetude* does not formally abrogate a law, the latter easily falls into oblivion and loses its force in practice. "Laws are repealed not only by the will of the legislator but also by disuse through the tacit consent of all men" (D. 1.3.32.1). In connection with the compilation of the Digest, Justinian ordered that laws which had vanished by *desuetude* should not be taken into consideration – *In desuetudinem abire = to pass out of use.*' Adolf Berger, *Encyclopedic Dictionary of Roman Law. New Series* – volume 43, part 2 (Philadelphia: The American Philosophical Society, 1953, reprinted in 1989).

[44] Cf. Franck, T.M., 'Who Killed Article 2(4)? Or: Changing Norms Governing the Use of Force by States', in: *American Journal for International Law*, Vol. 64, No. 5 (Oct., 1970) 809-837.

[45] Rosemary Righter (1995) 326-327.

[46] Security Council resolution 487 (1981), Adopted at its 2288th meeting on 19 June 1981. Available online at http://daccess-dds-ny.un.org/doc/RESOLUTION/GEN/NR0/418/74/IMG/

Third, the US-led invasion on October 25th, 1983, of the small Caribbean Island of Grenada. At the time, Grenada was led by the communist Maurice Bishop, and according to United States intelligence, it was establishing a Cuban military base. A resolution 'deeply deploring' the armed intervention in Grenada, 'which constitutes a flagrant violation of international law and of the independence, sovereignty and territorial integrity of that State',[47] was adopted in the General Assembly by a vote of 122 in favor to 9 against, with 27 abstentions (a similar resolution was debated in the Security Council, but not surprisingly it was vetoed by the United States).

None of these military interventions were indisputably unjust. One was carried out in part to put an end to genocide; two were carried out by developed, Western democracies on the basis of an assessment of their vital national interests. It is unlikely that countries will refrain from such interventions in the future, while it is equally unlikely that the UN Security Council will carry them out as a collective body. It is therefore unlikely that the half-hearted interpretation of the prohibition of the use of force in the UN Charter will change in the foreseeable future.

However, after the collapse of the Soviet regime, there was a moment of dramatic optimism. On September 11th, 1990, George H. Bush announced a 'new world order', in which international interventions would be sanctioned by the Security Council. Less than a year after the fall of the Berlin Wall, Bush declared in his speech to Congress, that:

> Clearly, no longer can a dictator count on East-West confrontation to stymie concerted United Nations action against aggression.[48]

Bush said that 'a new partnership of nations has begun', and that 'we stand today at a unique and extraordinary moment. The crisis in the Persian Gulf, as grave as it is, also offers a rare opportunity to move toward an historic period of cooperation. Out of these troubled times, (…) a new world order can emerge: A new era – freer from the threat of terror, stronger in the pursuit of justice and more secure in the quest for peace'. Bush expected the emergence of

> a world quite different from the one we've known. A world where the rule of law supplants the rule of the jungle. A world in which nations recognize the shared responsibility for freedom and justice. A world where the strong respect the rights of the weak.

All of this was the case, according to Bush, because:

NR041874.pdf?OpenElement.

[47] General Assembly resolution 38/7 of 1983, available online at http://daccess-dds-ny.un.org/doc/RESOLUTION/GEN/NR0/443/99/IMG/NR044399.pdf?OpenElement.

[48] George H. W. Bush, *Toward a New World Order*. Speech given to a joint session of the United States Congress, Washington DC, 11 September 1990.

> We're now in sight of a United Nations that performs as envisioned by its founders.

These words surely reflect a dream that lies at the foundation of much enthusiasm for supranationalism: a community of nations, all equally just, coming together to cooperate for the shared destiny of mankind. But after the 'success' in obtaining UN support for the invasion of Iraq, the aftermath turned out to be as frustrating as in the other operations in which the UN had been in charge. Saddam Hussein continued to flout the conditions of the ceasefire. The organization charged with overseeing the discontinuation of the Iraqi program of weapons of mass destruction, UNSCOM, reported time and again on the obstruction that prevented it from doing its work properly. Yet the UN failed to impose effective sanctions.

Nor did the UN show leadership during the Rwandan genocide in 1994, and though the Security Council admitted responsibility in 2000 'for failing to stop the killings',[49] and the Undersecretary General responsible for peacekeeping operations at the time, Kofi Annan, later admitted that he 'could and should have done more',[50] he was nevertheless appointed Secretary General in 1996.[51]

But in any case: the Security Council exercises two supranational powers: first, it can begin a war when it believes international peace and security have been threatened, and second, it can condemn the use of force by member states, ultimately by imposing sanctions on them and employing military intervention against them.

A third major power of the Security Council, however, is that it can also decide on the implementation of sanctions when it believes certain countries have seriously violated obligations under international law. An example is the Nicaraguan case before the International Court of Justice,[52] in which the United States was condemned to pay indemnification to Nicaragua for its aggression in supporting rebels that opposed the pro-communist regime. But the United States had withdrawn from the case, rejecting the ICJ's jurisdiction (see also chapter 4.4). The Security Council then proposed a resolution demanding that the United States comply with the rulings of the ICJ. Of course, the United States was able to veto this resolution. But if a non-veto power had been in the position of the US in this case, sanctions might have been imposed on it. And this is not confined to the deliberations of the ICJ, but may also be applied to rulings of

---

[49] Cf. the report of the *Independent Inquiry into United Nations actions during the 1994 Rwanda genocide*, accepted by the Security Council on 14 April, 2000, available online at http://www.un.org/sc/committees/918/htm/6843e.html.

[50] Kofi Annan, *Speech at the memorial conference of 26 March 2004, New York*. Available online at http://www.un.org/News/Press/docs/2004/sgsm9223.doc.htm.

[51] Cf. http://www.un.org/sg/annan.shtml.

[52] Military and paramilitary activities in and against Nicaragua *(Nicaragua v. United States of America)*, Merits, Judgment, ICJ Reports 1986.

other arbitration mechanisms endorsed or recognized by the UN, for instance, the International Labor Organization, the World Health Organization, or the Human Rights Council. Surely, this places an instrument of enormous power in the hands of its 15 members.

Now, it is highly unlikely that the Security Council will rule against vital interests of Western states. Their veto powers and strong alliances with one another will probably prevent the 'international community' from waging a war against any of them. But this is so only as long as they have their three veto powers (in the hands of the US, the UK and France). Should any of the 'reforms' that are regularly being proposed be accepted, making, for instance, veto powers rotate on a periodical basis upon recommendation by the General Assembly, the Security Council will have supranational powers that will enable it to actually develop dangerously unpredictable policies.[53]

5.3. THE EUROPEAN UNION

The EU is the most complex of the supranational organizations discussed in this book. It has many different levels of functioning and its internal structure has grown in a somewhat haphazard way, which, like an old city, leads to many surprising shortcuts, meandering pathways, and sudden dead-ends.[54]

There are, moreover, three 'readings' of the EU, of which only the third is the supranational one. First, there are those who argue that the current EU is, however imperfectly, a first step towards a 'United States of Europe', that is to say, a European federal state. They are therefore not, as I have explained, advocates of supranationalism, though of course they may in some cases accept the EU's current supranationalism as a necessary intermediary stage between the old nation states and a new European nation state to come.[55] They take what I call the 'federal approach' to the EU.

---

[53] Yehuda Z. Blum, 'Proposals for UN Security Council Reform', in: *The American Journal of International Law*, Vol. 99, No. 3 (July, 2005) 632-649; Jacqueline London, 'The reform of the United Nations Security Council: What role for the European Union?', *Conference Working Paper: United Nations and Security Council Reform: Proposals for the future.* (Madrid, INCIPE Assembly Hall, 29th June, 2007) available online at http://www.incipe.org/UNSCreform.html.

[54] See for example Luuk van Middelaar, *De passage naar Europa* (Amsterdam: Amsterdam University Press, 2009); Stanley Henig, *The Uniting of Europe. From discord to concord* (London: Routledge, 1997). An insightful and more general account of Europe's post-1945 political history is Tony Judt, *Postwar. A history of Europe since 1945* (London: Pimlico, Random House, 2007).

[55] An example is A.A.M. Kinneging, 'United we stand, divided we fall, a case for the United States of Europe', in: *Ibidem* (ed.), *Rethinking Europe's Constitution* (Nijmegen: Wolf Legal Publishers, 2007). Cf. K. Nicolaidis and R. Howse (eds.), *The Federal Vision, Legitimacy and levels of governance in the United States and the European Union*, (Oxford: Oxford University Press, 2001); A.G. Harryvan and J. van der Harst (eds.), *Documents on European Union* (London: Macmillan Press ltd., 1997).

Then there are those who see the EU as a project of primarily economic intergovernmental cooperation, conceptually not much different from a free trade zone, who desire to minimize its supranational powers, like those related to the single currency and the open borders agreement of Schengen. I call this the confederal approach.

Both the federalists and the confederalists do not advocate supranationalism in the sense that it is understood in this book. Both accept the logic of the traditional idea of sovereignty (as discussed in part I) – the first applying it on a larger scale, the second, though accepting minor supranational powers, attempting to retain it at the level of the member states. Moreover, for both federalists and confederalists the present EU is hardly satisfactory. While the EU does far more than merely streamline cooperation between its member states, and thereby antagonizes the confederalists, it officially professes no ambition to assume the full responsibilities of a federal state (though surely there are steps in this direction even if tentative and unsuccessful).

Indeed, by rejecting both federalism and confederalism – by renouncing sovereignty for itself while simultaneously denying it to its member states – the European Union is the quintessential supranational project. Its official aim, as abundantly described and advocated by the national European elites that support it, is 'the negation of the concept of statehood';[56] the EU exists not to create a European sovereignty, but to dissolve the borders, sovereignty and statehood of its members. Thus in speeches and writings about the European Union, the phrases are often untoned that 'the EU will never be a state' and 'we need a strong, united Europe', as if there were not an obvious contradiction between the two.[57]

To be sure, there is nothing new or supranational in the acknowledgment of a shared European culture and a common European interest. Historically, the shared lot of the European peoples has been recognized from a very early stage onwards.[58] In descriptions of the battle of Poitiers of 732, for instance, we already find references to 'les gens d'Europe', who see the tents of the invading Sarrasins,

---

[56] Karl Jaspers, *Freiheit und Wiedervereinigung*, (München: Piper, 1969) 53: 'Die Geschichte des deutschen Nationalstaats ist zu Ende, nicht die Geschichte der Deutschen. Was wir als grosse Nation uns und der Welt leisten können, ist die Einsicht in die Weltsituation heute: dass der Nationalstaatsgedanke heute das Unheil Europas und nun auch aller Kontinente ist. Während der Nationalstaatsgedanke die heute übermächtige zerstörende Kraft der Erde ist, können wir beginnen, ihn in der Wurzel zu durchschauen und aufzuheben.' See also: Wolfgang J. Mommsen, 'Varieties of Nation State in Modern History', in: Michael Mann, *The rise and decline of the Nation State* (Oxford: Basil Blackwell, 1990).

[57] See for example Robert Cooper, 'Oorlog en vrede: de geboorte van de Europese identiteit', in: Leonard Ornstein & Lo Breemer (eds.), *Paleis Europa. Grote denkers over Europa* (Amsterdam: De Bezige Bij, 2007) 55-76; Laurens Jan Brinkhorst, *Speech for the European Week Eindhoven*, 27 May, 2009; Glyn Morgan, *The idea of a European Superstate. Public Justification and European Integration* (Princeton: Princeton University Press, 2005), especially chapter 6: 'A postsovereign Europe'.

[58] Cf. Rémi Brague, *Europe. La voie Romaine* (Paris: Gallimard, 1992).

or who fear an ambush.[59] This sense of a common European identity (and not,
as the legend has Bismarck say, as a merely 'geographical concept'[60]), continued
to exist throughout the centuries – from the coronation of Charlemagne to the
crusades and the discovery of the 'New' World. Though the Reformation and
the religious wars that followed broke the political power of the Vatican, the
battles of Vienna (1521) and Lepanto (1571), and the siege of Vienna (1683), clearly
inspired those living in the West to recognize their common Roman-Christian
heritage. Pope Pius II wrote a book entitled *Europe* in 1458, describing this cultural
sphere, and he advocated a new crusade against the Turks who had conquered
Constantinople a few years before.[61] The Duke of Sully, minister of the French
King Henry IV, likewise proposed the setting up of a 'High Council' in which
the heads of the European states would come together, and which would meet
in Venice. The Council would take direct command of troops that would help
the members defend themselves against the Ottoman Empire.[62]

Napoleon went further. During his exile in St.-Helena, he reflected that the
terrible and endless wars he had brought to Europe had served the purpose of
unifying the several states of the continent. His biographer and companion to
St.-Helena, Emmanuel comte de Las Cases, noted that 'what [Napoleon] had
wanted for the prosperity, for the interests and for the well-being of Europe
was the same principles, identical everywhere, a European legal code, a single
European court of appeals, to correct all mistakes like our court of appeals
corrects the mistakes of our district courts, a single currency, the same weights,
the same measures, the same laws, etc.'.[63] According to Las Cases, Napoleon
expected Europe to

---

[59] 'les gens d'Europe voient les tentes du camp (...) les gens d'Europe craignent que, caches le
long des sentiers, les Sarrasins ne tendent des embuscades.' Jean-Henry Roy and Jean Deviosse,
La Bataille de Poitiers. ... October 733 (Paris: Gallimard, 1966) 294: 'Extrait de l'Anonyme de
Cordoue (Vers 1376 à 1437)'.
[60] Bismarck, November 1876, as quoted in: Timothy Garton Ash, *In Europe's name. Germany
and the divided continent* (London: Jonathan Cape, 1997) 387. Cf. Luuk van Middelaar, *De Passage
naar Europa. Geschiedenis van een begin* (Amsterdam: Historische uitgeverij, 2009) 31.
[61] Jacques Le Goff, *The Birth of Europe*. Translated by Janet Lloyd (Oxford: Blackwell Publishing,
2005) 186.
[62] Cf. Arthur Nussbaum, *A Concise history of the law of nations* (New York: The Macmillan
Company, 1961) 113ff.
[63] 'Ce qu'il eût proposé pour la prospérité, les intérêts et le bien-être de l'association européenne:
il eût voulu les mêmes principes, le même partout, un code européen, une cour de cassation
européenne, redressant pour tous les erreurs comme la nôtre redresse celles de nos tribunaux, une
même monnaie sous des coins différents, les mêmes poids, les mêmes mesures, les mêmes lois, etc'.
As quoted in Marcel Dunan, 'La veritable place de Napoléon dans l'histoire de l'Europe', in: André
Puttemans (ed.), *Napoléon et l'Europe* (Paris: Éditions Brepolis, 1965) 152. The classical source for
Napoleon's eurofederalist ideas is formed by his conversations on St.-Helena, written down by
his companion: Emmanuel comte de Las Cases, *Le Mémorial de Sainte-Hélène. Première edition
intégrale et critique établie par Marcel Dunan* (Paris: Flammarion, 1951). For a critical analysis of
the historiography on Napoleon's ideas, see Natalie Petiteau, 'Débats historiographiques autour

soon become a truly single nation, and everyone, freely travelling the continent, would find himself always in the same fatherland.[64]

There was a lot of enthusiasm for a united Europe in the 19th century, too, though it has often been dismissed as 'the nationalist century'. From Madame de Staël to Oswald Spengler, from Victor Hugo to Ernest Renan (see chapter 3):[65] all discussed the cultural unity of Europe and the possible future of the different nations within a common framework. There remained, moreover, a common European aristocracy throughout the 19th century. The major stylistic developments in the arts have been Europe-wide, and there was a European *haute couture*. European royal and aristocratic families routinely intermarried as well.[66]

In 1923, Count Richard Coudenhove-Kalergi published a manifest called *Paneuropa*.[67] In it, he argued for the political unification of Europe because, after the First World War, the separate European states that together represented the European culture and way of life, were in his view not strong enough to stand up any longer to 'den wachsenden aussereuropäischen Weltmächten'[68] – and in a conversation with the Finnish foreign minister, R. Witting, on November 28th, 1941, Adolf Hitler was recorded to have said that 'it was gradually becoming clear that the nations of Europe belonged together like a great family of nations' (see also chapter 8).[69]

The strong vision of a unified Europe that the Americans, Churchill, the Alsatian Robert Schuman and the Frenchman Jean Monnet (as well as many others) had after the Second World War was therefore nothing new.[70] In the original plans – the pre-supranational phase –, the idea of a federal United

---

de la politique européenne de Napoléon', in: Jean-Clément Martin (ed.), *Napoléon et l'Europe. Colloque de la Roche-sur-Yon* (Rennes: Presses Universitaires, 2002) 19-31, and Roger Caratini, *Napoléon, une imposture* (Paris: Michel Lafon, 1998).

[64] 'L'Europe, disait-il, n'eût bientôt fait de la sorte, véritablement qu'un même peuple, et chacun, en voyageant partout, se fût trouvé toujours dans la patrie commune'.

[65] Cf. Oswald Spengler, *Der Untergang des Abendlandes. Umrisse einer Morphologie der Weltgeschichte* (Düsseldorf: Albatros, 2007) 196.

[66] It is worth mentioning here as well the similar styles of dress across Europe, as well as the speed of communication of for instance scientific and other new discoveries.

[67] The movement that this manifest gave birth to gathered a great number of prominent followers, including Albert Einstein, Pablo Picasso, Sigmund Freud, Thomas Mann, Paul Valery, and Guillaume Apollinaire. Cf. Christopher Booker and Richard North, *The Great Deception. Can the European Union survive?* Second Edition (London: Continuum, 2005) 11.

[68] Richard Nicolaus Coudenhove-Kalergi, *Paneuropa* (Wien-Leipzig: Paneuropa Verlag, 1926).

[69] Walter Hewel, 'record of conversation between Hitler and the Finnish foreign minister, R. Witting, 28 November 1941', in: Walter Lipgens (ed.), *Documents on the History of European Integration* (Berlin and New York: De Gruyter, 1985) 94.

[70] Although Churchill did not think the United Kingdom would be part of this. In his speech at the University of Zurich in 1946, he declared: 'We British have our own Commonwealth of Nations. (…) And why should there not be a European group which could give a sense of enlarged patriotism and common citizenship to the distracted peoples of this turbulent and mighty continent? (…) In all this urgent work, France and Germany must take the lead together. Great Britain, the British Commonwealth of Nations, mighty America and (…) Soviet Russia (…) must

States of Europe was prominent. Robert Schuman, in his speech on the 9th of May, 1950, had said:

> The contribution, which an organised and living Europe can bring to civilisation, is indispensable to the maintenance of peaceful relations.
>
> (…)
>
> The pooling of coal and steel production should immediately provide for the setting up of common foundations for economic development as a first step in the federation of Europe.
>
> (…)
>
> This proposal will lead to the realisation of the first concrete foundation of a European federation indispensable to the preservation of peace.[71]

Aiming at a European federation, Jean Monnet is said to have stated in a memo of 3 April 1952: 'The fusion (of economic functions) would compel nations to fuse their sovereignty into that of a single European State'. Already in 1943, Monnet had argued that 'There will be no peace in Europe if states are reconstituted on a basis of national sovereignty (…) Prosperity and vital social progress will remain elusive until the nations of Europe form a federation or a 'European entity' which will forge them into a single economic unit'.[72]

It was not only an ideal to proceed to a federal structure of a united Europe. It was also a felt necessity. As the Cold War deepened, a demilitarized Germany was gradually becoming impossible to sustain. The re-militarization of Germany was combined with a plan to dilute the sovereignty of Germany, so that a new war between Germany and France would be, in Robert Schuman's words, 'not only unthinkable, but also impossible'.[73] The initial plan – the plan for a federal Europe – consisted in the establishment of three institutions: a coal and steel community, a defense community, and a political community.

First, the European Coal and Steel Community (ECSC). It established a common market for the two essential products of a war economy, coal and steel. A 'High Authority', based in Luxembourg, would ensure that the same prices were charged for these products in all member states, with no import or export duties or restrictions.

---

be the friends and sponsors of the new Europe and must champion its right to live and shine.' Available online at http://www.peshawar.ch/varia/winston.htm.

[71] Robert Schuman, *Speech of 9 May 1950*, available online at http://europa.eu/abc/symbols/9-may/decl_en.htm.

[72] Note of 5 August 1943, Algiers. Reprinted in: Pascal Fontaine, *Jean Monnet. A grand design for Europe* (Luxembourg: Office for Official publications of the European Communities, 1988) 41.

[73] Schuman declaration, May 9th, 1950. Cf. http://www.eppgroup.eu/Activities/docs/divers/schuman-en.pdf.

Second, a European Defense Community (EDC), to establish a supranational European defense force whose procurement and operations would be united.[74]

Third, a European Political Community (EPC), that would establish a directly elected assembly ('the Peoples' Chamber'), a Senate appointed by national parliaments and a supranational executive accountable to the parliament.

If combined, these three institutions would have formed an almost complete federal structure (thereby, in the terminology explained in earlier chapters of this book, ceasing to be 'supranational').[75]

The least far-reaching of the aforementioned proposals, the ECSC, was the only one to be brought into existence. Though both the EDC and the EPC treaties were drafted, the EDC was discarded after the French parliament – upon initiative by General De Gaulle's patriotic party – began singing the *Marseillaise* in 1954 when the EDC was presented.[76] The EPC treaty was not even debated further.

The architect of the three treaties was Jean Monnet, an unschooled son of a Cognac producing family. He had dreamed of a united Europe from an early age, and acknowledged that the three treaties taken together would have produced the political integration of Europe (historical research also suggests that Monnet may have received covert support from the CIA[77]). Now that this project had obviously failed, Monnet devoted his energies to economic integration, resulting in the European Economic Community, founded by the Treaty of Rome in 1957.[78]

From then on, the ultimate goal of European integration became blurred. Jean Monnet himself, though he had previously been clear about the final form of the European project (i.e. a federal state), now professed an open future, into which it was even harmful to enquire, and the following quote is typical of the prose thenceforth produced by proponents of the European project:[79]

> We want the Community to be a gradual process of change. Attempting to predict the form it will finally take is therefore a contradiction in terms. Anticipating the

---

[74] Van Middelaar (2009) 206ff.

[75] Stanley Henig, *The Uniting of Europe. From discord to concord* (London: Routledge, 1997) 25ff.

[76] The position of Winston Churchill towards the EDC may not have been entirely without influence. He was recorded picturing 'a bewildered French drill sergeant sweating over a platoon made up of a few Greeks, Italians, Germans, Turks, and Dutchmen, all in utter confusion over the simplest orders …'. Dean Acheson, *Present at the creation. My years in the State Department* (New York: W.W. Norton and Company, 1970) 765.

[77] Christopher Booker and Richard North, *The Great Deception. Can the European Union survive?* Second Edition (London: Continuum, 2005) 87.

[78] The Treaty of Rome established a wide-ranging package of economic cooperation with supranational governance, to be unfolded in the decades to come. For instance, it arranged for a customs union within 12 years after adoption.

[79] The vagueness of the prose of proponents of the European projects reminds of Mrs. Gradgrind in Charles Dickens' novel *Hard Times*, who said when asked if she was in pain: 'I think there's a pain in the room, but I couldn't positively say that I've got it'. Cf. for the deliberate manipulation of language for political purposes: Viktor Klemperer, *The Language of the Third Reich* (London: Continuum, 2006).

outcome kills invention. It is only as we push forwards and upwards that we will discover new horizons.[80]

It is no longer the official aim of most advocates of the European Union to move ultimately towards a 'United States of Europe'. Thus Paul de Grauwe, former economic advisor to the European Commission's President José Barroso, for instance said in an interview with the Belgian daily *De Morgen* on 18 March 2006, 'With the exception of a Don Quixote like Guy Verhofstadt (…), I see nobody who is pushing the case for a political union'.[81]

Time and again, supporters of the EU argue for supranationalism, not federalism. They go to great lengths to make clear that 'the European Union is not a state and (…) will never be one',[82] in the words of Robert Cooper, senior advisor to Javier Solana, in 2007; that federalism is not the envisaged endpoint of the European unification or that such an endpoint would be completely unrealistic;[83] that, as the Dutch Queen Beatrix has said, 'Europe is a development process of which the contours are not clearly definable in advance, nor even exactly predictable'; and that 'the further unification of Europe does not mean that national culture and national identity lose importance. On the contrary: national language, national culture, in short, singularity and self-consciousness are of vital importance.'[84]

According to those defending the current EU's political arrangement, any country in Europe could become a member of this hybrid, supranational construction since the European Union 'will never become a state'. Thus Tony Blair in his speech to the European Parliament on June 23rd, 2005, spoke of 'the new rules to govern a Europe of 25 and in time 27, 28 and more member states',[85] and expressed his fear that Europe might stop expanding and confine itself to members that shared a cultural inheritance (thereby excluding Turkey), because, if so, 'Europe will become more narrow, more introspective and those

---

[80] Pascal Fontaine (1988) 25.

[81] http://www.free-europe.org/english/2006/07/the-euro-will-collapse-without-political-union-forecasts-top-adviser-to-commission-president-barroso/. Cf. Laurens Jan Brinkhorst, 'National Sovereignty in the EU: an outdated concept', in: M.K. Bulterman, L. Hancher, A. McDonnell and H. Sevenster (eds.), *Views of European Law from the Mountain. Liber amicorum for Piet Jan Slot* (Alphen aan den Rijn: Kluwer Law, 2009) 327-333, who writes that the EU 'is not a state, nor a state in the making'.

[82] Robert Cooper (2007) 55-76.

[83] Kemal Dervis, 'Het ene Europa is het andere niet', in: Leonard Ornstein & Lo Breemer (eds.) (2007).

[84] HRH Beatrix, Queen of the Netherlands, *Voorbeschouwing*, in: Leonard Ornstein & Lo Breemer (eds.) (2007).

[85] Tony Blair, *Speech of 23 June, 2005*, published on http://news.bbc.co.uk/1/hi/uk_politics/4122288.stm.

who garner support will be those not in the traditions of European idealism but in those of outdated nationalism and xenophobia.'[86]

There is even a European commissioner for 'enlargement'. The Finnish economist Olli Rehn, who held this position from 2004 till 2009, perhaps not surprisingly given his job to focus on 'enlargement', expressed a desire that Europe should continue expanding. In his speech of April 28th, 2009, he said:

> If the positive experience of the 12 Central and Eastern new member states is anything to go by, then clearly the future potentially holds equally beneficial developments for the Western Balkans and Turkey.[87]

The EU has not taken steps to take over entirely the national sovereignty of its member states, but 'to pool their sovereignty'[88] (as if sovereignty could be pooled without being destroyed).

Also remarkable in this context is that the 9th of May, the day on which Robert Schuman delivered his speech calling for a 'united Europe', has now become 'Europe day', the annual day of the collective celebration of the European Union. Yet in order to illustrate that the ideal of a 'United States of Europe' – of which Schuman had dreamed – has been abandoned, the slogan of that day is: 'Unity in Diversity' – thereby immediately contradicting the idea of something that would 'unite' the Europeans (as the only thing that unites them is apparently their 'diversity' – a logical impossibility[89]).

Nor is there in the speeches and documents of most European politicians and policy makers much reference to the shared culture, to the shared history, indeed to anything that would provide any kind of new national identity for a united Europe;[90] the enthusiasm for Turkey's accession into the EU is an excellent illustration of this.[91] Questions of cultural resemblance, social cohesion, sense of belonging, political allegiance, are all brushed aside, for Europe would not become a state itself, nor merely be an international, intergovernmental organization.

---

[86] *Ibidem.*

[87] And he continued: 'So what's next? Even the fastest scenario for the next accession of a new member state, likely to be Croatia, is clearly slower than the slowest envisaged scenario for the ratification of the Lisbon Treaty. Time is on our side: we can pursue deepening and widening in parallel. This has been and still remains the best recipe to build a strong and united Europe. Today Europe is truly whole and free. Let us keep it that way.' Olli Rehn, *Speech of 28 April 2009*, Berlin, available online at http://europa.eu/rapid/pressReleasesAction.do?reference=SPEECH/o 9/205&format=HTML&aged=0&language=EN&guiLanguage=en.

[88] This has been repeated time and again. For instance: Bruno Waterfield, 'Barroso hails the European "empire:"', *The Telegraph*, July 18th, 2007.

[89] And standing in great contrast with the American slogan, 'e pluribus unum'.

[90] Striking is in this respect the discussion over recognizing in the European Constitutional treaty of 2005, a reference to the shared 'Judeo-Christian' or the 'Classical-Humanistic' traditions of the European culture.

[91] Roberto de Mattei, *Turkey in Europe: benefit or catastrophe?* Translated by John Laughland (Herefordshire: Gracewing, 2009).

Europe would be something in between, of its own kind: *sui generis*. And so the integration has proceeded, the EU has acquired more members, and new treaties have marked the next steps in this increasingly self-confident project of economic, though allegedly not political, integration.[92]

Yet strangely enough, the rhetoric of political integration continues to pop up every now and then, as if arising, like the British Empire once allegedly had, in a fit of absence of mind.[93] A remarkable conference of the European Council, held in Stuttgart in 1983, amounted to a so-called 'solemn declaration of the European Union', containing such phrases as:

> The Heads of State or Government of the Member States of the European Communities meeting within the European Council resolved to continue the work begun on the basis of the Treaties of Paris and Rome and to create a united Europe, which is more than ever necessary in order to meet the dangers of the world situation, capable of assuming the responsibilities incumbent on it by virtue of its political role, its economic potential and its manifold links with other peoples (...)

And:

> The Heads of State or Government, on the basis of an awareness of a common destiny and the wish to affirm the European identity, confirm their commitment to progress towards an ever closer union among the peoples and Member States of the European Community.

There is an obvious contradiction between this 'solemn declaration' and the continuous efforts of political leaders to stress that Europe will never become a federal state. The 'European identity' that ought to be 'affirmed', the 'ever closer union' and the 'political role' of a 'united Europe' are irreconcilable with the claim that no such unification was ever on the agenda in the first place.

---

[92] As Ernst B. Haas, whose work will be further discussed below, put it: 'Federalism was the initial watchword. European unity was hailed with glowing phrases by Winston Churchill, Léon Blum, Alcide de Gasperi, Salvador de Madariaga. A "European Movement" was formed that sought to achieve federation by stressing the cultural unity of Western civilization and that drew heavily on the misery of Europe, overshadowed by the new giants of East and West. The pan-European ideal first enunciated by Count Coudenhove-Kalergi in 1923, extolling Europe to seek survival in a world increasingly dominated by the United States and the Soviet Union, was hailed once more. The result was failure: no federal institutions were created, no uniform enthusiasm for federation could be mobilized in equal measure on the continent, in Britain, and in Scandinavia. The record of failure stretched from the creation of the far-from-federal Council of Europe through the defeat of the European Defense Community treaty to the burial of the European Political Community project in 1954. Something else happened instead. Not cultural unity but economic advantage proved to be an acceptable shared goal among the Six. The failure of the federalist European Movement saw the rise of the "functionalist" school of techocrats led by Jean Monnet (...)'. In: Ernst B. Haas, *The Uniting of Europe. Political, social and economic forces 1950-1957* (Stanford: Stanford University Press, 1968) xix: 'Author's preface, 1968'.

[93] Sir John Robert Seeley, *The Expansion of England* (1883), 'We seem, as it were, to have conquered and peopled half the world in a fit of absence of mind'.

One explanation for this contradiction lies in the functionalist approach to institutions, which is a philosophy that studies 'processes' and indeed 'functions' rather than accountability and democratic mandates, and is specifically designed to evade questions of legitimacy.[94] As Ernst Haas, one of the key analysts of this approach, wrote in 1968: '… the fact of the matter is that Europe did not have a Bismarck in 1948 or 1950. In the absence of the statesman who can weld disparate publics together with the force of his vision (…) we have no alternative but to resort to gradualism, to indirection, to functionalism if we wish to integrate a region'.[95] (Who is the 'we' here, one may ask? And is the whole of Europe implicitly being compared to the German states before their unification?)

Haas continues: 'the functionalist who relies on gradualism and indirection in achieving his goal must choose a strategy that will unite many people and alienate few. He can only move in small steps and without a clear logical plan, because if he moved in bold steps and in masterful fashion he would lose the support of many'.[96]

Though present-day advocates of the EU believe, or profess to believe, that concerns over sovereignty are largely irrelevant, and that there is no essential difference between 'statehood', 'intergovernmental cooperation', 'internationalism', 'supranationalism', and 'federalism'[97] – because what matters is the goals that are to be achieved, not the institutional structures by which they are achieved[98] – Ernst Haas nevertheless makes no mistake in the inevitable outcome of the 'gradual' and 'indirect' strategy, and recognizes that following the 'functionalist' path would make integration 'nearly automatic' and culminate from 'a mere customs union to an economic union and a political entity'.[99]

This seems to have been entirely accurate. There has been an exponential growth of EU competencies over the past decades. Protecting the common market has proved an excellent pretext for the most far-ranging rules and harmonization. The EU has issued tens of thousands of regulations and directives concerning such matters as safety regulations for cars, rules for bed and breakfasts, specifications for cheese and wine, social standards for laborers, the maximum sound grass-mowers may make, the kind of warning systems required

---

[94] Cf. Ernst B. Haas, *The Uniting of Europe; Political, Social, and Economic Forces, 1950-1957* (Stanford: Stanford University Press, 1958); Ernst B. Haas, *Beyond the Nation state: Functionalism and International Organization* (Stanford: Stanford University Press, 1964).
[95] Haas (1968) xxiii-xxiv: 'Author's preface, 1968'.
[96] Haas (1968) xxiii-xxiv: 'Author's preface, 1968'.
[97] Essential, therefore, in supranationalist writings is the term 'governance', which, in contradistinction to 'government', is used to denote a form of administration that, like the EU, does not have an organized and recognized form of opposition.
[98] See for instance Thomas O. Hueglin, 'From Constitutional to Treaty Federalism: a comparative perspective', in: *Publius* (Fall 2000).
[99] Haas (1968) xxv-xxvi: 'Author's preface, 1968'.

to assess swimming conditions in open water, and so on.[100] In the near future, it may even legislate mandatory safety jackets for cyclists all through Europe.[101]

The trick is that safeguarding a 'level playing field' can be used to declare every field of national policy within the administration's reach.[102] Indeed, similarly to protecting 'fundamental human rights', the wish to establish a 'level playing field' is potentially limitless. Like setting out to achieve absolute 'equality of opportunity' or complete 'non-discrimination', it is endless in its application. Meanwhile, the European Court of Auditors has refused to approve the budgetary estimates of the EU in February 2009 for the 14th successive time.[103]

But it is not only the EU politicians in Brussels that have expanded the power of the EU. As with the rise of state power in the Middle Ages (as discussed in chapter 1), it is to a large extent through law that the EU has tightened its grip on member states. The Luxembourg Court's expansion of power began with the *Van Gend en Loos v. Netherlands* case (1963), when it declared that 'the Community constitutes a new legal order of international law for the benefit of which the states have limited their sovereign right, albeit within limited fields', and ruled that states must apply community law as if it were national law.[104] In the *Costa v. Enel* case (1964), it ruled that Community law overrides any national law that conflicts with it.[105] In the case of *Simmenthal v. Commission* (1980) the Court then reinforced this ruling. Though under Italian law, only the Constitutional Court can declare a national rule void, it was nonetheless decided by the ECJ that 'every national court must (…) apply Community law in its entirety (…) and must accordingly set aside any provision of national law which may conflict with it (…). A national court, according to the ECJ, 'is under a duty to give full effect to [Community law], if necessary refusing (…) to apply any conflicting provision of national legislation'.[106] In the *Von Colson v. Nordrhein-Westfalen* Case (1984), moreover, the Court held that 'the domestic court should interpret all national laws in the light of directives, even if the law

---

[100]   Hendrik Vos and Rob Heirbaut, *Hoe Europa ons leven beïnvloedt*, 3de geactualiseerde druk (Standaard, Antwerpen, 2008).

[101]   The report calling for such legislation was adopted by the European parliament on 21 June, 2011. Information available online at http://www.europarl.europa.eu/document/activities/cont/201106/20110627ATT22630/20110627ATT22630EN.pdf

[102]   While it could also simply have meant opening up the borders between the member states, letting them decide for themselves whether and how to adjust their regulations. The resulting competition would have enabled member states to decide for themselves which measures they would adopt to make it attractive (or unattractive, depending on their interests) for foreign investors and labor forces to move there. The current EU policy of abolishing restrictive measures could in theory mean the abolition of the different languages of the EU member states.

[103]   According to the Court of Auditors the estimates continue to lack transparency to an unacceptable extent. *NRC Handelsblad*, 14 May 2009.

[104]   *Van Gend en Loos v. Nederlandse Administratie der Belastingen* (Case 26/62); [1963] ECR 1.

[105]   *Laminio Costa v ENEL* (Case 6/64)[1964] ECR 585.

[106]   *Simmenthal S.p.A. v Commission of the European Communities* (Case 243/78) [1980] ECR 2391.

in question was not based on the directive'.[107] The examples are endless, and the recurrent theme is the gradual expansion of fields of influence, with little or no institutional developments.

Thus the remarkable thing is that although the European Union started as an attempt at the federalization of Europe, it is now a partial unitary state which micromanages for example the economy, but does not have the essential features of sovereignty, such as an army, or a foreign policy, or powers of direct taxation.

Still less has it developed much of a democratic or even constitutional structure. The Commission's powers are not limited to specific tasks and the principle of subsidiarity has been used to centralize – not decentralize – ever more aspects of policy.

The Court in Luxembourg has interpreted the EU regulations in such a way as to arrogate to itself maximum power, and it has always interpreted such regulations to apply analogically to an ever-wider number of circumstances.

The European Parliament, while formally 'democratic', in reality is completely disconnected from the political debate in the countries it professes to represent. One simple reason for this is that the powers of the Parliament are still severely limited, and that it does not have an opposition. But there is a more structural reason as well, which is that for linguistic reasons if for no others, a European-wide public debate is inconceivable, and the European Parliament therefore operates in a political vacuum. It is odd, to put it no higher, that in the continent of its origin, representative and limited government should be so comprehensively undermined as they are in the present EU.

Nor is this situation even widely noticed let alone criticized by most who involve in discussions on the European Union. Although many claim to be 'severe critics' of the EU's legal expansion, very few actually desire their country to leave this supranational mega-project. Moreover, if we consider the three major spheres in which the EU operates – the common market, the common currency and acting as a bloc on the global scene – it is unquestionably assuming, very gradually, very stealthily, the responsibilities of statehood. This is the case because of at least three reasons.

Firstly, a common market with open internal borders requires, ultimately, a common immigration policy and defense of external borders, as national decisions to allow immigration have direct consequences for all member states. When Spain granted a 'general amnesty' to some 700 thousand illegal immigrants in 2005, or decided to accept former Guantanamo Bay detainees, the whole of Europe had to accept their right to reside anywhere in Europe. In the *R. v. Bouchereau* case (1981),[108] the criteria for the legal deportation of non-EU

---

[107] *Von Colson and Kamann v. Land Nordrhein-Westfalen* (Case 14/83)[1984] ECR 1891.
[108] *R. v. Bouchereau* (Case 30/77) [1977] ECR 1999.

citizens for an EU country were laid down. From now on, it was declared that 'free movement of persons' ultimately meant that the ECJ decide whether there was 'a genuine and sufficiently serious' threat to public order if states desired to disrupt such free movement of persons.

Secondly, the monetary union has now been shown to necessitate a common budgetary policy and therefore a powerful European ministry of Finance. The financial crisis and the situation in Greece demonstrated this clearly in the first half of 2011. As Christian Noyer, the president of the Bank of France said in an interview with *Le Figaro* in July 2011: 'It is necessary to go further and strengthen integration for the proper functioning of a monetary union'. He continued that the European Commission was working on it at the moment. In other words, a body of functionaries without any democratic credentials whatsoever was preparing a financial government for 350 million people.[109]

And thirdly, to act as one on the global scene requires a common foreign policy. Not surprisingly, the EU has begun to establish a diplomatic service and has appointed a 'high representative of the union' on foreign relations. Meanwhile, steps are constantly being taken to increase the possibilities for European armies to operate jointly.

Thus, we may conclude that while most advocates of the EU profess not to be striving for a united, federal Europe, what is in fact coming to pass is undoubtedly just that (if, of course, the project does not fall apart). The EU proves that the idea of supranationalism is untenable if brought to its logical conclusion, and inevitably leads back to sovereign statehood (but translated to a vast conglomerate).

---

[109] Bertille Bayart and Jean-Pierre Robin, 'Pour Noyer, la crise doit conduire à renforcer l'intégration financière de l'Europe', in: *Le Figaro* (2-3 July, 2011) 22: 'Il faut aller plus loin et renforcer l'intégration pour le bon fonctionnement d'une union monétaire. La Commission Européenne y travaille actuellement'.

CHAPTER SIX

MULTICULTURALISM

6.1. *Introduction*

In the previous two chapters, I have attempted to show, in a general overview, the extent to which supranational developments already dilute the sovereignty of European states. Supranational courts and organizations have, in their several ways, surreptitiously expanded their powers, taking over more and more elements of national policy and law. These supranational courts and organizations form a web of institutions that, even though each might still be limited in its powers, in their totality severely – and increasingly – limit national self-government.

Many present-day academics and politicians see no essential problem in these supranational tendencies – on the contrary, they are embraced, if not as a relief from ultimate national responsibility, then as 'inevitable'. As the American commentator George F. Will remarked: 'European elites believe that Europe's nations are menaced by their own sovereignty'.[1] There are interesting intellectual roots to this idea. But before we take up this discussion and examine both the background and the merits of the supranational idea, we will discuss multicul-turalism, because it is a manifestation of the same world-view, and an integral part of the assault on borders. Indeed: supranationalism and multiculturalism are not only consistent with one another, but in fact logically connected. It is impossible to defend supranationalism without supporting multiculturalism, while multiculturalism is perfectly compatible with supranationalism.

But it is important to define multiculturalism carefully, as it is to be distin-guished from the *multicultural nationalism* that I defend in this book. Moreover, even more than supranationalism, multiculturalism has touched a raw nerve in our societies. Its supporters often brand those who question it as racist, because opposition to multiculturalism is confused with multiracialism. However, the accusation is itself genuinely racist, for it assumes that race and culture are coterminous.[2]

The modern world brings us all in contact with much cultural and ethnic diversity: globalized economic activity, migration, the liberty of differing life

---

[1] George F. Will, 'The Slow undoing: the Assault on, and Underestimation of, Nationality', in: Irwin Stelzer (ed.), *Neoconservatism. Edited with an introduction by Irwin Stelzer* (London: Atlantic Books, 2004) 132.
[2] Cf. Christopher Caldwell, *Reflections on the Revolution in Europe* (Allen Lane, Penguin Books, London, 2009) 267-268.

styles, and so on. To some extent, this diversity has always existed. As discussed in chapters 1 and 3, the socially cohesive nation state is a fairly recent phenomenon, and there is nothing intrinsic in its philosophy that opposes a pluralist society.

Differences between people in the countryside and the cities have always existed as well. And no doubt the gastronomic varieties within nation states have increased beyond imagination in the past decades. All this 'multiculturality'– in the sense of diversity in a pluralist, modern society – is wonderful and not what is addressed in this chapter. The ideal of a *multicultural nationalism* that I support, also explicitly acknowledges this. As H.E. Baber writes:

> Critics of multiculturalism get bad press because the common perception is that we object to these harmless customs and practices. That is not what is at issue. When it comes to the harmless, superficial features of culture – food, costume, music and dance, language, entertainment, and crafts – the more the better.[3]

Interesting societies are always to some extent a melting pot of cultures and practices, seeking to cherish 'the best that has been thought and said'.[4] That is also why I propose a *multicultural nationalism* in the concluding chapters of this book – a diverse and pluralist society, held together nevertheless by a monocultural core.

Proponents of multiculturalism, on the contrary, do not seek to merely defend such pluralism. They make it clear that their philosophy is not simply the recognition of the empirical fact of diversity (in which case almost everyone would be a 'multiculturalist'), or the applauding of a greater choice in what to have for dinner. On the contrary, multiculturalism, its defenders explain, is a quite specific, and indeed novel thing.[5]

Multiculturalism, properly understood, denies that society has or should have a *Leitkultur*, a dominant culture – a set of core values, a shared common ground. Multiculturalists believe that 'the idea of national culture makes little sense, and the project of cultural unification on which many past societies and all modern states have relied for their stability and cohesion is no longer viable today'.[6] It is the view of society that emphasizes the differences between people within a state, instead of their similarities.[7] It tends towards legal pluralism

---

[3] H.E. Baber, *The multicultural mystique. The liberal case against diversity* (New York: Prometheus Books, 2008) 43.

[4] The phrase comes from Matthew Arnold, *Culture and Anarchy* (1882) (Oxford: Oxford University Press, 2006).

[5] Charles Taylor, *Multiculturalism, examining the politics of recognition*, Edited and introduced by Amy Gutman (Princeton: Princeton University Press, 1994). Bikhu Parekh, *Rethinking Multiculturalism, Cultural Diversity and Political Theory* (Palgrave, 2006). Will Kymlicka, *Multicultural Citizenship, A liberal theory of minority rights* (Oxford: Oxford University Press, 1996), Will Kymlicka, *Liberalism, Community and Culture* (Oxford: Oxford University Press 1991).

[6] Parekh (2006) 8.

[7] See on this for example: Baber (2008) 36-37: '... multiculturalists reject assimilation as an ideal, holding instead that multiethnic societies should support the persistence of cohesive ethnic

based on the presence of people of different cultural backgrounds and legal traditions, and applauds the efflorescence of different cultures at the expense of the shared national cohesion.

In his book *Culture and Equality*, Brian Barry concludes that for Bhikhu Parekh and other multiculturalists 'group identities and group loyalties have primacy over any broader, society-wide identity and loyalty'.[8] On this definition, multiculturalism would be a new phenomenon, previously unknown to political science. As Bikhu Parekh writes:

> As a political movement [multiculturalism] is just over thirty years old, and as a theoretical exploration of it only half as old.[9]

Parekh however polemicizes with Brian Barry concerning the precise meaning of the doctrine:

> Barry takes me to be an 'excellent example' of the preposterous view that 'group identities and group loyalties have primacy over any broader, society-wide identity and loyalty' (p. 301). He offers no evidence and there is none. I take this view to lie at the basis of the Ottoman millet system and its contemporary analogues, and explicitly reject it.[10]

Parekh then goes on to explain that rather than establishing *either* the primacy of group loyalties over a society-wide identity, *or* establishing the primacy of a single, society-wide identity over group loyalties (as Brian Barry proposes), multiculturalists take an all-inclusive approach, recognizing the importance of both. 'Multiculturalists cherish intercultural exchanges and fusions at all levels, propose policies and institutional structures conducive to them, and expect the state to play a judicious and supportive role.'[11] He continues:

> Although political obligations generally override ethnic and religious obligations, this is not always the case.[12]

---

communities, which coexist peacefully and interact without coalescing. They hold immigrants and members of ethnic minorities should not be expected to assimilate to the dominant culture and reject the melting pot in favor of a salad bowl model of cultural diversity'.

[8] Brian Barry, *Culture and Equality, An egalitarian critique of Multiculturalism* (Cambridge, MA: Harvard University Press, 2002) 301.

[9] Parekh (2006) 349.

[10] Parekh (2006) 352. The Millet system offered a dhimmi status to Christians and Jews in the Ottoman empire, who were then allowed to conduct their affairs and solve their legal issues through their own courts and representative organs.

[11] Parekh (2006) 350.

[12] Parekh (2006) 352. The whole quotation is a follows: 'What I maintain is that citizenship represents one of the individual's several identities, and does not automatically trump others. As human beings, we have moral obligations to people outside our political community, and these may modify, limit and in exceptional circumstances override our obligations as citizens. Although political obligations generally override ethnic and religious obligations, this is not always the case. If the state were to require me to betray my parents and friends, spy on or malign my ethnic or religious community, or convert to another religion, I would find its demands unacceptable. This

The trouble is that what Parekh precisely means by 'generally' and what by 'not always' remains unclear. And we are left in the dark as to the meaning and origins of 'ethnic' obligations (for what obligation could one possibly derive from one's 'ethnicity'?). Moreover, what Parekh is pointing at is something with which no one could really disagree. Clearly, this cannot mark the fundamental divide between advocates and critics of multiculturalism: for who would deny that political obligations can sometimes be overridden by other obligations?

According to Parekh, who seems to recognize this point, and goes on to admit that 'Barry and the multiculturalists then agree on many of the substantive issues thrown up by a multicultural society',[13] the important 'theoretical difference' is, he says, that

> Barry does not appreciate the value of cultural diversity and dialogue as I do. Nor does he see the importance of the right to cultural self-expression as Kymlicka, I and others do.[14]

Though Parekh suggests that this is a 'theoretical' difference, in fact it is clearly a 'practical' or gradual difference, and his definition of multiculturalism is therefore not very helpful in an attempt to understand multiculturalism conceptually.

If the extent to which one values 'cultural diversity and dialogue' is what distinguishes multiculturalists from non-multiculturalists, then Parekh speaks of 'multiculturalism' in a sense different from what is meant in this chapter. For if it is just a matter of valuing cultural diversity and enjoying cultural self-expression or 'dialogue', then we would all be 'multiculturalists' the moment we enjoy the Chinese restaurant around the corner, play the Persian game of chess, or 'dialogue' about rap music.

Certainly, multiculturalists take a favorable position towards diversity. But if Parekh acknowledges the need for shared, national political obligations too, then multiculturalism means little more than just a nuance. If multiculturalists are simply those people who are 'pro-diversity' and who tend to take a positive view towards manifestations of 'otherness', than it hardly needed to be discussed here.

Charles Taylor has given a different and much clearer definition to multiculturalism, with obvious policy implications. In his much praised essay *The politics of recognition* (1992), Taylor advocates 'the equal status of cultures and of genders'.[15] Taylor also accepts that an opposing concept to multiculturalism

---

is a very different view to the one Barry ascribes to me'. But this is a problem of any government, always, and evades the particular questions of multiculturalism.

[13] Parekh (2006) 355. It is typical for multiculturalists to confuse – or mix up – 'society' and 'state' all the time.

[14] Parekh (2006) 355.

[15] Taylor (1994) 27.

exists – very useful if not indispensible when it comes to defining things[16] – which is 'nonrecognition or misrecognition', through a form of 'homogenization'.[17] With Taylor, we can say that the opposite of multiculturalism is some form of monoculturalism, which has also been described as the recognition of a *Leitkultur:*[18] the attempt to define and defend not only shared values but also a shared culture, a shared political loyalty, and ideas of legitimacy shared by all members of society, despite whatever differences may exist between them. The question that multiculturalism poses is the extent to which it is desirable to share the same laws and customs within a single society (and not, as Parekh suggested, the extent to which we 'enjoy' or 'value' those different customs).

According to Taylor, and here he speaks for multiculturalism, 'what is to be avoided at all costs is the existence of "first-class" and "second-class" citizens' on the basis of different cultural practices or backgrounds.[19] Taylor continues:

> The politics of difference often redefines nondiscrimination as requiring that we make these distinctions the basis of differential treatment. So members of aboriginal bands will get certain rights and powers not enjoyed by other Canadians (...) and certain minorities will get the right to exclude others in order to preserve their cultural integrity, and so on.[20]

The idea of equal citizenship of multiculturalists, then, is not to be understood as formal equality. On the contrary. Multiculturalism claims that no society has the right to impose cultural or social norms on other groups within its territory: and that the strength of future societies lies exactly in their lack of a shared culture or core values (except that a lack of core values itself is of course a value, if viewed as desirable). 'Certain minorities will get the right to exclude others', and 'members of aboriginal bands will get certain rights and powers not enjoyed by other[s]', as Taylor states.

Society: a community of communities. The sense of shared membership of the state comes from the tolerance of the other's otherness, not from recognition of the other's kinship with oneself.[21] The official slogan of the European Union, 'United in Diversity', is multiculturalism distilled (and is, as mentioned before, in complete contrast to that of the United States, 'E Pluribus Unum', out

---

[16] 'Omnis determinatio negatio est': it is only possible to define something when you are also prepared to say what it is *not*. It is a fundamental problem of the 'all-inclusive' approach that both supranationalists and multiculturalists take, that by its very nature, it is difficult if not impossible to clearly delineate what it means. I discuss this theme more extensively in chapter 9.

[17] Taylor (1994) 25 and 71.

[18] Cf. Bassam Tibi, *Europa ohne Identität? Leitkultur oder Wetebeliebigkeit* (München: Siedler, 1998); Bassam Tibi, *Euro-islam: Die Lösung eines Zivilisationskonfliktes* (Darmstadt: Primus Verlag, 2009).

[19] Taylor (1994) 36.

[20] Taylor (1994) 40.

[21] See on group rights: Caroline Fourest, *La dernière utopie: menaces sur l'universalisme* (Paris: Editions Grasset, 2009).

of many, one). Not 'united *despite* diversity', or 'united *on core issues, diverse on matters of secondary importance*'; the feeling is that of belonging to a society as a 'multicultural mosaic' or even kaleidoscope.[22]

In 1991, Charles Taylor proposed that Canadians 'take the road of deep diversity together',[23] hoping that citizens 'might find it exciting and an object of pride' to work together to build a society *founded* on deep diversity.[24] In this view, diversity *is the basis* of society, not just a fact about it.

This entails tension between multiculturalism and constitutional rights. Taylor acknowledges this, when he writes: 'There would be no question of cultural differences determining the application of *habeas corpus*, for example. But [multiculturalists] distinguish these fundamental rights from the broad range of immunities and presumptions of uniform treatment that have sprung up in modern cultures of judicial review. [Multiculturalists] are willing to weigh the importance of cultural survival, and opt sometimes in favor of the latter.'[25]

Politically, Taylor's type of multiculturalism has two main consequences for social policy. First, it grants different rights and obligations to people by virtue of their cultural background. This leads to legal pluralism. Second, multiculturalism entails state sponsorship or support for expressions of minority cultures. The state supports different groups according to their size or alleged needs, in order to reflect and preserve the variety of cultural identities within its territory.[26]

---

[22]   Charles Taylor, 'Shared and Divergent Values', in: Ronald Watts and D. Brown (eds), *Options for a New Canada* (Toronto: University of Toronto Press, 1991), 53-76.

[23]   Taylor (1991) 53-76.

[24]   Taylor (1991) 53-76. Discussed by Kymlicka (1996) 190.

[25]   Taylor (1994) 61. Taylor does not specify exactly why there would be no question of the principle of *habeas corpus* to be mitigated according to the cultural traditions of a certain group.

[26]   It has been tempting for proponents of multiculturalism to suggest that the famous 'pillarization' of the Dutch society was in fact a form of multiculturalism as well. While to some extent there may be truth in this suggestions, Arend Lijphart, one of the most eminent scholars of this phenomenon, has nevertheless argued that despite the great differences and even animosity between the several 'pillars' of Dutch society during the second half of the twentieth century, there was consensus on core issues and a desire to preserve the authority of the central state, as well as a certain amount of shared nationalism between the several pillars. Arend Lijphart, *The politics of accommodation. Pluralism and democracy in the Netherlands* (Berkeley and Los Angeles: University of California Press, 1968) 78-79: 'The Netherlands cannot be called a consensual society, not even by the most generous stretch of the imagination. Consensus exists within each of the subcultures rather than among all four blocs. No state can exist without some degree of consensus on matters of fundamental concern, however, and Holland is no exception. (...) In the Netherlands, both the degree and extent of political consensus are very limited, but one vitally important element of consensus is present: the desire to preserve the existing system. Each bloc tries to defend and promote its own interests but only within the confines of the total system and without the threat of secession or civil war. (...) The most important factor behind this element of consensus is Dutch nationalism: the feeling of belonging to a common nation as well as to one's own bloc. The strength of this nationalism must not be exaggerated, but it certainly does exist. National independence was achieved at a relatively early date, and feelings of nationalism can be traced back to the early stage of the struggle for independence: the end of the sixteenth century. The separate Catholic, Calvinist, and secular subcultures also had their origin in this period, but

The first consequence of multiculturalism is the 'stronger' one, the second its 'weaker' one.[27] It is easier to take a categorical position on the question of legal plurality, whereas state support for minority expressions is perhaps more a question of nuance. The 'weak' form encompasses all sorts of appraisals for minorities' ways of life and values, often combined with disdain for and even suppression of national customs – a practice Roger Scruton denotes as 'oikophobia', or fear of what is one's own.[28] Hence the typical reproach to those who do not share enthusiasm for multiculturalism as being 'provincials', 'xenophobes', 'little Englanders' in the British case[29] or 'cheeseheads' in Holland. Official support for minority cultures encourages citizens to focus not on what they have in common, but on what they *do not* have in common.[30] Over time, this may clearly reinforce the demand for legal pluralism; for not only will groups that have been granted different rights continue to emphasize their distinctness from other groups or the majority of society; those who have been discouraged to integrate and so live separated from the rest of society, will come to think it only natural that they should have their own laws, too. Indeed, what does multiculturalism mean if it is not backed by a flexible law that can provide different remedies, in accordance with the different cultural backgrounds of those invoking it? Nevertheless, it is important to investigate the two elements of multiculturalism separately, as will be done below.

---

the blocs did not become thoroughly organized until the nineteenth century. In other words, nationalism and the nation state antedated by several centuries the outburst of organizational differentiation by the various subcultures.'

[27] Daniel I. O'Neill, 'Multicultural Liberals and the Rushdie Affair: A Critique of Kymlicka, Taylor, and Walzer', in: *The Review of Politics*, Vol. 61, No. 2 (Spring, 1999) 219-250, writes on 222: 'Of course, the very term multiculturalism is a vexed one, so it is important to define my use of it here. I want to distinguish two levels of commitment to multiculturalism. The first I call "strong" multiculturalism, and is the position I associate with Kymlicka, Taylor, and Walzer. Strong multiculturalists are committed, in certain circumstances, to the defense of differential (or special) citizenship rights for minority groups based on their culture. Put simply, strong multiculturalists are willing to defend cultural rights. The second level of multicultural argument I refer to (for lack of a better term) as "weak" multiculturalism. Weak multiculturalists do not argue for differential citizenship rights, but seek a range of different goals. In the United States, these have included, for example, expanding the academic curriculum to reflect more fully the contributions of minorities'.

[28] Cf. Roger Scruton, *A political philosophy. Arguments for Conservatism* (London: Continuum, 2006) 23ff, and Roger Scruton, *Green Philosophy. How to think seriously about the planet* (London: Atlantic Books, 2012) 247ff. An interesting organization that has taken up discussion on this phenomenon is the *Alliance Générale contre le Racisme et pour le respect de l'Identité Française et chrétienne (AGRIF)*. *AGRIF strives to curtail the anti-national and anti-French tendency in public debate, and objects to the extra protection that minorities' cultural values enjoy as compared to that of the majorities' values.*

[29] Cf. Scruton (2006) 23ff.

[30] See on this: Arthur M. Schlesinger, Jr., *The Disuniting of America, reflections on a multicultural society*, Revised and enlarged ed. (New York: W.W. Norton & Company, 1998) 118.

6.2. *Legal Plurality*

In a provisional decision in March 2007, a judge in Frankfurt rejected the petition for summary divorce of a woman who had been severely maltreated by her husband. According to German divorce law,[31] such a summary divorce is possible only if there is 'Härtefall': hardship. The judge considered that the spouses came from 'the Moroccan cultural sphere', and that it was 'not unusual' for them, 'that the man exercizes a right of corporal punishment against the woman'. She continued: 'the German born petitioner had to take this into account when she married the Moroccan-born respondent'.[32]

When the attorney of the woman complained against this provisional decision, the judge further explained her point of view. In a letter dated 4 February 2007, the judge wrote that by concluding the marriage in Morocco, the spouses had accepted that they would be submitted to 'the provisions of the Quran (…) and thereby also to Quran [verse] 4.34. Quran [verse] 4.34 entails apart from the right of the man to discipline his disobedient wife also the recognition of the superiority of the husband over his wife'. She continued to say that to her mind, it followed from the Quran that:

> The honor of the man, simply put, is connected to the chastity of the woman; this is to say that basically, for a man who was raised as a Muslim, the life of a woman according to Western cultural standards is already a loss of honor.[33]

This judgment caused international outrage,[34] and the judge was replaced.[35]

But it was not an isolated incident. Some of the reactions, such as those of Ali Kizilkaya, then president of the *Islamrat für die Bundesrepublik Deutschland*,

---

[31] The disputed article was § 1565 of the Bürgerliches Gesetzbuch.
[32] 'Dem marokkanischen Kulturkreis (…) nicht unüblich dass der Mann gegenüber der Frau ein Züchtigungsrecht ausübe'. (…) 'Hiermit musste die in Deutschland geborene Antragstellerin rechnen als sie den in Marokko aufgewachsenen Antragsgegner geheiratet hat'. Correspondence of judge Christa Datz-Winter, Richterin am Amtsgericht, Frankfurt am Mainz, to the attorney of the woman demanding divorce, Barbara Becker-Rojczyk, dated January 12th, 2007, Aktenzeichen 460 F 9405/06. I am grateful to Barbara Becker-Rojczyk for kindly placing the correspondence at my disposal.
[33] 'Den Vorschriften des Korans (…) und damit auch Koran 4.34. Koran 4.34 enthält neben dem Züchtigungsrecht des Mannes gegenüber der ungehorsamen Ehefrau auch die Feststellung zur Überlegenheit des Mannes gegenüber der Frau'. (…) '[Dass] die Ehre des Mannes, einfach ausgedrückten die Keuschheit der Frau angebunden ist, d.h. im Grunde genommen für einen islamisch erzogenen Mann, das Leben einer Frau nach westlichen Kulturregeln bereits diesen Tatbestand der Ehrverletzung erfüllt'. Correspondence of judge Christa Datz-Winter, dated February 4th, 2007.
[34] Following an article in *Der Spiegel*: Veit Medick and Anna Reimann, 'Justiz-Skandal. Deutsche Richterin rechtfertigt eheliche Gewalt mit Koran', in: *Der Spiegel*, 20 March 2007. Available online at http://www.spiegel.de/politik/deutschland/0,1518,472849,00.html.
[35] Because the judge, Christa Datz-Winter, was replaced, the whole procedure was delayed long enough for the ordinary divorce procedure to apply. Cf. Barbara Becker-Rojczyk, 'Der "Koran-fall" - Ein Erlebnisbericht', in: *Streit. Feministische Rechtszeitschrift*, vol. 23, no. 3 (3, 2007) 121-123.

the Islamic council of Germany, were telling. Kizilkaya declared that 'the physical disciplining of a woman by her husband is not supported by Islam'.[36] This was relevant because according to Kizilkaya, presumably, Islamic culture and religion now had a place in the German legal system. Not seeing the law as the expression of the shared national culture and therefore upholding it for every citizen in the same manner, the judge's challenge became to figure out what exactly was the cultural practice of those standing in court.

If it is not persons, but cultures, that are equal before the law, then the judges' role becomes that of an anthropologist, deciding what is or is not customary within cultures. A judge, then, will also have to consider what constitutes 'hardship' within different cultures (as the Frankfurt situation demonstrates), for the experience of hardship is dependent upon expectations, which themselves are cultural.

Multicultural ideas were also applied a few months later in a case in Amsterdam, on May 24th, 2007. A Muslim woman who wore a burqa had been living on welfare, as she had been unemployed from April 2006 onwards. In the Dutch welfare system, the benefit is conditional on the recipient searching actively for work and not declining suitable job offers, on pain of losing his or her benefit for a period of three months.

The woman concerned applied for several jobs, mostly in the field of telephonic sales. Two companies showed an interest in hiring her. One, however, demanded that she remove her burqa, as the garment made communication with her colleagues impossible and would prevent the management from identifying her in person. The other company, a telemarketeer, accepted the burqa, but demanded that she sell lottery tickets, which she considered to be against her faith.

As a result of the rejection by her of these two job offers, the social service withdrew her unemployment benefit, upon which she filed a complaint in court. The judge considered, in accordance with the regulations, that the withdrawal of the benefit was justified, the woman having declined 'generally accepted work'. But the judge went on to consider that, since it was 'a matter of common knowledge' that 'it is not permitted for Muslims to gamble', it could not be expected of the petitioner, who was obviously a Muslim, 'to provide an occasion for gambling through the sale of lottery-tickets'.[37]

---

[36] 'Die körperliche Züchtigung einer Ehefrau durch ihren Mann wird nicht vom Islam gedeckt'. 'Gewalt in der Ehe. Richterin bedauert Koran-Verweis', in: *Frankfurter Allgemeine Zeitung*, March 22nd, 2007. See also: Landler, Mark, 'Germany cites Koran in rejecting divorce, *New York Times*, March 22nd, 2007.

[37] LJN: BA6917, Rechtbank Amsterdam , AWB 07/1635 WWB, 24-05-2007. 'De rechter acht van algemene bekendheid dat het voor moslims niet is toegestaan om te gokken. Van verzoekster, die moslima is, kan daarom ook niet worden verwacht dat zij gelegenheid geeft tot gokken door het verkopen van loten voor een loterij.'

With regards to the other rejected job, in which it was demanded that the woman remove her burqa, the judge considered that it was 'disproportional' to punish the woman for declining this job, because the burqa was a 'direct expression' of the woman's faith. After only two job offers, both of them objectioned to by her on religious grounds, there was not enough justification for withdrawal of her welfare benefit.[38]

This is another example of the multicultural approach to law and politics. The state now has to determine which religious or cultural practices are 'direct expressions' of faith or culture, and is then obliged to give legal weight or protection to them. The woman in this case was clearly understood as belonging to a culture, who can therefore claim a different set of rights and obligations from those who do not share her cultural (or religious) background. For non-Muslims, meanwhile, selling lottery-tickets is still considered 'generally accepted work'.

The question is what the precedent means. Would working in a non-halal butcher's-shop, in a shop that sells alcohol, or indeed, working in any situation that is in contradiction with sharia law, now also not be considered 'generally accepted work' for Muslims? The implication is there, and the problems that arise from it are potentially endless.

Even more interesting for our purpose is the remark that the burqa was a 'direct expression' of the woman's faith. It is generally held by Muslims that there is no official rule in Islam obliging women to wear a burqa. The fact that the judge acknowledged the burqa to be a 'direct expression' of the applicant's faith, implies that not only the 'official' rules of a religious group can be taken into consideration in deciding a case, but also traditions and customs that are peculiar to subcultures and branches or sects of religions. Indeed, the implementation of multiculturalism might lead to legal exceptions for almost any conduct, provided it was sanctioned by a 'culture'.

A third example of legal pluralism consequent upon multiculturalism is the permission given to Dutch civil servants to deny gay couples the execution of their right to marriage by appeal to their Christian faith. The *Algemene Wet Gelijke Behandeling*, the general law on equal treatment, provides the legal basis for this unequal treatment: civil servants can appeal to their 'conscience' and then do not have to contract the marriage. This does not mean that *any* civil

---

[38] In translation: 'Verweerders stelling dat verzoekster haar boerka zou kunnen afdoen om de bemiddeling naar arbeid (beter) te doen slagen, acht de rechter voorshands disproportioneel. Niet is gebleken dat de bemiddelingsmogelijkheden reeds in zoverre zijn uitgeput, dat van verzoekster kan worden gevraagd om afstand te doen van het kledingstuk dat voor haar een rechtstreekse uitdrukking is van haar godsdienstige overtuiging (vergelijk: Commissie Gelijke Behandeling 20 maart 2003, LJN: AN7464, m.nt. BPV). De rechter neemt hierbij tevens in aanmerking dat verzoekster haar boerka reeds droeg bij aanvang van het traject naar arbeid en dat dat gegeven haar destijds niet is tegengeworpen. De rechter acht het voorshands onredelijk om verzoekster dit nu – na slechts vier sollicitaties – te verwijten'.

servant is now allowed to reject marrying gay couples. Only when they can refer to a cultural or religious background may civil servants do so: and so here we see yet another example of legal pluralism.

Many more examples can be given, of course, and it is not necessary to go into that at this point. We could look at family and inheritance law (where debates are ongoing on accepting some aspects of sharia law), mortgage law (where debates are ongoing of allowing an interest free mortgage to Muslims), and even penal law (as proposals have been made to approach honor killings more mildly and female genital mutilation leniently).

More individual rights are not always the result. Freedoms of citizens who happen to have a certain cultural background are frequently curtailed as a result of multiculturalism. In her essay *Is Multiculturalism bad for Women?*, Susan M. Okin provides several examples of women's individual rights and liberties being curtailed through the quiet permission of cultural practices that conflict with the law.[39] She discusses for instance the policy of the French state to allow multiple wives into the country, amounting to an estimated 200.000 *de facto* polygamous families now living in Paris – a situation the women in question 'regarded as an inescapable and barely tolerable institution in their African countries of origin, and an unbearable imposition in the French context'.[40]

In the Netherlands, a young ex-Muslim was viewed with disdain (not only by people from his own community, but also, most remarkably, by the multi-culturalist elites) when he spoke openly about his loss of belief in Islam.[41] Many multiculturalists observed that one had to be more considerate with the sensitivity to apostasy in Islam, and implied that the 'right to freedom of religion' – which the ex-Muslim invoked –, did not apply unmitigated to immigrants.[42]

The London-based Centre for Social Cohesion published a report in 2008 which described how all through Europe, people from immigrant backgrounds were threatened and intimidated when they spoke out critical of their communi-ties. The report, entitled *Victims of Intimidation,* notes:

> When many of these individuals began to receive threats from members of their own communities and their co-religionists, many governments began to treat them not as full citizens who deserved the full support of the law but as a people

---

[39] Susan Moller Okin, *Is Multiculturalism Bad for Women? With respondents* (Princeton: Princeton University Press, 1999).

[40] Okin (1999) 9-10.

[41] Eshan Jami, *Het recht om ex moslim te zijn* (Amsterdam: Uitgeverij Ten Have, 2007); Ibn Warraq, *Weg uit de Islam: Getuigenissen van afvalligen.* Met een inleiding van Afshin Ellian (Amsterdam: J.M. Meulenhoff, 2008).

[42] Douglas Murray and Johan Pieter Verwey, *Victims of Intimidation. Freedom of Speech within Europe's Muslim Communities* (London: Center for Social Cohesion, 2008).

apart; as people who are not expected to enjoy the same rights and freedoms as native Europeans ...[43]

A curious shift has thus occurred as a result of the multicultural mindset. No longer do minorities receive the right to integrate, but, instead, the right to maintain their own culture. 'The era that began with the dream of integration', as columnist Richard Rodriguez observed, 'ended up with scorn for assimilation'.[44]

This shift in less than half a century from an ideal of emancipation to an ideal of segregation is very remarkable indeed. And it is quite unclear where the boundaries of the right to exercise one's culture lie. What if, at some point in the near future, two-thirds of the civil servants reject gay marriages by reference to their faith? Or what if homosexual civil servants will start, as a counter reaction, to reject marriages of Christian fundamentalists?

The complications are certainly endless. The legislative power having effectively been put aside, it is clear that the path of legal pluralism can easily go astray as claims to cultural traditions reign unchecked. As the Berlin-based attorney Seyran Ates has put the dilema: 'We are at a crossroads, everywhere in Europe. Do we allow structures that lead straight into a parallel society, or do we demand assimilation into the democratic constitutional state?'[45]

6.3. CULTURAL DIVERSITY

Legal pluralism is still rather an exception than a rule. Even though the extent to which sharia courts have already established *de facto* jurisdiction in certain areas and among certain parts of the population should not be underestimated,[46] legal plurality is still a marginal phenomenon and the national judges still hold, over all, a general authority for most of the European population. Most people believe that core constitutional values should be upheld for all, and that freedoms granted to native populations should not be withheld to immigrants.

The second element of multiculturalism, by contrast, though theoretically not entirely separable from the first, can count on general applause. The discourse of 'diversity', and the concomitant scorn for the national culture and traditions, has remained fashionable. Because of the inflow of substantial numbers of immigrants with a different cultural background into Europe over the past decades,

---

[43] Murray and Verwey (2008) 91.

[44] Quoted in: Schlesinger (1998) 118.

[45] Quoted in: Matthias Bartsch, Andrea Brandt, Simone Kaiser, Gunther Latsch, Cordula Meyer and Caroline Schmidt, 'German Justice Failures' (Translated from the German by Christopher Sultan), in: *Spiegel Online International*, 27 March 2007. Available online at http://www.spiegel.de/international/germany/0,1518,474629-8,00.html.

[46] Cf. Douglas Murray, 'To what extent is sharia already operating in Britain?', in: *The Times*, December 30th, 2009.

the question now stands high on the agenda whether or not the national culture should be defended, propagated and thereby generally be upheld against the parallel claims of those immigrants. We see this for instance in the debates over national festive days, language, modes of behavior and standards of social interaction, but also much more pertinently in whole areas or neighborhoods becoming predominantly Moroccan, Algerian, Turkish, and native populations moving out.[47]

One way to avoid having to acknowledge this reality is to claim that no such thing as a 'national identity' existed in the first place, and therefore that immigration is not affecting any such thing as a national culture (because there is none). Though this point of view is not in itself an argument for multiculturalism, it may clearly support it (as will be discussed in chapter 8).

The tendency to move away from social cohesion and clear allegiance to the national state, towards a society that consists of multiple groups, not necessarily identifying themselves with one another, stands in any case at odds with the very idea of a national identity. Opposed to a common *Leitkultur* stands the image Theodore Roosevelt described in a speech in 1915: 'a tangle of squabbling nationalities, an intricate knot of German-Americans, Irish-Americans, English-Americans, French-Americans, Scandinavian-Americans, or Italian-Americans, each preserving its separate nationality'.

For Roosevelt, this was 'the one absolutely certain way of bringing this nation to ruin, or preventing all possibility of its continuing to be a nation at all'.[48] Arthur Schlesinger comments:

> Three quarters of a century later we must add a few more nationalities to T.R.'s brew. This only strengthens his point. But what was a nightmare for T.R. is the dream of multicultural ideologues today. If that dream were fulfilled, if each of our manifold groups were huddled in its own enclave, holding itself apart from the rest in the sacred name of diversity, would this really be a more equable, peaceful, strong, unified, happy country?[49]

As the chief rabbi of the British Commonwealth, Jonathan Sacks, puts it: 'Multiculturalism has led not to integration but to segregation. It has allowed groups to live separately, with no incentive to integrate and every incentive not to. It was intended to promote tolerance. Instead the result has been, in countries where it has been tried, societies more abrasive, fractured and intolerant than they once were'.[50]

---

[47] This is what Martin Bosma calls the 'demographic turn-table', or 'demografische draaischijf', in: Martin Bosma, *De schijn-élite van de valse munters. Drees, extreem-rechts, nuttige idioten, Groep Wilders en ik* (Amsterdam: Bert Bakker, 2010) ii.

[48] Quoted in Schlesinger (1998) 124. A report of the speech is available online at http://query.nytimes.com/mem/archive-free/pdf?_r=1&res=9901E0DD1239E333A25750C1A9669D946496D6CF.

[49] Schlesinger (1998) 124.

[50] Jonathan Sacks, *The home we build together. Recreating Society* (London: New York, 2007) 3.

The latest political developments suggest that Western politicians have abandoned the discourse of diversity. Over a period of a few months, several Western-European heads of government renounced multiculturalism. In 2004, then opposition leader and president of the CDU Angela Merkel had already said that 'multiculturalism has failed utterly', and she was heavily criticized for saying so by amongst others the then Chancellor of the German Federal Republic, Gerhard Schröder.[51] But when she repeated this statement in October 2010,[52] Merkel found wide response.

Former prime minister of Spain Jose Maria Aznar, British Prime Minister David Cameron, French president Nicolas Sarkozy, as well as Dutch vice-prime minister Maxime Verhagen all declared that multiculturalism had failed as well.[53]

Nevertheless, the debate goes on. Support for multiculturalism and for the continuation of mass-immigration is still considerable in Europe. Nor is it certain that current leading politicians will not be outvoted in upcoming elections, rendering power again to those defending multiculturalism. For instance, when David Cameron spoke out against multiculturalism, he was openly criticized by a large number of public intellectuals, artists and politicians, amongst whom at least two MP's, declaring that 'We believe David Cameron's statement that multiculturalism has failed was a dangerous declaration of intent. (…) David Cameron is attempting to drive a wedge between different communities by linking Britain's multicultural society with terrorism and national security. (…) The prime minister is aping attacks by other European leaders like France's Nicolas Sarkozy, who passed legislation banning the veil, and Angela Merkel, who has also made statements denouncing multiculturalism in Germany. We believe our multicultural society and the respect and solidarity it is built on is a cause for pride, and reject any moves by this government to undermine and destroy it.[54] Multiculturalism thus remains a major theme of political disagreement and is likely to continue to be so over years to come.

[51] Cf. 'Integrationsdebatte. Schröder warnt vor Kampf der Kulturen', in: *Frankfurter Allgemeine Sonntagszeitung*, 21 November 2004. Available online at http://www.faz.net/artikel/C30189/integrationsdebatte-schroeder-warnt-vor-kampf-der-kulturen-30198894.html.

[52] Matthew Weaver et al., 'Angela Merkel: German multiculturalism has 'utterly failed'. Chancellor's assertion that onus is on new arrivals to do more to integrate into German society stirs anti-immigration debate', in: *The Guardian*, 17 October 2010. Available online at http://www.guardian.co.uk/world/2010/oct/17/angela-merkel-german-multiculturalism-failed.

[53] Cf. 'Nicolas Sarkozy declares multiculturalism had failed. French president Nicolas Sarkozy on Thursday declared that multiculturalism had failed, joining a growing number of world leaders or ex-leaders who have condemned it', in: *The Telegraph*, 11 February 2011; http://www.telegraph.co.uk/news/worldnews/europe/france/8317497/Nicolas-Sarkozy-declares-multiculturalism-had-failed.html.

[54] Available online at http://www.guardian.co.uk/politics/2011/feb/09/more-division-over-multiculturalism.

CONCLUSION

Over several decades now, the dominant trend in politics and academia has been to defend supranationalism and multiculturalism. In the previous three chapters, I have attempted to sketch what this means in practice, by pointing out the powers of three supranational courts and three supranational organizations that have been installed over the past decades, as well as the extent to which multiculturalism has manifested itself in society and to what consequences this may lead.

In their several ways, supranational institutions take away from their member states elements of national sovereignty. As a result, member states can be bound by rules or decisions they never intended to or have never agreed upon, that may go against their interests or their preferences.

Not all of these decisions are of landmark importance. Nor are all supranational institutions necessarily powerful and wide-ranging. The WTO has a limited field of competence. The ECHR has few means of enforcing its dicta. But seen in their totality, each of them taking away perhaps only a small portion of the national power to decide in certain fields of policy, a web of supranational commitments has been spun up in the past decades, that, viewed in its entirety, now performs a significant part of all political and judicial decisions that have effect in European states.

All these organizations emerged fairly recently and their powers are still relatively limited. But if nothing changes, they will continue to expand their hold over their member states, and ultimately may come to dominate national law and overshadow national policies for years to come. Forming a network of decision making institutions, the supranationalism these organizations exercize poses problems of several kinds.

Firstly, it implies that national governments can be outvoted by majorities of other nations. Secondly, it implies that non-national judges are entrusted with decisions on matters of law and morals that national judges are not anymore. Thirdly, these supranational majorities and non-national judges are not, and cannot, be submitted to the kind of checks and balances that national parliaments and judges are, as long as no integrated political structure, i.e., a world state, exists.

While this supranationalism has increasingly become a reality, most Western states have embraced to a smaller or larger extent a policy of multiculturalism accompanying the influx of considerable numbers of immigrants from different cultural backgrounds since the 1960s and 70s. As a result, national cohesion and the idea of a national identity has now become questionable in most of these countries. While proposals for legal pluralism are still limited, in practice there have already been set up informal sharia courts and other parallel systems of solving conflicts that pass by the national laws.

Moreover, there is a general tendency to applaud cultural diversity and to stress the equal value of separate communities within nation states. As a consequence, as will be discussed more in depth in chapter 8, it has now become questionable even whether 'such a thing as *the* Dutch identity exists'[1] – or, for that matter, *the* Frenchman, *the* German, or *the* Dane.

My argument in this book is that these developments are, despite all their resonance of bringing people together and respecting others, ultimately incompatible with representative government and the rule of law.

It may be important to stress once again that although I have gone in some length to describe the actual functioning of the several supranational institutions and the policy of multiculturalism, my argument against supranationalism and multiculturalism is not dependent on any currently existing arrangements; the problems related to them are conceptual and apply to their very nature. I have attempted to present a flavor of the developments European countries have involved themselves with, and to point out the extent to which these organizations and courts may override national preferences, as well as the extent to which multiculturalism may – and does – dilute national cohesion.

It also seems worthwhile to stress one more time that the idea that borders should be effaced is to be distinguished from the idea that the nation state should enlarge its scope. Supranationalism and multiculturalism do *not* amount to the belief that, as economic interests span present borders, and national differences diminish, peoples of different national origins may over time recognize neighbors as members of their own tribe and join into new, more encompassing, i.e. *larger* nation states. This would mean a continuation of national sovereignty, but applied on a larger scale.

By contrast, supranationalism and multiculturalism are the philosophies of abolishing borders *altogether*, not of expanding them. Moving beyond borders means leaving the whole idea of a nation state behind in favor of a political system of overlapping loyalties and jurisdictions, of communities, double or even triple or quadruple passports, and 'deep diversity'.

This confusion seems to bring together commentators of entirely different persuasion under the thesis that 'the nation state is finished'. Take the example

---

[1] Princes Máxima, *Speech of 24 September 2007*, '(…) "de" Nederlandse identiteit? Nee, die heb ik niet gevonden'. Available online at http://archief.koninklijkhuis.nl/Actueel/Toespraken/ Toesprakenarchief/2007/Toespraak_van_Prinses_Maxima_24_september_2007.

of Kenichi Ohmae and Henry Grunwald, who both subscribe to the view that 'the nation state will have to dissolve'.

Ohmae, a frequent writer for the *Wall Street Journal, Foreign Affairs*, and *The Economist*, and the author of such works as *The Borderless World* and *The End of the Nation State: The Rise of Regional Economies*, wrote in his 1993 essay, *The Rise of the Region State*:

> The nation state has become an unnatural, even dysfunctional, unit for organizing human activity and managing economic endeavor in a borderless world.[2]

A borderless world. Indeed, that is the idea of supranational multiculturalism: not *enlarging* borders, but *removing* them. The late political commentator Henry Grunwald, in a January 2000 op-ed for *The Wall Street Journal* entitled *A World Without a Country?*, predicted that the 'nation state will undergo sharp limitations of its sovereignty' and that 'just as the old, petty principalities had to dissolve into the wider nation state, the nation state will have to dissolve into wider structures.'

These two ideas, though seemingly bearing much resemblance, are fundamentally different. The first is in line with the assault on borders, the second is simply a continuation of national sovereignty, but on a larger scale. Although we will come to speak of problems of scale, that is not the essential theme of the dispute.

Firstly, the dispute is about whether any form of national sovereignty should be maintained or pursued (as could be the case with a future 'United States of Europe'), or whether, as we have witnessed the results of multiculturalism and supranationalism, centralized decision-making and relatively harmonious sociological communities should be abandoned on the whole. To begin answering that question, we will now commence discussing representative government and the rule of law.

---

[2] Kenichi Ohmae, 'The Rise of the Region State', in: *Foreign Affairs*, vol. 17, no. 2 (Spring 1993) 79-85.

PART III

THE NEED FOR BORDERS

Representative Government and the Rule of Law

Free institutions are next to impossible in a country made up of different nationalities.

J.S. Mill, *Considerations on Representative Government* (1861)

CHAPTER SEVEN

GOVERNMENT

7.1. *Introduction*

As pointed out in part II, national sovereignty has been undermined by supra-nationalism, and national identities have been weakened through the policy of multiculturalism. The ideal of political independence has been replaced by an ideal of political *inter*dependence. Supranational policy-making has increased, at the cost of national self-government, and multiculturalism has promoted the idea that the societies of the future should not be united through a set of shared values, but – in the words of Charles Taylor – through 'deep diversity' and solely the acknowledgment of the 'radical otherness' of others.[1]

We will now reconsider sovereignty and national loyalty as well as their opposites, supranationalism and multiculturalism, from the perspective of representative government and the rule of law. I will argue that representative government and the rule of law require centralized decision-making and social cohesion, i.e. sovereignty and nationality, and that therefore, supranationalism and multiculturalism are, in their very principle, irreconcilable with them.

7.2. *Representation*

Every form of organization, including political organization, implies a mechanism of representation. The salesman who sells coffee machines represents his company when he makes a deal; the army commander who waves the white flag represents the soldiers under his command; the teacher represents the university when he grades an exam, and so on. Division of labor, a characteristic of every organization, requires an acknowledgement of the individual agent as a *pars pro toto*.

In this sense, a political leader is by definition a 'representative' of the people under his solicitude. An example S.E. Finer discusses is that of the emperor of China who 'represented' the people of China at the international scene: 'Clearly', Finer writes, 'this view of "representation" does not require the representative to

---

[1] Taylor (1991) 53-76. This ultimately amounts to an attempt to move beyond thinking in terms of 'us' and 'them', the logical consequence of borders. Cf. Carl Schmitt, who saw it as the essential characteristic of 'the political', 'Der Begriff des Politischen', in: Carl Schmitt, *Frieden oder Pazifismus?* (Berlin: Ducker & Humblot, 2005).

be elected; anyone performing a function on behalf of a group is a representative of that group'.[2]

To understand representation in this strictly formal sense tells us something about the representation with regards to *external* parties only. The salesman, the army commander, the teacher and the dictator are representatives of, respectively, their business, their army, their school or their country – but only for those outside their group: the business partner, the enemy's army, the student, or other states and international organizations.

What is therefore not included in this understanding of 'representation' is *internal* 'representativeness': the extent to which the conduct of the dictator may be viewed as representative of the desires or opinions of his people. In political affairs, representation must enable, as Finer puts it, a small group or a single individual to 'somehow *stand for* a larger collectivity'.[3] Representation in this sense poses the question of legitimacy. An army commander may be the external representative of his army – and so bind his soldiers to decisions he makes on behalf of them –, but these decisions may not be 'representative' of the views of the soldiers nor even be experienced as legitimate by them. Ultimately, they may no longer feel 'represented' by him. The same goes for the dictator who may rule against the ideas of the people, making it obvious for some or many of them to say, as did *Nasawiya*, a group of feminist activists in Lebanon in February 2011, that the then first-lady of Egypt, Suzan Mubarak, 'does not represent Egyptian women'.[4] When speaking of representative government in this sense, we mean *legitimate* government.

Theoretically, this could be entirely undemocratic,[5] taking again the example of the army commander – this time a successful one: he is unelected, but may be experienced as an entirely legitimate 'representative' of the interests of the soldiers. When it comes to government, it is however quite unlikely that without the subjects having a say in the policies pursued, the politicians will endurably be considered as representative and legitimate.[6] This also brings us to what seems to be underlying in every conception of representation, which is the need for

---

[2] Finer (1997) vol. II, 1032. This is to be distinguished from Eric Voegelin's conception of 'existential representation', as explored in Volume IV of *Order and History: The Ecumenic Age* (Baton Roughe: Louisiana State University, 1974).

[3] Finer (1997) vol. II, 1025. Finer adds that 'this is not a sufficient condition for what we would call "representative government" today, but it is a necessary one'.

[4] Website of Epress.am, 23 February 2011. Available online at http://www.epress.am/en/2011/02/23/suzan-mubarak-does-not-represent-egyptian-women-egypts-coalition-of-womens-ngos/.

[5] As David Apter analyzes, for instance, in: 'Notes for a theory of nondemocratic representation', in: J.R. Pennock and J.W. Chapman (eds.), *Representation. Yearbook of the American Society for Political and Legal Philosophy* (New York: Atherton Press, 1968) 278-317.

[6] Cf. Hamilton, Madison and Jay, *The Federalist Papers. With an introduction and commentary by Garry Wills* (New York: Bantam Classics, 1982).

social cohesion among those who are to be represented. But we will come to speak of that below.

R.H. Lord argues that 'the development of the representative system and of parliaments' was 'one of the greatest achievements of the Middle Ages.'[7] According to most observers, the kind of political representation that we are familiar with today did not exist before Medieval times: the Greeks and the Romans are generally regarded to have known 'something like "delegated" or "vicarious" government' – enabling only direct agency for concrete purposes (and not the general kind of representation for all sorts of purposes known at present).[8] Thomas Bisson writes that 'the uniqueness of the medieval evolution is not in doubt; historians agree that the circumstances and forms of European representation bear little resemblance to those known in antecedent or non-European societies.'[9] Lord continues on the rise of the modern form of representation in the Middle Ages:

> The hallmark of it is the fact that the power of the crown was then more or less extensively limited by that of assemblies, in part elective, whose members, though directly and immediately representing only the politically active classes, were also regarded as representing in a general way the whole population of the land.[10]

Finer argues that 'during the thirteenth and fourteenth centuries (...) there sprang up a multitude of conciliar bodies to give consent to but also – by the same token – to exert some control over their rulers.'[11] Their names differed from country to country,

> some countries, like England, Ireland, Scotland, Sicily, the Papal States, and the great Kingdom of Naples called them parliaments or *parlamenti*. In the Iberian peninsula they were called *cortes* or *corts*. In France and the Lowlands they went under the name of Estates- or States-General. In Germany they were called *landtage*, in Denmark and Norway the assembly was the *Rigsdag*, in Sweden the *Riksdag*, and in Poland the *Sejm*.[12]

In his 1851 book entitled *Histoire des origines du gouvernement representatif en Europe*, the French statesman and historian François Guizot wrote that 'almost everywhere [in Europe], the representative form of government is demanded, allowed, or established'. He connected this to the development of central power,

---

[7] R.H. Lord, 'The Parliaments of the Middle Ages and the Early Modern Period', in: *The Catholic Historical Review*, Vol. 16, No. 2 (July, 1930) 125-144. Cf. P. Spufford, *The origins of the English Parliament: Readings* (Longman, London, 1967) 21.

[8] Finer (1997) *vol. I*, 380-381. An exception is J.A.O. Larsen, *Representative government in Greek and Roman history, Sather classical lectures, vol. 28* (Berkeley: University of California Press, 1955) 86ff.

[9] T.N. Bisson (ed.), *Medieval representative institutions. Their Origins and Nature* (Illinois: The Dryden Press, 1973) 1.

[10] Lord (July, 1930) 125-144.

[11] Finer (1997) vol. II, 1024.

[12] Finer (1997) vol. II, 1024.

as 'the first movement towards a representative government appear[ed] at the same time with the efforts of a central power which aims at becoming general and organized (...)'.[13] Ample reflection shows that this is entirely in line with logic: for without organized, centralized power, it is impossible to conceive of political representation. If representative bodies do not possess sovereignty, they have nothing to be representative about.

But the analytical question remains what exactly is to be understood by 'representation'. We may further our understanding of this difficulty by distinguishing representation from two related concepts: that of delegation, and that of mandation.

Delegation is the – in principle temporary – transfer of concrete decision-making powers, authorizing the delegate 'to act only in accordance with specific instructions, or a specific ideology'.[14] States send 'delegates' to the assemblies of the United Nations, for instance, to lobby in accordance with specific instructions from the minister of foreign affairs. Delegates also appear on behalf of interest groups at national legislative bodies to influence legislation or processes of decision-making. A delegate has less freedom of operation than a 'representative'. As Burke suggested:

> A delegate merely mirrors and records the views of his constituents, whereas a representative is elected to judge according to his own conscience.[15]

It is an interesting discussion whether, due to modern party rule, members of parliaments may have come to resemble more the characteristics of a delegate (of their party), to the detriment of their representativeness of the people at large.[16] Nevertheless, the idea of representative government is that parliaments consist of members with the individual capacity to make decisions, rendering their freedom of action wider than that of a delegate.

---

[13] François Guizot, 'European History as the history of representative institutions', in: Bisson (1973) 9-12.

[14] Scruton, *The Palgrave Macmillan dictionary of political thought*. 3rd Edition (London: Palgrave Macmillan 2007) 168 under 'delegation'.

[15] Quoted in: Scruton (2007) 591 under 'Representation'.

[16] Cf. Frank R. Ankersmit, 'De hedendaagse politieke partij, van representatie van de kiezer naar zelfrepresentatie', in: *Jaarboek DNPP 2000;* M. Gallagher et al., *Representative Government in Modern Europe,* 3rd edition (Boston: McGrall-Hill, 2001); Gerhard Leibholz, *Strukturprobleme der Modernen Demokratie* (Karlsruhe: Verlag C.F. Müller, 1958); Arend Lijphart, *Electoral Systems and Party Systems,* (Oxford: Oxford University Press, 1994); Arend Lijphart, *Democracy in the Twenty-First Century: can we be optimistic?,* (Wassenaar: NIAS, 2000); J. Steiner, *European Democracies,* (London & New York: Longman Inc., 1986); J.J.A. Thomassen, *Kiezers en gekozenen in een representatieve demokratie* (Alphen aan den Rijn: Samsom, 1976); E. Witte, *Politiek en democratie, omtrent de werking van de westerse democratieën in de 19de en 20ste eeuw* (Brussel: VUB press, 1990). I have explored the subject in relation to the Dutch situation: Thierry Baudet, 'Tegen de partij-oligarchie', in: Joop Hazenberg, Farid Tabarki and Rens van Tilburg (eds.), *Dappere Nieuwe Wereld. 21 jonge denkers over de toekomst van Nederland* (Amsterdam: Van Gennep, 2011) 117-124.

A mandate, then – originating from the Latin *mandare*, i.e. to instruct – may mean two things. It may imply a concrete command to do something. For instance in a mandate to buy goods up to a certain amount at an auction; or, in the case of the army commander again, the mandate to use a certain type of weaponry. Yet the word is also used to denote the authority to act: as in a 'mandate of an electorate'. Representatives need such a 'mandate' of their electorate for their actions to be perceived as legitimate.

To clarify this second understanding of representation – in the sense of a mandate from an electorate –, J. Roland Pennock distinguishes between a delegate and a trustee. 'For a representative to act purely and simply as a delegate would be to make him functionless most, if not all, of the time, for it is seldom clear precisely what a constituency, or even its majority, wishes'.[17] On the contrary, indeed, the representative is *entrusted* to make decisions on behalf of his constituents in their name but not necessarily with their consent. The mandate, then, pertains to the period of entrustment, but – and here arises difficulty – also to the content of the general concern of the representative. Surely, many would consider it a breach of the 'mandate of the electorate', if a politician was voted in office because of a strong opposition to, say, immigration or transfer of sovereignty, but then promoted the bringing about of either.

Another approach to this difficulty can be found in Edmund Burke's famous speech delivered on November 3rd, 1774, when he had been elected as one of the representatives of Bristol in the British parliament. Burke contended that 'to be a good member of parliament is (…) no easy task; (…) all [the] wide-spread interests must be considered; must be compared; must be reconciled, if possible',[18] and he went on to argue that:

> It ought to be the happiness and glory of a representative to live in the strictest union, the closest correspondence, and the most unreserved communication with his constituents. Their wishes ought to have great weight with him; their opinion, high respect; their business, unremitted attention. It is his duty to sacrifice his repose, his pleasures, his satisfactions, to theirs; and above all, ever, and in all cases, to prefer their interest to his own.[19]

Burke then continues:

> But his unbiased opinion, his mature judgment, his enlightened conscience, he ought not to sacrifice to you, to any man, or to any set of men living. These he does not derive from your pleasure; no, nor from the law and the constitution. They

[17] J. Roland Pennock, 'Political Representation: an overview', in: R.J. Pennock and J.W. Chapman (eds.), *Representation. Yearbook of the American Society for Political and Legal Philosophy* (New York: Atherton Press, 1968) 3-27, there 15.
[18] Edmund Burke, 'Speech to the Electors of Bristol', in: *Ibidem, Speeches and Letters on American affairs. Introduction by very rev. Canon Peter McKevitt* (London: J.M. Dent & Sons LTD, 1908, reprinted in 1961) 74.
[19] Burke (1961) 72.

are a trust from Providence, for the abuse of which he is deeply answerable. Your
representative owes you, not his industry only, but his judgment; and he betrays,
instead of serving you, if he sacrifices it to your opinion. (...) Parliament is not a
congress of ambassadors (...) but parliament is a *deliberative* assembly (...) you
choose a member indeed; but when you have chosen him, he is not member of
Bristol, but he is a member of *parliament*.[20]

Burke thus emphasizes the autonomous judgment a representative is entitled,
indeed required, to make. Because the direct form of representation has become,
in practice, impossible in modern times, this seems necessary for any form of
democracy in advanced societies. Organization implies a hierarchy:[21] this is what
Robert Michels calls the 'iron law of oligarchy'.[22] 'Rule by the people' – the literal
meaning of 'democracy' – is therefore necessarily dependent upon the Burkean
idea of representation. But again this poses the problem of social cohesion in
the relation between constituents and representatives.

For representative government presupposes two things. The first is the
possibility of the people to be actively involved in the government through
periodical, free elections among a wide franchise, and the possibility to partake
in political decision making, to stand for election, and to have freedom of
expression in political debate. I call these first presumptions of representative
government its 'formal' prerequisites. Concerned only with the institutional
reality, these could be installed on every level: municipal, national, European,
global; or anything in between.

Yet representative government also presupposes something else, which I call its
'material' prerequisites. This is the *experience* of representation in governmental
institutions, requiring not merely a right to vote as well as all the other formal
institutions that allow political participation, but also a collective identity that can
be represented as a whole. The term democracy may easily be understood as a
formal, legalistic arrangement. However, to speak of 'representative government'
leads to the question of what it is that can be represented. It poses the question
of collective identity since it poses the question why a majority decision would
be experienced as legitimate. This 'material' aspect of representation proves far
more problematic than its formal aspect.

For it is self-evident that formal representation can exist in any central body
where decisions can be made. As John Stuart Mill writes in his *Considerations
on Representative Government*: 'the meaning of representative government is,
that the whole people, or some numerous portion of them, exercise, through

---

[20] *Ibidem.*
[21] Cf. the works of Moisey Ostrogorski, who has written about the depth of experienced loyalties
among members of political parties.
[22] Cf. James Burnham, *The Machiavellians* (Chicago: The John Day Company, Inc., 1943) esp.
180ff: 'The iron Law of Oligarchy'.

deputies periodically elected by themselves, the ultimate controlling power …'.
He continues: 'This ultimate power they must possess in all its completeness.'[23]

The point Mill here makes is evident. If the national government is tied to
all kinds of supranational entanglements, such as the ones described in the
previous part of this book, there is no guarantee that the laws and policies it
has to enforce are representative of its people's wishes or perceived interests. It
must be clear where and by whom rules and decisions have been made or could
be made for representative government to be able to exist.

But a deeper question related to representative government is: who *are* the
people? Why could an elected supranational structure, such as the European
Parliament, not attain the same level of representation? This leads to the material
aspect of representative government: the *experience* or *perception* of representation. It refers not just to the institutional reality, but to the social reality. Ronald
Dworkin presents an instructive thought-experiment on this subject in a chapter
entitled 'Who are the People?', in his book *Justice for Hedgehogs* (2011). 'One
day', he imagines, 'Japan grants equal voting rights to the citizens of Norway
so that they can elect a small party of Norwegians to the Japanese Diet if they
wish. Then the Diet by majority vote levies taxes on Norwegian oil and directs
its transfer to Japanese refineries.' Obviously, this would not satisfy the criteria
for representative government. Dworkin concludes:

> If some form of majoritarian process is to provide genuine self-government, it
> must be government by a majority of the *right* people.[24]

The question who are the *right* people comes down to a more simple one: who
are 'the people'? Who fall in the group considering themselves represented, and
who fall out of it? This question is of a sociological nature, and depends on the
experience of membership: 'we' are the people, if we believe we share the same
identity and the same loyalty. And it was this, that we identified as 'the nation'
in the first part of this book.

When it comes to the experience of membership, the famous 1928 Thomas
theorem applies: 'if men define situations as real, they are real in their consequences'[25] – meaning in this case that whatever subjective experience of
membership exists, determines the reality of material representation.

Should the Scots regard their political representation threatened by governing
together with the English, then that is a fact one has to deal with. This could
change of course, depending on political climate, financial stability, economic

---

[23] John Stuart Mill, *Considerations on Representative Government* (New York: Prometheus
Books, 1991) 97: Chapter V, 'Of the proper functions of representative bodies'.
[24] Ronald Dworkin, *Justice for Hedgehogs* (Cambridge, MA: Harvard University Press, 2011) 380.
[25] W.I. Thomas and D.S. Thomas, *The child in America: Behavior problems and programs* (New
York: Knopf, 1928) 571-572.

and cultural factors, and so on. Defending representative government could therefore mean supporting a return to govern on a smaller scale than the scope of current nation states; equally, it could mean the rendering of full sovereignty to a federal United States of Europe: provided the material experience of membership is in place. For while representative government can well go hand in hand with a division between matters of regional importance and matters of national importance;[26] it can also mean moving on to an even larger scale (in this case to that of a European representative federation). Yet then again, the point becomes evident that a European-wide social cohesion – a continental collective identity – would be required. In both cases, therefore, the experience of membership provides the material 'representativeness' of the formal representation.

But as government encompasses more than merely parliamentary rule, there is also more to representative government than merely parliamentary representation. The entire political structure, with its balance of powers and several different branches, requires rootedness in a collective identity. This is especially problematic when it comes to judges, typically unelected officials of the state, as we will see in the next paragraph. For what is the role of judges in representative government? What is required of them to fit in the scheme of representative government? And what may it imply, to have a body of judges appointed by different national governments, as is the case in the ECHR?

7.3. LAW

Rule of law is in place when at least three principles are applied to the government of a society:

1. In its actions, the state is bound by the law;
2. In passing laws or changing the law, the state is bound by procedural prerequisites;
3. There is an impartial judiciary applying the laws.

The first criterion ensures that state action is not arbitrary but that the law provides for the state's competencies. It also implies that a subject, 'however placed, [may] enforce that law', even against the state itself.[27] In this way the state, however powerful or encompassing its rule may be, can be held accountable under the same laws as it applies to its citizens, in the same courts, by the same judges.

---

[26] Cf. John Stuart Mill, *Considerations on representative government* (New York: Prometheus Books, 1991) 286ff: Chapter XV, 'Of local representative bodies'.
[27] Scruton, *The Palgrave Macmillan dictionary of political thought.* 3rd Edition (London: Palgrave Macmillan, 2007) 611 under 'rule of law'.

The second principle forbids that arbitrary changes in the law be made; laws must be enacted before they become valid, and have to be debated in public and voted upon by a legislative assembly.

An important element in both these aspects of the rule of law is that it helps to realize 'legal certainty'. For it means that no judgment is binding unless based on a previously encoded law. In passing laws or changing the law, the state must be bound by certain procedural prerequisites, and legislation must not have retrospective effect.[28] But it is precisely at this point, however, that it becomes increasingly clear why the whole concept of the rule of law already implies a nation state. For in practice all legal certainty is dependent on the predictability of legal judgments, which in turn depends, to speak with Oliver Wendell Holmes, on 'the prophecies of what the courts will do'.[29]

Without some degree of certainty about the judges that will administer the law, people grope in the dark as to the content of the law.[30] Therefore, legal certainty in reality implies being judged by judges who understand the often vague terms of the law in a foreseeable way. The rule of law for that reason does not merely mean the rule of previously issued rules (a merely formal meaning), but also some extent of uniformity and trust in how they may be understood (a material meaning).

This is partly realized through the third criterion: the impartial judiciary branch, which ensures that the courts reach their decisions autonomously. But the 'impartiality' or 'autonomy' of the judiciary is as much restrained by their connection to a shared sense of community. While the law that rules is, naturally, the law of society, the judges that administer it are for that reason supposed to be a part of that society.

In principle, one might say, there should be no reason why different judges should not come to the same conclusions in a given dispute; for what is 'legal' should be subject to the abstract and neutral logic of the profession. But in reality, the vaguer – or more 'fundamental' – the principles concerned, the more leeway judges have.

Take as an example the 'right to life'. Many people would say that this right is among the most fundamental principles of justice, and that respect for it should lie at the core of any sensible notion of the 'rule of law'. But what does it mean in practice? What are the boundaries of police action, for instance, when dealing with terrorists or armed criminals? Or what positive obligation to protect life

---

[28] See on this: Scruton, 'Rechtsgefühl and the Rule of Law', in: J.C. Nyiri and B. Smith (eds.), *Practical Knowledge: outlines of a Theory of Traditions and Skills* (London: Croom Helm, 1988) 61ff.
[29] Oliver Wendell Holmes, jr., 'The path of the law', in: *Harvard Law Review* vol. 10, no. 8 (1897) 457.
[30] Cf. Benjamin N. Cardozo, *The nature of the judicial process* (New York: Dover publications, 2005).

follows from the 'right to life'? What may this mean in the future concerning abortion and euthanasia? And concerning access to healthcare and medicines?

Indeed, if we take the 'right to life' seriously, should certain political measures curtailing the welfare state not be regarded as a violation of it? Leaving someone starving or freezing to death on the street without providing a remedy amounts to murder, a random collective of judges might say.

Or take the principle of non-discrimination. Again something that sounds 'fundamental' and important, but that can impossibly be neutrally administered. For consistent application of this principle should mean the prohibition of just about anything, for example the abolition of all hereditary monarchies, as well as the constitutional rule that to become American president, one has to be born in the US. The privileged position that many states – for a variety of social, cultural and historical reasons – preserve for a specific religious denomination, for instance the Anglican Church in Britain, or the Lutheran in Denmark, or clubs that discriminate on the basis of sex: all may theoretically be found to be in violation of this principle. Because no two people are entirely the same, the principle of non-discrimination is endless in its application (just as 'equal opportunity' would theoretically require a ban on private property and the dissolution of families). The prohibition of discrimination in any case, inevitably clashes with classic civil liberties such as those of expression, conscience and religion.

This is by no means a theoretical discussion only. Consider the dissenting opinion of judge Pavlovschi in the case of *O'Halloran and Francis v. the United Kingdom* at the European Court of Human Rights in 2007,[31] who believed speed limits were a violation of fundamental human rights:

> In my opinion, if there are so many breaches of a prohibition, it clearly means that something is wrong with the prohibition. It means that the prohibition does not reflect a pressing social need, given that so many people choose to breach it even under the threat of criminal prosecution. And if this is the case, maybe the time has come to review speed limits and to set limits that would more correctly reflect peoples' needs. We cannot force people in the twenty-first century to ride bicycles or start jogging instead of enjoying the advantages which our civilization brings. Equally, it is difficult for me to accept the argument that hundreds of thousands of speeding motorists are wrong and only the government is right.[32]

As this example shows, judges can – and will – easily stretch the rights and principles they rule upon to cover the most far-reaching phenomena; their task is not confined to merely applying the law to presented facts. There are many obvious examples from the United States as well.[33] From the *Dred Scott*

[31] Case of *O'Halloran and Francis v. The United Kingdom (Applications 15809/02 and 25624/02)* Judgment Strasbourg 29 June 2007.
[32] *Ibidem*, dissenting opinion of Judge Pavlovschi.
[33] Cf. Bork (1990).

v. Sandford case (1856), in which the Supreme Court ruled that people of African descent, whether former slaves or not, were not citizens as meant in the Constitution;[34] to the *Roe v. Wade* case (1973), in which the right to abortion was found implicit in a person's rights (Fourteenth Amendment); to the *Regents of the University of California v. Bakke* case (1978), in which *affirmative action* was found constitutional (and therefore not in violation of the constitutional right of equality).[35]

The freedom judges have is precisely the reason why becoming one is often a very selective process, and why nominations for supreme courts are almost everywhere *political* decisions (by royal resolution upon nomination by Parliament, for example, in the Netherlands[36]). American presidents nominate judges with views consistent with their own. The Senate, which must ratify the appointments, can oppose the nomination when the majority has a different political opinion (as happened in 1987 when the candidate of Ronald Reagan was rejected). Americans know where the judges of the Supreme Court stand and weigh their chances to push for certain political changes when a judge is replaced. Democrats hope to replace Republican judges, and vice versa (as has been discussed in chapter 4.2).[37]

Now, precisely because different judges may interpret the same rules differently, legal certainty is threatened when different judges, from a different nation, are invited to pass judgment. It is unpredictable what different judges will say. While it is certainly true that different judges of the same nation may also disagree, placing the judiciary outside the national context no doubt multiplies this problem exponentially.

But there is also another side to this point. For legal certainty not only requires that the conduct of the judges is to a large extent predictable; it also presupposes that the expectations of those subjected to the same laws are to a large extent congruent. Ordinary people do not have profound knowledge of jurisprudence; they act on the basis of a *Rechtsgefühl* that certain things may be expected from

---

[34] '... We think they [people of African ancestry] are ... not included, and were not intended to be included, under the word 'citizens' in the Constitution, and can therefore claim none of the rights and privileges which that instrument provides for and secures to citizens of the United States ...'. (Chief Justice Roger B. Taney, speaking for the majority).

[35] '... Race or ethnic background may be deemed a 'plus' in a particular applicant's file, yet it does not insulate the individual from comparison with all other candidates for the available seats ...'. (Justice Powell, Speaking for the Court).

[36] Cf. Articles 117 and 118 of the Dutch constitution.

[37] At present, of course, debates are raging as to the proper role of the supreme court. Cf. Stephen Breyer, *Making our democracy work. A judge's view* (New York: Alfred A. Knopf, 2010); Erwin Chemerinsky, *The conservative assault on the constitution* (New York: Simon & Schuster, 2010); Jeffrey Toobin, *The Nine. Inside the secret world of the supreme court* (New York: Anchor Books, 2008).

others, and certain corresponding duties demanded.[38] If you and I have entirely different ideas of what 'equity' means, or what constitutes a threat to my 'honor' or 'good name', then there can be no legal certainty between us in our ordinary interactions (unless we constantly consult our lawyers).

Moreover, as the courtroom is never more than an ultimate remedy, the 'rule of law' really implies that the individuals in a society generally have a shared, internalized idea of morality and that they live more or less according to it.

This also works the other way round. For how could a judge determine what equity or 'good faith' or 'grave reasons' or 'casting a slur on a person's honor' (legitimizing self-defense) mean, if he could not refer to a general – dominant, *Leitkulturliches* – viewpoint or tradition in society?[39]

For these reasons – the need for congruence in both the viewpoints of judges and in the expectations of the people – the content of the law itself is in practice mostly congealed culture. However abstract legal reasoning may be, and however intellectual the arguments may be: properly understood, the rule of law is only the tip of the iceberg of social cohesion. The very idea implies a *Leitkultur*.

To be a judge is therefore inescapably a representative function on behalf of a community. The judge has been granted the confidence of the members of the community to voice and co-determine their way of life.[40] Even the administration of 'fundamental' values requires a judge to choose position: between being reserved and being activist, between keeping in line with past cases or changing course, between defining racism in the strict etymological meaning or in a more wide-ranging, 'cultural' sense; or between interpreting the right to life as prohibitive of the death penalty, of abortion or of assisted suicide.

Judges cannot give arbitrary opinions, and the aim is to give a judgment that would win the consent of other independent rational observers. But this does not remove all subjective elements from the activity of judges.[41] As David Pannick writes: 'However knowledgeable judges may be about their biases, we cannot expect them to give other than an informed and intelligent but never-

---

[38] Cf. Scruton (1988) 61ff.

[39] As indeed multiculturalism has shown, it becomes increasingly difficult for judges to condemn so-called 'honor killings' as these acts were sanctioned by a culture that had been granted the same rights as the dominant national culture (See chapter 6).

[40] It is precisely because of this proper function of judges, that a portrait of the Queen is present in every Dutch courthouse: to emphasize that judges bear the authority of the majesty, and that the duty of obedience arises from that in which all Dutch citizens are represented – the sovereign. If judges did not have such authority, the losing party should have no reason to accept their verdict. Who would those men and women in gowns be to tell them what they should or should not do? Again: 'What right have you, a foreigner, to come to me and tell me what I must do?' Ernest Hemingway, *For whom the bell tolls* (London: Vintage Books, 2005) 17.

[41] See on this: Arie-Jan Kwak, 'Het (on)persoonlijke gezicht van het recht; de rechter tussen objectiviteit en gezag', in: *Trema* (Special 2, 2008) 428-431; Arie-Jan Kwak (ed.), *Holy Writ: Interpretation in Law and Religion* (Surrey: Ashgate, 2009).

theless subjective view of the facts and the law. It is therefore a matter of great importance who is appointed to the Bench'.[42]

Their role as a counterweight against mere majority rule,[43] may thus easily be perceived as a 'tyranny of the minority'. His decision can only have authority, if the judge is recognized and accepted by the parties seeking a remedy through him. Although his 'impartiality' is an important feature for him, it is only 'impartiality' as to the conflicting parties; he has to be at the same time recognized by both as part of the community; as part of their 'we'. In this way, tyranny of the majority and tyranny of the minority are the Scylla and Charybdis a wise constitutional system has to navigate its way through.[44]

This observation is also relevant for our discussion of multiculturalism. For the national judges can only be accepted as such by cultural and religious minorities, if there is a sense of shared community that gives the judge in question his authority and enables him to speak in this particular case (hence the enthusiasm of some Muslim communities for Sharia courts with *their own* judges, see also chapter 9.3). Thus in fact, a judge is not so much supposed to be 'objective' as to be 'authoritative': and that can only be the case when he is part of a larger whole, of which the conflicting parties are also members. And only the nation provides the territorial context for such authority.

---

[42] David Pannick, *Judges* (Oxford: Oxford University Press, 1987) 44 (and backflap).
[43] Cf. J. Hampton, 'Democracy and the rule of law', in: Ian Shapiro (ed.), *The Rule of Law: Nomos XXXVI. Yearbook of the American society for Political and Legal Philosophy* (New York: New York University Press, 1994) 13-44.
[44] Cf. Thierry Baudet, 'De achilleshiel van de rechtsstaat', in: *NRC Handelsblad,* 16 December, 2011.

CHAPTER EIGHT

THE FALLACIES OF UNIVERSALISM

8.1. *No More War*

Three fallacies accompany the assault on borders. I call them the fallacies of universalism. They return time and again at defences of supranational or multicultural projects. The first is, that the First and Second World Wars have taught us that 'nationalism' is inherently war bound, and that supranational – universalist – projects, such as the EU, are the answer to that inherently bellicose nature of man, dangerously surfacing through national democracies, which must therefore be curtailed.

The second is, that the universal society, based solely on abstract principles of justice that all people could agree with, could be an actuality. At least since the Enlightenment, this idea has been fashionable among liberal philosophers, and those adhering to it have thenceforth dreamed of superseding the particularities of different cultures and of installing a world government that would make such arbitrary national arrangements obsolete.

The third fallacy is the idea of the all-inclusiveness (or, which amounts to the same thing, the non-exclusiveness) of political loyalties, suggesting that it is entirely unproblematic to hold several passports; to feel loyal to several different states; and to have, generally, no particular attachment to any particular nation, but rather to subgroups or even virtual communities, that may transgress borders, as in the philosophy of multiculturalism.

Serving as arguments to legitimize the assault on borders, these fallacies of universalism are being brought forward regularly by advocates of supranationalism or multiculturalism. This chapter attempts to show why they are in fact fallacies, commencing with the first: that nationalism is inherently war bound.

To be sure, one of the leading themes of the second half of the 20th century was '*Nie wieder Krieg*': never again the loss of lives and the destruction that the First and the Second World Wars had brought about. It was widely felt that nationalism had been one of the primary causes of these wars, and this makes it hardly surprising that European intellectuals have taken a sceptical approach towards national sovereignty. The nation state seemed to produce nationalism, which had, in turn, produced war, destruction, and the holocaust. The German philosopher Karl Jaspers wrote in 1951 that it was the task of the 'great' German nation to 'negate' nationality. Apparently oblivious to the obvious contradiction, he contended that 'the history of the German nation state has come to an end.

As a great nation we can do but one thing for us and the world: to make people realize that today the idea of the nation state spells disaster for Europe and all the other continents'. He concluded:

> The idea of the nation state is today a destructive force in the world of mighty proportions. We may begin to lay bare its roots and effect its negation.[1]

His perspective was widely shared by European elites, and still is until this day. The former French president François Mitterrand received a great applause, for instance, when he announced in 1995 that 'le nationalisme, c'est la guerre!'[2] Ten years later, in 2005, Tony Blair warned the European Parliament that if Europe would cease its expansion and stick with the members that shared some cultural inheritance (by for instance excluding Turkey), it would 'become more narrow, more introspective', and what would await Europe was 'outdated nationalism and xenophobia.'[3]

'Nationalism was identified as the problem', concludes the British journalist Douglas Murray, 'and as the nation was responsible for nationalism, it was obviously the cause of the problem.'[4] It was precisely from this perspective, that the former President of the European Parliament (1994-1997), the German Klaus Hänsch,[5] said: 'Never again must a state be so sovereign that it can decide between weal and woe, between war and peace.'[6] This is a clear attack on the idea of sovereignty itself, of course, and as such illustrative of the supranational idea – which does not aim at creating a new sovereign entity, but, as I have explained, at negating the concept of sovereignty altogether.

At the time of the 60th anniversary of the end of World War II, EU Commissioner Margot Wallström tried to persuade the people to vote for the European constitutional treaty, arguing that 'politicians who resisted pooling national sovereignty risked a return to Nazi horrors of the 1930s and 1940s'.[7] In her speech, not coincidentally organized at the site of the former concentration camp Theresienstadt (Terezin) in the Czech Republic, she blamed the Second World War on

---

[1] Jaspers (1969) 53: 'Die Geschichte des deutschen Nationalstaats ist zu Ende, nicht die Geschichte der Deutschen. Was wir als grosse Nation uns und der Welt leisten können, ist die Einsicht in die Weltsituation heute: dass der Nationalstaatsgedanke heute das Unheil Europas und nun auch aller Kontinente ist. Während der Nationalstaatsgedanke die heute übermächtige zerstörende Kraft der Erde ist, können wir beginnen, ihn in der Wurzel zu durchschauen und aufzuheben.'

[2] François Mitterrand, *Speech of 17 January 1995* at the European Parliament, available online at http://www.lours.org/default.asp?pid=375.

[3] Tony Blair, *Speech of 23 June 2005*, published on http://news.bbc.co.uk/1/hi/uk_politics/4122288. stm.

[4] Douglas Murray, *Neoconservatism: why we need it* (London: Social Affairs Unit, 2005) 178.

[5] Klaus Hänsch presided the European Parliament from 1994 till 1997.

[6] *Frankfurter Allgemeine Zeitung*, 16 October 1995, as quoted in Laughland (1997) 77.

[7] 'Vote for EU Constitution or risk new Holocaust, says Brussels', *Daily Telegraph*, 9 May 2005.

nationalistic pride and greed, and (…) international rivalry for wealth and power.

According to Wallström, the EU had replaced such rivalry with an historic agreement to share national sovereignty.[8]

Two years later, in 2007, when the EU was celebrating its 50th birthday, the motto was: 'The EU: 50 years of peace', indeed suggesting that there was a causal connection between the two. In his speech to the University of Washington (Seattle), deputy spokesperson for the European Commission to the United States, Mattias Sundholm, remembered that 'some 65 years ago, the world was in flames (…) Europeans fought each other, and in the rest of the world people were starving and millions of people died'.

What a contrast with the summer of 2006, Sundholm contended, when Germany was hosting the World Soccer Championship. He was struck by people coming 'from all over Europe, with the common currency – the Euro – in their pockets, travelling there without passports – because those are not needed in a Europe without borders – and waving their own respective national flags – and this without violence or holding grudge against each other'. Coming to his conclusion, Sundholm said:

> Now, how did all this happen, and in only some 50 years? Well, to a large extent it is thanks to an economist from Cognac in France, Robert Schuman (…).[9] [never mind that it was the brandy salesman Jean Monnet who came from Cognac, while Schuman, the economist, was an Alsatian]

Imaginatively as it may be presented (although one may doubt the lack of 'grudge' to be found in football supporters) the question of congruence with reality is pressing. How true is all this? What is really the connection between the Second World War and nationalism? And to what extent can the EU – and other supranational projects – be credited for whatever 'lasting peace' may have come about since 1945?

---

[8] *Ibidem.*
[9] 'Let me start off by briefly sharing two pictures with you: Some 65 years ago, the world was in flames, to a large extent because of and orchestrated from Nazi-Germany and Berlin. Europeans fought each other, and in the rest of the world people were starving and millions of people died. And this was not the first time the very same European countries were fighting each other; some of them had been in war at least 3 times in the last 75 years. Please keep this picture in your heads for a second. Last summer, the very same country – Germany – and its capital – Berlin – hosted the World Soccer Championships. People came from all over Europe, with the common currency – the Euro – in their pockets, travelling there without passports – because those are not needed in a Europe without borders – and waving their own respective national flags – and this without violence or holding grudge against each other. Now, how did all this happen, and in only some 50 years? Well, to a large extent it is thanks to an economist from Cognac in France, Robert Schuman, who later became French foreign minister and who said that "Europe will not be made all at once, or according to a single plan. It will be built through concrete achievements which first create a *de facto* solidarity."' Available online at http://www.eurunion.org/eu/2007-Speeches-and-Press-Conferences-/THE-EUROPEAN-UNION-CELEBRATING-50-YEARS-OF-PEACE-PROSPERITY-AND-PARTNERSHIP.html.

Was Nazism even a form of nationalism? Though generally contended, this view is not entirely undisputed either. One historian who has questioned the all too quick identification of Nazism with nationalism is the renowned Oxford historian and Special Operations veteran of the Second World War, Hugh Seton-Watson. In his classic account on *Nations and States,* Seton-Watson analyzed that 'it may be argued that Hitler was himself a nationalist, resolved to perfect the union of all Germans which had been left incomplete in 1870'.[10] Hitler succeeded in

> annexing the great majority of 'unredeemed' Germans in 1938 without war (Austria and the Bohemian borderlands of Czechoslovakia), but he was unable to annex the million and a half Germans of Poland and the city of Danzig without going to war with the Poles, and this let loose a European war which in turn became a world war.

Giving further credit to this 'standard' view of history, Seton-Watson continues that it can well be argued, that 'a series of conflicts, concerned with the status of unsatisfied nations (Croats and Slovaks) or of divided nations (Hungarians in Czechoslovakia, Yugoslavia and Romania; Bulgarians in Yugoslavia, Romania and Greece), created in Central Europe an atmosphere of mutual hatred between states which caused each in turn to succumb either to the blandishments or to the aggression of Hitler'.[11] Seton-Watson concludes that 'Thus, nationalism played an important part.' He nevertheless goes on to say that:

> It is equally clear that Hitler's aims were not limited to anything which, even if the phrase be stretched to the utmost, can be described as German nationalism. His aim was to conquer all Europe and a good deal more besides. Mussolini aimed to create a new Roman empire in the Mediterranean, the Japanese a Greater East Asia Co-Prosperity Sphere embracing hundreds of millions who were not Japanese.[12]

Seton-Watson thus emphasizes the important distinction between *nationalism* on the one hand, and *imperialism* on the other. Though the latter may follow from the former, they are not identical phenomena.

In his polemical work *The tainted source,* John Laughland goes further, and analyzes the eurofederalist tendencies inherent in Fascism and Nazism itself. 'It is false', he writes, 'to say that the ideology of European unification (...) post-dates the Second World War, or even that it was only ever conceived in opposition to its worst excesses. On the contrary, not only the Nazis, but fascists and collaborators from many European countries, made very widespread use of

---

[10] Seton-Watson (1977) 467-469.
[11] Seton-Watson (1977) 468.
[12] Seton-Watson (1977) 469.

European ideology'.[13] Joseph Goebbels, for instance, asserted in a speech entitled 'Das Europa der Zukunft', that

> European peoples are realizing more and more clearly that many of the issues between us are mere family quarrels compared to the great problems that today require to be solved as between continents.[14]
> (…)
> I am convinced that in fifty years people will no longer think in terms of countries – many of today's problems will have faded into obscurity, and there will be little left of them.[15]

In a conversation with the Finnish foreign minister, R. Witting, held on November 28th, 1941, Adolf Hitler was recorded to have said that 'it was gradually becoming clear that the nations of Europe belonged together like a great family of nations. France, too, would come to realize this, and he hoped that England, too, would recognize this; it was to be hoped that it would not be too late. England had to realize that the only group of powers which had an interest in maintaining the British Empire was Europe and never America.'[16]

> He [the Führer] did not belong to those who were ready to leave to circumstances a very difficult task with which they had been confronted. The task of bringing together the European family had to be performed now. With modern military technology small nations could no longer exist independently. In a time when 600 km could be covered by an airplane in an hour, a great territorial integration of nations was necessary. [17]

In a memorandum, probably written for the Nazi top-diplomat Cecil von Renthe-Fink, the NSDAP journalist and secretary Karl Mergele developed a number of guidelines on Europe, which included the observation that

> The new order in Europe will largely remove the causes that have led to internal European wars in the past. The nations of Europe will no longer be one another's enemies. The age of European particularism will be gone for ever.[18]

The memo concluded that

> The new Europe will be tolerant in matters of religion and personal philosophy. It will permit each and everyone.[19]

---

[13] Laughland (1998) 12.
[14] Goebbels, "'Das Europa der Zukunft": speech to Czech intellectual workers and journalists', 11 september 1940, reprinted in: Walter Lipgens (ed.), *Documents on the History of European Integration* (Berlin and New York: De Gruyter, 1985) 73. Discussed and analyzed by Laughland (1998) 25.
[15] *Ibidem.*
[16] Walter Hewel, 'record of conversation between Hitler and the Finnish foreign minister, R. Witting, 28 November 1941', in: Lipgens (1985) 94.
[17] *Ibidem.*
[18] Karl Mergele, 'European themes', probably autumn 1941, reprinted in Lipgens (1985) 95.
[19] *Ibidem.*

Von Ribbentrop, too, wrote in a note in 1943 that 'I am of the opinion that, as already proposed to the Führer in my previous minutes, we should at the earliest possible date, as soon as we have scored a significant military success, proclaim the European Confederation in quite a specific form.'[20]

Mussolini had already announced in 1933 that 'Europe may once again grasp the helm of world civilization if it can develop a modicum of political unity',[21] and several thinkers who were also charmed and fascinated by Fascist, corporatist or national socialist initiatives, such as Bertrand de Jouvenel and Pierre Drieu la Rochelle, supported a European federalist cause.[22]

Others have argued that these references to a United Europe were primarily a matter of propaganda.[23] Propaganda may certainly have played an important part in fascist and national-socialist references to a 'united', a 'peaceful' and a 'tolerant' Europe, but to regard it all as merely that is not an entirely satisfactory explanation. For not only were references to a united Europe often not made in public but rather in private conversations and memoranda, the enthusiasm was also generally shared among not only political leaders but also intellectual supporters.

Whatever is the case, however, the point here is not that what Nazi's and fascists had in mind with the future of Europe was necessarily the same as what Jean Monnet and his followers desired. The point is that it is certainly not self-evident that fascism and Nazism were 'nationalisms'. Their pan-European plans were much more *imperialisms* than strict nationalisms.

It may furthermore be emphasised, as Laughland quite rightly does, that racialism 'as a form of materialist determinism', of the pseudo-scientific kind expounded by Nazi-theorists such as Alfred Rosenberg,[24] 'is a non-national

---

[20] Ribbentrop, 'European Confederation', 21 March 1943, reprinted in Lipgens (1985) 122-123. Discussed and analyzed by Laughland (1998) 33.

[21] Benito Mussolini, 'Discorso pre lo stato corporativo', in: Eduardo and Duilio Susmel (eds.), *Opera omnia, XXVI: Dal Patto a Quattro all'inaugurazione della Provincia di Littoria* (Florence: La Fenice, 1958) 91, quoted in Laughland (1998) 47.

[22] Bertrand de Jouvenel authored a book in 1930 entitled *Vers les États Unis de l'Europe*; in the following years, he joined the Parti Populaire Francais, an anti-parliamentary party led by Jacques Doriot, and partly funded by the Italian fascists. Pierre Drieu la Rochelle wrote an essay in 1928, entitled *Genève ou Moscou* (Paris: Gallimard, 1928), in which he advocated strong European cooperation, and he supported the collaboration with Germany from 1942 onwards. Cf. Daniel Knegt, 'Ni droite, ni gauche? Debatten over het Franse fascisme', in: *Tijdschrift voor Geschiedenis*, 124.3 (2011) 206-219. There was also considerable support among communist thinkers for the European idea; Altiero Spinelli is an example. Indeed, the very core idea of Jean Monnet – that cultural unity follows economic unity – is essentially Marxist.

[23] As is done for example by Christopher Booker and Richard North, in *The Great Deception. Can the European Union survive?* Second Edition (London and New York: Continuum, 2005) 22-40.

[24] Alfred Rosenberg, *Der mythos des 20. Jahrhunderts. Eine Wertung der Seelisch-geistigen Gestaltenkämpfe unserer Zeit* (München: Hoheneichen-Verlag, 1930).

concept'.[25] Indeed, 'race transcends the boundaries of the nation and of the state, and racialist theory is thus, by definition, an international doctrine'.[26]

Nationalism in the sense that we have defined it in chapter 3 – as an imagined and territorial loyalty, to be distinguished from universal loyalties on the one hand, and tribal loyalties on the other – is in any case certainly not easily connected to some of the more obscure doctrines of Nazism, such as its emphasis on 'Aryan'-supremacy. As Tzvetan Todorov writes, for nationalism 'the notion of the stranger (…) says nothing about the physical characteristics of the designated individual'.[27] Indeed, from a nationalist point of view, strangers are simply those 'who are not citizens', Todorov recognizes.[28] Opposed to this is the viewpoint of the racist, as illustrated by how the Ku-Klux-Klan approaches African- or Jewish-Americans:

> The racist (…) sees the man, not the citizen: the blacks or the jews in America partake in the same nation as the member of the Ku-Klux-Klan, but are not part of the same 'race'. We can change our nationality, not our race (the first notion is moral, the second physical).[29]

If we take that view, thus, Nazism was not even a nationalism. But even when taking the view that Nazism grew out of a pathological kind of nationalism associated in chapter 3 with national humiliations (as the German nation clearly had to face after the dictate of Versailles), it is clearly not easily understood as a defense of national sovereignty – but rather, as mentioned above, as imperialism. It seems safe to contend indeed, as does Seton-Watson, that 'Hitler's aims were not limited to anything which, even if the phrase be stretched to the utmost, can be described as German nationalism'.[30]

Apart from references to the Second World War, mention is often made of the First World War as an example of the atrocities committed in the name of nationalism. But again the German objective in the First World War was not only to defend or expand the German nation state, but also to establish a German imperial yoke on non-German parts of Western Europe.

As Seton-Watson notes, the First World War 'started by a conflict between Austria-Hungary and Serbia, which was directly caused by the unsatisfied movement of the South Slavs for national unity'.[31] Serbia had been recognized as an

---

[25] Laughland (1997) 15.
[26] Ibidem.
[27] Todorov (1989) 333: 'la notion d'étranger (…) ne dit rien des caractéristiques physiques de l'individu incriminé'.
[28] Ibidem: 'qui ne sont pas citoyens'.
[29] Ibidem: 'Le raciste, en revanche, voit l'homme, non le citoyen : les Noirs ou les juifs américains appartiennent à la même nation que le membre du Ku-Klux-Klan, mais non à la même « race ». On peut changer de nation, non de race (la première notion est morale, la seconde physique)'.
[30] Seton-Watson (1977) 468.
[31] Ibidem.

independent state at the Congress of Berlin of 1878, but a large proportion of the Serbian population remained under the Ottoman and the Habsburg empires.[32] The southern part of Serbia was won from the Ottomans at the first Balkan war of 1912-3, but attempts to reunite the Habsburg parts of Serbia – especially Bosnia – failed, motivating a group of 'Young Bosnians' to plan the assassination of archduke Franz Ferdinand upon his visit to Sarajevo in June 1914. This was carried out by Gravilo Princip on the 28th of that month.

But the Serbs were certainly not the only nationalities within the Habsburg empire to strive for more recognition or even independence. 'Different national aspirations began to clash head on', writes Oliver Zimmer.[33] The nationalisms in the Habsburg Monarchy, according to Seton-Watson, 'had been largely provoked by the policy of the Hungarian government which sought to create a single Magyar nation out of several other nations by a policy dictated from above.'[34]

Again Zimmer:

> Magyarisation – the cultural nationalism of the Magyar majority that dominated the state – was 'motivated by a sense of cultural superiority' on the part of the dominant group. Its impact was particularly marked in education, where the laws of 1879, 1883, 1891 and 1893 made Hungarian the official language in state and confessional schools. Another pillar of Magyarisation was electoral politics: Magyars took over 90 per cent of parliamentary seats, while Romanians, Slovaks and Serbs remained grossly under-represented. A law of 1898 determined that each town or village could have only one official (Magyar) name, to be approved by the Minister of the Interior. The tombstones of local cemeteries had to be engraved in Magyar.[35]

The different nationalities were widely considered to be problematic,[36] and 'Hungary's state-building nationalism caused considerable resentment among the economically and culturally less advanced ethnic minorities in the border areas.'[37]

Thus while it is undoubtedly true that nationalism has been important in the origins of the First World War, it seems equally true that 'forcible repression of national aspirations has also been',[38] and indeed this has been one of the major lessons that many observers drew from the First World War. An example is

---

[32] A. Sked, *The decline and fall of the Habsburg Empire, 1815-1918* (London: Pearson, 2001) esp. 216-222.

[33] Oliver Zimmer, *Nationalism in Europe, 1890-1940* (New York: Palgrave Macmillan, 2003) 56.

[34] Seton-Watson (1977) 468.

[35] Zimmer (2003) 56.

[36] Cf. E. Niederhausen, 'The national question in Hungary', in: Teich and Porter (eds.), *The national question in Europe in historical context* (Cambridge: Cambridge University Press, 1998) 248-269.

[37] Zimmer (2003) 59.

[38] Seton-Watson (1977) 469.

Woodrow Wilson, whose 'principle of self-determination' implies respect for the different nationalities rather than the desire for their dissolution.[39]

Going back further in history, moreover, it is clear that it was after the humiliation of 1870-1 that the pathological kind of nationalism emerged in France in which the Dreyfus affaire became possible; or that it was right after the march of the French *armée* underneath the Brandenburg gate in 1806, that Fichte called for the German nation to gather militarily, and that Herders ethnic nationalism grew to great popularity (as discussed in chapter 3). It is true that nationalism has been a potent force in modern political history: but it has only been responsible for war if it was confronted with an imperial (or supranational) power, or when it turned into imperialism itself, which, again, only seems to have happened after national humiliation (again, by other imperial or supranational powers).

Another question is to what extent the EU can be credited for a supposed lasting peace after 1945. It is widely claimed that this is the true novelty that European integration has brought. Although there can be no doubt that the First and Second World War were of unprecedented horror, it is not self-evident that the time before 1914 was equally insecure, violent and conflict bound. The contrast between pre-1914 and post-1945 is not as big as it is often presented.

After the battle of Waterloo and the Vienna Congress, Western Europe has experienced three serious armed conflicts in the 19th century: the Franco-Austrian war of 1859, the Prusso-Austrian war of 1866, and the Franco-Prussian war of 1870. There have been several wars with external parties, of course, such as the Balkan wars, the Russo-Turkish wars, the Crimean war, and several wars in the colonies; but external wars have also occurred regularly since 1945.

All three intra-European wars of the 19th century were, moreover, relatively limited in scale and losses. The Franco-Austrian war of 1859, which would amplify the Italian unification, lasted only a few months, and although bloody at times – the atrocities at the battle of Solferino even inspired Henri Dunant to found the International Red Cross – the number of casualties remained limited. The Prusso-Austrian war lasted even shorter: only seven weeks, between July and August 1866. The war took no more than a total of approximately 100 thousand casualties, and resulted in Prussian hegemony in the German lands as well as an enlargement of the territory of Italy at the cost of Austria. Thirdly, there was the Franco-Prussian war of 1870-1, which was the longest and most bloody conflict on European soil since the Napoleonic wars. It lasted about 8 months, and took an approximate total of 350 thousand casualties.

The casualties of these wars are lamentable, but international involvement remained limited and much of European life went untouched by it. For most

---

[39] Cf. Henry William Brands, *Woodrow Wilson* (New York: Henry Holt and Company, 2003) esp. 80-81.

Europeans, then, the period between the end of the Napoleonic wars and the First World War had been a century of peace. While the three wars of the 19th century certainly infused nationalistic pride among the populations of the belligerents (although Napoleon III for instance was heavily criticized by his own people as well), the wars were initiated not by the people but by undemocratic rulers – Napoleon III, Bismarck – who sought, in the words of Seton-Watson, 'to make their states dominant on the European continent'.[40]

The Napoleonic wars, which had followed almost immediately on the French Revolution and the downfall of the *ancien régime*, spanned almost twenty years and took several millions of casualties – from Western as well as Eastern European countries, from Russia and from northern Africa. Were these wars inspired by nationalism? Was it 'nationalistic pride and greed, and (…) international rivalry for wealth and power' that infused this horror?[41] Quite the contrary.

The Napoleonic wars were inspired not by some nationalist particularism, but by the universalist ideals of the Enlightenment and the dream to build a new *imperium romanum*. The Napoleonic wars were non-nationalistic, and precisely in that quality resided their limitless character. Napoleon aimed to bring the whole of Europe under his Enlightened empire (as has been discussed in chapter 5.3), an objective so unattainable that constant war was the result.

Preceding the revolutionary wars – that is to say, in the 18th century and before – few standing armies existed and a universal draft was unheard of. Wars were for that reason by definition limited in scale. The view was that glory could be obtained on the battlefield, and as territorial gain still formed a realistic perspective (since states were not national states, see part I), the general idea of war was not necessarily negative: indeed, warfare was the primary means for aristocrats to prove their honor, and glorifications of conduct on the battlefield form a major part of world literature. From Caesar's *De bello gallico* to the Duke of Saint Simon's descriptions of Louis XIV's quest 'pour la gloire' and Napoleon's memoir, lay two millennia of enthusiasm for the virtues of the battlefield and the importance of military might. Anyone visiting Paris or London or any other major European capital will be struck by the abundance of military monuments, statues of former army leaders, streetnames referring to military victories or fields of combat, and so on.

Moreover, because of premodern technological limitations, wars were incomparably less destructive in the 18th century and before, than after. Indeed, 'war' in the twentieth century is an entirely different thing from what it used to be in the past. Although of course it is true that destruction of villages and lives occurred on a tremendous scale during the religious wars of the 16th and

---

[40] Seton-Watson (1977) 467.
[41] 'Vote for EU Constitution or risk new Holocaust, says Brussels', in: *Daily Telegraph*, 9 May 2005.

17th centuries: these were so problematic largely because they could hardly be called wars properly but rather civil wars. And it were precisely these wars that led to the birth of modern statehood in order to prevent them in the future (as discussed in chapter 1). Thus: to say that the EU should have coincided with a stop to some horrific historical continuity caused by 'nationalism' is to make a hollow claim; to say that the EU should have even *caused* this, is simply grotesque, and reminds of the more obscure forms of African shamanism in which rain is believed to result from hallucinating dances around a fire.

But there is yet more. For to emphasize constantly that the countries of the European Union have experienced half a century of peace is to miss out on one essential reality: that the countries of the European Union were for most of that time at war with the Soviet Union – the expression, itself, of a 'post-national' philosophy *par excellence*: communism. The fact that members of the European Union have not engaged in a war against each other, then, since the end of the Second World War, is a bit like being surprised that members of the same soccer team did not commit violations against one another. The countries of the European Union were major allies in a deadly and global nuclear conflict; *of course* they would not bother to fight amongst themselves! Nor was it the European Union that provided an adequate response in this war; it was the NATO alliance and the presence of formidable American weaponry on every bordering country in Europe (brought about, as I have explained, without supranational powers, see Part II, *Introduction*).

Nor should we attribute the deterring power of nuclear bombs to the European Union, or to a fading of 'nationalism'. The fact is that with the invention of the atomic bomb, full-scale wars between countries have become impossible. This is not only the case for the atomic bomb specifically, but also for the whole of modern warfare as first deployed in the First World War.[42] The scale of destruction brought about through modern warfare is unbearable – and since modern architecture has declared it impossible to rebuild destructed houses and city-centers but has consistently replaced them with the most horrific building-blocks in Novosibirsk-style, it is clear that no one is prepared to pay the price of war anymore.

And it is connected with all these considerations that Germany has, after so much destruction, settled – at least for the time being – for its present borders and gave up its envy of Alsace-Lorraine. This may also be due to the fact that since the Second World War, population growth has stagnated in Europe and

---

[42] This is also one of the reasons why the First World War took such an incredible number of casualties. The generals were unfamiliar with the new reality of the battlefield and combat strategies did not take into account, for instance, that one machine gun can cover an entire valley (such as the Somme).

therefore, there is absolutely no economic possibility to have a massive war anymore either.

In short, the claim that nationalism inherently leads to war, and that the EU has caused lasting peace is untrue for five reasons. Number one, the contrast between pre-1914 and post-1945 political life is not so great as to legitimize the self-congratulation. A hundred years of mostly peace had passed in Europe before the outbreak of World War I, while of course no EU existed during the 19th century. Two, there is no reason to believe that the First World War, as well as the wars of the 19th century, came about more because of the glorification of nationalism than because of the suppression of it. Three, the Second World War may have been triggered by national humiliation, but Nazism is certainly not easily classified as a 'nationalism' and the aims of the Axis powers far exceeded the possible scope of a nation state. Four, the fact that Western-European countries have not been engaged in a war with each other is clearly connected to the Cold War and the NATO alliance, rather than with the regulations from Brussels.[43] Five, what really makes war increasingly impossible is the unbearable destructiveness of modern weaponry. Combined with a highly prosperous population with, moreover, declining birth-rates, as well as the horrors of modern architecture that can surely be expected to replace every destructed building, there is simply no impetus to militarily solve problems anymore.

But there is yet another element to be mentioned. Far from being inherently conflict bound, aiming for national sovereignty is in fact the only stable and inherently peaceful political form. The only types of wars nation states can – by their very nature – aim for are defensive. This could be understood in terms of direct or collective self-defense, or of defense of interest or spheres of influence. If they aim for national leadership, however, the governments of nation states will not fight wars of territorial conquest, there being no reason for them to wish to expand their territory beyond the borders of their nation.

8.2. *The Universal Society*

The idea to move beyond borders implies, as we have seen, the assumption that no preconceived social condition of membership is needed for legitimate political decisions. As defenses of national loyalty and sovereignty are logically connected – so are defenses of supranationalism and multiculturalism. Both supranationalism and multiculturalism take root in the idea of the universal

---

[43] Cf. Carl Schmitt, *Das politische Problem der Friedenssicherung* (Wien: Karolinger Verlag, 1993). In this essay, Schmitt poses the question what – if peace is the opposite of war – a state of peace really means. He states that the current 'pax Americana' in effect means that the world complies with American wishes. As soon as rivalling powers arise, the pax Americana will turn out to be a *bellum Americanum,* Schmitt argues.

society, of rational individual agents and abstract, 'objective' criteria of justice. In opposition to the particularism of the nation state, supranationalism and multiculturalism can only be properly understood when we take into account the Enlightenment conception of the social contract. As we shall see, the philosophy of the social contract provides a means to legitimize political decisions entirely separated from social – national – preconditions, and indeed introduces, through its strong emphasis on natural law, a test to the legitimacy of existing arrangements.

Social contract theory is 'a general label for views which try to found all ideas of legitimacy and political obligation in a contract'.[44] 'The essence of this view', Scruton continues, is that 'since to contract is to put oneself under an obligation, the grounds of political obligation would be objectively determined if all such obligations could be traced to a contractual promise'.[45] The philosophy of the social contract thus teaches that the order of society relies solely on rational self-interest; that it is not in a shared identity, in shared ideals, but in a shared individual rationale that man decides to join into society with others.

This obviously implies that there is no foundation for the existence of different states, as the terms of the contract are – at least in the most pure form of social contract theory – supposed to be universal and to apply to the conditions of human nature, not to any specific needs of the Frenchmen or the Germans.[46] Moreover, social contract theory also diminishes the legitimacy of existing states as their sole task as well as their sole reason of existence is supposed to be their realization of the individual's interests.

Though born in stages, the understanding of the state as the result of some form of contract was ingrained in the very theory of the modern, centralized state. Jean Bodin takes as his initial premise, as we saw in part I, a 'war of all against all',[47] and so does Thomas Hobbes. When the latter wrote his *Leviathan* (1651), it was in many respects a logical follow-up of earlier works scrutinizing the relation of man to nature, and man to man.[48] Hobbes worked, in the typical Enlightenment manner, *ab initio.* One source of inspiration for this had been, of course, the works of the Dutchman Hugo Grotius (1583-1645), who in his *De*

---

[44] Scruton (2007) 641 under 'Social contract'.

[45] *Ibidem.*

[46] Or indeed to the Alsatian, the Bavarian, or the Saxon: a generalization already implied in the idea of nationality.

[47] Bodin (1995) book I, ch. VI, 59-60: 'Reason and common sense alike point to the conclusion that the origin and foundation of commonwealths was in force and violence (…) such being the origin of commonwealths, it is clear why a citizen is to be defined as a free subject who is dependent on the sovereignty of another.'

[48] Cf. Thomas Hobbes, *The Elements of Law. Natural and Politic* (1640).

jure belli ac pacis (1625) had already discerned fundamental principles of natural law that applied to the individual vis-à-vis the state (i.e. 'inalienable' rights).[49]

For Hobbes, the most threatening political situation was the anarchy in the state of nature. In the first part of Leviathan, *Of Man*, Hobbes sets out his view of needy human nature and the state of war of all against all *(bellum omnium contra omnes)* when there is no sufficiently powerful state. In the second part, *Of Common-wealth*, he then proceeds to sketch the outlines of what would have to be required to let man step out of this state of nature and into the civilized condition. Essential for this stage would be, according to Hobbes, the loss of virtually all natural rights. Therefore, although Hobbes accepts the premise of the social contract, the outcome does not deligitimize the existing political order.

In many ways his successor, John Locke (1632-1704), took Hobbes' treaty as the basis, but added, in the second part of his *Two treatises on Government*, inalienable rights that are derived from man's natural entitlements in the state of nature, but that continue to apply even after having entered into the civilized state. Locke acknowledges that 'wherever (…) any number of men are so united into one society, as to quit every one his executive power of the law of nature, and to resign it to the public, there, and there only, is a political, or civil society'.[50] But he adds that the aim of entering into civil society is to set up

> a judge on earth with authority to determine all the controversies and redress the injuries that may happen to any member of the commonwealth

in order that the member's 'life, liberty and estate' be protected.[51] Locke warns for the 'breach of trust in not preserving the form of government agreed on, and in not intending the end of government itself, which is the public good and preservation of property'. Should this happen indeed, then

> a king has dethroned himself and put himself in a state of war with his people.[52]

In such a case, the legislative power 'reverts to the society, and the people have a right to act as supreme, and continue the legislative in themselves; or erect a new form, or under the old form place it in new hands, as they think good'.[53]

It was the French writer Jean-Jacques Rousseau (1712-1778), then, who introduced the concept of the 'volonté générale' in his Enlightenment work *Du Contrat Social*. The 'general will', he contended, could decide whether there was

---

[49] Grotius, *The rights of war and peace, including the law of nature and of nations. Translated from the original Latin* (New York: M. Walter Dunne, 1901). This has been discussed in chapter 1.
[50] Locke, *The second treatise of Government* (1690) chapter VII: 'Of political or civil society', par. 89.
[51] Locke (1690) chapter VII: 'Of political or civil society', par. 87.
[52] Locke (1690) chapter XIX: 'Of the dissolution of government', par. 239.
[53] Locke, *The second treatise of Government* (1690) chapter XIX: 'Of the dissolution of government' , par. 243.

such a violation of rights described by Locke. According to Rousseau, society was to be an expression of the continuing redrawing of the social contract: 'the people, who are subjected to the laws, should be their author'.[54]

And this contributed decisively to the view of society that dominated the French Revolution. In the words of Raymond Aron, 'the French Constituents wrote that the aim of all political associations is the preservation of the natural and inalienable rights of man'.[55]

Supranationalism and multiculturalism take root in the universal social contract as laid out by these Enlightenment doctrinaires. As a result, both supranationalists and multiculturalists hold an unproblematic conception of what a society is: a society of man, not of people. As T.S. Eliot sarcastically voiced the Enlightenment view of political society in 1934: we are 'dreaming of systems so perfect that no one will need to be good'.[56]

This is evident in the writings of Bernard de Mandeville, who suggested that 'private vices' lead to 'public benefits',[57] as well as in those of Kant, who argued that the perfect laws would even turn devils into good citizens – thus leaving no room for the individual to be either good or bad.[58]

While the Enlightenment introduced this idea of the universality of human desires and the rationality of self-interest, it was romanticism that gave rise to the worship of cultural identities that we see in multiculturalism. As the romantics

----

[54] Du contrat social, II, 6. Cf. L.G. Crocker, *Rousseau's social contract. An interpretive essay* (Cleveland: Press of Case western reserve university, 1968) 73.

[55] Raymond Aron, 'Is multinational citizenship possible?', in: *Social Research. An international quarterly of the social sciences,* Volume 41, no. 4 (Winter 1974) 638-656, there 641.

[56] 'Why should men love the Church? Why should they love her laws? / She tells them of Life and Death, and of all that they would forget. / She is tender where they would be hard, and hard where they like to be soft. / She tells them of Evil and Sin, and other unpleasant facts. / They constantly try to escape / From the darkness outside and within / By dreaming of systems so perfect that no one will need to be good. / But the man that is will shadow / The man that pretends to be.' T.S. Eliot, 'Choruses from "the Rock"' (1934), in: *The complete poems and plays of T.S. Eliot* (London: Book Club Associates, 1977) 159: 'VI'.

[57] Bernard de Mandeville, *The fable of the bees, or, private vices, public benefits* (1714).

[58] Kant held that a good organization of the state forces the human agent 'to be a good citizen even if not morally a good person': '… es [kommt] nur auf eine gute Organisation des Staats an (…), jener ihre Kräfte so gegeneinander zu richten, das seine die anderen in ihrer zerstörenden Wirkung aufhält, oder diese aufhebt: so dass der Erfolg für die Vernunft so ausfällt, als wenn beide gar nicht da wären, und so der Mensch, wenngleich nicht ein moralisch-guter Mensch, dennoch ein guter Bürger zu sein gezwungen wird. Das Problem der Staatserrichtung ist, so hart wie es auch klingt, selbst für ein Volk von Teufeln (wenn sie nur Verstand haben) auflösbar und lautet so: "Eine Menge von vernünftigen Wesen, die insgesamt allgemeine Gesetze für ihre Erhaltung verlangen, deren jedes aber insgeheim sich davon auszunehmen geneigt ist, so zu ordnen, und ihre Verfassung einzurichten, dass, obgleich sie in ihren Privatgesinnungen einander entgegenstreben, diese einander doch so aufhalten, dass in ihrem öffentlichen Verhalten der Erfolg eben derselbe ist, als ob sie keine solche böse Gesinnungen hätten'. Kant (2005) 31, Zweiter Abschnitt. Die definitivartikel. Erster Zusatz. As is noticed by Harry van der Linden, *Kantian ethics and Socialism* (Indianapolis: Hackett Publishing Company, 1988): 'A more fundamental consideration is that intelligent devils realize that coercion is a rational response …'.

tended to ethnic conceptions of nationality (as discussed in chapter 3), they were also quick to regard the culture of immigrants as something 'inalienable'. Rousseau – with one foot in the Enlightenment, and one in Romanticism – has been important in this too, when he expressed the influential idea that *l'homme est un être naturellement bon, aimant la justice et l'ordre.*[59] Indeed, the idea of the natural goodness of man – itself admittedly as old as civilization and the conception of loss of innocence in the garden of Eden[60] – rises to a level of general acceptance in the eighteenth century, and as the idea of original sin is discarded, and evil is no longer taken to come from man himself, but from the bad arrangements of society, it becomes possible to conceive peace as a far more natural condition of man to live in, than war.[61]

With this idea that man is good out of himself, and that it is through the vested interests that he becomes corrupted, rather than through his own wicked nature, the necessity for *Bildung* loses much of its legitimacy. *'Be yourself, no matter what they say'*, has become the new creed.[62] And just as the Enlightenment idea that a perfect system would even turn devils into good citizens, this belief in man's natural goodness, too, easily results in the idea, that the particularities of each culture could happily flourish next to one another.

Having thus sketched the roots of the idea to move beyond borders as this combination of rationalism that can be found in the Enlightenment, and the conception of man's natural goodness and cultural predetermination that was enshrined in much of Romanticist ideas, fast forward again to the 20th century.

In an influential book in 1971, *A Theory of Justice*, John Rawls formulated the ultimate consequences of these intellectual currents. In this book, Rawls

---

[59] Jean-Jacques Rousseau, 'Lettre a C. de Beaumont' (1763), in: *Euvres completes* (Paris: Pléiade, Gallimard, 1964) 925-1028, there 936: 'Le principe fondamental de toute moral, sur lequel j'ai raisonné dans tous mes Ecrits, et que j'ai développé dans ce dernier avec toute la clarté dont j'étais capable, est que l'homme est un être naturellement bon, aimant la justice et l'ordre ; qu'il n'y a point de perversité originelle dans le coeur humain, et que les premiers mouvements de la nature sont toujours droits.'

[60] See on this: Henri Baudet, *Paradise on Earth. Some thoughts on European images of Non-European man.* Translated by Elizabeth Wentholt (Middletown: Wesleyan University Press, 1988) 9ff.

[61] Compare in this respect: Oswald Spengler, 'Ist Weltfriede möglich?', in: *Ibidem, Reden und Aufsätze* (München, Beck Verlag, 1937): 'Der Friede ist ein Wunsch, der Krieg eine Tatsache (…). Das Leben (…) ist ein Kampf um die Macht, seinen Willen, Vorteil oder seine Meinung vom Nützlichen oder Gerechten durchzusetzen, und wenn andre Mittel versagen, wird man immer wieder zum letzten greifen, der Gewalt. (…) Wenn ganze Völker pazifistisch werden, ist es ein Symptom von Altersschwäche. (…) So lange es menschliche Entwicklung gibt, wird es Kriege geben'. And Carl Schmitt, *Das politische Problem der Friedenssicherung* (Wien, Karolinger Verlag, 1993): 'Heute erscheint uns eine Befriedigung der ganzen Erde praktisch nur dadurch möglich, dass mehrere Weltmächte sich verständigen. Sie müssten dann die Erde unter sich verteilen'. And: Carl Schmitt, 'Machiavelli-Zum 22. Juni 1927', in: *Kölnische Volkszeitung*, Jg. 68, No. 448 (June 21, 1927) 1: 'If men were good, my views would be wicked; but men are not good', as quoted in: Joseph W. Bendersky, *Carl Schmitt, Theorist for the Reich* (Princeton: Princeton University Press, 1983) 87.

[62] Sting, chorus from the song *Englishman in New York*.

defended the idea – indeed a logical consequence of the aforementioned developments – that 'different conceptions of the good' would not be a problem for joining into society together. *A Theory of Justice* forms the highpoint and the standard reference for the new approach to borders: limitless universalism, and limitless particularism combined. This, as we have observed now, stands opposed to the compromise of universalism and particularism that the nation state seeks to make, in which the law is universal in the sense that it applies to all citizens, yet particularist in the sense that it is the expression of *this* particular people, living on *this* particular territory, with this particular history and set of values and customs.

Rawls explains in the introductory chapter of his *A Theory of Justice* that he sets out to devise a theory of justice that applies to every society. His aim is to sketch the contours of justice as it is in every time and every place. To do so, Rawls takes the idea of the social contract, 'as represented by Locke, Rousseau, and Kant',[63] and sets out to 'generalize it' and to carry it 'to a higher order of abstraction',[64] of such a nature, that 'a theory can be developed that is no longer open to the more obvious objections often thought fatal to it.'[65]

With these 'obvious objections', Rawls means the fact that people from a different starting situation will prefer different contractual arrangements. To overcome this problem, he invents the 'original position', a fictional condition in which all contractual parties will not only be equal, but also afflicted with a 'veil of ignorance' over the position in society that will be theirs. Rawls contends that by applying this principle consistently, we will be able to retrieve those arrangements that make a universally just society possible.

However attractive this idea may be, there is one premise in the whole undertaking that is easily overlooked, but deeply problematic. That premise is of course that in order for Rawls' project to work, it should be *possible* that all differences between human agents, be it of social, economic, cultural or religious nature, be included in a single society.

> Among the essential features of this situation is that no one knows his place in society, his class position or social status, nor does any one know his fortune in the distribution of natural assets and abilities, his intelligence, strength, and the like.

So far so good: Rawls is presenting some system of distribution of wealth and of social arrangements within an existing society that one can agree or disagree with.[66] But then he continues:

---

[63] John Rawls, *A Theory of justice* (Clarendon Press, Oxford, 1972) preface, vii.
[64] Rawls (1972) viii.
[65] Rawls (1972) viii.
[66] Even though quite what kind of arrangement never becomes even remotely clear, as has been convincingly argued by: Brian Barry, *The liberal theory of justice: a critical examination of the principle doctrines in: A theory of justice by John Rawls* (Oxford: Clarendon Press, 1973);

> I shall even assume that the parties do not know their conceptions of the good or their special psychological propensities.[67]

Indeed, for Rawls to come to just terms, 'they are to presume that even their spiritual aims may be opposed, in the way that the aims of those of different religions may be opposed.'[68] It becomes clear, that Rawls is really not talking so much of a particular distribution of wealth for an already in-place society, but rather setting up the principles of the universal society (though he always talks of 'a' society, as though of one among several).[69]

The contractual parties in the original position, he stresses once more, 'do not know, of course, what their religious or moral convictions are, or what is the particular content of their moral or religious obligations as they interpret them (...) the parties do not know how their religious or moral views fare in their society, whether, for example, it is in the majority or the minority.'[70]

All those who follow, in their several ways, this Rawlsian idea, be it on the social-democratic side, the liberal side, or the libertarian side (as such wide-ranging social-economic arrangements have been defended in its name),[71] will naturally come to view borders as obstacles, as impractical, inherently illegitimate and outdated residues that do not serve any particular interest in the sense that rational contemplation can bring forth higher principles of universal justice, and therefore there being no need for divisions. In line with Eleanor Roosevelt, they contemplate the 'Magna Carta for all mankind',[72] rather than that of specific peoples.

And it is certain that not only a generation of politicians and philosophers has grown up on this idea; social contract theory as a universal system of justice is presently by far the most important philosophy on the theory of statehood taught and discussed in schools and academic curricula,[73] so much so that it

---

Brian Barry, *Theories of justice. A treatise on social justice*, Vol. 1 (London: Harvester-Wheatsheaf, 1989); N. Daniels (ed.), *Reading Rawls: critical studies on Rawls' A theory of justice* (Oxford, 1975); Robert Nozick, *Anarchy, state, and utopia* (New York: Basic Books, 1974); J.H. Wellbank (ed.), *John Rawls and his critics; an annotated bibliography* (New York, 1982).

[67] Rawls (1972) 12.
[68] Rawls (1972) 14.
[69] The fact that in his later publication, *The law of peoples* (Cambridge, MA: Harvard University Press, 1999), Rawls simply assumes the existence of nations without questioning them, does not affect this.
[70] Rawls (1972) 206.
[71] M.J. Trappenburg analyzes the different political views that can be defended on the basis of the 'original contract', in: Trappenburg, M.J., 'John Rawls', in: Cliteur, P.B., Van der List, G.A. (eds.), *Filosofen van het hedendaags liberalisme* (Kampen: Kok Agora, 1990) 91-105.
[72] Eleanor Roosevelt, *Speech for the United Nations at the announcement of the Universal Declaration of the Rights of Man*, 9 December 1948. Available online at http://www.udhr.org/history/ergeas48.htm.
[73] See for instance Will Kymlicka's widely used handbook of political philosophy. Kymlicka, *Contemporary Political Philosophy: An introduction* (Oxford: Oxford University Press, 2002).

seems to many now impossible to conceive of legitimate statehood and just political arrangements in other than contractual terms.[74] As has been discussed above, all versions of social contract theory, as Hobbes, Locke, Rousseau and others in their several ways argue, ignore the question of community, as they start with a gathering of random people agreeing on the terms of a contract by which all of them will be bound – we already saw this. Yet this universalistic idea that is implicit in every form of social contract theory (as it is implied in its very premise of a 'precontractual phase' and the rational principles on which a society is supposed to have to be founded if it is to be 'just') presupposes a shared idea of community.

Roger Scruton has analyzed that if the people that are drawing up a contract 'are in a position to decide on their common future, it is because they already have one: because they recognize their mutual togetherness and reciprocal dependence, usually as a result of an already common past,[75] which makes it incumbent upon them to settle how they might be governed under a common jurisdiction in a common territory.' Therefore, Scruton suggests a social experience of cohesion (i.e. nationality) that precedes the discussion over dividing rights and duties and of redistributing wealth. He continues:

> In short, the social contract requires a relation of membership, and one, more-over, that makes it plausible for the individual members to conceive the relation between them in contractual terms. Theorists of the social contract write as though it presupposes only the first-person singular of free rational choice. In fact it presupposes a first-person plural, in which the burdens of belonging have already been assumed.[76]

Once the idea had caught ground that a society could be formed by any human agent reasonable enough to come to a certain rational understanding of his self-interest, the presupposed social experience of membership became easily neglected. Basically anyone, it was now held, would agree with the principles of a wise social contract. However, to sit together at a table and decide on a common future requires a loyalty preceding that political reality: a 'we' that is not defined as self-interest rightly understood, but, quite the contrary, in the words of Raymond Aron,

> Individuals cannot become citizens of the same state unless they feel a common destiny.[77]

---

[74] Even though impressive critique on this idea has been formulated by equally modern political philosophers, for example by Burke in his *Reflections on the Revolution in France*, by Hegel in his *Philosophy of Right*, and by Michael Oakeshott in *Rationalism and Politics*.

[75] Compare Renan and Fustel de Coulanges on the 'nation' in chapter 3.

[76] Scruton, *England and the need for nations* (London: Civitas, 2004) 9.

[77] Raymond Aron, 'Is multinational citizenship possible?', in: *Social Research. An international quarterly of the social sciences*, Volume 41, no. 4 (Winter 1974) 638-656, there 655.

Because this 'common destiny', this 'we', not defined by rational self-interest, is necessary – there being otherwise no reason to accept the political say of others – social contract theory is ultimately in need of a preceding fundament. Whatever claims to economic redistribution or social justice one may justify on the basis of a theory of social contract: it always presupposes the experience of membership and could therefore not be used to legitimize whatever world government may be desired.

8.3. *The All-Inclusiveness of Loyalties*

A third fallacy that serves to defend supranationalism and multiculturalism is that it is possible to have multiple political loyalties. In this view, it is not the compulsory blueprint of universalism that seeks to delegitimize the nation state, but quite the contrary: the supposed non-contradictory nature of particularities. If there is no reason to defend the membership of one particular nation at the cost of another, what legitimacy does the idea of a 'Leitkultur' still possess?

Usually, two arguments are presented preliminary to this viewpoint, which are, however, internally contradictory: first, that no national 'core identity' exists, and second, that it is impossible to 'turn back the clock'. An example of how these contradicting arguments are presented is the speech of the Dutch crown princess Máxima, held in 2007, at the presentation of a report by the WRR, the Scientific Council for Government Policy in the Netherlands. The report was called *Identification with the Netherlands*.[78] It addressed the problems related to national identity that have arisen in the past decades 'as a result of internationalization and mass-immigration'.[79]

Princess Máxima declared that '*the* Dutch identity does not exist',[80] and quoted with sympathy her father in law, the late Prince Claus, husband of the Queen of the Netherlands, who had allegedly spoken the remarkable words: 'I have several loyalties and I am a citizen of the world, a European, and a Dutchman'.[81] The

---

[78] WRR, *Identificatie met Nederland* (Amsterdam: Amsterdam University Press 2007).

[79] WRR (2007) 24-26. The WRR makes a different kind of distinction, though, recognizing *four* developments: 'Globalisation, Europeanization, Individualisation and Multiculturalization'.

[80] Princes Máxima, *Speech of 24 September 2007*, 'Zo'n zeven jaar geleden begon mijn zoektocht naar de Nederlandse identiteit. Daarbij werd ik geholpen door tal van lieve en wijze deskundigen. Ik had het voorrecht met veel mensen kennis te maken. Heel veel te zien, te horen en te proeven van Nederland. Het was een prachtige en rijke ervaring waarvoor ik enorm dankbaar ben. Maar 'de' Nederlandse identiteit? Nee, die heb ik niet gevonden'. Available online at http://archief.koninklijkhuis. nl/Actueel/Toespraken/Toesprakenarchief/2007/Toespraak_van_Prinses_Maxima_24_september_2007.

[81] *Ibidem*: '"Eén vraag die heel moeilijk te beantwoorden is en die mij herhaaldelijk gesteld werd, is hoe het voelt Nederlander te zijn. Mijn antwoord is: "Ik weet niet hoe het is Nederlander te zijn. Ik heb verschillende loyaliteiten en ik ben wereldburger en Europeaan en Nederlander." Woorden die ik nooit ben vergeten. Om de identiteit en loyaliteit van een mens zijn geen hekken te plaatsen. Ik denk dat veel mensen het zo voelen'.

princess, who mentioned that she was trained as an economist,[82] stressed that the world has 'open borders',[83] and that

> it is not either-or. But and-and'.[84]

This plea for 'and-and' was largely in lines with the positions defended in the report of the scientific council. Proposing to move away from the idea of 'one national identity',[85] the council pointed at three 'perspectives' on national 'identification': functional, normative, and emotional.

With 'functional identification', the Council denoted the kind of identification that results from utilitarian interaction. Typical areas in which this can be realized, according to the academics of the WRR, are 'neighborhoods, working places, and schools'.[86]

With 'normative identification', the authors of the report denoted the importance not only of adaptation 'to the norm', but also meant to stress that there should be room and platform for newcomers to effect 'adaptations of the norm', ultimately in the political arena as well.[87]

'Emotional identification', finally, is what the authors call 'a sense of belonging', on which according to them the public debate had focused too much in recent years. As a result, according to the council, instead of amplifying this emotional identification, newcomers had been discouraged, and retreated into their culture of origin.[88]

---

[82] *Ibidem*: 'Daarom zeg ik ook als econoom: het is goed als je organisatie mensen in huis heeft die van elkaar verschillen. Diversiteit loont'.

[83] *Ibidem*: 'Het rapport van de WRR geeft veel aandacht aan functionele identificatie. Dat betekent heel simpel: elkaar leren begrijpen omdat je samen een belang deelt. Denk aan een sportclub. Of een bedrijf. Of een school. Of een buurt. Het goede daarvan is dat de nadruk niet ligt op de zichtbare verschillen tussen mensen. Maar op het gezamenlijke doel. En op ieders persoonlijke kwaliteiten. Zo kunnen vooroordelen wegsmelten. Samen spelen. Samen studeren. Samen werken. Dat geeft jonge mensen met verschillende achtergronden een gezamenlijk perspectief. Dat is enorm belangrijk in een wereld van open grenzen'.

[84] *Ibidem*: 'We vervallen gemakkelijk in zwart-wit denken. Maar daarmee doen we onszelf en anderen te kort. Mensen hebben altijd méér dimensies. Mensen veranderen ook. Dat is wat mensen zo bijzonder maakt: het vermogen zich te ontwikkelen. Het is niet 'of, of'. Maar 'en, en''.

[85] WRR (2007) 196ff. 'De raad kiest op basis van zijn bevindingen echter voor een nieuwe benadering en bepleit een wisseling van het perspectief waarin één nationale identiteit centraal staat, naar een perspectief waarin wordt onderkend dat het bij vragen van identiteit altijd gaat om meervoudige processen van identificatie.'

[86] WRR (2007) 204.

[87] WRR (2007) 206, 'Normatieve identificatie houdt in dat mensen de mogelijkheid hebben voor hen betekenisvolle normen te volgen, publiekelijk te articuleren en dat er voldoende gelegenheid is om conflicten over die normen democratisch op te lossen. Het aanpassen aan de norm gaat in de meeste gevallen vanzelf. Het veranderen van normen is veel lastiger. De ruimte om dat te kunnen doen en andere normen in te brengen in de publieke arena is echter wel een noodzakelijke voorwaarde voor identificatie en is ook belangrijk om processen van disidentificatie te voorkomen.'

[88] WRR (2007) 207, 'Emotionele identificatie gaat over gevoelens van verbondenheid met anderen en in abstractere zin met Nederland, over een 'sense of belonging'. We hebben laten zien dat burgers in een veranderende samenleving zoals de Nederlandse meerdere loyaliteiten hebben

All things viewed together, the WRR stated that 'with our plea for an and-and approach, we presuppose the existence and importance of multiple identities and identifications'.[89] According to the authors,[90] no core identity exists in societies or in individuals: on the contrary, societies and individuals alike are in a constant flux. This may be true to a certain extent, but it is quite something else to conclude from this that no national identity exists, no such thing as '*the* Dutchman'. By drawing that conclusion, the authors obviously attempted to thwart criticism of multiculturalism. For if no original national culture existed – how could one oppose the presence of new cultures?

Further down, however, the authors of the report, while attempting to score a rhetorical success, were apparently unaware of fundamentally contradicting themselves:

> As if the Netherlands still have a realistic option to withdraw from the world and from Europe, and to reverse the multicultural society. As if the Netherlands, through processes of globalization, Europeanization, and continuing immigration, would lose their own identity and perish their own core.'[91]

It seems to go largely unnoticed that this familiar argument in defense of multiculturalism – that we won't 'perish our core' – is entirely incompatible with the aforementioned argument that 'no core identity' exists.[92] If we follow the line of argument, the Netherlands, thus, do not have a realistic option to withdraw from the world and to reverse the multicultural society anymore, as one cannot 'turn back time'; yet at the same time, however, the Dutch are

---

zonder dat dat een probleem hoeft te zijn voor hun verbondenheid met Nederland. Van belang is dat deze hybride identificaties erkend en gewaardeerd worden en niet onmiddellijk ter discussie worden gesteld. Juist als dat laatste wel gebeurt – zoals nu steeds vaker het geval is – wordt meer of minder expliciet een keuze geëist, een keuze die in een emotionele zin niet gemaakt kan worden, en die naar ons oordeel ook niet verlangd hoeft te worden.'

[89] WRR (2007) 200ff: 'Onderscheid maken betekent niet noodzakelijkerwijs dat er tegenstellingen zijn: wij en zij denken is iets anders dan wij of zij denken. Met dit pleidooi voor een én-énbenadering gaan wij uit van het bestaan en van het belang van meervoudige identiteiten en identificaties.'

[90] The authors of this report were in fact a group of 'experts' under the presidency of a member of the council. The president was prof. dr. Pauline Meurs, and the members of the group were drs. Dennis Broeders (who was also the coordinator of the project), dr. mr. Fouzia Driouichi, dr. Monique Kremer, drs. Erik Schrijvers and Fleur Sleegers.

[91] WRR (2007) 201ff: 'Alsof Nederland nog een reële optie heeft om zich terug te trekken uit de wereld en Europa, en de multiculturele samenleving zou kunnen terugdraaien. Alsof Nederland door processen van globalisering, europeanisering en voortdurende immigratie zijn eigen identiteit zou verliezen en zijn eigen kern kwijt zou raken.'

[92] WRR (2007) 63: 'In deze theoretische verkenning kwam naar voren dat in plaats van te spreken over nationale identiteit het vruchtbaarder is te spreken over meerdere vormen van identificatie. Identificaties kunnen dynamisch, sociaal, alledaags, nationaal en gelaagd zijn – denk bijvoorbeeld aan het onderscheid tussen functionele, normatieve en emotionele identificatie. Maar er is nog een reden om te willen spreken over identificatie (met Nederland) in plaats van over nationale identiteit.'

apparently unrealistically worried, because the Netherlands is not in danger of 'perishing its own core'.

Must we conclude that the academics of the WRR think that firstly, the Netherlands *do not* have a realistic option to withdraw 'from the world and from Europe' anymore, nor to 'revert the multicultural society', but secondly, that these processes *do not* threaten the Netherlands with the loss of its own identity and the perishing of its own core[93]? How can that be, when the WRR had argued that *no such core* existed in the first place?

It is clear that we simply can't escape some positive definition of, as Samuel Huntington put it, 'who we are'.[94] In any case, to state that no 'core identity' exists while at the same time contending that multiculturalism does not affect that core identity, is logically inconsistent.

This was also the essence of the criticism that burst out upon the publication of the WRR-report (and the accompanying speech of the Argentinean Crown Princess of the Netherlands). The historian Frank Ankersmit for example stated that thinking about national identity came up as a reaction 'to the a-historical worldview of the Enlightenment. For the Enlightenment, people of all times and all places and all parts of the world are in principle equal; and that leaves indeed little or no room for national identity.' This is what we have been discussing in chapter 3 on the Enlightened approach to the nation, amongst others in the words of Sieyès. Ankersmit continued:

> Our national identity is not to be found in a certain set of general and unchangeable characteristics that social scientists should be able to find in the conduct of the Dutch.

This is also nothing new for us, having discarded the Romantic reaction to the Enlightenment, as Herder and Fichte and others have voiced it. Ankersmit then concludes:

> One only comes on track with that if one takes note of the big tracts of Dutch history (...) What our national identity actually consists in, is not fixed for ever. It is always a matter of debate. But the fact that we debate our national identity, does not mean that it doesn't exist. That is the mistake princess Máxima makes. For who reasons in such a way, should also have to abolish history itself. And moral norms and values, for those are also the subject of ongoing debates.[95]

---

[93] WRR (2007)) 201ff.: 'Nog los van het feit dat er weinig empirisch bewijs ter onderbouwing van deze stelling is, is zij ook weinig productief, want weinig toekomstgericht.'

[94] Samuel Huntington, *Who Are We: The Challenges to America's National Identity* (Simon & Schuster, New York, 2004). Cf. the works of Coos Huijsen, Robert Bellah, Rudiger Safranski, and many others.

[95] Frank Ankersmit, 'Prinses Máxima maakt denkfout', in: *NRC Handelsblad*, 2 October 2007, '(...) Onze nationale identiteit moet je niet zoeken in een bepaalde set van algemene en onveranderlijke eigenschappen die sociale wetenschappers zouden ontwaren in het gedrag van de Nederlanders. Nee, die komt men pas op het spoor door te letten op de grote lijn in de Nederlandse geschiedenis

Ankersmit chooses the third approach to nationality: it is open, but requires effort (and debate). It is the view of Renan and Fustel de Coulanges that I have also discussed in Chapter 3. The WRR tried to step over any positive definition of national identity because it believed this to focus on differences instead of bridging them. Yet what the WRR did not realize, is that it is logically impossible to talk about 'a renewal of Dutch identity' and a 'core' of Dutchness without presupposing the existence of such a thing.

Moreover, far from a means to exclude newcomers, can a shared national identity in fact bridge the differences in a diverse and cosmopolitan society.[96]

This is indeed contrary to what is generally believed, and probably the reason why defenders of multiculturalism go to such length to argue against national identity: they perceive it as something *exclusive* to newcomers, instead of something uniquely capable of *including* them.

Now of course strictly speaking, nationality is not identical with citizenship. While citizenship involves for example the right to vote, nationality involves the right to a passport. This is illustrated by the American Samoans, for instance, who possess the American 'nationality' and have a right to travel the US freely, but may not vote. The same goes for the Dutch from Aruba, who do not posses the right to vote either.

As these are exceptions to the general identification of 'citizenship' with 'nationality', however, in the following, as in the preceding chapter, the two will continue to be used as synonyms – as the WRR does as well. The council, while contending that 'an unjustified mingling' had occurred 'between nationality and loyalty', stated in its report that

> having one, two, or more passports in itself does not say anything about one's loyalty to the Netherlands.[97]

Supporting the right to hold more than one nationality and thereby possess more than one passport[98] while stating that this would not have to affect the

---

en op wat historici daarover gezegd hebben. Wat onze identiteit is, ligt daarom niet voor eeuwig en altijd vast. Die is altijd inzet van debat. Maar het feit dat we onze nationale identiteit ter discussie stellen, betekent nog niet dat die niet zou bestaan. Dat is de denkfout van prinses Máxima. Wie zo redeneert, zou ook de geschiedenis moeten afschaffen. En ook alle normen en waarden, want daar discussiëren we ook eindeloos over.'

[96] Following this article by Ankersmit, the weekly journal *Opinio* published a series of essays, mostly by historians, defending the same point of view. In this series were included analyses by amongst others Johan Huizinga, Hans Wansink, Willem Velema, A. Th. Van Deursen, and H.W. von der Dunk. Opinio, 12-18 October 2007 (yr 1, number 39), Opinio, 4-10 January 2008 (yr 2, number 1), Opinio, 18-24 January 2008 (yr 2, number 3).

[97] WRR (2007) 208: 'Er is een onterechte vermenging ontstaan tussen loyaliteit en nationaliteit. Het hebben van een, twee of meer paspoorten zegt op zichzelf niets over iemands loyaliteit aan Nederland.'

[98] WRR (2007) 208: 'Dit betekent dat de WRR hier een pleidooi houdt voor het formeel toestaan van dubbele nationaliteit door het laten vallen van de afstandseis.'

'loyalty to the Netherlands', one would expect the WRR to believe one primary political loyalty to be desirable (for why bothering to disconnect *loyalty* from *nationality* otherwise?). Yet the report then intends to show 'that citizens in a changing society like the Dutch have plural loyalties without this having to be a problem for their connection to the Netherlands'.[99] They thus call upon citizens to disconnect nationality from loyalty, and yet to accept that both are non-exclusive, overlapping and 'dynamic'. Apparently, the WRR thinks that it is perfectly possible to be a national without being loyal, and vice versa.

But is it really unproblematic to have no loyalty towards one's nationality, or to hold several different nationalities? Is there no logical – indeed necessary – connection between political loyalty and nationality? What is, in fact, required of a subject of a state?

The classical approach was that a citizen earned his 'rights', such as the right to partake in political decision-making, through the fulfillment of 'duties', such as paying taxes and partaking in the common defense. In the Greek *Polis* and the major part of the history of the Roman Empire, citizenship was regarded as a high responsibility, open and fit only for the privileged few.[100]

In the modern, democratic state, the emphasis has strongly been placed on the rights of citizenship, rather than the duties. Generally, citizenship is no longer viewed as something that must be 'earned', nor is it regarded as a heavy responsibility. Until well into the nineteenth century, the right to vote, for instance, was still confined to a small upper layer of society. Voting was regarded as a serious task that could be properly fulfilled only by those who belonged to the more or less financially independent and educated classes.[101] Partly as a result of the discourse of 'rights' gaining worldwide momentum, amongst others through the *Universal Declaration of Human Rights*, the idea that citizenship implies first and foremost the fulfillment of *duties* rather than the entitlement to *rights*, was lost.[102]

Although the duties of the citizen have thus moved somewhat to the background, it is by no means certain that they are no longer to be upheld. On the contrary, it will be argued in the remaining part of this chapter that the

---

[99] WRR (2007) 16: 'Dit rapport laat zien dat burgers in een veranderende samenleving zoals de Nederlandse meerdere loyaliteiten hebben zonder dat dit een probleem hoeft te zijn voor hun verbondenheid met Nederland.'

[100] Cf. J.P.V.D. Balsdon, *Romans and aliens* (London: Duckworth, 1979).

[101] See on this, for instance, Gerhard Leibholz, *Strukturprobleme der Modernen Demokratie*, (Karlsruhe, 1958) 80ff; Burke (1961) 186-210. Maurice Duverger, *Les Partis Politiques* (Paris: 1951) 466ff. Concerning the Dutch situation: Theo J. Veen, *De Staten-Generaal vertegenwoordigen het gehele Nederlandse volk* (Nijmegen, 2000) 34ff.

[102] It is clear, too, that this development is consequent upon the view of political order as resulting from a mere social contract.

fulfillment of duties continues to play a pivotal – however implicit – role in the well functioning of democratic states.

The discussion on this has focused for instance on whether 'double passports' should be allowed. In 1976, the 'passport office' of the American department of state published a report on *The United States Passport. Past, present, future.*[103] Tracing the first mention of a passport to Nehemiah 2.7,[104] the report analyzes that the 'development of formal travel documents [has] always been necessary (…) in the relationship among nations.'[105]

Until well into the nineteenth century, however, international travel was not very common. In a perhaps prophetic part of his *Mémoires d'outre tombe*, Chateaubriand wonderfully attached the rise of the passport to the coming of the modern world when he arrived on May 19th, 1833 in Ulm, Baden-Wurttemburg:

> We were halted at the gate of a village; the gate opened; they investigated my passport and my luggage (…) The vulgarity, the modernity of the customs and of the passport contrasted with the thunder, the gothic gate, the sound of the horn and the noise of the torrent (…)[106]

On his way to Prague, Chateaubriand arrived at the Austrian border village Waldmünchen two days later. However, his passage was refused:

> – You will not pass.

> – Pardon, I will not pass, and why? The explication commences:

> – Your details are not on your passport. – My passport is a passport for foreign affairs. – Your passport is old. – It doesn't have a date; it should therefore still be valid. – it has not been visa'd by the Austrian ambassador in Paris. – You are mistaken, it has. – It does not have the dry stamp. – The embassy must have forgotten; besides, you will see the visa of other foreign delegations. I have just travelled the canton of Bâle, the grand-duchy of Bade, the kingdom of Wurtemberg, the whole of Bavaria, without the slightest difficulty. Upon simply stating my name, they did not even inquire in my passport. – You are a public figure? – I have been minister in France, ambassadeur of his Very Christian Majesty in Berlin, in London and in Rome. I am a personal acquaintance of your sovereign and of the prince of Metternich.

> – You will not pass …[107]

---

[103] *The United States Passport. Past, present future* (Department of State Publication 8851, department and foreign service series 153, released July 4, 1976).

[104] 'And I said to the king, "If it pleases the King, let letters be given me to the governors of the province Beyond the River, that they may let me pass through until I come to Judah".'

[105] *The United States Passport* (1976) 1.

[106] François-René de Chateaubriand, *Mémoires d'outre-tombe* (Paris: Classiques Garnier Multimédia, 1998) 221: book 36, chapter 6: 'Nous étions arrêtés à la porte d'une ville; la porte s'ouvre; on s'enquiert de mon passeport et de mes bagages (…) La vulgarité, la modernité de la douane et du passeport contrastaient avec l'orage, la porte gothique, le son du cor et le bruit du torrent (…).'

[107] *Ibidem:* '– Vous ne passerez pas. – Comment, je ne passerai pas, et pourquoi? L'explication commence: – Votre signalement n'est pas sur le passeport. – Mon passeport est un passeport des

For the most part of the second half of the 19th century 'there continued the confusing practice by governments of issuing passports not only to their own subjects, but also to aliens traveling within the country'. Moreover, despite these troubles that Chateaubriand had ended up in, 'many European countries abolished passport requirements by mutual agreement'. This definitely changed with the First World War, 'with the need for both belligerents and neutrals to determine the identity of travelers in their territories'.[108] When the Great War had finished, the League of Nations consequently organized a conference on Passports in Paris: the 1920 *International Conference on Passports, Customs Formalities, and Through Tickets*.[109]

The conference would result in some general agreements on registering luggage, international train stations, and acceptance of foreign travel documents, and marks the global acceptance of the idea of the passport as, in the definition of the US passport office, 'a travel document (...) issued under the authority of the Secretary of State attesting to the identity and nationality of the bearer'.[110]

It is both with regard to the 'nationality' as well as to the 'identity' of the bearer that the supposed all-inclusiveness of passports proves inconsistent.

Let us first discuss nationality as such. The idea that multiple citizenship would only consist in an amplification of rights, rather than a multiplying of duties, shows a lack of understanding of the meaning of rights.

It is in the fulfillment of duties, not in the enjoyment of rights, that citizenship can only be attached to one state,[111] as the Dutch constitutional scholar Twan Tak has argued.[112] He said in an interview with the weekly *Opinio* that 'logically speaking, a double nationality is just as impossible as a double gender or a double religion. (...) Because let us not forget: having a nationality means being subject to a particular sovereign state'.[113] He continued:

---

affaires étrangères. – Votre passeport est vieux. – Il n'a pas un an de date; il est également valide. – Il n'est pas visé à l'ambassade d'Autriche à Paris. – Vous vous trompez, il l'est. – Il n'a pas le timbre sec. – Oubli de l'ambassade ; vous voyez d'ailleurs les *visa* des autres légations étrangères. Je viens de traverser le canton de Bâle, le grand-duché de Bade, le royaume de Wurtemberg, la Bavière entière, on ne m'a pas fait le moindre difficulté. Sur la simple déclaration de mon nom, on n'a pas même déployé mon passeport. – Avez-vous un caractère public ? – J'ai été ministre en France, ambassadeur de sa Majesté Très Chrétienne à Berlin, à Londres et à Rome. Je suis connu personnellement de votre souverain et du prince de Metternich. – Vous ne passerez pas ....'.

[108] *The United States Passport* (1976) 4.
[109] Mark B. Salter, *Rights of Passage: The passport in International Relations* (Colorado: Lynnie Rienner Publishers, 2003) 77ff.
[110] 22 Code of Federal Regulations 51.1 (d).
[111] Indeed, in terms of 'rights' it seems to be very convenient to have a second or even third passport. It makes it possible, for instance, to dispose of one passport and rely on the other, the duties of the one state are conceived as too heavy.
[112] Bart-Jan Spruyt, 'Dubbele Nationaliteit is een gedrocht, interview met Twan Tak', in: *Opinio*, 23 February 2007.
[113] *Ibidem*: 'Een dubbele nationaliteit is logisch net zo onmogelijk als een dubbele sekse of een dubbele religie. En wat onmogelijk is, moet je niet per decreet alsnog voor mogelijk verklaren.

The most important problem is conflicting duties. The relation between state and subject does not only imply rights, but also duties. Who is the subject of a particular sovereign state, not only retrieves advantages from it, but also burdens and duties. With a double nationality, one can accumulate rights, but one has to take conflicting duties into account as well. For someone with a double nationality is subjected to two legal systems, with two systems of duties too.[114]

This is most clearly seen in a situation of war, when the state may call upon its citizens to perform military duties.[115] As Raymond Aron observed: 'How could a citizen possibly belong to several political entities at once? (...) Surely, (...) one cannot claim the rights of citizenship without accepting its duties, such as military service'.[116]

One possible reply to this would be that professional armies have to a large extent replaced military service. But it is not evident that this has been a permanent transition. It is, in any case, easy to doubt the political or moral advantages of a professionalized military. Again Raymond Aron:

> I for one am not at all convinced that the replacement of a citizen army with a professional army represents any political or moral progress. It was the sending of a partially conscripted army to Algeria which foreshadowed the triumph of those in France who stood for an independent Algeria. In the United States it seems that popular demonstrations, if not popular indignation, died down as soon as college students were no longer being called up for service in Vietnam.[117]

But the state may assert its rights over its citizens in less extreme situations as well. Since citizenship means being subjected to the legal system of a state, the moment the two legal systems collide, the double citizen finds himself in a difficult situation. Imagine a French citizen who also holds a Turkish passport:

Het is belachelijke onzin. Want laten we niet vergeten: het hebben van een nationaliteit betekent dat je onderdaan bent van één bepaalde, soevereine staat.'

[114] Spruyt, 'Dubbele Nationaliteit is een gedrocht¸ interview met Twan Tak', in: *Opinio*, 23 February 2007: 'Het belangrijkste probleem is een conflict van plichten. De relatie tussen staat en onderdaan kent niet alleen rechten maar ook plichten. Wie onderdaan is van één bepaalde soevereine staat, ontleent daaraan niet alleen voordelen maar ook lasten en plichten. Je kunt bij een dubbele nationaliteit rechten gaan opstapelen, maar je moet ook rekening houden met botsende plichten. Iemand met een dubbele nationaliteit is immers onderdaan van twee rechtssystemen, met ook twee systemen van plichten. En dat leidt al snel tot botsingen. Een dubbele nationaliteit suggereert in feite dat het feit dat je onderdaan bent van land X geen consequenties heeft voor het feit dat je ook onderdaan bent van het land Y. Met andere woorden: je Nederlanderschap heeft geen consequenties voor de eisen die de Marokkaanse nationaliteit aan jou als onderdaan stelt.'

[115] The history of military service is – from the point of view of national identity – tremendously interesting indeed. As Carl Schmitt notices, the reflections of the economist and sociologist Emil Lederer: 'Wir können sagen, dass sich am Tage der Mobilisierung die *Gesellschaft*, die bis dahin bestand, in eine *Gemeinschaft* umformte', in: Carl Schmitt, 'Der Begriff des Politischen', in: *Ibidem, Frieden oder Pazifismus?* (Ducker & Humblot, Berlin, 2005) 204n7.

[116] Raymond Aron, 'Is multinational citizenship possible?', in: *Social Research. An international quarterly of the social sciences*, Volume 41, no. 4 (Winter 1974) 638-656, there 638.

[117] Aron (Winter 1974) 638-656, there 656.

there have been attempts in France to legally forbid denying the Armenian Genocide, whereas it is forbidden for every Turkish citizen – even to those living abroad – to acknowledge it. Or imagine the Dutchman who also holds an American passport and may be prosecuted upon traveling to the United States because he has sold half a gram of Marihuana.

Nor do states with a large immigrant population in Europe labour to free their former citizens from their nationality. The Moroccan nationality is inalienable and will be passed on indefinitely. While it is theoretically possible to give up Turkish nationality, for instance, those who do so can count on reprisals from the Turkish government such as no longer being allowed in for a family visit. In line with this, the Turkish Prime Minister Erdogan told the Turks in Europe on his visit to Germany in October 2010 that they should not assimilate into their new nations, and that 'assimilation is a crime against humanity'.[118] What is even more surprising is that Turkish Dutchmen are called up for an eighteen months military service in Turkey. They can buy themselves out for 5.000 euros, but cannot escape a 21-day stint, on pain of a prison sentence. Nor does Turkey turn a blind eye when it comes to breaches of the Turkish penal code committed by Dutchmen of Turkish descent in Holland.

As long as they are officially subjects of the Moroccan state, Rabat could similarly call up even those who have – for several generations now – been living abroad, to perform military service and claim jurisdiction over them. In theory, this could mean criminal prosecution for acts performed in the Netherlands, where no Moroccan interest was concerned, and which were entirely in compliance with Dutch law. Examples are criticizing the Moroccan king, the performance of an abortion, the use of soft drugs, homosexual behavior, or apostasy.

We have so far discussed the problems of double nationality with citizens. But in the Netherlands, a vehement discussion burst out in 2007 on the question whether an executive official may have a double nationality. Apart from the above-mentioned problems, which exist in the same degree for politicians and non-politicians, some additional questions remain when secretaries of state and other persons holding official positions, have a double nationality. Even when the primary political loyalty may not be in question, it is especially problematic as a politician can be held accountable, in the last instance, by another state.

What is also at stake with the rights-based conception of citizenship is the inflation of the passport as a guarantee of the issuing state that foreign governments can trust the holder of it. This is the 'identity' question related to passports.

---

[118]   Erdogan had already said the same thing two years before, upon is visit in 2008: cf. 'Erdogan's Visit leaves German conservatives fuming', in: *Spiegel Online*, 2 December 2008. Available online at: http://www.spiegel.de/international/germany/0,1518,534724,00.html.

Free passage and hospitality are offered as a gesture of friendship from the one state and its citizens to the other. There is no such thing as a 'right' to enter the territory of another state: quite the contrary, the rule is that strangers are forbidden to enter the territory of another state; through international agreements, however, states have mutually opened up their borders to friendly citizens. This implies that the citizen holding a passport of the state whose citizens are allowed into a certain country can also to some extent be held accountable. When one state is at war with another, no travelers from that country are allowed in. Visas are not a right, but a gift, granted under the trust that the guest will behave well.

If states have no idea who holds a passport of a certain state, other states have no idea who they are admitting into their country. What this could mean *in extremis* was shown in the mid-90s, when the Oceanic state of Tonga offered its nationality for sale on the market. Anyone who paid a certain amount of money was offered Tongan citizenship and a passport. By doing this, the Island state hoped to attract foreign investors (and no doubt it offered low taxes and other business advantages), but as a result, many countries did not allow Tongan travelers to pass through their customs anymore. Once again, we discover that behind the legal formalities lie sociological and cultural preconditions that enable the formal legal approach in the first place. But once this legal formality is in place, we are easily led to believe that that is all that is needed.[119]

And that observation also bridges us to another aspect of the passport, which is not legal but cultural. Its symbolic value. The large numbers of immigrants from non-Western countries that European states have received in the last decades have led to serious pressure on its social cohesion. If immigrants retain the passport of their country of origin, this inevitably implies a conditional integration. They may always use the second passport to go back. That is another reason why a double passport may be problematic. For representative government and the rule of law require not merely *loyalty*, but a loyalty to the exclusion of other loyalties, at least when they conflict. This will be further explored in the next chapter.

---

[119] Cf. the 'Nottebohm' case of the ICJ (*Liechtenstein v. Guatemala*, April 6th, 1955), in which the ICJ ruled that 'a genuine link' must exist between a citizen and a state in order to claim nationality of a state and insist that other states recognize the claim.

CHAPTER NINE

THE PARTICULARISM OF CITIZENSHIP

9.1. *Loyalty*

Life is not merely about the approximately eighty years the individual spends on earth. Although it may be true, that those eighty years are all there actually are, and that, as Sartre put it, at the end of the day we are all *seul sans excuse*,[1] it is certainly not true that for the individual person, himself and his eighty years are all that matter.

Indeed, not only are we inherently historical beings, who derive meaning from being entrenched in a web of past and future, we are also inherently social beings, defining our lives in terms of what surrounds us. That is why family histories are almost universally cherished, why procreation or 'leaving something behind' is in the top level of priorities in life, and why being disconnected from the world, even when it is in a very comfortable place, as it is in Dr. Johnson's fable Rasselas[2] and in the story of Robinson Crusoe[3] (or for example in reasonably comfortable prisons), is universally perceived as a terrible misfortune.

However, it is also true for all of us that these ties that reach beyond us and connect us to the larger realm of existence, constantly pose constraints and lead us into conflicts. It seems that an unrelenting effort is required to mediate between the conflicting demands of our individual desires and expectations, and those of the many associations we are part of; or between one of our associations and another (for instance a conflict between an ancient family and the village council over claims on a certain piece of land).

The common way out of these all too familiar conflicts is through a compromise: the importance of the individual's demands are weighed against those of the family, or another group, and the desire to stick together as a whole, is reaffirmed through mutual concessions. That is how, in everyday life, we manage

---

[1] Jean-Paul Sartre, *L'Existentialisme est un Humanisme* (Paris: éditions Nagel, 1946) 36-38.
[2] Samuel Johnson, *The history of Rasselas. Prince of Abissinia* (1759) (London: Oxford University Press, 1971). Cf. Theodore Dalrymple, 'Samuel Johnson (1709-1784)', in: Thierry Baudet and Michiel Visser (eds.), *Revolutionair Verval. En de conservatieve vooruitgang in de 18de en 19de eeuw* (Amsterdam: Bert Bakker, 2011).
[3] Daniel Defoe, *Robinson Crusoe. His life and strange surprising adventures* (1791) (London: The Nonesuch Press, 1968).

to live together in a generally peaceful manner – and how, when this goes wrong, associations are destroyed (as, for example, in a family feud).[4]

Associations express a form of loyalty, and as discussed in chapter 3, there are at least three types in which this loyalty can manifest itself politically: tribal, national, or religious. National – imagined and territorial – loyalty is by no means a given: indeed, in large parts of the world, people do not experience such a national loyalty – or at least not very strongly. Their loyalties are often primarily tribal or religious (or a combination of the two) – and as a result, it has proven utterly difficult to establish a political order in which minorities were accepted and civil wars were not incumbent, and in which representative institutions managed to speak for the whole. This is not surprising: in situations where such non-national loyalties prevail, the individual is under constant pressure to submit to tribal or religious laws and customs; the free market will continuously be inclined to degenerate into a system of monopolized guilds and nepotistic favours;[5] and the administration of politics and justice will be menaced by corrupted civil servants who prefer the moral codes of their tribe or creed to the ones of the state.

In Western Europe, to be sure, class-justice and a predominance of religious loyalties over national ones have continually existed throughout the centuries as well. Jews, for example, until well into the nineteenth century, were denied many citizens' rights. Catholics, in protestant countries such as the Netherlands, were regarded as not to be trusted because of supposed 'loyalties' to Rome.[6] And exclusion on the basis of race remained a big issue in large parts of the United States until well into the 1960s. The development and flourishing of the territorial, imagined loyalty, that we have identified as the *national* loyalty, was an achievement, realized at the cost of tribal and creedal ones, and demanding a constant effort. National loyalties have been taught and developed, in families and schools, through national festive days and commemorations, and they have been tamed, too, by the traumatic experiences that several over-affirmed, imperialist nationalisms have rendered.

All this brings us to the problems concerning nationality again, and brings the much-debated concept of *citizenship* in view. For what is essential in this idea, is the recognition that the others with whom we live together on the same territory are essentially members of the same political project (and it is immediately clear

---

[4] See on this for instance Amartya Sen, *Identity and Violence: The Illusion of Destiny* (New York: W.W. Norton & Company, 2006).

[5] Cf. Andreas Kinneging, 'Loyalty in the modern world', in: *Modern Age* vol. 46 (2004) 66-73.

[6] And not necessarily without reason, as William of Orange was, for instance, killed by the religiously inspired Balthasar Gérard in 1584. See on this: Cliteur (2007) 164ff, and: Jardine (2005), who writes on 51: 'This act of assassination was, it appeared, the deed of a solitary fanatic, a loner with an intense commitment to the catholic Church and a faithful upholder of the legitimacy of the rule of Philip II in the Netherlands ...'.

that in this, sovereignty is implied too). Conceiving of ourselves as sharing the same nationality means that, despite all our differences in custom, religion, ethnicity, and background, we share a fundamental loyalty towards a territory and inherent therein, a loyalty towards the way of life on that territory (despite, of course, a great deal of differences).

It is this that enables us to live together with all our differences. It provides a reason for being bound by the same laws; for treating one another equally in equal circumstances; for holding up public virtue and a sense of care for both the human and the natural environment.[7] It is only with a constant reference to the shared nationality, that the fierce political debates in France are resolved; it was only because Barack Obama was experienced as a member of the same nation, that many Americans who had a different ethnicity and may have had a different religious background than him, nevertheless warmly accepted him as their president in 2008; and only in nation states would such a thing have been possible.

The American and French Revolutions (1776 and 1789 respectively) can be regarded as the definite breakthrough of the idea of a national citizenship. Instrumental in that development has been the change in how the people were understood: from being 'subjects' – who owe allegiance to the crown –, they became 'citizens', with a right to co-decide. As such a right to co-decide, however, is always – indeed by definition –, carried out in a collective form, it is implied in national citizenship that the citizen is not just an atomized individual, with 'inalienable rights', but also part of a larger community or group. (Hence the birth of the idea of a 'nation' as discussed in chapter 3).

Indeed, it was with the French Revolution, that besides all the universalist ideals, the *'principe des nationalités'* was introduced, which was the ideal that nations should have the right to political independence and self-determination. The French *National Convention*, the legislative assembly established in 1792, declared that it was ready to assist oppressed peoples to overthrow their rulers, a statement that caused much unrest in the pan-national empires of the Habsburgs and the Ottomans.[8]

But as we have seen throughout this book, European countries have now abandoned this ideal of a prevailing national loyalty. As a consequence, nation states are dissolving again into the pan-national empires that characterized the Middle Ages: internally divided, politically decentralized.

---

[7] See on the relationship between local attachment and care for the environment: Theodore Dalrymple, *Litter: How other people's rubbish shapes our lives* (London: Gibson Square Books), and Scruton (2012).

[8] Martin Lloyd, *The Passport, the history of man's most traveled document* (Sutton Publishing, Gloucestershire 2005) 171. Not much later this principle was abandoned by the universalist imperial ambitions of revolutionary and Napoleonic France, as discussed in chapters 3.2, 3.3 and 8.1.

A telling illustration of how national loyalties are upset in practice, is the way in which the Dutch tradition to commemorate those who died in the Second World War has been turned around in recent years. The ceremony is traditionally carried out on the 4th of May, the day before the German capitulation of 1945. Every year at 20:00 o'clock, the Dutch Queen lays a garland on the national monument on Dam square, whereupon the mayor of Amsterdam says a few words to announce two minutes of silence. On many other squares in Amsterdam and in other cities, and in almost every village in the country, a comparable ceremony is carried out: garments are laid down, and local dignitaries voice the purpose of the commemoration before the gathered people silently contemplate the dead. In 1995, however, the *National Committee 4 and 5 May*[9] announced a shift in accent:

> No longer only the victims of the Second World War are being commemorated, but also the Dutch people that have fallen in wars, armed conflicts, and peace operations after the Second World War.[10]

At the commemoration on Dam square, the mayor of Amsterdam from now on announced that

> we practice two minutes of silence for all – civilians and soldiers – who have perished in the Kingdom of the Netherlands or wherever else in the world since the outbreak of the Second World War, in situations of war and at peace operations.[11]

The phrase 'or wherever else in the world' seems to mean that the Dutch are now, – in what appears to be an attempt to 'universalize' the national memorial –, commemorating the deaths of their national soldiers *as well as* the deaths of the ones those soldiers might have killed in combat. It reminds of the 'and-and-approach' to loyalties of the WRR (as discussed in the previous chapter).

To have a universalist commemoration of the dead of armed conflict, however, is impossible. As armed conflict is necessarily about an adversary – a 'them' –, the attempt to include everyone in the commemoration will inevitably contradict the very idea of such a commemoration in the first place. The Committee, realizing that 'since the end of the Second World War, worldwide not a day has passed without war', and that 'since 1945, more than 200 wars and armed

---

[9] This is the committee that organizes the yearly commemoration. In Dutch: het *Nationaal Comité 4 en 5 Mei.*

[10] From the website of the National Committee 4 and 5 May: 'Accentverschuiving. In de loop van de jaren is de herdenking verbreed. Niet alleen de slachtoffers van de Tweede Wereldoorlog worden herdacht, maar ook de Nederlanders die zijn omgekomen bij oorlogen, gewapende conflicten en vredesoperaties na de Tweede Wereldoorlog'. Available online at http://www.4en5mei.nl/herdenken/achtergronden/achtergronddetail/_pid/kolom2_1/_rp_kolom2_1_elementId/1_90676.

[11] 'Allen – burgers en militairen – die in het Koninkrijk der Nederlanden of waar ook ter wereld zijn omgekomen sinds het uitbreken van de Tweede Wereldoorlog, in oorlogssituaties en bij vredesoperaties'.

conflicts have been fought', explained its reasons for the aforementioned shift in accent as follows:

> In the Netherlands live many who have experienced these actual situations of war, suppression, and unfreedom. Especially for young people who lack historical reference to the Second World War, commemorating can relate to the present or the recent past.[12]

At the national commemoration on May 4th, 2003, some possible consequences of this all-inclusive approach became visible. In the Amsterdam neighbourhood *De Baarsjes*, a group of Islamic youth shouted 'We must kill the Jews!',[13] during the two minutes of silence. On the *Sierplein* in the neighbourhood *Slotervaart Overtoomse Veld*, young Moroccans started playing soccer with the garlands. In the centre of Amsterdam, cars klaxoned in order to show disdain for the commemoration at the *gay monument*.

The trouble is that based on a literal understanding of the ideas of the *Committee 4 and 5 May*, these immigrants were not entirely unjustified to behave as they did. Many of them, it appears, regard Jewish people as the enemy (because of anti-Semitism in the Quran and in their culture, and because of the presence of the Jewish state in territories they perceive to be theirs, i.e. Israel), and some conceive the allied victory over Nazi-Germany as synonymous with the installation of Israel.[14] Comparable confusion arose when a high school in Amsterdam-West wanted to hold two minutes of silence on the day after the terrorist attack on the Twin Towers in New York on September 11th, 2001. The school-children started rioting and said they would not commemorate the victims of this attack. They shouted: 'Sorry for you! We have shown the Americans something!'.

From the point of view of multiculturalism, they in fact had a point. If we accept the *Committee's* commemoration of 'all who have perished', why commemorate the dead from the Twin Towers, and *not* commemorate Muhamed Atta and the other suicide terrorists indeed?[15] Why mourn the fallen Dutch

---

[12] 'De actualiteit geeft betekenis aan herdenken en vieren. Sinds het einde van de Tweede Wereldoorlog is er wereldwijd nog geen dag zonder oorlog geweest. Vanaf 1945 zijn er meer dan 200 oorlogen en gewapende conflicten uitgevochten. In Nederland leven ook velen die deze actuele situaties van oorlog, onderdrukking en onvrijheid aan den lijve hebben meegemaakt. Vooral voor jongeren zonder historisch referentiekader met betrekking tot de Tweede Wereldoorlog kan herdenken betrekking hebben op het heden of recente verleden.'
[13] 'Joden moeten we doden'.
[14] 'Had Hitler maar gewonnen, dan hadden de Palestijnen nu een leven gehad. Dat is wat je hoort in de klas', in: 'Juf, wordt het fout gerekend dat ik Joden vergeten ben!', *NRC Handelsblad*, 29 April 2006.
[15] 'Marco Strang – leraar geschiedenis, voorheen sportschoolmedewerker, openlijk homoseksueel – keek er niet van op toen in mei 2003 een paar Marokkanen met bloemenkransen gingen voetballen. Maar hij was nog wel verbaasd toen zijn school – het Meridiaan College in Amsterdam-West – op de dag na 11 september twee minuten stilte zou houden voor de doden in de Twin Towers. "Er waren leerlingen die zeiden dat ze dat niet deden. Ze gingen herrie maken." De euforie. De blik waarmee naar hem gekeken werd. Jammer voor jullie, nou hebben wij de

resistance fighters and bring homage to the British and Americans who had to put out hundreds of thousands of Germans in order to liberate the Netherlands and other countries, while condemning those who killed only a few thousand Americans in an attempt to 'liberate' what they believed to be the 'Palestinian' lands, on September 11th, 2001? If all cultures are equal, and if all conflicts are equally just, and if all victims equally deplorable – there should be no reason to make a distinction, should there? When the Dutch proclaim to commemorate *all deaths*, on *all sides of conflicts*, why should these immigrants not express their grief over the loss of the supposed 'Palestinian' lands? And given some anti-homosexual trends in much of Muslim culture, is it really surprising that when they are granted the moral right to commemorate whichever value they choose, they might choose a condemnation of gays?

As a nation state, it is simply not possible to commemorate universally, as much as it is not possible to fight on both sides of an armed conflict.

This mistake of the *Committee* should, however, not blind us to its good intentions. Its idea has clearly been to reshape the national commemoration in a way that may actually *include* immigrants. They supposedly wanted the 4th and 5th of May to be more than a merely historical commemoration, but an actual, *national* commemoration. But what is necessary for that, again, is some positive formulation of values. A better rephrasing of the commemoration announced could have been:

> We practice two minutes of silence for all – civilians and soldiers – who have perished in defense of the Kingdom of the Netherlands or its allies or its way of life since the outbreak of the Second World War.

This too, is a universalistic approach to the nation, open to newcomers, yet living up to the need for particularism that is intrinsic in the whole concept of commemorating.

Nor was the *Committee* right in supposing that newcomers in the Dutch nation can have no connection to the ancestors who gave their lives in wars of the past. Because in fact these Dutch ancestors gave their lives for the national culture and the national territory, and by living on those grounds, and having membership of that same nationality, one enjoys precisely what they have fought for and died for – so not being heir to them by blood, is not a reason at all not to be grateful for their sacrifice. It only shows the ethnic misconception of nationality.

One final example of the mistaken approach of the *Committee of 4 and 5 May*: the 'theme' of the commemoration of 2009 was 'Freedom and Identity'. Why? Because:

Amerikanen eens wat laten zien', in: 'Juf, wordt het fout gerekend dat ik Joden vergeten ben!', *NRC Handelsblad*, 29 April 2006.

it was shown in the Second World War how thoughts about identity can affect freedom.

Conclusion, apparently: abolish national identity, and you will get unmitigated freedom.[16]

In France, a comparable debate about national commemorations and national identity exists. In an attempt to reaffirm the national spirit amongst the younger generation of Frenchmen, President Sarkozy announced shortly following his installation in the Elysée in May 2007, that on October 22nd of each year, the letter of 17 year old communist-resistance activist Guy Moquêt, written just before his execution in the prison camp in the French village of Chateaubriant, would be read out in every school class throughout France.

On May 16th, Sarkozy went to the Bois de Boulogne, where the Gestapo had shot 35 resistant fighters in 1944, and announced:

> I wanted to hold my first commemoration in my capacity as President of the Republic here, in this place where young Frenchmen were murdered because they could not conceive of France turning its back on all of its history and all of its values. I wanted to use the first day of my term to honour these young resistant fighters to whom France was more important than their party or their church. I wanted to have the moving letter that Guy Môquet wrote to his parents on the eve of his execution read out loud. I wanted these things because I believe it is critically important to explain to our children what a young Frenchman is, and to explain how the sacrifice of some of these anonymous heroes who have been left out of the history books can show us the greatness of a man who devotes himself to a greater cause.[17]

Then he concluded: 'Children of France, remember that admirable men have sacrificed much to conquer the freedom that you enjoy.'[18]

Analogous to this French – national – approach, the mayor of Amsterdam in the Netherlands could for example announce on the yearly Dutch commemoration on the 4th of May: 'Children of the oldest free Republic of the world, children

---

[16] 'In de Tweede Wereldoorlog is gebleken hoe gedachten over identiteit de vrijheid kunnen aantasten.'

[17] 'Si j'ai tenu à faire ici ma première commémoration en tant que Président de la République, dans ce lieu où de jeunes Français furent assassinés parce qu'ils ne pouvaient pas concevoir que la France reniât toute son histoire et toutes ses valeurs, si j'ai tenu au premier jour de mon quinquennat à rendre hommage à ces jeunes résistants pour lesquels la France comptait davantage que leur parti ou leur Eglise, si j'ai voulu que fût lue la lettre si émouvante que Guy Môquet écrivit à ses parents à la veille d'être fusillé, c'est parce que je crois qu'il est essentiel d'expliquer à nos enfants ce qu'est un jeune Français, et de leur montrer à travers le sacrifice de quelques-uns de ces héros anonymes dont les livres d'histoire ne parlent pas, ce qu'est la grandeur d'un homme qui se donne à une cause plus grande que lui.'

[18] The translation comes from the official website of the Elysée, http://www.elysee.fr/elysee/elysee.fr/anglais/speeches_and_documents/2007/speech_by_nicolas_sarkozy_president_of_the_republic_at_the_memorial_ceremony_for_the_bois_de_boulogne_martyrs.76687.html.

of Holland, remember! Wherever you come from, whatever your religion or ethnicity … Remember! (etc.)'.

This approach to the nation, once again, is open to all, to newcomers as well as to those who have been in the Netherlands for generations, and so complies with the criteria of an open concept of nationality, as defended by Ernest Renan and Fustel de Coulanges (see chapter 3). Yet it does not jeopardize the idea of a shared community of which politics necessarily forms an expression if it is to remain representative and if a shared rule of law should continue to apply.

With Sarkozy's speech, however, the complicated issue of *patrimony* comes into play as well. *Patrimony* is the cultural heritage of a society, and as 'the freedom that [we] enjoy' is not isolated from social context and history, it is not unconnected to political arrangements either. As whatever 'freedom' that may be enjoyed is inevitably part of the complex fabric of society, an understanding of patrimony comes close to what Edmund Burke meant when he explored the relationship between convention – custom – and law. While going so far as to say that 'if civil society be the offspring of convention, that convention must be its law',[19] Burke realized that whatever *contract* this society may be, it would inevitably be a 'partnership not only between those who are living, but between those who are living, those who are dead, and those who are to be born'.[20] 'The state ought not to be considered as nothing better than a partnership agreement', according to Burke, as living together – and governing together – implies sharing a common culture, from which the political order and the law come forth.

If the state is the representative of the people that live on the territory over which it claims jurisdiction – which (as argued in part I) is the pretention of the nation state – it is natural for the state to conceive of itself as the herdsman of the culture, the customs, and in general the particular form of life that has taken shape on it.

9.2. *The Public Sphere*

This has consequences for what is commonly denoted as 'the public sphere'. Although generally conceived as 'neutral territory' to which the state ought to be indifferent, there is nevertheless an indisputable connection between the nation – and its history and identity – and this public sphere. A first element

---

[19] Edmund Burke, *Reflections on the Revolution in France. A critical edition.* Edited by J.C.D. Clark (Stanford: Stanford University Press, 2001) 218.

[20] Burke (2001) 261. Thomas Paine did not agree with Burke on this, see Thomas Paine, *Rights of Man, being an answer to mr. Burke's attack on the French Revolution* (1791) 8. Available online at http://www.iowagrandmaster.org/Books%20in%20pdf/Paine--Rights%20of%20Man.pdf. Cf. Craig Nelson, *Thomas Paine. Enlightenment, Revolution, and the Birth of Modern Nations* (New York: Viking, 2006) 181ff: 'Droits de l'Homme, ou Droits du Seigneur?'.

of the public sphere that comes to mind is the language spoken. France poses an interesting example of state support for that element of the public sphere in the form of the *Académie Française*, founded in 1614 by Richelieu, who also defended, as we have seen, the importance of a national political loyalty. With the official mission of 'watching over the French language',[21] the academy has, in its own words,

> worked in the past to stabilize the language, in order to create a common patrimony for all Frenchmen and for all those who use our language.[22]

Especially the reference to the French language in the Academy's mission statement as 'our language' ('notre langue') is interesting: French is not conceived of as a neutral, utilitarian *open source medium* merely serving the exchange of information, but as the possession of a nation, and the expression of a way of life.[23] To further support the French language worldwide, the French state founded the *Organisation International de la Francophonie* in 1970, organizing conferences, supporting initiatives, and generally promoting the French language. In line with this, the French constitution reads that 'the language of the Republic is French'.[24] This means that the French state openly speaks out for a particular language, and that it does not, by implication, just as happily see English or Arabic being spoken.

It is not surprising that nation states, seeking representative government and the rule of law, emphasize the importance of a shared language. For how would either be possible without such a shared means of communication? A national public debate is impossible amongst citizens who cannot understand one another, as it would be to follow the developments of government and parliament. Without a shared language, such institutions as national newspapers

---

[21] 'Veiller sur la langue française'.
[22] 'Travaillé dans le passé à fixer la langue, pour en faire un patrimoine commun à tous les Français et à tous ceux qui pratiquent notre langue http://www.academie-francaise.fr/role/index.html.
[23] Cf. the book of the current member of the Académie Française, Marc Fumaroli, *Quand l'Europe parlait Français* (Paris: Éditions de Fallois, 2011) 26-27: 'La grammaire française, le lexique du français, dont Voltaire n'avait pas peur de tourner en derision la relative pauvreté, la syntaxe française, la sémantique exigeante du français, sa versification dont Walpole voyait bien les défauts un siècle avant la "crise du vers" diagnostiquée par Mallarmé, les genres où notre langue excellait, notamment les genres intimes, la lettre, le journal, la poésie de circonstance, les *Mémoires*, et ce genre littéraire oral qu'est la conversation entre amis, tout cet apprentissage difficile avait le sens d'une initiation à une manière exceptionnelle d'être libre et naturel avec autrui et avec soi-même. C'était tout autre chose que de communiquer. C'était entrer "en compagnie"'.
[24] Constitution Française, Article 2: 'La langue de la République est le français. L'emblème national est le drapeau tricolore, bleu, blanc, rouge. L'hymne national est la "Marseillaise". La devise de la République est "Liberté, Egalité, Fraternité". Son principe est : gouvernement du peuple, par le peuple et pour le peuple'. The full text of the French constitution can be found at: http://www.legifrance.gouv.fr/affichTexte.do;jsessionid=64C8027EBFD9CE02B300CE6F0E48A C7F.tpdjo09v_1?cidTexte=LEGITEXT000006071194&dateTexte=20110518. The article was added to the constitution in 1992.

and national television channels would have severe difficulties to function.[25] They refer to a national public debate and reaffirm the idea that a shared public interest exists. Parliament, supposedly the reflection of the national debate and the place where the national interest is ultimately decided upon, needs to find reception in the nation in order to live up to its democratic claims.

The French state, in addition, performs a wide range of other promotional activities not only of its language, but also of its culture. And the French state is by no means unique in this. Just as France has the *Alliance française*, Germany has a network of *Goethe Institutes*, organizing lectures, inviting speakers, and generally promoting the German culture in other countries worldwide[26] – the Netherlands has a network of *Dutch institutes*, and so on. The examples are endless.

When it comes to the content of the national culture, the French state again choses an interesting approach. While the state formally possesses strict 'neutrality' towards all 'cults' (religions), it financially supports a great amount of church buildings, which are considered to be part of the *patrimoine* of the French nation. Indeed, in the years following the famous *law of 1905* that installed this secularism, the French state, having prided itself for centuries for being the *fille aînée de l'église,* the oldest daughter of the church, and being covered, in the words of Sarkozy, by a 'manteau de cathédrales',[27] realized an 'absorption of the old diocese buildings by the historical Monuments'.[28]

With the exception, to this day, of Alsace and Lorraine, which at the time were not part of France and have never accepted the law of separation since their reunion, the French state is considered to be neutral towards all religions, yet at the same time to remain a defender of the cultural heritage of the French nation, in which the churches inescapably play a large role.[29] In the course of the 20th century, a great number of additional laws have been passed bringing more and more elements of society – certainly not only religious ones – under the aegis of the French state.

---

[25] See on this for instance Benedict Anderson's analysis of the importance of national newspapers in the developments of *imagined communities*: Anderson (1991) 37ff.

[26] On its website the Goethe-institute announces: 'The Goethe-Institut is the Federal Republic of Germany's cultural institution operating worldwide'; available online at http://www.goethe.de/enindex.htm.

[27] Nicolas Sarkozy said this at a Speech held on 13 December, 2007. Cf. Catherine Gouëset, '8 ans d'idylle entre l'Elysée et les catholiques', in: *l'Express*, 8 October, 2010. Available online at http://www.lexpress.fr/actualite/politique/8-ans-d-idylle-entre-l-elysee-et-les-catholiques_925948.html.

[28] 'L'Absorption des anciens édifices diocésains par les Monuments historiques'. A. Auduc, 'L'héritage des croyants devient patrimoine national', in: *Hommes et Migrations*, vol. 1259, 'Les 100 ans d'une idée neuve, II. Culture(s), religion(s) et politique', Dossier coordonné par Alain Seksig (janvier-février 2006) 70-77.

[29] Cf. Olivier le Roy, *La laïcité face à l'Islam* (Paris: Stock, 2005); Gerard Noiriel, *A quoi sert l'identité nationale?* (Marseille: Agone, 2007). When still a government minister, Nicolas Sarkozy also authored a book partly on this subject, *La République, les religions, l'espérance* (Paris: Editions du cerf, 2004).

In their several ways, almost all Western nation states have developed comparable means to support a particular patrimony. From a strictly universalist perspective, then, they all discriminate. They discriminate firstly between citizens and non-citizens; but secondly, they favor a particular culture, and a particular way of life. Whether in the form of a language, or through the upkeep of architectural heritage, rarely have states remained indifferent to the way or ways of life of which they are the ultimate herdsmen.

This is not disconnected from the rule of law either. The law itself – as I have attempted to show in chapter 5 and 6 –, implies a choice for a *particular* law, and for particular values and approaches to such themes as free will, accountability, the relationship between men and women, the right form of punishment for criminal offenses, and so on. If a state upholds the rule of law, it is always a *particular* law – and it is to be hoped that this law is perceived by all who are submitted to it, to be *theirs*.

Underneath the discussion over the French protection of its Catholic heritage, lie, then, complicated questions concerning the right to confess one's religion in public. For not only is freedom of religion understood to mean freedom of conscience, it has also come to mean the freedom to express one's religion publicly. From that perspective, all faiths may be said to be equal. Yet at the same time, the churches and cathedrals in many European states are major anchor points of the national awareness. Since Chateaubriand, many have praised the church bells as possessing 'undoubtedly a beauty of the first rank, that what artists call *the great*',[30] even when they are no longer practicing believers. The bells have become a part, to some extend, of the cultural heritage of many nation states. They are reminiscent of an inherited religious tradition, of the great history and artistic achievements of Christian Europe; of a sense of provinciality, too, which many cherish as an antidote against modern hectic life.

To say that the state is the expression of a heritage is not to say, of course, that this heritage is fixed forever. However, to question the neutrality of the public sphere, and to regard it as an expression of a certain kind of heritage, is to understand it not only legally, but also sociologically. To see the public sphere as an expression of a certain social reality makes it self-evident that the social right to make a strong impact on the public sphere has to be 'earned'.

Again, France provides an interesting example, with the great mosque that was built in the centre of Paris in the 1920s. It was the first mosque to be built in France, and its construction was decided upon after the battle of Verdun, in which more than 50.000 Algerian Muslims had lost their lives while fighting

---

[30] 'Indubitablement une beauté de la première sorte: celle que les artistes appellent *le grand*'. Chateaubriand, *Génie du Christianisme. Ou beautés de la Religion Chrétienne* (1802) (Paris: Éditions Gallimard, 1978) 893: part 4, book 1, chapter 1. Cf. Ernest Renan, 'Souvenirs d'enfance et de jeunesse' (Paris 1883), in: Henriette Psichari (ed.), *Œuvres Complètes d'Ernest Renan* II (Paris 1949-1961) 723.

on the French side. It was strongly felt that through their sacrifices for the French nation, the Muslim community had earned the right to partake in the public sphere and so place a symbol of their culture and religion in the midst of French society. In any ordinary social situation, most people would regard this as a most common thing: to adapt to an existing social code, to a certain way of living, a certain architectural style, to gradually 'earn' the (social) right to influence the way things are done; these are amongst the immediate data of conscience, self-evident to all who have ever been a part of a society, a group of friends, a club, or a family.

Much abstract thought about rights, such as social contract theory of the kind expounded by John Rawls (as discussed in chapter 8), while emphasizing the importance of the 'neutrality' of the state, neglects the social experience that is implied in every form of political organization. But while it may or may not do justice to their similarities and differences to classify Judaism, Christianity and Islam under the same word 'religion' (Tocqueville for instance believed there were 'a thousand' reasons not to do so[31]), to have an impact on the public sphere raises not only theological and legalistic, but also sociological questions – ultimately culminating in that most fundamental question of all: will the others be tolerated? If human history shows one thing, it is that accepting our differences is never unproblematic. As Arthur Schlesinger puts it: 'The hostility of one tribe for another is among the most instinctive human reactions.'[32] A way to overcome this natural hostility is by creating a common point of reference – which in the past has often been a common enemy, but which can also be a common nationality, a common home. By emphasizing the shared nationality – an association that all members of society are a part of –, the different tribes, races and religions can actually manage to live together in a peaceful manner.

What happens when this unification around a shared nationality fails, is illustrated by the Dreyfus affair that I have discussed in chapter 3. Had the French self-image not been injured so fundamentally after the defeat in 1871, then it is unlikely that the fever to 'purify' the nation would have taken such a pathological shape. Moreover, hadn't the German self-consciousness been crushed in Versailles, then the popular support for such resentful movements as the Nazi-party, is, if not unimaginable, at least highly improbable.

It is not implausible that contemporary disdain for the ordinary, peaceful national feelings of the European peoples may cause them to be charmed by intolerantly nationalist or 'populist' politicians today. The all too severe emphasis

---

[31] Tocqueville, *Democracy in America*, vol. 2, book I, chapter 5. Cf. Cliteur, Paul, 'A Secular Reading of Tocqueville', in: Raf Geenens and Annelien de Dijn (eds.), *Reading Tocqueville: From Oracle to Actor* (Houndmills, New York: Palgrave, MacMillan 2007) 112-132.
[32] Arthur M. Schlesinger jr., *The Disuniting of America. Reflections on a Multicultural Society. Revised and enlarged edition* (New York: W.W. Norton & Company, 1998) 12.

of mainstream politicians on abstract and universalist principles, has possibly caused them to insufficiently accommodate the shared national identities of European states. Instead of debating the meaning of national identities, political fora have been permeated by what Mary Ann Glendon calls 'rights talk':[33] the rephrasing of disputes in terms of abstract, universal rights.

Especially the 'universal human right' to enjoy equal treatment proves to be problematic.[34] Reminding us of John Rawls' ideas of a just society, article 2 of the 'Universal Declaration of Human Rights' condemns distinctions 'of any kind, such as race, color, sex, language, religion, political or other opinion, national or social origin, property, birth or other status'.[35] The European Convention on Human Rights has put it almost identically, outlawing 'discrimination' (in its article 14) 'on any ground such as sex, race, color, language, religion, political or other opinion, national or social origin, association with a national minority, property, birth or other status.'[36]

The Dutch constitution has a comparable formulation, expressed in its very first article:[37] 'All persons in the Netherlands shall be treated equally in equal circumstances. Discrimination on the grounds of religion, belief, political opinion, race or sex or on any other grounds whatsoever shall not be permitted.'[38]

The list is so extensive and explicitly mentions 'all other forms' (i.e. all possible forms) of discrimination, that the grounds of distinction that are to be combated according to the universalist worldview are unlimited (rendering significant power to the judges at, for instance, Strasbourg to do so in accordance with their own political views).

But since laws are ultimately not to be supported by force but by heartfelt endorsement by the community that they apply to, a society that condemns all forms of discrimination, 'on the grounds of religion, belief, political opinion, race or sex or on any other grounds whatsoever', must necessarily implicate the citizens' *indifference* towards those criteria. The ideal citizen (for those who aim the banning of all forms of 'discrimination') is the one who says:

---

[33] Glendon (1991).
[34] Cf. N. Lerner, *The U.N. Convention on the Elimination of all Forms of Racial Discrimination* (Alphen aan den Rijn: Sijthoff en Noordhoff 1970) 46.
[35] The Universal Declaration of Human Rights was issued by the United Nations General Assembly, on December 10th, 1948.
[36] The European Convention for the Protection of Human Rights and Fundamental Freedoms was drafted in Rome, on 4 November 1950. This article got the heading "Prohibition of Discrimination" according to the Provisions of protocol 11 (ETS no. 155), 11 may 1994.
[37] Since 1983.
[38] This is the official translation of the Dutch text, provided by the Ministry of the Interior and Kingdom Relations, Constitutional Affairs and Legislation Department, in collaboration with the Translation Department of the Ministry of Foreign Affairs. www.minbzk.nl. The Dutch text reads: 'Allen die zich in Nederland bevinden, worden in gelijke gevallen gelijk behandeld. Discriminatie wegens godsdienst, levensovertuiging, politieke gezindheid, ras, geslacht of op welke grond dan ook, is niet toegestaan.'

to me, any religion, belief, political opinion, race, sex, or really any difference
between human beings is equal.

The non-discriminatory citizen has become a universal human being, without
preferences or particular attachments that he favors over others. The Rawlsian
society, that is indifferent to any 'conceptions of the good' the citizens may have,
has ceased to be a society. In the words of James Fitzjames Stephen:

> Complete moral tolerance is possible only when men have become completely
> indifferent to each other – that is to say, when society is at an end.[39]

As 'national identity' is necessarily something *particular*, it implies also that
certain forms of behavior or cultural practices are *not* part of it. A national
identity implies, in short, a distinction, which is a form of inequality that constitutes – strictly speaking – a form of discrimination.

It is implied in the modern conception of citizenship, which grants to all
the right to partake in democratic decision making, that those with citizenship
have a different status than those without. Guests or temporary visitors may
enjoy the hospitality of the community, but, as they do not bear the burdens of
membership (nor are demanded to fulfill the duties that go hand in hand with
it), they do not have a natural entitlement to all of its benefits either.

Indeed, from this perspective, to demand equal treatment and non-
discrimination to strangers, implies denying the legitimacy of the sense of
membership altogether. That is why the universal prohibition to discriminate
even to those who are not citizens – through the European Court of Human
Rights –, if applied consistently, is contradictory to the very idea of citizenship.
Or, put the other way round: citizenship necessarily discriminates between
those who possess it, and those who don't.

The right to partake in democratic decision-making is granted to all citizens,
yet, as a rule, denied to foreigners (though not always on the municipal level).
Properly understood, all nation states say, as does the Spanish guerrilla fighter
Pablo in Ernest Hemingway's *For Whom the Bell Tolls*:

> What right have you, a foreigner, to come to me and tell me what I must do?[40]

Much practice that is condemned as being 'discriminatory' concerns a different
treatment of immigrants as compared to natives. It is called 'discrimination', for
instance, when an immigrant with an unfamiliar name is rejected at a job for that
reason; or when Switzerland votes to ban the building of new minarets (while still
allowing the building of for instance church towers). Whereas the experience of
membership always poses demands on the members, the universal approach to

---

[39] James Fitzjames Stephen, *Liberty, Equality, Fraternity* (1874), quoted in: Roger Kimball,
Experiments against reality. The fate of culture in the postmodern age (Chicago: Ivan R. Dee, 2000) 159.
[40] Ernest Hemingway, *For whom the bell tolls* (London: Vintage Books, 2005) 17.

the 'fundamental rights' of the individual has made it incumbent upon Western states to ignore that element of membership. In this way, it would be possible to understand the 'non-discrimination' project not as a demand for 'equal rights in equal circumstances', but of 'equal rights in unequal circumstances'.

The question whether these equal rights for different groups and practices *should* in fact be given, leads to a discussion on the criteria of membership and the future of the identity of the community again.

To demand equal treatment on the basis of race or ethnicity, moreover, is an entirely different thing than to demand it on the basis of faith, religion, way of life, and 'conceptions of the good'. For the former are not the result of a choice or a matter of moral significance. The latter, on the contrary, are subject to choice and imply a moral position. Rational beings can be held personally responsible for their 'conceptions of the good'. By implying that nations do not have a right to resist certain 'conceptions of the good', the general movement against discrimination has become, over the past decades, a one-sided battle for minorities' – and immigrants' – rights, and thus a tool for the political project to abandon borders and weaken national identities.[41]

There is also a crucial role for symbols to be played in this. As discussed in the previous chapter, most modern nation states have a number of official festive or memorial days. Usually there is a role for the national anthem and the national flag at the ceremonies that mark the beginning or conclusion of these happenings. In times of civil war, one of the very first things that the different factions do is develop their own flag. It seems to be difficult to have a political organization without such symbols. The first observation that seems important in relation to this is that group identity expresses itself through symbols. Flags, anthems, signs, colours or special words can thus carry meaning for members of a social group and so express their loyalty to that group.

After the publication of twelve cartoons that mocked the Islamic prophet on September 30th, 2005, in the Danish newspaper *Jyllands Posten*, Muslims felt that a symbol to which they were attached was desecrated and protested all over the world. Responses were, amongst others, the burning of the Danish flag. They were offended not by the mocking of themselves, but of their prophet; those who felt offended held the whole nation in which the publication had occurred, responsible. Thus understanding the Danish nation as to some extent a collective identity, they responded by attacking *the symbols* of that nation, such as the flag.[42]

---

[41] See on this, for instance, Christopher Lasch, *The Revolt of the Elites and the Betrayal of Democracy* (New York: W.W. Norton and Company, 1995).

[42] In contrast with many other countries, burning the flag is not illegal in Denmark. Section 110 (e) of the Danish penal code forbids to desecrate the flags or national symbols of foreign nations, while it doesn't prohibit to burn Denmark's own national flag. The reason for this is that the burning

As a matter of fact, this attachment to symbols, as illustrated by the unrest that followed the publication of the Danish cartoons, is what we all live by on a daily basis. National festive days, the flag, the anthem, and so on, express the collective identity that is necessary for representative government and the rule of law to make sense. When a judge puts a person in the wrong, he must do so with a reference to a law that this person must, in order to accept the judge's decision, also consider authoritative over him. This provides an additional argument for the wearing of uniforms by judges and others involved with upholding the law, such as police officers and prison guards, too: they are not supposed to be individual agents, but representatives of a collective body.[43]

A final aspect of modern citizenship and the conception of 'national identity' that is implied in it is connected to the facilities of the welfare state: the national health care, national welfare, national pensions, national aid programmes and tax cuts for donations to national development programmes. All such forms of state-funded or fostered solidarity imply a sense of national loyalty that provides legitimacy for it. Indeed, it is very difficult to imagine social democratic politics without presupposing the existence of a nation.[44] This is also the reason why many traditional left-wing parties have taken a sceptical position towards immigration (whereas many right-wing parties have been wary of the idea of a national identity and defended global free trade and open borders[45] – interestingly enough almost the exact opposite to the present!). But it cannot be denied that the welfare state rests upon a sense of national solidarity: a sense of community.

9.3. WITHOUT A 'WE', IT WON'T WORK

Ultimately, representative government and the rule of law are thus dependent upon a territorial loyalty that is sufficiently imagined to allow newcomers in, yet not so universal that it leaves its members without shared symbols or objects of identification. As national loyalty is connected to a collective identity, it is only natural that it also encompasses a certain claim on the public sphere. The inevitable consequence of supranationalism and multiculturalism is the development of parallel loyalties that will challenge the unity of the state, and

---

of foreign flags is a matter of foreign policy, as it could be understood as a threat to that country. In fact, according to Danish tradition, burning is also the proper way to dispose of a worn flag.

[43] See on this for example Cliteur, 'Ambtenaar en Politiek. Over de anarchie in ons openbaar bestuur', in: *Tegen de Decadentie, de democratische rechtstaat in verval* (De Arbeiderspers, Amsterdam, 2004)143ff.

[44] See on this for instance: Leszek Kolakowski, *Main Currents of Marxism* (London: Norton Publishers, 2005) 81.

[45] Although John Stuart Mill already recognized the necessity for a 'principle of cohesion' amongst the members of a state, as discussed in the previous part.

thus hollow out representative government and the rule of law (as well as the preconditions for any form of state-initiated welfare).

The WRR may be right that multiple loyalties – to religion, family, different cultural backgrounds, and so on – will always exist. It is undesirable that the state should seek to eliminate this entirely; such a state would be a totalitarian state, recognizing only itself as a legitimate purpose in the lives of its subjects.

Nevertheless, the opposite is undesirable to largely the same extent: if different institutions and authorities consequently present alternatives to the national law – ultimately challenging the monopoly to the legitimate use of force of the state[46] –, representative government and the rule of law will effectively be hollowed out. The double problem that may, moreover, be rising in Western Europe is this: while multiculturalism sets in motion a centrifugal tendency out of the national idea, supranationalism offers the tools to defend a non-national law. Most clearly in the form of the ECHR and the ICC, supranational law presents, at a deeper level, the ongoing example that ultimately, reference is not to be made to the national law, but to the universal rights that every single individual is supposedly always entitled to.

When taking the perspective of multiculturalism, emphasizing the equality of each cultural group, and the right to an equal share in the state's cultural foundations, there is no reason why Muslims would not be encouraged to accept *their* form of non-national universal jurisdiction: *sharia* law. It is not unlikely that increasing numbers of Muslims, seeking a home in the modern world, will retreat into fundamentalism and derive from the language of universal jurisdiction the tools to defend divine commands. Then what may be evolving in the slipstream of the spread of 'human rights' is a concept of universal jurisdiction of the same nature as the religious jurisdiction that was finally abandoned – after more than a century of devastating warfare – in the 17th century.[47] This is a problem related to 'universal' human rights that lies below their superficial attractiveness. Not only do they seem to generate a rights- rather then a duties-based conception of citizenship (as discussed in chapter 8.3), but they also bear an innate justification of divine law, and thereby diminish the authority and indeed legitimacy of a shared, national law.

And this applies not only to the European Court of Human Rights, or the human rights discourse generally, but to the entire supranational idea. Supranational – i.e. global, universal – jurisdiction actually nourishes the idea that national law is of no particular authority and could be easily overridden. The

---

[46] As seems to be a tendency in the suburbs of many large European cities, from Paris and Amsterdam to Berlin and Marseille.

[47] Cf. Karin Jespersen and Ralph Pittelkow, *Islamisten en Naïvisten*. Met een introductie van Afshin Ellian (Amsterdam: Uitgeverij Nieuw Amsterdam, 2008).

weakening of national authority that this leads to is a dangerous development.[48] National loyalty is the common point of reference for the rule of law and representative government, and provides the sense of home into which strangers can be welcomed.[49] It is impossible to collectively deliberate and ultimately decide upon political questions, unless an assembly may speak for a collective whole: the people. It is unlikely that disputing parties will accept the verdict of a judge, if they do not experience both themselves and the judge as part of the same community. Globalization, migration, virtualization and so on pose great opportunities and chances. The twenty-first century seems to become a most exciting and international century, full of exchanges and unexpected developments. Yet if we want to continue living under representative governments with a shared rule of law, political organization will have to continue to focus on strengthening national loyalties, for 'without a we, it won't work'.[50]

---

[48] Again the French example is relevant. Each year on the morning of the fourteenth of July, in every French city and village, the inhabitants come together to play the *Marseillaise*, run their eyes over the lists of *Morts pour la Patrie*, and celebrate the hoisting of the flag. The French 14th of July may be compared with the several national festivities and commemorations in the Netherlands: April 30th (Queen's day), May 4th (the national commemoration of the dead), May 5th (Liberation day). The rituals attached to these festivities and commemorations can and should reaffirm the sense of membership, not only of particular communities, but also of the political whole, which ultimately comes down to the nation, which in turn is expressed through representative institutions and the shared rule of law. In France, of course, much (intellectual) weight is given to the French Revolution and the ideals that surfaced with it; but the celebrations on the 14th of July are not about the triumph of certain intellectual ideas. This day is, just as the symbols of the flag and the anthem, clearly the expression of a common home.

[49] Evidence from the *European Value Studies* suggests that for inhabitants of the EU, national loyalty still takes clear precedence over their loyalty to the union: '[F]or Europeans, nation comes first, then Europe. Europe has only been accepted in an instrumental and utilitarian way; no emotional or affective attachment exists towards the Union. Europeans perceive themselves first and foremost as French, Italian or Polish. They cherish their language, their habits and national culture" (Halman et al. 2005: 15)'.

[50] Paul Scheffer, *Het land van aankomst* (Amsterdam: De Bezige Bij, 2007).

CONCLUSION

This book has argued that representative government and the rule of law require nation states; or, put the other way round, that it is only in a nation state, that these institutions can properly function.

The significance of borders lies in their ability to define jurisdictions, and so separate one political community from another. In doing so, borders enable the formation and protection of a national loyalty as well as the exercise of sovereignty. Representative government and the rule of law need such a loyalty and such sovereignty. The gradual dismantlement of borders, brought about by supranationalism from above, and by multiculturalism from below, dilutes sovereignty and weakens nationality, and so hollows out representative government and the rule of law.

It is unfortunate that the significance of borders has been neglected. Instead of the *sovereign cosmopolitanism* that I propose, a policy of supranationalism has been pursued. Three supranational courts – the ICC, the ECHR, and the ICJ –, as well as three supranational organizations – the WTO, the Security Council and the EU – are unaccountable to the national community, while presenting the nation with law that is not from itself. Nor is this supranational law being administered, in the last instance, by the nation itself. In this way, the national sense of membership is weakened. The law is no longer 'ours' or 'from within', but from 'out there'. The judges that administer the law are no longer from within either. They are out of the reach of the national balance of powers and the pressures of public opinion. These supranational judges may have different ideas on how legal provisions should be interpreted, and their political persuasions are often unknown.

Indisputably, then, the national community has a limited say in the creation and application of supranational law. And while it inevitably becomes harder for the national community to accept the right of say of the supranational bodies as their powers increase, in the fact that no national assembly decides on the most important political decisions anymore, the reaffirmation of collective identity through collective decision-making is weakened as well.

Meanwhile, the response to mass-immigration has been one of multiculturalism, encouraging the differences between the diverse ethnic and religious groups, rather than their similarities. Instead of focusing on what the community of strangers may have in common, or should have in common, as in the ideal of a *multicultural nationalism* that I defend, multiculturalism advocates the lack of such a core-identity. While legal pluralism is still an exception, there can be no doubt that this is a logical next step on the line that starts with denying the existence of a single, shared national identity. As a result of this, the sense of overarching membership that is required for representative government and the rule of law, is severely eroded.

If representative government and the rule of law are to be preserved, or restored, it is important to change course. Because representative government and the rule of law require a collective, national identity as well as political sovereignty, nation states should be reaffirmed. Powers should gradually be taken back from the supranational institutions that now possess and exercise them; and the importance of national loyalty in the face of the multiethnic and multireligious societies of today, should be thoroughly reflected upon.

There are clearly many alternatives to current supranational entanglements. With regards to the World Trade Organization, the compulsory jurisdiction of the panels could be reversed, and the jurisdiction of the Appellate Body could be restricted, so giving back the power to ultimately interpret trade agreements to member states themselves. The International Criminal Court could accept Security Council veto power over decisions to commence investigations. It could also narrow the scope of crimes it has jurisdiction over, to for instance genocide or the use of weapons of mass destruction only. The European Court of Human Rights, too, could narrow its jurisdiction and restrict itself to what it was originally intended for: protecting individuals against the most basic injustices in terms of physical violence and gross cruelties, and standing up for the most elementary principles of democracy only, such as the liberty of the press and free elections. It could thus apply a more formalized principle of subsidiarity. Also, the ECHR could accept that a two-thirds majority should be reached amongst its judges before states can be convicted. An annual report with leading cases could be produced by the Parliamentary Assembly, which could then be reviewed and questioned by national parliaments.

One could easily go on in this fashion: the possibilities to reshape supranational organizations in a less supranational – more intergovernmental – way, or to curtail and limit their powers, are legion and the many possibilities deserve serious debate. A *sovereign cosmopolitanism*, exercised by nation states that are open to international cooperation and global developments, but retain the ultimate say in their obligations and policies, can take shape in many different forms, too, and therefore merits further exploration.

To argue – as has been the main purpose of this book – that representative government and the rule of law can exist only within nation states, however, does not necessarily mean that those nation states that presently exist should also be held on to. There is nothing in this book that specifically defends current borders: it has been a defense of borders in general. For that reason, representative government and the rule of law would not necessarily be undermined by a change of presently existing borders. The states that today exist do not necessarily reflect existing national identities, and the separation of Scotland from Great Britain, for instance, or the splitting up of Belgium into two nation states, may well improve the functioning of representative government and the rule of law, rather than undermine it. Nor is there in principle any objection to the merger of present-day nation states into larger nation states (the merger of Germany and Austria, for example, or, theoretically speaking, of even all European states into one United States of Europe). The point is that sovereignty and nationality uniquely enable representative government and the rule of law – not that we should hold on stiffly to historically contingent boundaries.

Nevertheless, I have tried to point out – in chapters 1, 3 and 9 especially – that there are great difficulties connected to creating the national membership that is required for representative government and the rule of law. It is certain that the kind of national loyalties that – however imperfectly – exist today, have been shaped at tremendous costs, over a long period of time, and that European states have made a great effort in building them. The idea that a European national-ity could be created seems to me to be frivolous and completely out of touch with reality. The difficulties that uniting East- and West-Germany in the 1990s already posed are illustrative: if unification asked already such effort from two countries with the same history, language and culture, after only half a century of separation – how on earth could this be done on a European scale? And if after more than 180 years of existence as a state, still hasn't led to the formation of a generally experienced Belgian nationality – what can we really, realistically speaking, expect from the packing together of Poles, Spaniards, Dutchmen, Frenchmen and Bulgarians?

There are, moreover, many plausible intergovernmental alternatives to the present supranational EU. The powers of the European Union could be severely diminished by for instance reconsidering the interpretation of the common market, the Schengen-agreement on open borders, as well as the euro currency. Gradually dismantling the politico-economic structure of the EU and moving back to the idea of a free trade zone is not difficult to imagine and might prove to be a stable format for European cooperation.

This hypothetical intergovernmental Europe, an open network of intensively cooperating, yet sovereign states, would have many attractive elements. If border controls were restored, it would make cooperation with non-European countries much easier. One result could be the opening up of the old continent to the vast markets in the Middle East and Northern Africa. By granting these countries, which could include Turkey, Egypt, Morocco, Russia, and even Turkmenistan and Kazakhstan, a status of 'peripheral benevolent countries', the richer and technologically more advanced (Western-) European countries could ensure access to cheap production in those countries, while maintaining control over their national economies and immigration. As national sovereignty would be restored, European states would cease to be obliged to converge their several foreign policies. International relations would again be determined on the basis of the historical loyalties, the national interests, and the policy decisions of the elected national governments.

The main argument against such an intergovernmental EU seems to be that, as the foreign policies of European countries could diverge, it would disable Europe to secure its 'common' global interests in the longer term (if there even exists such a thing). What some people fear is that by not installing an overarching political structure, the European states may become subject to policies of *divide et impera* by such great powers as India, China and the United States, thereby dwarfing the political clout of the European continent on the international scene. Recent events suggest that this might indeed be the case. Gas contracts with Russia which will be given to only a limited number of European countries; Chinese trade deals and customs agreements denounced as a result of some European state's critique on Chinese international geopolitical behavior; hardly are European political leaders being listened to in military conflicts around the globe; and so on.

The defender of an intergovernmental EU would argue that all these difficulties are the problem of the European nations themselves; and that it is their challenge to deal with them, as a federal European Union is – for lack of a single European nationality – unattainable. The European federalist, on the other hand, would argue that the formation of such a single European nationality is nevertheless possible. To form such a federal union, it would be necessary to transfer political sovereignty to the European political centre. Choosing this option would mean the end of the current, supranational EU and with it the thousands of regulations and directives that the Monnet method has produced, and the beginning of a new, democratic European nation state.

European foreign policy would have to converge. France would have to give up its permanent seat in the Security Council to be replaced by a common, 'European' seat; Germany and France must accept the possibility of being outvoted by former Communist countries in the East of Europe when it comes to questions of foreign policy and support for American military interventions around the globe; the Italians would have to fight in the same army as the Spaniards, the Germans, the Dutch and the Danes. The significantly less liberal majorities in Middle and Eastern European countries may outvote Dutch ideals on gay rights, abortion, euthanasia, drugs and so on. A European *lingua franca*, which will most certainly be English, would eclipse the importance of the great culture-languages of the continent. And so on.

As I have said, to my mind this is grotesque and indeed absurd, and I don't see how this could possibly be believed to be a realistic scenario. Moreover, I fear that going this way would incite an intolerant and closed nationalism – of the kind that also helped to bring about the explosion of Yugoslavia – rather than invoke enthusiasm for yet more 'Europeanization'. But whether this is so or not, and whether the process of unifying Europe politically must therefore be set in motion or not, goes beyond the scope of this book. The point here has been that the present, supranational 'in between' concept of European integration, with an EU that is stuck somewhere halfway between a federation and mere intergovernmental cooperation, is unsustainable. Sovereignty and national identity must coincide for representative government and the rule of law to exist.

BIBLIOGRAPHY

BOOKS, ARTICLES, CHAPTERS IN EDITED VOLUMES AND SPEECHES

'Café berispt om ladies' night-korting', *NOS*, 30 June 2011, http://nos.nl/artikel/252403-cafe-berispt-om-ladies-nightkorting.html.

'Council of Europe blasts burqa ban', in: *www.euractiv.com*, 20 july 2011, available online at: http://www.euractiv.com/en/culture/council-europe-blasts-burqa-ban-news-506689.

'De Nederlander bestaat: Johan Huizinga, Hans Wansink, Willem Velema, A. Th. Van Deursen, and H.W. von der Dunk', in: *Opinio*, 12-18 October 2007 (yr 1, number 39), *Opinio*, 4-10 January 2008 (yr 2, number 1), *Opinio*, 18-24 January 2008 (yr 2, number 3).

'Erdogan's Visit leaves German conservatives fuming', in: *Spiegel Online*, 2 December 2008. Available online at: http://www.spiegel.de/international/germany/0,1518,534724,00.html.

'Europese begroting moet drastisch worden herzien', in: *NRC Handelsblad*, 14 May 2009.

'Gewalt in der Ehe. Richterin bedauert Koran-Verweis', in: *Frankfurter Allgemeine Zeitung*, 22 March, 2007.

'Integrationsdebatte. Schröder warnt vor Kampf der Kulturen', in: *Frankfurter Allgemeine Sonntagszeitung*, 21 November 2004. Available online at http://www.faz.net/artikel/C30189/integrationsdebatte-schroeder-warnt-vor-kampf-der-kulturen-30198894.html.

'Juf, wordt het fout gerekend dat ik Joden vergeten ben!', in: *NRC Handelsblad*, 29 April 2006.

'Many rights, some wrong', in: *The Economist*, 22 March, 2007.

'More division over multiculturalism', *The Guardian*, 9 February 2011, Available online at http://www.guardian.co.uk/politics/2011/feb/09/more-division-over-multiculturalism.

'Nicolas Sarkozy declares multiculturalism had failed', in: *The Telegraph*, 11 February 2011. Available online at http://www.telegraph.co.uk/news/worldnews/europe/france/8317497/Nicolas-Sarkozy-declares-multiculturalism-had-failed.html.

'Penalising women who wear the burqa does not liberate them', in: *The Council of Europe Commissioner's Human Rights Comment*, 20 July 2011. Available online at: http://commissioner.cws.coe.int/tiki-view_blog_post.php?postId=157.

'Poll: almost two-thirds of Czechs support capital punishment', in: *Prague Daily Monitor*, 13 July 2009.

'Professor Rick Lawson nu zelf onzorgvuldig', on: *Dagelijkse Standaard* (weblog), 1 July, 2011. Available online at http://www.dagelijksestandaard.nl/2011/07/professor-rick-lawson-nu-zelf-onzorgvuldig.

'Suzan Mubarak does not represent egyptian women', on: *Epress.am* (weblog), 23 February 2011. Available online at http://www.epress.am/en/2011/02/23/suzan-mubarak-does-not-represent-egyptian-women-egypts-coalition-of-womens-ngos/.

'The Maastricht Guidelines on Violations of Economic, Social and Cultural Rights' in *Human Rights Quarterly, vol. 20* (Summer 1998) 691-730.

The United States Passport. Past, present future (Department of State Publication 8851, department and foreign service series 153, released July 4, 1976).

'Vote for EU Constitution or risk new Holocaust, says Brussels', *Daily Telegraph*, 9 May 2005.

Acheson, Dean, *Present at the creation. My years in the State Department* (New York: W.W. Norton and Company, 1970).

Althusius, Johannes, *Politics*, in: F.S. Carney, *The politics of Johannes Althusius*. An abridged translation of the Third Edition of Politica Methodice Digesta, atque exemplis sacris et profanes illustrata and including the prefaces to the First and Third editions (London: Eyre & Spottiswoode, 1965).

Anderson, Benedict, *Imagined Communities. Reflections on the Origin and Spread of Nationalism*. Revised Edition (New York: Verso, 1991).

Anderson, Sarah, 'US immigration policy on the table at the WTO', in: *Global Politician*, 12 March 2005. Available online at http://www.globalpolitician.com/21446-immigration.

Ankersmit, Frank R., 'De hedendaagse politieke partij, van representatie van de kiezer naar zelfrepresentatie', in: *Jaarboek DNPP 2000*; M. Gallagher et al., *Representative Government in Modern Europe*, 3rd edition (Boston: McGrall-Hill, 2001).

Ankersmit, Frank, 'Prinses Máxima maakt denkfout', in: *NRC Handelsblad*, 2 October 2007.

Annan, Kofi, *Speech of 26 March 2004, New York*. Available online at http://www.un.org/News/Press/docs/2004/sgsm9223.doc.htm.

Amnesty International, *Report 2006*. Available online at http://www.amnesty.org/en/library/info/POL10/001/2006.

Apter, David, 'Notes for a theory of nondemocratic representation', in: J.R. Pennock and J.W. Chapman (eds.), *Representation. Yearbook of the American Society for Political and Legal Philosophy* (New York: Atherton Press, 1968) 278-317.

Aquinas, Thomas, *Summa Theologiae* (1265).

Arendt, Hannah, *Eichmann in Jerusalem: a report on the banality of evil* (New York: Penguin Books, 1992).

Aristotle, *Politics* (London: Penguin Classics, 1992).

Arnold, Matthew, *Culture and Anarchy* (Oxford: Oxford University Press, 2006).

Aron, Raymond, 'Is multinational citizenship possible?', in: *Social Research. An international quarterly of the social sciences*, Volume 41, no. 4 (Winter 1974) 638-656.

Atkinson, W.H., *A History of Spain and Portugal* (Harmondsworth: Penguin, 1960).

Auduc, A., 'L'héritage des croyants devient patrimoine national', in: *Hommes et Migrations*, vol. 1259, 'Les 100 ans d'une idée neuve, II. Culture(s), religion(s) et politique', Dossier coordonné par Alain Seksig (janvier-février 2006) 70-77.

Baber, H.E., *The multicultural mystique. The liberal case against diversity* (New York: Prometheus Books, 2008).

Bache, I., *Europeanization and multilevel governance. Cohesion policy in the European Union and Britain* (Maryland: Rowman & Littlefield Publishers Inc., 2007).

Bairoch, Paul, 'European Trade Policy, 1815-1914', in: P. Mathias and S. Pollard (eds.), *Cambridge Economic History of Europe*, vol. 8, 'The industrial economies: the development of social and economic policies' (Cambridge University Press: 1989) 103-126, 'Colonial trade policies'.

Baldacchino, G., and Milne, D. (eds.), *The Case for Non-sovereignty: Lessons from Sub-national Island Jurisdictions* (London: Routledge, 2008).

Baldwin, S., 'Jean Bodin and the League', in: *The Catholic Historical Review* Vol. 23, No. 2 (July 1937) 160-184.

Balsdon, J.P.V.D., *Romans and aliens* (London: Duckworth, 1979).

Banton, M., *West African City. A Study of Tribal Life in Freetown* (London: Oxford University Press, 1957)

Barfield, Claude E., *Free trade, sovereignty, democracy. The future of the World Trade Organization* (Washington DC: IAE Press, 2001).

Barrès, Maurice, *Scènes et doctrines du Nationalisme* (Paris: Émile-Paul, 1902).

Barry, Brian, *Culture and Equality. An egalitarian critique of Multiculturalism* (Cambridge, MA: Harvard University Press, 2002).

Barry, Brian, *The liberal theory of justice: a critical examination of the principle doctrines in: A theory of justice by John Rawls* (Oxford: Clarendon Press, 1973).

Barry, Brian, *Theories of justice. A treatise on social justice*, Vol. 1 (London: Harvester-Wheatsheaf, 1989).

Bartsch, Matthias, Brandt, Andrea, Kaiser, Simone, Latsch, Gunther, Meyer, Cordula, and Schmidt, Caroline, 'German Justice Failures' (Translated from the German by Christopher Sultan), in: *Spiegel Online International*, 27 March 2007. Available online at http://www.spiegel.de/international/germany/0,1518,474629-8,00.html.

Baudet, Henri, *Paradise on Earth. Some thoughts on European images of Non-European man*. Translated by Elizabeth Wentholt (Middletown: Wesleyan University Press, 1988).

Baudet, Thierry, 'De achilleshiel van de rechtsstaat', in: *NRC Handelsblad*, 16 December 2011.

Baudet, Thierry, 'De vrijspraak van Geert Wilders is uniek in Europa', in: *Trouw*, 25 June 2011.

Baudet, Thierry, 'Geert Wilders, a Voltaire for our times?', 26 June 2011, available online at http://www.presseurop.eu/en/content/article/743751-geert-wilders-voltaire-our-times.

Baudet, Thierry, 'Tegen de partij-oligarchie', in: Joop Hazenberg, Farid Tabarki and Rens van Tilburg (eds.), *Dappere Nieuwe Wereld. 21 jonge denkers over de toekomst van Nederland* (Amsterdam: Van Gennep, 2011) 117-124.

Beatrix, HRH the Queen of the Netherlands, *Voorbeschouwing*, in: Leonard Ornstein & Lo Breemer (eds.), *Paleis Europa, Grote denkers over Europa* (Amsterdam: De Bezige Bij, 2007).

Becker-Rojczyk, Barbara, 'Der "Koran-fall" - Ein Erlebnisbericht', in: *Streit. Feministische Rechtszeitschrift*, vol. 23, no. 3 (3, 2007) 121-123.

Beever, Antony, 'They raped every German female from eight to 80', in: *The Guardian* (1 May 2002), available online at http://www.guardian.co.uk/books/2002/may/01/news.features11.

Beevor, Antony, *Berlin. The Downfall 1945* (London: Viking Penguin, 2002).

Belien, Paul, 'Why Belgium is an artificial state', in: *The Brussels Journal*, August 27, 2007, available online at http://www.brusselsjournal.com/node/2369.

Belien, Paul, *A throne in Brussels. Britain, the Saxe-Coburgs and the Belgianisation of Europe* (Exeter: Imprint Academic, 2005).

Bendersky, Joseph W., *Carl Schmitt, Theorist for the Reich* (Princeton: Princeton University Press, 1983).

Benz, A., and Zimmer, C., 'The EU's competences: The "vertical" perspective on the multilevel system', in: *Living Reviews in European Governance*, Vol. 3 (2008) available online at: http://www.livingreviews.org/lreg-2008-3.

Berger, Adolf, *Encyclopedic Dictionary of Roman Law. New Series - volume 43, part 2* (Philadelphia: The American Philosophical Society, 1953, reprinted in 1989).

Berlin, Isaiah, 'Joseph de Maistre and the Origins of Fascism', in: Ibidem, *The crooked timber of humanity. Chapters in the history of ideas.* Edited by Henry Hardy (London: John Murray, 1990) 91-174.

Berlin, Isaiah, *Vico and Herder* (London: The Hogarth Press, 1976).

Bayart, Bertille and Robin, Jean-Pierre, 'Pour Noyer, la crise doit conduire à renforcer l'intégration financière de l'Europe', in: *Le Figaro* (2-3 July, 2011) 22.

Bisson, T.N., (ed.), *Medieval representative institutions. Their Origins and Nature* (Illinois: The Dryden Press, 1973).

Black, Jeremy, *A Military Revolution? Military Change and European Society, 1550–1800* (London: Macmillan education, 1991).

Blair, Tony, *Speech of 23 June 2005*, published on http://news.bbc.co.uk/1/hi/uk_politics/4122288.stm.

Bloom, Allan, *The closing of the American mind. How higher education has failed democracy and impoverished the souls of today's students* (New York: Simon & Schuster, 1987).

Blum, Yehuda Z., 'Proposals for UN Security Council Reform', in: *The American Journal of International Law*, Vol. 99, No. 3 (July, 2005) 632-649.

Bodin, Jean, *Six books of the Commonwealth.* Abridged and Translated by M.J. Tooley (Oxford: Basil Blackwell, 1955).

Bodin, Jean, *On Sovereignty. Four chapters from the Six books of the Commonwealth.* Edited and translated by Julian H. Franklin (Cambridge: Cambridge University Press, 1992).

Bolton, John R., 'The risks and weaknesses of the International Criminal Court from America's perspective', in: *Law and Contemporary Problems*, vol. 64, no. 1 (Winter 2001) 167-180. Available online at http://www.law.duke.edu/shell/cite.pl?64+Law+&+Contemp.+Probs.+167+(Winter+2001).

Booker, Christopher, and North, Richard, *The Great Deception. Can the European Union survive?* Second Edition (London and New York: Continuum, 2005).

Bork, Robert H., *The tempting of America. The political seduction of the law* (New York: The Free Press, 1990).

Bosma, Martin, *De schijn-élite van de valse munters. Drees, extreem-rechts, nuttige idioten, Groep Wilders en ik* (Amsterdam: Bert Bakker, 2010).

Bossche, Peter van den, *The Law and Policy of the World Trade Organization* (Cambridge: Cambridge University Press, 2008).

Brague, Rémi, *Europe. La voie Romaine* (Paris: Gallimard, 1992).

Brands, Henry William, *Woodrow Wilson* (New York: Henry Holt and Company, 2003).

Braudel, Fernand, *L'identité de la France. Espace et histoire* (Paris: Arthaus-Flammarion, 1986).

Brennan jr., William J., 'Why have a Bill of Rights?', in: *Oxford Journal of Legal Studies*, vol. 9, no. 4 (1989) 425-440.

Breyer, Stephen, *Making our democracy work. A judge's view* (New York: Alfred A. Knopf, 2010).

Brinkhorst, Laurens Jan, 'National Sovereignty in the EU: an outdated concept', in: M.K. Bulterman, L. Hancher, A. McDonnell, A., and Sevenster, H., (eds.), *Views of European Law from the Mountain. Liber amicorum for Piet Jan Slot* (Alphen aan den Rijn: Kluwer Law, 2009) 327-333.

Brinkhorst, Laurens Jan, *Speech of 27 May 2009 at the European Week in Eindhoven.*

Buckle, Henry Thomas, *History of Civilization in England.* 2nd edition, vol. 1 (New York: D. Appleton and co., 1859).

Budzinski, O., *Mehr-Ebenen-Governance, Leitjurisdiktionskonzepte und globaler Wettbewerb* (April 14, 2009) available online at http://ssrn.com/abstract=1379608.

Burgers, J.H., 'The Road to San Francisco: the revival of the Human Rights Idea in the Twentieth Century', in: *Human Rights Quarterly*, vol. 14 (1992) 447-477.

Burgi, Elisabeth, Cottier, Thomas, and Pauwelyn, Joost (eds.), *Human Rights and International Trade* (Oxford: Oxford University Press, 2005).

Burke, Edmund, 'Speech to the Electors of Bristol', in: Ibidem, *Speeches and Letters on American affairs.* Introduction by very rev. Canon Peter mcKevitt (London: J.M. Dent & Sons LTD, 1908, reprinted in 1961) 68-75.

Burke, Edmund, *Reflections on the Revolution in France. A Critical Edition.* Edited by J.C.D. Clark (Stanford: Stanford University Press, 2001).

Burnham, James, *The Machiavellians* (Chicago: The John Day Company, Inc., 1943).

Bush, George H. W., *Toward a New World Order Speech*, given to a joint session of the United States Congress, Washington DC on 11 September 1990.

Caldwell, Christopher, *Reflections on the Revolution in Europe* (Allen Lane, Penguin Books, London, 2009).

Campbell, Peter R. (ed.), *The Origins of the French Revolution. Problems in Focus* (New York: Palgrave Macmillan, 2006).

Cannadine, David, *Class in Britain* (New Haven: Yale University Press, 1998).

Canovan, Margaret, *Nationhood and political theory* (Massachusetts: Edward Elgar Publishing Limited, 1996).

Caratini, Roger, *Napoléon, une imposture* (Paris: Michel Lafon, 1998).

Cardozo, Benjamin N., *The nature of the judicial process* (New York: Dover publications, 2005).

Cassese, Antonio, 'Flawed International Justice for Sudan', in: *Project Syndicate*, 15 June 2008, available online at http://www.project-syndicate.org/commentary/cassese4/English.

Cassese, Antonio, *International Law* (Oxford: University Press, 2001).

Charnovitz, Steve, 'The moral exception in trade policy', in: *Virginia Journal of International Law*, vol. 38 (Summer 1989) 686.

Chateaubriand, François-René de, *Mémoires d'outre-tombe* (1809-1841) (Paris: Classiques Garnier Multimédia, 1998).

Chateaubriand, François-René de, *Génie du Christianisme. Ou beautés de la Religion Chrétienne* (1802) (Paris: Éditions Gallimard, 1978).

Chemerinsky, Erwin, *The conservative assault on the constitution* (New York: Simon & Schuster, 2010).

Church, W.F., *Constitutional thought in sixteenth-century France. A study in the evolution of ideas* (New York: Octagon Books, 1969).

Churchill, Winston, *Speech of 19 September 1949*, University of Zurich, available online at http://www.peshawar.ch/varia/winston.htm.

Cliteur, Paul, 'A Secular Reading of Tocqueville', in: Raf Geenens and Annelien de Dijn (eds.), *Reading Tocqueville: From Oracle to Actor* (Houndmills, New York: Palgrave, MacMillan, 2007) 112-132.

Cliteur, Paul, 'Afschaffing van de doodstraf als nationale folklore', in: ibidem, *Moderne Papoea's. Dilemma's van een multiculturele samenleving* (Amsterdam: De Arbeiderspers, 2002) 106-136.

Cliteur, Paul, 'Ambtenaar en Politiek. Over de anarchie in ons openbaar bestuur', in: *Tegen de Decadentie, de democratische rechtstaat in verval* (Amsterdam: De Arbeiderspers, 2004) 143-160.

Cliteur, Paul, 'De onafhankelijkheid van de rechterlijke macht: acht vormen', in: J.P. Loof (ed.), *Onafhankelijkheid en onpartijdigheid. De randvoorwaarden voor het bestuur en beheer van de rechterlijke macht* (Leiden: Stichting NJCM-boekerij 36, 1999) 9-31.

Cliteur, Paul, *Constitutionele toetsing*. Met commentaren van R.A.V. van Haersolte, J.M. Polak en T. Zwart ('s Gravenhage: Geschrift 74 van de Prof. mr. B.M. Teldersstichting, 1991).

Cliteur, Paul, *Moreel Esperanto. Naar een autonome ethiek* (Amsterdam: De Arbeiderspers, 2007).

Cliteur, Paul, *Rechtsfilosofie. Een thematische inleiding* (Amsterdam: Ars aequi libri, 2001).

Cliteur, Paul, *Tegen de Decadentie. De democratische rechtstaat in verval* (Amsterdam: De Arbeiderspers, 2004).

Cliteur, Paul, *The Secular Outlook. In Defense of Moral and Political Secularism* (London: Wiley Blackwell, 2010).

Conot, R.E., *Justice at Nuremberg* (New York: Harper & Row Publishers, 1983).

Cooper, Robert, 'Oorlog en vrede: de geboorte van de Europese identiteit', in: Leonard Ornstein & Lo Breemer (eds.), *Paleis Europa. Grote denkers over Europa* (Amsterdam: De Bezige Bij, 2007) 55-76.

Cooper, Robert, *The breaking of nations. Order and chaos in the twenty-first century* (London: Atlantic Books, 2004).

Coskun, Deniz, 'Constitutioneel patriottisme voor Europa. Wat Ernst Cassirer bepleitte in Weimar', in: Ernst John Kaars Sijpesteijn (ed.), *Het Volk en Europa* (Amsterdam: Vereniging Democratisch Europa, 2004) 83-92.

Coudenhove-Kalergi, Richard Nicolaus, *Paneuropa*, (Wien-Leipzig: Paneuropa Verlag, 1926)

Crawford, James, *The Creation of States in International Law*. Second Edition (Clarendon Press, Oxford, 2006).

Crocker, L.G., *Rousseau's social contract. An interpretive essay* (Cleveland: the press of case western reserve university, 1968).

Dale, Reginald, 'Thinking ahead: Old lines appear on Europe's map', in: *International Herald Tribune*, 17 January 1995.

Dalrymple, Theodore, 'Samuel Johnson (1709-1784)', in: Thierry Baudet and Michiel Visser (eds.), *Revolutionair Verval. En de conservatieve vooruitgang in de 18de en 19de eeuw* (Amsterdam: Bert Bakker, 2011).

Dalrymple, Theodore, 'The demoralization of abortion', in: Claire Fox (ed.), *Abortion: whose right?* (London: Hodder & Stoughton, 2002).

Dalrymple, Theodore, *Litter: How other people's rubbish shapes our lives* (London: Gibson Square Books).

Daniels, N. (ed.), *Reading Rawls: critical studies on Rawls' A theory of justice* (Oxford, 1975).

Daum, Werner, 'Universalism and the West. An agenda for understanding', in: *Harvard International Review*, vol 23 (2) (Summer 2001) 19-23.

Davies, Norman, *Europe. A History* (Oxford: University Press, 1996).

Daniel Defoe, *Robinson Crusoe. His life and strange surprising adventures* (1791) (London: The Nonesuch Press, 1968).

Delsol, Chantal, *Unjust Justice. Against the tyrany of international law* (Wilmington, Delaware: ISI Books, 2008).

Dervis, Kemal, 'Het ene Europa is het andere niet', in: Leonard Ornstein & Lo Breemer (eds.), *Paleis Europa. Grote denkers over Europa* (Amsterdam: De Bezige Bij, 2007).

Dicey, Albert Venn, *Introduction to the study of the law of the constitution* (London: Macmillan and Co., 1939).

Doern, G.B., and Johnson, R. (eds), *Rules, Rules, Rules, Rules: Multi-Level Regulatory Governance* (Toronto: University of Toronto Press, 2006).

Doorman, Maarten, *De Romantische orde* (Amsterdam: Bert Bakker, 2004).

Douzinas, Costas, *The end of Human Rights* (Portland: Hart Publishing, 2000).

Drieu la Rochelle, Pierre, *Genève ou Moscou* (Paris: Gallimard, 1928).

Duby, George, *The Three Orders: Feudal Society Imagined*, translated by Arthur Goldhammer (Chicago: University of Chicago Press, 1980).

Dunan, Marcel, 'La veritable place de Napoléon dans l'histoire de l'Europe', in: André Puttemans (ed.), *Napoléon et l'Europe* (Paris: Éditions Brepolis, 1965) 139-152.

Dupuy, Pierre-Marie, *Droit International Public* (Paris: Editions Dalloz-Sirey, 1992).

Durchhardt, 'Münster/Osnabrück as a short-lived peace system', in: Goudoever (ed.), *Great Peace Congresses in History 1648-1990*, Utrechtse Historische Cahiers: year 14, issue 2 (1993) 16.

Duverger, Maurice, *Les Partis Politiques* (Paris 1951).

Dworkin, Ronald, *Freedom's Law. The moral reading of the American Constitution* (Cambridge, MA: Harvard University Press, 1996).

Dworkin, Ronald, *Justice for Hedgehogs* (Cambridge, MA: Harvard University Press, 2011).

Dzehtsiarou, K., 'Consensus from within the Palace Walls: UCD Working Papers in Law, Criminology & Socio-Legal Studies Research Paper No. 40/2010' (September 17, 2010) available online at http://papers.ssrn.com/sol3/papers.cfm?abstract_id=1678424.

Eastman, Max, 'The Manifesto of the Communist Party', in: Max Eastman (ed.), *Captial. The Communist Manifesto and other Writings* (New York: The modern library, 1932).

Eliot, T.S., 'Choruses from "the Rock"' (1934), in: *The complete poems and plays of T.S. Eliot* (London: Book Club Associates, 1977).

Ellian, Afshin, *Een onderzoek naar de Waarheids- en Verzoeningscommissie van Zuid-Afrika* (Nijmegen: Wolf Legal, 2003).

Elton, G.R., *England under the Tudors*. Third Edition (London: Routledge, 1991).

Evans, Malcolm D. (ed.), *International Law* (Oxford: University Press, 2003).

Evron, B., *Jewish state or Israeli Nation?* (Bloomington and Indianapolis: Indiana University Press, 1995).

Farrow, R., 'Beware of the U.N. Human Rights Council; Obama should be careful about lending legitimacy to bad actors', in: *The Wall Street Journal*, 5 April 2009.

Fennema, Meindert, *De Moderne Democratie. Geschiedenis van een politieke theorie* (Amsterdam: Het Spinhuis, 2001).

Fichte, Johann Gottlob, *Reden an die Deutsche Nation* (Hamburg: Felix Meiner Verlag, 1978).

Fichte, Johann Gottlob, *Addresses to the German nation*. Edited with an introduction and notes by Gregory Moore (Cambridge: Cambridge University Press, 2008).

Fichtner, Paula S., *Protestantism and Primogeniture in Early Modern Germany* (New Haven: Yale University Press, 1989).

Finer, Samuel E., *The History of Government from the earliest times, Volume I. Ancient Monarchies and Empires* (Oxford: Oxford University Press, 1997).

Finer, Samuel E., *The History of Government from the earliest times, Volume II. The Intermediate Ages* (Oxford: Oxford University Press, 1997).

Finer, Samuel E., *The History of Government from the earliest times, Volume III. Empires, Monarchies, and the Modern State* (Oxford: Oxford University Press, 1997).

Finkielkraut, Alain, *Remembering in Vain. The Klaus Barbie trial and crimes against humanity*. With an introduction by Alice Y. Kaplan (New York: Columbia University Press, 1989).

Finkielkraut, Alain, *The defeat of the mind*. Translated by Judith Friedlander (New York: Columbia University Press, 1995).

Fish, Stanley, *There's No Such Thing As Free Speech. And It's a Good Thing, Too* (Oxford: Oxford University Press, 1994).

Fontaine, Pascal, *Jean Monnet. A grand design for Europe* (Luxembourg: Office for Official publications of the European Communities, 1988).

Fourest, Caroline, *La dernière utopie: menaces sur l'universalisme* (Paris: Editions Grasset, 2009).

Franck, T.M., 'Who Killed Article 2(4)? Or: Changing Norms Governing the Use of Force by States', in: *American Journal for International Law*, Vol. 64, No. 5 (Oct., 1970) 809-837

Franklin, J.H., 'Introduction, An outline of Bodin's career', in: Bodin, *On Sovereignty* (Cambridge: Cambridge University Press, 1992).

Friedrich, J., *Der Brand. Deutschland im Bombenkrieg 1940-1945* (München: Propyläen Verlag, 2002).

Fumaroli, Marc, *Quand l'Europe parlait Français* (Paris: Éditions de Fallois, 2011).

Fustel de Coulanges, Nouma Denis, 'L'Alsace, est-elle allemande ou français?', in: ibidem, *Questions Historiques* (Paris: Librairie Hachette 1893) 505-512.

Garner, Bryan A., (ed.), *Black's Law Dictionary*, 8th edition (Los Angeles: West Group, 2004).

Garton Ash, Timothy, *In Europe's name. Germany and the divided continent* (London: Jonathan Cape, 1997).

Gellner, Ernest, *Nations and Nationalism* (Oxford: Basil Blackwell, 1983).

Gilbert, Martin, *The Somme. Heroism and Horror in the First World War* (New York: Henry Holt and Company, 2006).

Gillingham, John, and Griffiths, Ralph A., *Medieval Britain. A very short introduction*, (Oxford: Oxford University Press, 2000).

Glendon, Mary Ann, *Rights Talk. The impoverishment of political discourse* (New York: The Free Press, 1991).

Goebbels, Joseph, '"Das Europa der Zukunft": speech to Czech intellectual workers and journalists, 11 September, 1940', reprinted in Walter Lipgens (ed.), *Documents on the History of European Integration* (Berlin and New York: De Gruyter, 1985).

Gouëset, Catherine, '8 ans d'idylle entre l'Elysée et les catholiques', in: *l'Express*, 8 October, 2010. Available online at http://www.lexpress.fr/actualite/politique/8-ans-d-idylle-entre-l-elysee-et-les-catholiques_925948.html.

Grant, N., *Oxford Children's History of the World* (Oxford: Oxford University Press, 2000)

Grauwe, Paul de, 'The euro will collapse without political union', *De Morgen*, 18 March 2006, http://www.free-europe.org/english/2006/07/the-euro-will-collapse-without-political-union-forecasts-top-adviser-to-commission-president-barroso/.

Grewe, W.G., *Epochen der Völkerrechtsgeschichte* (Baden-Baden: Nomos Verlagsgesellschaft, 1984).

Grotius, Hugo, *The rights of war and peace, including the law of nature and of nations* (1625). Translated by David J. Hill (New York: M. Walter Dunne, 1901).

Guizot, François, 'European History as the history of representative institutions', in: T.N. Bisson (ed.), *Medieval representative institutions. Their Origins and Nature* (Illinois: The Dryden Press, 1973) 9-12.

Haas, Ernst B., *Beyond the Nation state: Functionalism and International Organization* (Stanford: Stanford University Press, (1964).

Haas, Ernst B., *The Uniting of Europe. Political, Social and Economic forces 1950-1957* (Stanford: Stanford University Press, 1958).

Haas, Ernst B., *The Uniting of Europe. Political, Social and Economic forces 1950-1957* (Stanford: Stanford University Press, 1968).

Hafen, Thomas, *Staat, Gesellschaft und Bürger im Denken von Emmanuel Joseph Sieyes* (Wien: Haupt, 1994).

Hall, Stuart, 'The state in question', in: McLennan, Gregor, Held, David, and Hall, Stuart (eds.), *The idea of the modern state* (Philadelphia: Open University Press 1984) .

Hamilton, Alexander, Madison, James, and Jay, John, *The Federalist Papers. With an introduction and commentary by Garry Wills* (New York: Bantam Classics, 1982).

Hampson, Norman, *Will and Circumstance. Montesquieu, Rousseau and the French Revolution* (London: Duckworth, 1983).

Hampton, J., 'Democracy and the rule of law', in: Ian Shapiro (ed.), *The Rule of Law: Nomos XXXVI. Yearbook of the American society for Political and Legal Philosophy* (New York: New York University Press, 1994) 13-44.

Harryvan, A.G., and Harst, J. van der, (eds.), *Documents on European Union* (London: Macmillan Press ltd., 1997).

Harvey C. Mansfield jr., 'On the impersonality of the modern state: a comment on Machiavelli's use of Stato', in: *The American Political Science Review*, Vol. 77, No. 4. (Dec., 1983) 849-857.

Hegel, Georg Wilhelm Friedrich, *Grundlinien der Philosophie des Rechts* (1821) (Frankfurt am Main: Suhrkamp Verlag, 1974).

Heinz Duchhardt, 'Münster/Osnabrück as a short-lived peace system', in: A.P. van Goudoever (ed.), *Great Peace Congresses in History 1648-1990*, Utrechtse Historische Cahiers: issue 2, year 14 (1993).

Held, David, *Political theory and the modern state. Essays on state, power and democracy* (Cambridge: Polity Press, 1989).

Hemingway, Ernest, *For whom the bell tolls* (London: Vintage Books, 2005).

Henderson, Alasdair, 'Al-Skeini v. United Kingdom (7 july 2011)', in: *Human Rights and Public Law Update* (14 July 2011), available online at http://www.1cor.com/1315/?form_1155.replyids=1402.

Henig, Stanley, *The Uniting of Europe. From discord to concord* (London: Routledge, 1997).

Henkin, L., *International Law: Politics and values* (Dordrecht: Martinus Nijhoff Publishers, 1995).

Herder, Johann Gottfried, *Auch eine Philosophie der Geschichte zur Bildung der Menschheit*. Nachwort von H.G. Gadamer (Frankfurt am Main: Suhrkamp Verlag, 1967).

Herder, Johann Gottfried, 'Another philosophy of history', in: Ioannis D. Evrigenis and Daniel Pellerin (eds.), *Another Philosophy of History and Selected Political Writings* (Indianapolis: Hackett Publishing, 2004).

Herder, Johann Gottfried von, 'This too a Philosophy of History for the Formation of Humanity', in: Ibidem, *Philosophical Writings*. Translated and edited by Michael N. Forster (Cambridge: Cambridge University Press, 2002).

Herzl, Theodor, *Der Judenstaat* (Osnabrück: Otto Zeller 1968).

Hewel, Walter, 'Record of conversation between Hitler and the Finnish foreign minister, R. Witting, 28 November 1941', in: Walter Lipgens (ed.), *Documents on the History of European Integration* (Berlin and New York: De Gruyter, 1985).

Hobbes, Thomas, *Leviathan* (1651). Edited with an introduction by C.B. Macpherson (London: Penguin Books, 1985).

Hobbes, Thomas, *The Elements of Law. Natural and Politic* (1640) Edited with a preface and cirtical notes by Ferdinand Tönnies (London: Frank Cass & Co, 1969).

Hobsbawm, Eric, *Nations and nationalism since 1780. Programme, myth, reality* (Cambridge: Cambridge University Press, 1990).

Hoek, A. van, et al. (eds.), *Multilevel governance in enforcement and adjudication* (Antwerpen: Intersentia, 2006).

Hoffmann, Leonard, 'Foreword', in: Michael Pinto-Duschinsky, *Bringing Rights Back Home. Making human rights compatible with parliamentary democracy in the UK* (London: Policy Exchange, 2011).

Hoffmann, Leonard, *The Universality of Human Rights* (Judicial Studies Board Annual Lecture, 19 March 2009), available online at www.shrlg.org.uk/wp-content/plugins/download.../download.php?id=15.

Holland, B., 'Sovereignty as *Dominium*? Reconstructing the Constructivist Roman Law Thesis', in: *International Studies Quarterly*, vol. 54, issue 2 (June 2010) 449–480.

Holmes, jr., Oliver Wendell, 'The path of the law', in: *Harvard Law Review* vol. 10, no. 8 (1897) 457.

Hondagneu-Sotelo, Pierrette, *God's heart has no borders. How religious activists are working for immigrant rights* (Berkeley: University of California Press, 2008).

Hooghe, L., and Marks, G., 'Unraveling the central state, but how? Types of Multi-Level Governance', in: *The American Political Science Review*, Vol. 97, No. 2 (May, 2003) 233-243.

Howden, Daniel, 'International justice and Congo "warlord" on trial', in: *the Independent* (23 November 2010): 'Mr. Bemba's supporters in the DRC have accused the ICC of allowing itself to be used to remove the political rivals of the President Joseph Kabila.' Available online at http://www.independent.co.uk/news/world/europe/international-justice-and-congo-warlord-on-trial-2141135.html.

Howse, Robert, 'The WTO and Protection of Workers' Rights', in: *Journal of Small and Emerging Business Law*, vol. 3 (1999) 131-172.

Hueglin, Thomas O., 'From Constitutional to Treaty Federalism: a comparative perspective', in: *Publius* (Fall 2000).

Hueglin, Thomas O., 'State and Church in the Political Thought of Althusius', available online at http://polis.unipmn.it/seminari/calvino2009/files/Hueglin7_05_09.pdf.

Huizer, M., *Hoofd en hoogste overheid. De soevereiniteit in Nederland sinds 1543* (Amsterdam: J.M. Meulenhoff, 1967).

Huntington, Samuel, *Who Are We: The Challenges to America's National Identity* (New York: Simon & Schuster, 2004).

Jami, Eshan, *Het recht om ex moslim te zijn* (Amsterdam: Uitgeverij Ten Have, 2007).

Jardine, Lisa, *The Awful end of Prince William the Silent. The first Assassination of a head of state with a Handgun* (Londen: HarperCollins, 2005).

Jasay, A. de, *The State* (Oxford: Basil Blackwell, 1985).

Jaspers, Karl, *Freiheit und Wiedervereinigung* (München, Piper, 1969).

Jespersen, Karin, and Pittelkow, Ralph, *Islamisten en Naivisten*. Met een introductie van Afshin Ellian (Amsterdam: Uitgeverij Nieuw Amsterdam, 2008).

Johnson, Samuel, *The history of Rasselas. Prince of Abissinia* (1759) (London: Oxford University Press, 1971).

Joly, Maurice, *Dialogue aux enfers entre Machiavel et Montesquieu ou la politique de Machiavel au XIXe siècle* (Bruxelles, A. Mertens, 1865).

Jouvenel, Bertrand de, *Sovereignty, an enquiry into the political good* (Cambridge: Cambridge University Press, 1957).

Jouvenel, Bertrand de, *Sovereignty. An inquiry into the political good* (Indianapolis: Liberty Fund, 1997).

Jouvenel, Bertrand de, *Vers les États Unis de l'Europe* (1930).

Judt, Tony, *Postwar. A history of Europe since 1945* (London: Pimlico, Random House, 2007).

Kagan, Robert, *Of Paradise and Power. America and Europe in the New World Order* (New York: Alfred A. Knopf, 2003).

Kant, Immanuel, *Zum ewigen Frieden. Ein philosophischer Entwurf* (Stuttgart: Philipp Reclam, 2005).

Kant, *The metaphysics of morals*. Translated and edited by Mary Gregor (Cambridge: Cambridge University Press, 1996).

Kant, Immanuel, 'Perpetual Peace', in: *Political Writings*. Edited with an introduction and notes by Hans Reiss. Second, enlarged edition (Cambridge: Cambridge University Press, 1991).

Kelsen, Hans, 'Sovereignty and International Law', in: *The Georgetown Law Journal*, vol. 48, no. 4 (1960) 627-640.

Kennedy, John F., *Profiles in Courage* (New York: Harper & Row, 1963).

Kimball, Roger, *Experiments against reality. The fate of culture in the postmodern age* (Chicago: Ivan R. Dee, 2000).

Kinneging, Andreas, 'Loyalty in the modern world', in: *Modern Age* vol. 46 (2004) 66-73.

Kinneging, Andreas, *Aristocracy, Antiquity, and History, Classicism in political thought* (New Brunswick and London: Transaction Publishers, 1997).

Kinneging, Andreas, 'United we stand, divided we fall, a case for the United States of Europe', in: ibidem (ed.), *Rethinking Europe's Constitution* (Nijmegen: Wolf Legal Publishers, 2007) 37-61.

Kissinger, Henry, 'The Pitfalls of Universal Jurisdiction', in: *Foreign Affairs*, vol. 80, no. 4 (July/August 2001) 95.

Klemperer, Viktor, *The Language of the Third Reich* (London: Continuum, 2006).

Klerk, Y.S. en Poelgeest, L. van, 'Ratificatie a contre Coeur: de reserve van de Nederlandse regering jegens het Europees Verdrag voor de Rechten van de Mens en het individueel klachtrecht', in: *RM Themis* 5 (1991) 220-246.

Knegt, Daniel, 'Ni droite, ni gauche? Debatten over het Franse fascisme', in: *Tijdschrift voor Geschiedenis*, 124.3 (2011) 206-219.

Knoops, Geert-Jan, *Blufpoker. De duistere wereld van het internationaal recht* (Amsterdam: Uitgeverij Balans, 2011).

Kolakowski, Leszek, *Main Currents of Marxism* (London: Norton Publishers, 2005).

Kooijmans, Peter H., *Internationaal Publiekrecht* (Deventer: Kluwer, 2000).

Koschaker, Paul, *Europa en het Romeinse Recht*. Nederlandse editie verzorgd door Theo Veen (Devener: W.E.J. Tjeenk Willink, 2000).

Koskenniemi, Martti, *From Apology to Utopia. The structure of international legal argument* (Cambridge: Cambridge University Press 2005).

Kossmann, Ernst, 'Soevereiniteit in de Zeven Verenigde Provinciën', in: *Theoretische Geschiedenis*, vol. 18, issue 4 (dec. 1991) 413-422.

Kreijen, Gerard, *State Failure, Sovereignty, and Effectiveness. Legal Lessons from the Decolonization of Sub-Saharan Africa* (Leiden, Martinus Nijhoff Publishers, 2004).

Krugman, Paul, *Pop Internationalism* (Cambridge, MA: MIT Press, 1997).

Kwak (ed.), Arie-Jan, *Holy Writ: Interpretation in Law and Religion* (Surray (GB): Ashgate, 2009).

Kwak, Arie-Jan, 'Het (on)persoonlijke gezicht van het recht; de rechter tussen objectiviteit en gezag', in: *Trema* (Special 2, 2008) 428-431.

Kymlicka, Will, *Contemporary Political Philosophy: An introduction* (Oxford: Oxford University Press, 2002).

Kymlicka, Will, *Liberalism, Community and Culture* (Oxford: Oxford University Press 1991).

Kymlicka, Will, *Multicultural Citizenship, A liberal theory of minority rights* (Oxford: Oxford University Press, 1996).

Landler, Mark, 'Germany cites Koran in rejecting divorce, *New York Times* (22 March 2007).

Lang, Tim, and Hines, Colin, *The New Protectionism: Protecting the Future against Free Trade* (London: Earthscan Publications, 1993).

Lapitskaya, Julia, 'ECHR, Russia, and Chechnya: two is not company and three is definitely a crowd', in: *International Law and Politics* (NYU, Vol. 43, 2011) 479-547.

Larsen, J.A.O., *Representative government in Greek and Roman history, Sather classical lectures, vol. 28* (Berkeley: University of California Press, 1955).

Las Cases, Emmanuel comte de, *Le Mémorial de Sainte-Hélène. Première edition intégrale et critique établie par Marcel Dunan* (Paris: Flammarion, 1951).

Lasch, Christopher, *The Revolt of the Elites and the Betrayal of Democracy* (New York: W.W. Norton and Company, 1995).

Laughland, John, *A History of political trials. From Charles I to Saddam Hussein* (Oxford: Peter Lang, 2008).

Laughland, John, *The Tainted Source. The undemocratic origins of the European Union* (Boston: Little Brown & Company, 1997).

Laughland, John, *The Tainted Source. The undemocratic origins of the European Union* (London: Warner Books, 1998).

Laughland, John, *Travesty. The trial of Slobodan Milosevic and the corruption of international justice* (London: Pluto press, 2007).

Lawson, R.A., and Schermers, H.G., *Leading cases of the European Court of Human Rights* (Leiden: Ars Aequi 1995).

Lawson, Rick, 'Werd Islamcritici de mond gesnoerd? Helemaal niet', in: *Trouw* (June 28th, 2011).

Lawson, Rick, 'Wild, wilder, wildst. Over de ruimte die het EVRM laat voor de vervolging van kwetsende politici', in: *NJCM-Bulletin*, vol. 33, no. 4 (2008).

Le Goff, Jacques, *The Birth of Europe*. Translated by Janet Lloyd (Oxford: Blackwell Publishing, 2005).

Leibholz, Gerhard, *Strukturprobleme der Modernen Demokratie* (Karlsruhe: Verlag C.F. Müller, 1958).

Lerner, N., *The U.N. Convention on the Elimination of all Forms of Racial Discrimination* (Alphen aan den Rijn: Sijthoff en Noordhoff 1970).

Lesaffer, 'The Westphalia Peace Treaties and the Development of the Tradition of Great European Peace Settlements prior to 1648', in: *Grotiana*, New Series Vol. 18 (1997) 71-96.

Lesaffer, Randall, 'Peace treaties from Lodi to Westphalia', in: Randall Lesaffer (ed.), *Peace treaties and international law in European History, From the Late Middle ages to World War One* (Cambridge: Cambridge University Press, 2004).

Lief, Michael S., Caldwell, H. Mitchell, and Bycel, Benjamin, *Ladies and Gentlemen of the Jury: Greatest arguments in Modern Law* (New York: Simon & Schuster, 1998).

Lijphart, Arend, *Democracy in the Twenty-First Century: can we be optimistic?*, (Wassenaar: NIAS, 2000).

Lijphart, Arend, *Electoral Systems and Party Systems*, (Oxford: Oxford University Press, 1994).

Lijphart, Arend, *The politics of accommodation. Pluralism and democracy in the Netherlands* (Berkeley and Los Angeles: University of California Press, 1968).

Linden, Harry van der, *Kantian ethics and Socialism* (Indianapolis: Hackett Publishing Company, 1988).

Lloyd, Martin, *The Passport, the history of man's most traveled document* (Sutton Publishing, Gloucestershire 2005).

Locke, John, *The second treatise of Government* (1690) (Mineola, NY: Dover Publications, 2002).

Lokin, J.H.A. and Zwalve, W.J., *Hoofdstukken uit de Europese Codificatiegeschiedenis. Derde, geheel herziene druk* (Den Haag: Boom Juridische Uitgevers, 2006).

London, Jacqueline, 'The reform of the United Nations Security Council: What role for the European Union?', *Conference Working Paper: United Nations and Security Council Reform: Proposals for the future*. (Madrid, INCIPE Assembly Hall, 29th June, 2007) available online at http://www.incipe.org/UNSCreform.html.

Lord, R.H., 'The Parliaments of the Middle Ages and the Early Modern Period', in: *The Catholic Historical Review*, Vol. 16, No. 2 (July, 1930), 125-144.

Lovejoy, Arthur O., *The great chain of being. A study of the history of an Idea* (New York: Harper & Brothers, 1936).

Luchaire, A., *Histoire des institutions monarchiques de la France sous les premiers Capétiens (987-1180)* (Paris: Alphonse Picard, 1891).

Lyttelton, Adrian, 'The national question in Italy', in: Teich and Porter (eds.), *The national question in Europe in historical context* (Cambridge: Cambridge University Press, 1993) 63-105.

MacIntyre, Alasdair, 'Is Patriotism a Virtue?', in: Beiner, R. (ed.), *Theorizing Citizenship* (New York: State University of New York Press, 1995) 209-228.

Mackenzie, W.J.M., and Chapman, B, 'Federalism and Regionalism. A Note on the Italian Constitution of 1948', in: *The Modern Law Review*, Vol. 14, No. 2 (Apr., 1951) 182-194.

Mackenzie, Ruth, Maleson, Kate, Martin, Penny, and Sands, Philippe, *Selecting International Judges. Principle, Process and Politics* (Oxford: Oxford University Press, 2010).

Madison, James, 'Examination of the British Doctrine which subjects to capture a neutral trade not open in time of peace', in: Gaillard Hunt (ed.), *The writings of James Madison, vol. 2* (The Rnickerboch Press, 1901).

Maistre, Joseph de, 'Considérations sur la France', in: *Oeuvres complètes* (Lyon: Vitte, 1884, reprinted: Genève, Slatkine, 1979).

Maitland, John, *The constitutional history of England* (Cambridge: Cambridge University Press, 1961).

Mandeville, Bernard de, *The fable of the bees, or, private vices, public benefits* (1714) Newly edited, with an introduction by Irwin Primer (New York: Capricorn Books, 1962).

Mann, Heinrich, *Die Jugend des Königs Henri Quatre* (Reinbek bei Hamburg: Rowohlt Taschenbuch, 1964).

Marshall, J.M., 'Death in Venice: Europe's Death-penalty Elitism, in: *The New Republic* (July 31, 2000).

Marwell, Jeremy C., 'Trade and Morality: the WTO Public Morals Exception after *Gambling*', in: *New York University law review*, vol. 81 (May 2006) 802-842.

Marx, Karl, and Engels, Friedrich, *Manifesto of the Communist Party* (1848). Authorised English translation of 1888, edited and annotated by Frederick Engels (London: Lawrence and Wishart, 1888).

Mattei, Roberto de, *Turkey in Europe: benefit or catastrophe?* Translated by John Laughland (Herefordshire: Gracewing, 2009).

Maurras, Charles, *Mes idées politiques* (Paris: Arthème Fayard, 1937).

Maxima, HRH the Princess of the Netherlands, *Speech of 24 september 2007*, Available online at http://archief.koninklijkhuis.nl/Actueel/Toespraken/Toesprakenarchief/2007/Toespraak_van_Prinses_Maxima_24_september_2007.

Mayer, F.C., 'Multilevel Constitutional Jurisdiction', in: A. von Bogdandy and J. Bast (eds.), *Principles of European Constitutional Law* (Oxford and München: Hart Publishing and Verlag C.H. Beck, 2010).

McCready, W.D., 'Papal Plenitudo Potestatis and the Source of Temporal Authority in Late Medieval Papal Hierocratic Theory', in: *Speculum*, Vol. 48, No. 4 (Oct., 1973) 654-674.

McFarlane, Alan, *The Savage Wars of Peace: England, Japan and the Malthusian Trap* (Oxford: Blackwell Publishers, 1997).

McLennan, Gregor, Held, David, and Hall, Stuart (eds.), *The idea of the modern state* (Philadelphia: Open University Press, 1984).

Medick, Veit, and Reimann, Anna, 'Justiz-Skandal. Deutsche Richterin rechtfertigt eheliche Gewalt mit Koran', in: *Der Spiegel*, 20 March 2007. Available online at http://www.spiegel.de/politik/deutschland/0,1518,472849,00.html.

Mendes de Leon, Pablo, *Cabotage in International Air Transport Regulation* (PhD thesis Leiden: Leiden University Press, 1992).

Mergele, Karl, 'European themes', probably autumn 1941, reprinted in Lipgens, Walter (ed.), *Documents on the History of European Integration* (Berlin and New York: De Gruyter, 1985).

Middelaar, Luuk van, *De passage naar Europa* (Amsterdam: Amsterdam University Press, 2009).

Mill, John Stuart, *Considerations on Representative Government* (New York: Prometheus Books, 1991).

Minahan, James B., *One Europe, many nations. A historical dictionary of European national groups* (Greenwood Press, London, 2000).

Minogue, Kenneth R., *Nationalism* (Maryland: Penguin Books, 1968).

Mitterrand, Francois, *Speech of 17 January 1995*, at the European Parliament, available online at http://www.lours.org/default.asp?pid=375.

Molier, Gelijn, 'De soevereine staat en het international recht', in: Gelijn Molier and Timo Slootweg (eds.), *Soevereiniteit en Recht, rechtsfilosofische beschouwingen* (Den Haag: Boom Juridische Uitgevers, 2009).

Mommsen, 'Lettere al sig. Clemente Maraini', in: *Il Diritto*, September 17th, 1870. Available online at http://www.mommsenlettere.org/Letter/Details/323.

Mommsen, Christian Matthias Theodor, *Römische Geschichte* (1854-1856).

Mommsen, Theodor, 'Lettere al sig.Clemente Maraini', in: *Il Diritto*, September 17th, 1870. Available online at http://www.mommsenlettere.org/Letter/Details/323.

Mommsen, Wolfgang J., 'Varieties of Nation State in Modern History', in: Michael Mann, *The rise and decline of the Nation State* (Oxford: Basil Blackwell, 1990).

Monnet, Jean, *Mémoires* (Paris: Fayard, 1976).

Montesquieu, Charles-Louis de Secondat, Baron de la Brède et de, *De l'esprit des lois* (1748) (Paris: Éditions Garnier Frères, 1961).

Moorman, Yasmin, 'Integration of ILO Core Rights Labor Standards into the WTO', in: *Columbia Journal of Transnational Law*, vol. 39 (2001) 555.

Mora, F.O., and Cooney, J.W., *Paraguay and the United States: Distant Allies. The United States and the Americas* (Athens: University of Georgia Press, 2007).

Moravchik, A., 'The new abolitionism: why does the U.S. practice the death penalty while Europe does not?', in: *European Studies* (September 2001)' See also: J.M. Marshall, 'Death in Venice: Europe's Death-penalty Elitism', in: *The New Republic* (July 31, 2000).

Moreno-Ocampo, Luis, statement made on 9 February, 2006. http://www2.icc-cpi.int/NR/rdonlyres/F596D08D-D810-43A2-99BB-B899B9C5BCD2/277422/OTP_letter_to_senders_re_Iraq_9_February_2006.pdf.

Morgan, Glyn, *The idea of a European Superstate. Public Justification and European Integration* (Princeton: Princeton University Press, 2005).

Münch, R., *European Governmentality. The Liberal Drift of Multilevel Governance* (London: Routledge, 2010).

Murray, Douglas, 'To what extent is sharia already operating in Britain?', in: *The Times*, December 30th, 2009.

Murray, Douglas, and Verwey, Johan Pieter, *Victims of Intimidation. Freedom of Speech within Europe's Muslim Communities* (London: Center for Social Cohesion, 2008).

Murray, Douglas, *Neoconservatism: why we need it* (London: Social Affairs Unit, 2005).

Mussolini, Benito, 'Discorso pre lo stato corporativo', in: Eduardo and Duilio Susmel (eds.), *Opera omnia*, XXVI: *Dal Patto a Quattro all'inaugurazione della Provincia di Littoria* (Florence: La Fenice, 1958).

Nadeau, Jean-Benoît, and Barlow, Julie, *The Story of the French* (London: Anova Books, 2006).

Nader, Ralph, et al., *The Case against "Free Trade": GATT, NAFTA, and the Globalization of Corporate Power* (Berkeley: North Atlantic Books, 1993).

Neillands, Robin, *The Hundred Years War, revised edition* (London and New York: Routledge, 1990).

Nelson, Craig, *Thomas Paine. Enlightenment, Revolution, and the Birth of Modern Nations* (New York: Viking, 2006).

Nicolaidis, K., and Howse, R., (eds.), *The Federal Vision, Legitimacy and levels of governance in the United States and the European Union,* (Oxford: Oxford University Press, 2001).

Niederhausen, E., 'The national question in Hungary', in: Teich and Porter (eds.), *The national question in Europe in historical context* (Cambridge: Cambridge University Press, 1998) 248-269.

Nisbet, Robert, *Prejudices: A philosophical dictionary* (Cambridge, MA: Harvard University Press).

Nisbet, Robert, *The quest for community. A study in the ethics of order and freedom* (Oxford: Oxford University Press, 1953).

Noble, T.F.X., et al., *Western Civilization. The continuing experiment* (Boston: Houghton Mifflin Company 1998).

Noiriel, Gerard, *A quoi sert l'identité nationale?* (Marseille: Agone, 2007).

Nozick, Robert, *Anarchy, state, and utopia* (New York: Basic Books, 1974).

Nugent, Neill, *The Government and Politics of the European Community* (London: Macmillan, 1991).

Nussbaum, Arthur, *A Concise history of the law of nations* (New York: The Macmillan Company, 1961).

O'Neill, Brendan, 'Down with the Dalai Lama. Why do western commentators idolise a celebrity monk who hangs out with Sharon Stone and once guest-edited French Vogue?', in: *The Guardian*, May 29th, 2008.

O'Neill, Daniel I., 'Multicultural Liberals and the Rushdie Affair: A Critique of Kymlicka, Taylor, and Walzer', in: *The Review of Politics*, Vol. 61, No. 2 (Spring, 1999) 219-250.

Oakeshott, Michael, *Rationalism and Politics*.

Ohmae, Kenichi, 'The Rise of the Region State', in: *Foreign Affairs*, vol. 17, no. 2 (Spring 1993) 79-85.

Okin, Susan Moller, *Is Multiculturalism Bad for Women?* With respondents. Edited by Joshua Cohen, Matthew Howard, and Martha C. Nussbaum (Princeton: Princeton University Press, 1999).

Oppenheim, Lassa, *International law. A treatise*. 4th Edition by A.D. McNair (London: Longmans, 1928).

Osiander, A., *Sovereignty, International Relations, and the Westphalian Myth*, in: *International Organization*, vol. 55, issue 2 (Spring 2001) 251–287.

Osiander, Andreas, 'Sovereignty, International Relations, and the Westphalian Myth', in: *International Organization*, vol. 55, issue 2 (Spring 2001) 251–287.

Paine, Thomas, *Rights of Man, being an answer to mr. Burke's attack on the French Revolution* (1791) 8. Available online at http://www.iowagrandmaster.org/Books%20in%20pdf/Paine--Rights%20of%20Man.pdf.

Pannick, David, *Judges* (Oxford: Oxford University Press, 1987) 44 (and backflap).

Parekh, Bikhu, *Rethinking Multiculturalism. Cultural Diversity and Political theory*. Second edition (London: Palgrave, Macmillan, 2006).

Parker, Geoffrey, *The Thirty Years War* (New York: Routledge, 1997).

Pennock, J. Roland, 'Political Representation: an overview', in: R.J. Pennock and J.W. Chapman (eds.), *Representation. Yearbook of the American Society for Political and Legal Philosophy* (New York: Atherton Press, 1968) 3-27.

Petiteau, Natalie, 'Débats historiographiques autour de la politique européenne de Napoléon', in: Jean-Clément Martin (ed.), *Napoléon et l'Europe. Colloque de la Roche-sur-Yon* (Rennes: Presses Universitaires, 2002) 19-31.

Phillips, Melanie, *Londonistan* (London: Gibson Square 2006).

Pufendorf, Samuel, *On the Duty of Man and Citizen* (Cambridge: Cambridge University Press, 1991).

Quinn, B., 'Prisoners' voting rights: government loses final appeal in European court. European court of human rights rules UK must draw up proposals to end ban on prisoners voting within six months', in: *The Guardian*, Tuesday 12 April 2011. Available online at http://www.guardian.co.uk/politics/2011/apr/12/prisoners-vote-government-loses-appeal?&.

Rabkin, Jeremy A., 'Nuremberg Misremembered', in: *SAIS Review*, The Johns Hopkins University Press, Vol. 19 no. 2 (1999) 81-96.

Rabkin, Jeremy A., *Law without nations? Why constitutional government requires sovereign states* (Princeton: Princeton University Press, 2007).

Rabkin, Jeremy A., *The case for Sovereignty. Why the world should welcome American independence* (Washington DC: The AEI Press, 2004).

Randall Lesaffer, 'The Westfalian Peace Treaties and the Development of the Tradition of Great European Peace Settlements prior to 1648', in: *Grotiana* NS 18 (1997) 71-96.

Rawls, John, *A Theory of justice* (Oxford: Clarendon Press, 1972).

Rawls, John, *The law of peoples* (Cambridge, MA: Harvard University Press, 1999).

Raymond Aron, 'Is multinational citizenship possible?', in: *Social Research. An international quarterly of the social sciences*, Volume 41, no. 4 (Winter 1974) 638-656.

Rees, J.W., *The theory of sovereignty restated*, in: Peter Laslett (ed.), *Philosophy, Politics and Society* (Oxford: Oxford University Press, 1975) first series.

Rehn, Olli, *Speech of 28 April, 2009, Berlin*, available online at http://europa.eu/rapid/press ReleasesAction.do?reference=SPEECH/09/205&format=HTML&aged=0&language=EN &guiLanguage=en.

Reich, Emil (ed.), *Selected Documents Illustrating Mediaeval and Modern History* (London: P.S. King & son, 1905), 230-232. Available online at http://pages.uoregon.edu/sshoemak/323/texts/augsburg.htm

Renan, Ernest, 'Lettre a M. Strauss', in: ibidem, *Histoire et parole. Oeuvres diverses* (Paris: Robert Laffont, 1984) 639-649.

Renan, Ernest, 'Nouvelle lettre à M. Strauss', in: ibidem, *Histoire et parole. Œuvres diverses* (Paris: Robert Laffont, 1984) 647-655.

Renan, Ernest, *Qu'est-ce qu'une nation?*, in: Philippe Forest, *Qu'est-ce qu'une Nation?* (Paris: Pierre Bordas et fils 1991).

Renan, Ernest, 'Souvenirs d'enfance et de jeunesse' (Paris 1883), in: Henriette Psichari (ed.), *Œuvres Complètes d'Ernest Renan* II (Paris 1949-1961) 711-931.

Ribbentrop, Joachim von, 'European Confederation', 21 March 1943, reprinted in Lipgens, Walter (ed.), *Documents on the History of European Integration* (Berlin and New York: De Gruyter, 1985).

Righter, Rosemary, *Utopia Lost* (New York: A twentieth century fund press, 1995)

Robert Bork, *The Tempting of America. The political seduction of the Law* (New York: The Free Press, 1990).

Roberts, Russel, *The Choice: A fable of free trade and protection*. Third Edition (New Jersey: Prentice Hall, 2006).

Rockler, Walter J., 'War crimes applies to U.S. too', in: *Chicago Tribune*, 23 May 1999.

Röling, B.V.A., *The Tokyo trial and Beyond. Reflections of a peacemonger.* Edited and with an Introduction by Antonio Cassese (London: Polity Press, 1993).

Roosevelt, Eleanor, *Speech of 9 December, 1948, for the United Nations at the announcement of the Universal Declaration of the Rights of Man.* Available online at http://www.udhr.org/history/ergeas48.htm.

Roosevelt, Theodore, *Speech of 13 October*, 1915, http://query.nytimes.com/mem/archive-free/pdf?_r=1&res=9901E0DD1239E333A25750C1A9669D946496D6CF.

Rosenberg, Alfred, *Der mythos des 20. Jahrhunderts. Eine Wertung der Seelisch-geistigen Gestaltenkämpfe unserer Zeit* (München: Hoheneichen-Verlag, 1930).

Rosenkrantz, N., *Journal du Congrès de Vienne 1814-1815* (Copenhague: G.E.C. Gad, 1953)

Roth, R., 'Iraq to chair disarmament conference', on: *CNN.com*, 29 January 2003. Available online at http://edition.cnn.com/2003/WORLD/meast/01/28/sprj.irq.disarmament.conference/

Rousseau, Jean-Jacques, 'Considérations sur le gouvernement de Pologne et la réforme projetée en avril 1772', in: Ibidem, *Oeuvres Choisies de J.J. Rousseau. Contrat Social ou Principes du Droit Politique.* Nouvelle édition (Paris: Garnier Frères, no year of publication mentioned).

Rousseau, Jean-Jacques, 'Lettre a C. de Beaumont' (1763), in: *Euvres completes* (Paris: Pléiade, Gallimard, 1964) 925-1028.

Rowen, H., *The King's State: Proprietary dynasticism in Early Modern France* (New Brunswick, N.J.: Rutgers University Press, 1980).

Roy, Jean-Henry, and Deviosse, Jean, *La Bataille de Poitiers. Octobre 733* (Paris: Gallimard, 1966).

Roy, Olivier le, *La laïcité face à l'Islam* (Paris: Stock, 2005).

Ruddy, Francis Stephen, *International Law in the Enlightenment. The background of Emmerich de Vattel's Le Droit des Gens* (New York: Oceana Publications, 1975).

Ruggie, John Gerard, 'Territoriality and Beyond: Problematizing Modernity in International Relations', in: *International Organization*, Vol. 47, No. 1. (Winter, 1993) 139-174.

Sacks, Jonathan, *The home we build together. Recreating Society* (London: New York, 2007).

Safranski, Rüdiger, *Romantik. Eine deutsche Affäre* (München: Hanser, 2007).

Salter, Mark B., *Rights of Passage: The passport in International Relations* (Colorado: Lynnie Rienner Publishers, 2003).

Sampson, Gary P. (ed.), *The role of the World Trade Organization in global governance* (New York: United Nations University Press, 2001).

Sampson, Gary P. (ed.), *The WTO and global governance: future directions* (New York: United Nations University Press, 2008).

Sarkozy, Nicolas, *La République, les religions, l'espérance* (Paris: Editions du cerf, 2004).

Sarkozy, Nicolas, *Speech of 16 May 2007*, available online at: http://www.elysee.fr/elysee/elysee.fr/anglais/speeches_and_documents/2007/speech_by_nicolas_sarkozy_president_of_the_republic_at_the_memorial_ceremony_for_the_bois_de_boulogne_martyrs.76687.html.

Sartre, Jean-Paul, *L'Existentialisme est un Humanisme* (Paris: Editions Nagel, 1946).

Scalia, Antonin, *A matter of interpretation. Federal courts and the law* (Princeton: Princeton University Press, 1997).

Scharf, Michael P., 'The ICC's jurisdiction over the nationals of non-party states: a critique of the U.S. position', in: *Law & Contemporary Problems*, vol. 64, issue 1 (Winter 2001) 67-118.

Scheffer, Paul, *Het land van aankomst* (Amsterdam: De Bezige Bij, 2007).

Schenk, H.G., *The Mind of the European Romantics: An Essay in Cultural History*, (London: Constable, 1966).

Schlesinger jr., Arthur M., *The Disuniting of America. Reflections on a Multicultural Society.* Revised and enlarged edition (New York: W.W. Norton & Company, 1998).

Schmitt, Carl, 'Der Begriff des Politischen', in: ibidem, *Frieden oder Pazifismus?* (Ducker & Humblot, Berlin, 2005).

Schmitt, Carl, 'Machiavelli-Zum 22. Juni 1927', in: *Kölnische Volkszeitung*, Jg. 68, No. 448 (June 21, 1927).

Schmitt, Carl, *Das politische Problem der Friedenssicherung* (Wien: Karolinger Verlag, posthumous 1993).

Schmitt, Carl, *Frieden oder Pazifismus?* (Berlin: Ducker & Humblot, 2005).

Schmitt, Carl, *Politische Theologie, Vier Kapitel zur lehre von der Souveränität* (München/Leipzig: Verlag von Duncker & Humboldt, 1934).

Schokkenbroek, Jeroen, 'The Basis, Nature and Application of the Margin of Appreciation Doctrine in the Case-Law of the European Court of Human Rights', in: *Human Rights Law Journal*, vol. 19, no. 1 (April 1998) 30-36.

Schulze, H., *Das Recht der Erstgeburt in den deutschen Fürstenhäusern und seine Bedeutung für die deutsche Staatsentwicklung* (Leipzig: Avenarius und Mendelsohn, 1851).

Schuman, Robert, *Speech of 9 May*, available online at http://europa.eu/abc/symbols/9-may/decl_en.htm.

Scruton, Roger, 'Man's Second Disobedience: Reflections on the French Revolution', in: Ibidem, *The Philosopher on Dover Beach* (Indiana: St. Augustine's Press, 1998) 196-226.

Scruton, Roger, 'Rechtsgefühl and the Rule of Law', in: J.C. Nyiri and B. Smith (eds.), *Practical Knowledge: outlines of a Theory of Traditions and Skills* (London: Croom Helm, 1988) 61-89.

Scruton, Roger, *A political philosophy. Arguments for Conservatism* (London: Continuum, 2006).

Scruton, Roger, *Animal Rights and Wrongs* (London: Continuum, 2000).

Scruton, Roger, *England and the need for nations* (London: Civitas, 2004).

Scruton, Roger, *England: an elegy* (London: Chatto & Wandus, 2000).

Scruton, Roger, *Green Philosophy. How to think seriously about the planet* (London: Atlantic Books, 2012).

Scruton, Roger, *The Palgrave Macmillan dictionary of political thought*. 3rd edition (London: Palgrave Macmillan, 2007).

Scruton, Roger, *The West and the Rest. Globalization and the terrorist threat* (Delaware: ISI Books, 2002).

Seeley, Sir John Robert, *The Expansion of England* (1883).

Sen, Amartya, *Identity and Violence: The Illusion of Destiny* (New York: W.W. Norton & Company, 2006).

Serres, Michel, *Le contrat naturel* (Paris: François Boudin, 1990).

Seton-Watson, Hugh, *Nations and States. An enquiry into the origins of nations and the politics of nationalism* (Colorado: Westview Press 1977).

Sewell jr., W.H., *Work and revolution in France: the language of labor from the Old Regime to 1848* (Cambridge: Cambridge University Press, 1980).

Shapiro, Steven J., 'The "Hart-Dworkin" Debate: A Short Guide for the Perplexed', *University of Michigan Public Law Working Paper No. 77* (February 2, 2007). Available online at http://ssrn.com/abstract=968657.

Sherriff, R.C., *Journey's End* (New York: Bretano's Publishers, 1929).

Siedentop, Larry, *Democracy in Europe* (London: Penguin Press 2000).

Sieyes, Emmanuel-Joseph, 'Préliminaire de la Constitution. Reconnoissance et exposition raisonnée des droits de l'homme et du citoyen. Lu les 20 et 21 juillet 1789, au comité de constitution', in: Ibidem, *Ecrits Politiques*. Choix et presentation de Roberto Zapperi (Paris: Editions des Archives Contemporaines, 1985).

Sieyes, Emmanuel-Joseph, *Qu'est-ce que le Tiers état?* (Geneve: Libraire Droz, 1970).

Sillen, Joost, 'Tegen het toetsingsrecht', in: *Nederlands Juristenblad*, vol. 43 (10 December 2010) 2231-2748.

Simonde de Sismondi, J.C.L., *Histoire des Français*. Vol. XXII (Paris: Treuttel et Würtz, 1839).

Sked, A., *The decline and fall of the Habsburg Empire, 1815-1918* (London: Pearson, 2001).
Spengler, Oswald, 'Ist Weltfriede möglich?', in: Ibidem, *Reden und Aufsätze* (München: Beck Verlag, 1937).
Spengler, Oswald, *Der Untergang des Abendlandes. Umrisse einer Morphologie der Weltgeschichte* (Düsseldorf: Albatros, 2007).
Spruyt, Hendrik, 'The origins, development, and possible decline of the modern state', in: *Annual Review of Political Science*, Volume 5 (2002) 127–49.
Spruyt, Hendrik, 'The Origins, Development, And Possible Decline Of The modern State', in: *Annual Review of Political Science* (2002, Volume 5).
Spruyt, Bart-Jan, 'Dubbele Nationaliteit is een gedrocht, interview met Twan Tak', in: *Opinio*, 23 February 2007.
Spufford, P., *The origins of the English Parliament: Readings* (Longman, London, 1967).
Stalin, Joseph V., *Works 1907-1913* (Moscow, 1953).
Steinberger, H., 'Sovereignty', in: R. Bernhardt (ed.), *Encyclopedia of Public International Law. Volume Four* (Amsterdam: Elsevier, 2000).
Steiner, J., *European Democracies*, (London & New York: Longman Inc., 1986).
Stephen, James Fitzjames, *Liberty, Equality, Fraternity* (1874).
Sternhell, Zeev, *La droite révolutionnaire : les origines françaises du fascisme, 1885-1914* (Paris: Editions du Seuil 1978).
Strauss, David Friedrich, *Krieg und Friede 1870. Zwei Briefe von David Friedrich Strauss an Ernst Renan und desen Antwort, mit einem Anhang: Carlyle an die Times* (Leipzig: Im Insel Verlag, 1870).
Strauss, Leo, *Natural Right and History* (Chicago: University of Chicago Press, 1953).
Strayer, J.R., *On the medieval origins of the modern state* (Princeton: University Press, 2005).
Strayer, Joseph R., *The Reign of Philip the Fair* (Princeton: Princeton University Press, 1980).
Struett, M.J., *The politics of constructing the International Criminal Court. NGOs, discourse, and agency* (New York: Palgrave Macmillan, 2008).
Sumption, Jonathan, *The Hundred Years War, Volume I. Trial by Battle* (London and Boston: Faber and Faber, 1990).
Sundholm, Mattias, Speech to the University of Washington (Seattle), available online at http://www.eurunion.org/eu/2007-Speeches-and-Press-Conferences-/THE-EUROPEAN-UNION-CELEBRATING-50-YEARS-OF-PEACE-PROSPERITY-AND-PARTNERSHIP.html.
Swart, Alexander de, 'Toch nog een raadsman bij het politieverhoor? Enkele ontwikkelingen na *Salduz/Panovits*', in: *Nederlands Juristenblad*, no. 4 (29 January 2010) 223-226.
Swart, Alexander de, 'Update *Salduz*-doctrine. Toch nog een raadsman bij het politieverhoor? Part II', in: *Nederlands Juristenblad*, no. 42 (4 December 2010) 2692-2695.
Tatar, M., 'Reading the Grimm's *Children's Stories and Household Tales*: Origins and Cultural effects of the Collection', in: *The Annotated Brothers Grimm* (New York: W.W. Norton & Company, 2004).
Taylor, Charles, *Multiculturalism, examining the politics of recognition*. Edited and introduced by Amy Gutman (Princeton University Press, 1994).
Taylor, Charles, 'Shared and Divergent Values', in: Ronald Watts and D. Brown (eds), *Options for a New Canada* (University of Toronto Press, Toronto) 53-76.
Taylor, Telford, *The anatomy of the Nuremberg trials. A personal memoir* (New York: Alfred J. Knopf, 1992).
Teich, Mikulas, and Porter, Roy (eds.), *The national question in Europe in historical context* (Cambridge: Cambridge University Press, 1993).
Teschke, Benno, *The Myth of 1648: Class, Geopolitics, and the Making of Modern International Relations* (London: Verso 2003).
Thomas, W.I., and Thomas, D.S., *The child in America: Behavior problems and programs* (New York: Knopf, 1928).
Thomassen, J.J.A., *Kiezers en gekozenen in een representatieve demokratie* (Alphen aan den Rijn: Samsom, 1976).
Thorbecke, J.R., *Bijdrage tot de herziening van de Grondwet* (1848).
Tibi, Bassam, *Euro-islam: Die Lösung eines Zivilisationskonfliktes* (Darmstadt: Primus Verlag, 2009).
Tibi, Bassam, *Europa ohne Identität? Leitkultur oder Wetebeliebigkeit* (München: Siedler, 1998).

Tilly, Charles, *Coercion, Captial, and European States, AD 990-1992* (Oxford: Blackwell, 1989).

Tocqueville, Alexis de, *De la démocratie en Amérique* (Paris: Éditions Gallimard, 1986).

Tocqueville, Alexis de, *Democracy in America*. The Henry Reeve Text as revised by Francis Bowen, 2 Volumes (New York: Vintage Books, 1990).

Tocqueville, Alexis de, *l'Ancien Régime et la Révolution* (Paris: Éditions Gallimard, 1953).

Todorov, Tzvetan, *Nous et les autres. La réflexion française sur la diversité humaine* (Paris: Éditions du Seuil, 1989).

Tombs, R. (ed.), *Nationhood and Nationalism in France. From Boulangism to the great war 1889-1918* (London: Harper Collins Academic, 1991).

Toobin, Jeffrey, *The Nine. Inside the secret world of the supreme court* (New York: Anchor Books, 2007).

Trappenburg, M.J., 'John Rawls', in: Cliteur, P.B., Van der List, G.A. (eds.), *Filosofen van het hedendaags liberalisme* (Kampen: Kok Agora, 1990) 91-105.

Tully, James, *Introduction*, in: Samuel Pufendorf, *On the Duty of Man and Citizen* (Cambridge: Cambridge University Press, 1991).

Vacher de Lapouge, George, *l'Aryen et son rôle sociale* (Paris: 1899).

Vattel, Emer de, *The Law of Nations, or principles of the Law of Nature, Applied to the Conduct and Affairs of Nations and Sovereigns, with Three Early Essays on the Origin and Nature of Natural Law and on Luxury*. Edited and with an introduction by Béla Kapossy and Richard Whatmore (Indianapolis: Liberty Fund, 2008).

Veen, Theo J., *De Staten-Generaal vertegenwoordigen het gehele Nederlandse volk* (Nijmegen, 2000).

Verhoeven, Joe, *Droit International Public* (Louvain: Larcier 2000).

Voegelin, Eric, *Order and History. Volume IV: The Ecumenic Age* (Louisiana State University Press, 1974).

Voltaire, 'Dialogue entre un plaideur et un avocat' (1751), in: *Oeuvres complètes de Voltaire*, vol. XXIII, 'Mélanges II' (Paris: Garnier Frères, 1879) 493-496.

Voltaire, 'Dictionnaire Philosophique: Lois' (1765), in: *Oeuvres complètes de Voltaire*, vol. 33. 'Dictionaire Philosophique – Tome I' (Paris: Antoine-Augustin Renouard, 1819) 169-187.

Vos, Hendrik, and Heirbaut, Rob, *Hoe Europa ons leven beïnvloedt*, 3de geactualiseerde druk (Standaard, Antwerpen, 2008).

Wallach, Lori, and Woodall, Patrick, *Whose Trade Organization? Corporate Globalization and the Erosion of Democracy* (New York: Public Citizen, 1999).

Warraq, Ibn, *Weg uit de Islam: Getuigenissen van afvalligen*. Met een inleiding van Afshin Ellian (Amsterdam: J.M. Meulenhoff, 2008).

Waterfield, Bruno, 'Barroso hails the European 'empire'', in: *The Telegraph*, July 18, 2007.

Weaver, Matthew, et al., 'Angela Merkel: German multiculturalism has "utterly failed". Chancellor's assertion that onus is on new arrivals to do more to integrate into German society stirs anti-immigration debate', in: *The Guardian*, 17 October 2010. Available online at http://www.guardian.co.uk/world/2010/oct/17/angela-merkel-german-multiculturalism-failed.

Weber, Max, *Economy and Society. An outline of interpretive sociology*. Edited by Guenther Roth and Claus Wittich (Berkeley: University of California Press, 1978).

Weber, Max, *Wirtschaft und Gesellschaft, Grundriss der Verstehenden Soziologie*. Studienausgabe herausgegeben von Johannes Winckelmann (Köln & Berlin: Kiepenheuer & Witsch, 1964).

Wedgwood, C.V., *The Thirty Years War* (New York: The New York Review of Books, 1938).

Wellbank, J.H., (ed.), *John Rawls and his critics; an annotated bibliography* (New York, 1982).

Wells, Stanley, and Taylor, Gary (eds.), *The Oxford Shakespeare. The Complete Works* (Oxford: Oxford University Press, 1999).

Will, George F., 'The Slow undoing: the Assault on, and Underestimation of, Nationality', in: Stelzer, Irwin (ed.), *Neoconservatism. Edited with an introduction by Irwin Stelzer* (London: Atlantic Books 2004) 127-140.

Witte, E., *Politiek en democratie, omtrent de werking van de westerse democratieën in de 19de en 20ste eeuw* (Brussel: VUB press, 1990).

WRR, *Identificatie met Nederland* (Amsterdam: Amsterdam University Press, 2007).

Yamamoto, H., 'Multi-level Governance and Public Private Partnership: Theoretical Basis of Public Management', in: *Interdisciplinary Information Sciences*, Vol. 13, No. 1 (2007) 65-88.

Yokota, Kisaburo, 'The Recent Development of the Stimson Doctrine', in: *Pacific Affairs*, Vol. 8, No. 2 (June, 1935) 133-143.

Zamoyski, Adam, *Rites of Peace. The fall of Napoleon & The Congress of Vienna* (London: Harper Perennial, 2007).

Zenner, M., 'Die Nation im Denken Ernest Renans', in: K. Kluxen and W.J. Mommsen, *Politische ideologen und Nationalstaatliche Ordnung. Studien zur Geschichte des 19. und 20. Jahrhunderts* (München: R. Oldenbourg, 1968) 219-238.

Ziegler, Karl-Heinz, 'Der westfälische Frieden von 1648 in der Geschichte des Völkerrechts' in Meinhard Schröder (ed.), *350 Jahre westfälischer Friede* (Berlin, 1999) 99-117.

Ziegler, Karl-Heinz, 'Die Bedeutung des westfälischen Friedens von 1648 für das europäisches Völkerreht', *Archiv des Völkerrechts 37* (1999), 129-51.

Zimmer, Oliver, *Nationalism in Europe, 1890-1940* (New York: Palgrave Macmillan, 2003).

Zimmern, Alfred, *The League of Nations and the Rule of Law, 1918-1935* (London: Macmillan, 1936).

Zleptnig, Stefan, 'The Standard of Review in WTO Law: An analysis of law, legitimacy and the distribution of legal and political authority', in: *European Integration online Papers (EIoP)*, vol. 6, no. 17 (2002) 24 October 2002. Available online at http://eiop.or.at/eiop/texte/2002-017.htm.

Zwalve, Willem, *De Staat en zijn Recht. Een hoorcollege politieke geschiedenis van het recht in West-Europa* (Den Haag: Home Academy Publishers, 2005).

LEGAL SOURCES

Cases of the ECHR

Case of *A. v. The Netherlands (Application no. 4900/06)* Judgment Strasbourg 20 July 2010.

Case of *Al-Skeini and Others v. the United Kingdom (Application no. 55721/07)* Judgment Strasbourg 7 July 2011.

Case of *Bankovic and others v. Belgium and Others (Application no. 52207/99)* Judgment Strasbourg 12 December 2001.

Case of *Christine Goodwin v. The United Kingdom (Application no. 28957/95)* Judgment Strasbourg 11 July 2002.

Case of *Greens and M.T. v. The United Kingdom (Applications nos. 60041/08 and 60054/08)* Judgment Strasbourg 23 November 2010.

Case of *Hatton and others v. The United Kingdom (Application no. 36022/97)* Grand Chamber Judgment Strasbourg, 8 July 2003.

Case of *Hirst v. The United Kingdom (no. 2) (Application no. 74025/01)* Judgment Strasbourg 6 October 2005.

Case of *J.A. Pye (Oxford) Ltd. v. The United Kingdom (Application no. 44302/02)* Judgment Strasbourg 15 November 2005; and Grand Chamber Judgment Strasbourg, 30 August 2007.

Case of *Kelly and others v. The United Kingdom (Application no. 30054/96)* Judgment Strasbourg 4 May 2001.

Case of *Lautsi and others v. Italy (Application no. 30814/06)* Judgment Strasbourg 3 November 2009; and Grand Chamber Judgment Strasbourg 18 March 2011.

Case of *Loizidou v. Turkey (Application no. 15318/89)* Preliminary Objections, Judgment Strasbourg 23 March 1995.

Case of *MSS v. Belgium & Greece (Application no. 30696/09)* Judgment Strasbourg 21 January 2011.

Case of *O'Halloran and Francis v. The United Kingdom (Applications 15809/02 and 25624/02)* Judgment Strasbourg June 29, 2007.

Case of *Osman v. United Kingdom (Application no. 87/1997/871/1083)* Judgment Strasbourg 28 October 1998.

Case of *Salah Sheekh v. The Netherlands (Application no. 1948/04)* Judgment Strasbourg 11 January 2007.

Case of *Salduz v. Turkey (Application no. 36391/02)* Judgment Strasbourg 27 November 2008.

Case of *Sanoma Uitgevers B.V. v. The Netherlands (Application no. 38224/03)* Judgment Strasbourg 14 September 2010.

Case of *Ternovszky v. Hungary (Application no. 67545/09)* Judgment Strasbourg 14 December 2010.

Case of *Tyrer v. The United Kingdom (Application no. 5856/72)* Judgment Strasbourg 25 April 1978.
Case of *Von Hannover v. Germany (Application no. 59320/00)* Judgment Strasbourg 24 June 2004.

Cases of the Permanent Court of International Law

PCIL, Lighthouses Case (*France v. Greece*), 1934 P.C.I.J. (ser. A/B) No. 62.
PCIL, Case of S. Lotus (*France v. Turkey*), 1927 P.C.I.J. (ser.A) No. 10.

Cases of the ICJ

ICJ, Corfu Channel Case (*United Kingdom v. Albania*), judgment 9 April, 1949.
ICJ, Nottebohm-case (*Liechtenstein v. Guatemala*), judgment 6 April, 1955.
ICJ, Military and paramilitary activities in and against Nicaragua (*Nicaragua v. United States*), judgment 27 June, 1986.

Cases of the European Court of Justice

ECJ *R. v. Bouchereau* (Case 30/77) [1977] ECR 1999.
ECJ *Van Gend en Loos v. Nederlandse Administratie der Belastingen* (Case 26/62); [1963] ECR 1.
ECJ *Laminio Costa v. ENEL* (Case 6/64)[1964] ECR 585.
ECJ *Simmenthal S.p.A. v. Commission of the European Communities* (Case 243/78) [1980] ECR 2391.
ECJ *Von Colson and Kamann v. Land Nordrhein-Westfalen* (Case 14/83)[1984] ECR 1891.

Cases of the Supreme Court of the United States of America

US Supreme Court, Case of *Dred Scott v. Sandford*, 60 U.S. 393 (1856).
US Supreme Court, Case of *Marbury v. Madison* (1803).

Cases of the Nuremberg Tribunal

Judgment of the International military tribunal for the trial of German major war criminals: *The Law Relating to War Crimes and Crimes Against Humanity.*
Judgment of the International military tribunal for the trial of German major war criminals: *The law of the Charter.*
'The Justice Case', United States *against* Josef Altstoetter, *et al.* (Washington DC: U.S. Government Printing Office, 1951), in: *Trials of war criminals before the Nuremberg Military Tribunal under Control Council Law No. 10*, Volume III, Case no. 3.
London Agreement of August 8th 1945, in: Nuremberg Trial Proceedings Vol. 1.

Cases of the Dutch (Advisory) Judiciary

LJN: AN7464, Commissie Gelijke Behandeling, 20 March, 2003.
LJN: BA6917, Rechtbank Amsterdam, AWB 07/1635 WWB, 24 May, 2007.
LJN: BK4547, Hoge Raad, 08/01354, 9 April, 2009.
LJN: BO3682, Gerechtshof 's-Gravenhage, 200.076.673/01. 8 November, 2010. Supported by the Supreme Court on 28 October, 2011.

Dispute Settlement of the WTO

WT/DS1, Malaysia – Prohibition of Imports of Polyethylene and Polypropylene.
WT/DS58, United States – Import Prohibition of Certain Shrimp and Shrimp Products.
WT/DS267, United States – Subsidies on Upland Cotton.
WT/DS285, United States – Measures Affecting the Cross-Border Supply of Gambling and Betting Services.
WT/DS291, European Communities – Measures Affecting the Approval and Marketing of Biotech Products.

WT/DS316, European Communities and Certain Member States - Measures Affecting Trade in Large Civil Aircraft.

Dispute Settlement of the ILO

Case of *Palme v. ICC*, International Labor Organization, Judgment No. 2757, 105th session.

Resolutions of the Security Council

UN Security Council Resolution 82 (1950), 25 June 1950, 'Complaint of aggression upon the Republic of Korea'.
UN Security Council Resolution 487 (1981), 19 June 1981, 'Iraq-Israel'.
UN Security Council Resolution 1593 (2005), 31 March 2005, 'Security Council Refers Situation in Darfur, Sudan, to Prosecutor of International Criminal Court'.

Resolutions of the General Assembly

UN General Assembly Resolution 38/7 (1983), 2 November 1983, 'The situation in Grenada'.

INDEX